T0323239

Agrifood Transitions in the Anthropocene

SAGE STUDIES IN INTERNATIONAL SOCIOLOGY

Series Editor Chaime Marcuello Servós (2016–ongoing)
Editor, Department of Psychology and Sociology,
Zaragoza University, Spain

Recent books in the series
Journey to Adulthood: East Asian Perspectives
Edited by Chin-Chun Yi & Ming-Chang Tsai

Power, Violence and Justice: Reflections, Responses and Responsibilities
Edited by Margaret Abraham

Sociologies in Dialogue
Edited by Sari Hanafi & Chin-Chun Yi

Global Childhoods in International Perspective: Universality, Diversity and Inequalities
Edited by Claudio Baraldi & Lucia Rabello De Castro

Key Texts for Latin American Sociology
Edited by Fernanda Beigel

Global Sociology and the Struggles for a Better World: Towards the Futures We Want
Edited by Markus S. Schulz

Sociology and Social Justice
Edited by Margaret Abraham

Facing An Unequal World: Challenges for Global Sociology
Edited by Raquel Sosa Elizaga

Agrifood Transitions in the Anthropocene

Challenges, Contested Knowledge, and the Need for Change

Edited by Allison M. Loconto and Douglas H. Constance

SSIS SERIES SAGE STUDIES IN INTERNATIONAL SOCIOLOGY: 70

1 Oliver's Yard
55 City Road
London EC1Y 1SP

2455 Teller Road
Thousand Oaks
California 91320

Unit No. 323-333, Third Floor, F-Block
International Trade Tower
Nehru Place, New Delhi – 110 019

8 Marina View Suite 43-053
Asia Square Tower 1
Singapore 018960

Library of Congress Control Number: 2023940204

British Library Cataloguing in Publication data

A catalogue record for this book is available from the British Library

Editor: Michael Ainsley
Editorial assistant: Sarah Moorhouse
Production editor: Victoria Nicholas
Copyeditor: Ritika Sharma
Proofreader: Girish Kumar Sharma
Indexer: TNQ Technologies
Marketing manager: Fauzia Eastwood
Cover design: Wendy Scott
Typeset by: TNQ Technologies

ISBN 978-1-5296-8015-7

We dedicate this book to the memory of Lawrence Busch, first President of the ISA's RC40 (the Sociology of Agriculture and Food). With this book we remain firmly planted in the spirit of this scientific community, which is dedicated to critical inquiry, activism and theoretical musings.

Contents

7 'Anti-fish' Campaign: Food Safety and Ethical Issues of Eating Fish From Indonesia 119

Wardah Alkatiri

8 Hunger, Obesity and Soy: The Corporate Agribusiness Diet in Argentina 153

Luis E. Blacha

9 Farmers, Autonomy and Biodiesel: What Can We Expect From Brazil's Experiment With Biodiesel for Rural Development Policy? 175

Sarina Kilham

12 'Planting Seeds' for 'Good Growth': Anthropocenic Performances of Responsibility 265

Allison M. Loconto

13 Interactive Innovation: New Ways of Knowing for the Anthropocene 290

Renée van Dis

About the Editors

Allison Marie Loconto (PhD, HDR in Sociology) is Co-Director of the Interdisciplinary Laboratory for Science, Innovation and Society (LISIS) and a Research Professor at the French National Institute for Research on Agriculture, Food and Environment (INRAE). Dr Loconto is a member of the Multi-stakeholder Advisory Committee of the Sustainable Food Systems Programme of the One Planet Network (UN Environment), a Board Member of Commerce Equitable France and a member of France's National Committee on Organic Agriculture (CNAB). She is an Executive Committee member of the International Sociological Association (ISA) and Past President of ISA's Research Committee on the Sociology of Agriculture and Food (RC40). Dr Loconto is the Chief Editor of the International Journal of the Sociology of Agriculture, an Associate Editor for the Journal of Rural Studies and an Editorial Board member of Agriculture and Human Values. Previously, she was a Science, Technology and Society Fellow at Harvard University and a Visiting Scientist at the Food and Agriculture Organization of the United Nations (FAO). Author of numerous academic and practitioner oriented publications, she focuses on the governance of transitions to sustainable food systems, specifically on the metrics, models, standards and systems of certification that are part of emerging institutional innovations.

Douglas H. Constance is a Professor of Sociology at Sam Houston State University in Huntsville, Texas, USA. His degrees are in Forest Management (BS), Community Development (MS) and Rural Sociology (PhD), all from the University of Missouri – Columbia. His research focuses on the impacts of the industrialisation and globalisation of the conventional agrifood system on rural communities and alternative agrifood systems. He has numerous journal articles, book chapters and books on these topics. His more recent co-edited books are *Alternative Agrifood Movements: Patterns of Convergence and Divergence* (2014) by Emerald Press and *Contested Sustainability Discourses in the Agrifood System* (2018) by Earthscan Press. He is the past President of the Southern Rural Sociological Association (2003) and the Agriculture, Food, and Human Values Society (2008), and the past Editor-in-Chief of the *Journal of Rural Social Sciences*. He is also the past Chair of the Administrative Council of the United States Department of Agriculture Southern Sustainable Agriculture Research Education Programme (USDA/SARE), where he served as the Quality of Life Representative.

About the Contributors

Wardah Alkatiri is an independent scholar and researcher in interdisciplinary studies on societal–environmental relations. She obtained her PhD in Sociology at the University of Canterbury, New Zealand, in 2016; a Postgraduate Certificate in Social Sciences in Environmental Studies at Lincoln University, New Zealand; a Master of Arts in Philosophy at Islamic College for Advanced Studies (ICAS) in Indonesia; and did her first degree in Chemical Engineering at Institut Teknologi Sepuluh Nopember Surabaya, Indonesia. She has been a volunteer environmental educator and sustainable food activist for many years. At present, she is working at Universitas Nahdlatul Ulama Surabaya, Indonesia.

Zerihun Yohannes Amare has diverse experience from humanitarian to academic in both rural and urban settings. Zerihun is lecturer, researcher and Development project specialist at Bahir Dar University, Institute of Disaster Risk Management and Food Security Studies. He holds his PhD in Environmental Management, Specialization on climate change and Development from Pan-Africa University talented youth scholarship program of African Union at the University of Ibadan campus, Nigeria in 2018. He has got academic excellence award from African Union on 22 February 2018. He designed and implement more than seven development projects funded by AfricaUniNet, USAID, and WFP. He has development project and academic collaborations with Austria, Indonesia, Somalia, South Sudan, Myanmar, Algeria, Nigeria, Zimbabwe, Kenya, Morocco, and Burkina Faso. His work is related to environment, agriculture, clean energy, livelihoods and food security.

Marc Barbier is a Research Professor at INRAE. He holds the following degrees: Agro-Economist Engineer SupAgro Montpellier

(1987) Master in Management Science EM Lyon & Univ. Lyon 3 (1993) PhD in Management Science, Univ. Lyon 3 (1998). Between 1998–2000 he was a Research Fellow at INRA Grenoble. From 2001 to 2010, he was a Permanent Researcher at INRA in Paris. From 2010 to 2015, he was the Founding director of the INRA SenS Unit. Since 2012, he is the President of the Société d'Anthropologie des Connaissances, which publishes an open access journal of the same name. He was the Director of the CorTexT Platform from 2009 to 2019, and since 2019 he is the Director of IFRIS and Labex SITES.

Florence Beaugrand is associate professor in management sciences at Oniris Vetagrobio, Nantes, France. Her research focuses on how agricultural and One Health transitions impact the animal health advisors' practices and stakeholders' coordination in industry and at regional levels. She has in peculiar worked on prudent use of antibiotics.

Claudia Bieling holds the Chair of Societal Transition and Agriculture at the University of Hohenheim, Germany. Her work is rooted in transdisciplinary sustainability research and focuses on the interface of ecological and social dimensions in land-use and food systems.

Jim Bingen is a Professor Emeritus (July 2013), Community, Food and Agriculture. With degrees in Political Science (UCLA) Jim works on range of food, farming and rural development issues in Michigan, Western Europe and French-speaking Africa. He collaborates with colleagues across the social and agricultural sciences on numerous applied research studies of: organic farming and place-named foods and development in the Great Lakes States. Jim was past President (2011–2012) of the Agriculture, Food and Human Values Society (AFHVS). He is an Associated Co-Director of the Working Group for Transdisciplinary Systems Research at BOKU. Jim holds the Chevalier d'Ordre du Mérite Agricole, (Order of Agricultural Merit) awarded by the Government of France and from October 2009 to January 2010 he was a Fulbright Distinguished Chair at the University of Natural Resources and Applied Life Sciences in Vienna.

Luis E. Blacha (PhD in Social Sciences, FSOC-UBA) is a Researcher at 'Consejo Nacional de Investigaciones Científicas y Técnicas

(CONICET)' and a Lecturer and Researcher at IESCT-UNQ, Argentina. His main areas of interest are the sociology of food, malnutrition and social inequalities in the nutritional field.

Marta Lopez Cifuentes is a post-doctoral research fellow at University of Natural Resources and Life Sciences [BOKU], Austria and a Visiting researcher at the Centre for Environment and Sustainability, University of Surrey FWF Schrödinger Fellowship. She works in the field of (urban) food systems. Her work mainly focuses on food policy and governance, food democracy and sustainable diets, with special attention to the role and perspectives of different actors in the food system. She has several years of experience in an inter- and transdisciplinary project in this field and is active in Vienna's food policy council.

Nathalie Couix is a Senior Researcher in the mixed research unit AGIR at INRAE in Toulouse.

Lucia Diez Sanjuan is a Postdoc University Assistant in the Division of Organic Farming at University of Natural Resources and Life Sciences [BOKU], Austria. She holds a PhD in Economic History (University of Barcelona), as well as a master degree in International Economics and Development and Bachelor degrees in Economics and Philosophy (Complutense University of Madrid). Her work focuses on social metabolism, ecological economics, agroecology, food sovereignty and sustainable food systems.

Pierre Ellssel is a Research Associate in the Department of Sustainable Agricultural Systems, at the University of Natural Resources and Life Sciences, Vienna. He holds a BSc in Landscape Management and Nature Conservation, an MSc in Organic Agricultural Systems & Agroecology, and is currently pursuing a PhD focused on agroecological intensification in smallholder farming in North and West Africa.

Valentin Fiala is a Researcher at the Environmental Policy Research Centre (FFU) of Freie Universität Berlin, Germany. He works on the project 'Inclusive Food System Transitions', funded by the Berlin University Alliance. The topic of his work is the transition towards sustainable and socially cohesive food systems. His work focuses on societal discourses on food systems and the participatory development of scenarios for their future development.

Nicolas Fortané is a Research Professor at the French Research Institute for Agriculture, Food and the Environment (INRAE), based at Paris Dauphine University. He works on animal health policies and the veterinary profession. His current research focuses on the problem of antimicrobial resistance and antibiotic use in livestock, the regulation of the veterinary drugs market and the current transformations of veterinary medicine.

Prof. Dr. Bernhard Freyer is a distinguished member of the Division of Organic Farming at the University of Natural Resources and Life Sciences, BOKU, Vienna, Austria, and head of the working group of Transdisciplinary Systems, and has been a Senior Fellow at the University of Minnesota in the United States since 2011. He has organised and has headed several national and international research projects, is guiding PhD and master thesis for more than 25 years. His research endeavors are centered on agro-food systems, with a particular focus on both European and African geographical contexts. His research covers a wide array of topics including soil science, cropping practices, fertilizer use, agroforestry, and various farming systems. Dr. Freyer employs diverse approaches in his research, such as systems thinking, transformation studies, ecosystem services analysis, social practice theories, and transdisciplinary case study research. In his teaching, Dr. Freyer aligns closely with his research interests, addressing real-world challenges such as food security, soil conservation, biodiversity, climate change and ethics. He places special emphasis on organic farming systems, including the conversion from conventional farming methods.

Harriet Friedmann is a Professor Emeritus of Sociology at University of Toronto and Visiting Professor of Agrarian, Food and Environmental Studies at the International Institute of Social Studies (ISS) of Erasmus University Rotterdam (The Hague). She is a food system analyst, writer and a Lecturer. Since retirement in 2012, she freely pollinates the worlds of academia, policy and activism across scales of organisation. Beginning at the intersection of Rural Sociology and World Systems, she has progressively engaged with natural sciences and ways of knowing, all through the lens of intertwined histories of monocultures and creative place-based foodways emerging in their shadows. She looks to the future by exploring transitions to sustainable ways of inhabiting places in the earth and connecting them across the whole earth, and to sustainable ways of organising all our relationships to be responsible foodgetters.

Florence Hellec is a researcher at the French Research Institute for Agriculture, Food and the Environment (INRAE) and the CESAER research unit at the Institut. Agro Dijon. She works on vulnerabilities of the livestock sector and innovation paths of innovation favoring its agroecological transition. Her latest work focuses on technical innovation in herd health and feed management, through two levels of analysis: the farmer's work in relation to his herd, and the role of agricultural socio-professional networks.

Nathalie Joly is an senior Lecturer in sociology at Institute Agro Dijon (France) and associate researcher in the research unit CESAER (INRAE, Dijon). She studies agri-food systems transitions through standards and management tools.

Sarina Kilham is a Rural Sociologist at Charles Sturt University, Wagga Wagga, Australia. Specialising in transdisciplinary research, she focuses on the intersection of sustainable rural livelihoods, autonomy of peasants and the ways in which people adapt, integrate or resist government-led development programmes.

Violet Kisakye an Associate Professor at Mountains of the Moon University, Fort Portal, Uganda with a background in Water resources management and Environmental management. She has extensive experience teaching and research in the area of environmental management totaling over 12 years at both under graduate and postgraduate level. Over the years, she has successfully implemented projects related to sustainable farming systems such as Agroecology, sustainable irrigation, and point-of-use water treatment systems.

Claire Lamine is a Research Professor in the research unit ECODE-VELOPPEMENT, at INRAE in Avignon. She is specialised in rural sociology, agroecology and agrifood transitions.

Nora McKeon studied history and political science at Harvard University and the Sorbonne before joining the UN Food and Agriculture Organization (FAO), where she was responsible for opening up the institution to cooperation with organisations of small-scale producers and civil society. She closely follows evolutions in global food governance including the reformed Committee on World Food Security and the current trend towards 'multistakeholderism'. She teaches at the International University College of Turin. She serves as technical advisor on international issues to the West African network of peasant and agricultural producer organizations (ROPPA). Publications include: Peasant Organizations in Theory and Practice (UNRISD 2004), The United Nations and Civil Society (Zed 2009), Global Governance for World Food Security (Heinrich-Böll Foundation, 2011) and Food Security Governance: empowering communities, regulating corporations (Routledge 2015).

Mathilde Paul is a Professor in Epidemiology at ENVT – Toulouse Veterinary School.

Elizabeth P. Ransom is an Associate Professor of the School of International Affairs and Senior Research Associate in the Rock Ethics Institute at The Pennsylvania State University. She holds an MA and PhD in sociology from Michigan State University. Ransom's research interests are in the areas of international development and globalisation, especially in Sub-Saharan Africa; gender; the political economy of agriculture and food systems; and social studies of science and technology in agriculture and food. Ransom has published articles and book chapters on these subjects, and she has two co-edited books *Rural America in a Globalising World: Problems and Prospects for the 2010s* (West Virginia University Press, 2014, with co-editors Conner Bailey and Leif Jensen) and *Global Meat: Social and Environmental Consequences of the Expanding Meat Industry* (MIT Press, 2019, with co-editor Bill Winders).

Hope Raymond is a Commodity Associate for the Americas Agriculture team at S&P Global Commodity Insights in Houston, Texas. Her degrees include a Bachelor of Science in Soil and Crop Sciences from Colorado State University and a Master of International Affairs from Pennsylvania State University. Her graduate studies focused on development policy and food system resilience in the face of global catastrophic events.

Thaís Rozas Teixeira holds a Master's in Sociology and BA degree also in Sociology from the University of Brasília, in Brasília, Brazil. During her academic trajectory, she participated in different research groups. In these groups, she collaborated with sociological inquiries on education and national public policies, as well as scientific and technological studies presented in national and international events and published in scientific journals. Since 2017, she is a member of the certified brazilian research group Ciências, Tecnologias e Públicos (CTP) led by PhD Tiago Ribeiro Duarte, in which she conducted most of her work. In her bachelor's conclusion work, she interviewed vegetarian and vegan students to understand their motivations and how they describe their food practices. Now, her dissertation is about a scientific controversy over climate mitigation technologies for pasture restoration and the co-production of science and politics in this debate. Her main research interests focus on the areas of climate change, sustainability and science and technology studies, particularly in the science/policy interface, sociotechnical controversies and geopolitics of knowledge.

Paul Thompson is the W.K. Kellogg Professor Emeritus of Agricultural, Food and Community Ethics in the Departments of Philosophy, Community Sustainability and Agricultural, Food and Resource Economics at Michigan State University. Thompson's research and teaching has focused on ethical and philosophical topics in food and agriculture. He is the author or co-author of over two hundred articles in refereed journals or scholarly books. His book *From Silo to Spoon: Global and Local Food Ethics* was published by Oxford University Press in 2023. Thompson has served on advisory boards at the US National Research Council, the US National Academy of Engineering, Genome Canada and for numerous academic journals, including Environmental Ethics and Agriculture and Human Values.

Renée van Dis is a post-doctoral researcher at the Laboratory for Interdisciplinary Science, Innovation and Society (LISIS) in France. She did her PhD in sociology as the French National Research Institute for Agriculture, Food and Environment (INRAE). Her thesis is about responsible research in the context of a French mission-oriented research programme about 'zero pesticides'. She explored how impact assessment in real-time helps researcher to responsibilise as they are guided in envisioning their contribution to the zero pesticides mission. Originally from the Netherlands, she holds an MSc in Organic Agriculture from Wageningen University, the Netherlands, and a master in History of Science, Technology and Society (2017) from EHESS in Paris, France. Prior to her PhD, she worked at the Food and Agriculture Organization of the United Nations (FAO) in Rome, Italy, as part of the team on Agroecology.

Christine Wieck is a Professor for agricultural and food policy at the University of Hohenheim. Her research, teaching and outreach centres on the quantitative and qualitative analysis of agricultural and food policies in a globalised world with a special focus on the sustainable transformation (greening) of the EU food system and EU–Africa relationships on agrifood matters. Prior to returning to academia, she worked in the years 2015–2018 for the German Development Agency (GIZ) as an agricultural trade policy advisor. She started her agricultural career with a vocational training as a farmer and worked for several years on organic dairy farms in the West of Germany. In 2020, she was appointed a member of the scientific advisory board of the German Federal Ministry of Food and Agriculture. From April 2018 to March 2019 she was appointed to the European Commission Task Force 'Rural Africa'.

1

Exploring Agrifood Transitions in the Anthropocene

Allison M. Loconto and Douglas H. Constance

Introduction

The greatest challenges of the 21st century are linked to the recognition that we are now living in a new epoch – the Anthropocene (Crutzen, 2006). The human footprint on the planet can no longer be denied, and one of the greatest human innovations – agriculture – is increasingly recognised as a leading contributor to climate change (Shukla et al., 2019). The most recent estimates identify food systems as being responsible for a third of global anthropogenic greenhouse gas (GHG) emissions, with 71 percent of these coming from agricultural land use/land-use change and 10 percent from the supply chain activities that bring food to eaters (Crippa et al., 2021). Despite the intensification of agriculture that has driven the sharp rises in GHG emissions, in 2017, the Food and Agriculture Organization of the United Nations (FAO) observed that the progress made in reducing food insecurity over the previous ten years had probably been reversed (FAO et al., 2017). Each year since, this downward trend has been confirmed despite changes to how food insecurity is measured (Loconto, 2022).

While global governance bodies have seemed to agree that the world will need to feed a predicted nine billion people by 2050 (cf. Fouilleux et al., 2017), the recognition of the Anthropocene reveals the need to reduce environmental externalities and inequalities in how these people will be fed. The surging push from social movements to foster more democratic food systems demonstrates that these sorts of debates must be social as well as technical, as the problems, as well as the solutions are highly contested (Constance et al., 2018). These contestations are often at the intersections of knowledge and governance as the ability to contest a proposed solution to a societal problem is often derived from the inability to find consensus in scientific and political definitions of the problem itself (Loconto and Fouillieux, 2019).

This knowledge–environment–governance nexus in studies of agriculture and food is encapsulated in the term agrifood. This term has been used – since 1960 – to refer to the continuum of practices and relations between actors from agricultural production to food consumption (the date of the first reference in a Google Scholar search that produced 134,000 results in 2022). The sub-field of the Sociology of Agriculture and Food has been active in what has long been referred to as 'agrifood studies' since the 1980s when the founders of the International Sociological Associations' (ISA) Research Committee on the Sociology of Agriculture and Food (RC40) began to systematically document and analyse questions of power, inequality, gender, knowledge and institutional change in a globalising agrifood system (Bonanno et al., 1994; Busch and Lacy, 1983; Buttel et al., 1990; Friedland, 1984; Friedland et al., 1981; Friedmann and McMichael, 1989). A specific programme within agrifood studies has been placing analyses of the dominant agrifood system actors (e.g., Constance and Bonanno, 2000) in dialogue with alternative agrifood movements (Goodman et al., 2012), which are actively co-constituting real utopias around the world (Cucco and Fonte, 2015; Wright, 2010). With the arrival of the global COVID-19 pandemic, it has become painfully obvious that our societies are ill-prepared to deal with the current conditions of life in the Anthropocene. The zoonotic virus that has crippled economies and exposed the weaknesses in democratic institutions is a direct result of how we produce and consume food (FAO, 2020). Thus, a volume that brings to light current societal struggles to transition towards more sustainable agrifood systems is particularly timely.

Knowing the Anthropocene

Discussions of the Anthropocene have been dominated by natural and life scientists, who have raised the alarm and have proposed technical solutions. Within the social sciences more broadly, a number of epistemic communities have been working on the political and economic questions of how to shift towards sustainability. Researchers in the fields of sustainability transitions, social movements, transformative innovation policy, and behavioural and institutional economics have all been putting forward proposals on how to encourage change that both creates sustainable societies and is itself sustainable as a process (Köhler et al., 2019; McGreevy et al., 2022). Anthropologists (Haraway et al., 2016) and historians (Hamilton et al., 2015) have explored what this epoch means for human–nature relations and how humans have and will shape history.

Sociologists have been surprisingly quiet in their engagement with, or theorising of, the Anthropocene. In the top ranked mainstream sociology journals, we found that the *American Sociological Review*, the *European Sociological Review*, and *Social Science Quarterly* have yet to publish a single article on the Anthropocene. The *Annual Review of Sociology* has published two review articles – both on Climate Change, which is only part of the story proposed by the term Anthropocene. The *American Journal of Sociology* published three book reviews (including Ulrich Beck's and David Pellow's theory-building books and a book about bees). Sociology published two book reviews (Donna Haraway and J.K. Gibson-Grahams' books that advance feminist theories) and two empirical papers that don't mention the Anthropocene except in passing. The *British Journal of Sociology* has published three original articles and three book reviews, while the ISA's two journals – *International Sociology* and *Current Sociology* – have published one and six articles, respectively. *The French Review of Sociology* has only three hits for the word – a book review of Bruno Latour's 'Modes of Existence' and two articles about climate science where the Anthropocene carries no empirical or conceptual weight. This dearth of attention in the mainstream journals would make one think that sociologists are not seriously engaging with this recently introduced social category, but that would not be correct.

Indeed, the sub-discipline of environmental sociology is where we find the majority of sociological contributions. *Society & Natural Resources* has published 19 articles (five book reviews and mostly the Anthropocene as context and not as object of research or theoretical development). The 25 articles published in *Environmental Sociology* since 2016 offer not just interesting empirical analyses of the Anthropocene as a changing human–nature condition but also theoretical propositions for how to deal with this new epoch in sociology. We also see that it is in the *European Journal of Social Theory* where we find the largest collection of articles (34) that deal with the Anthropocene as an object of sociological inquiry. These scholars have put forward challenges to the Anthropocene as a way to tell time, as a way to know and tell stories about the planet and as a condition of social change (Bowden, 2017; Lidskog and Waterton, 2016a).

This introduction engages with this literature[1] as a means to position the monograph within the traditions of environmental sociology and science and technology studies (STS), which have cross-fertilised the sub-discipline of the sociology of agriculture and food since their parallel emergences in the 1980s. The idea for the collection emerged when the editors organised bi-continental twin sessions on agrifood transitions in the Anthropocene at the International Rural Sociology Association (IRSA) World Congress in Cairns, Australia and the IV ISA Forum of Sociology in Porto Alegre, Brazil in 2020. Due to the COVID-19 pandemic we were not able to meet in person as planned, but instead we met virtually in 2021 to explore experiences from around the world. We then collaborated, again virtually, throughout 2021 and 2022 to prepare this volume. Each chapter in this collection focuses on a specific controversy (Venturini, 2010) within the Anthropocene in order to shed light on the political stakes of problem definitions and solutions, which is a classic technique used in the sociology of agriculture and food to study societal inequities (Carolan, 2021). By comparing the insights from each specific controversy, we offer a sociological analysis of the types of agrifood transitions that are currently underway and what societal concerns are at stake in the Anthropocene.

In this introduction, we first position the Anthropocene and the fundamental question that it poses about human–nature interactions. We then explore the core concerns related to agriculture and food and the debates around the need for agrifood system transitions. In the section that follows we draw upon the chapters in the book to explore the controversies that are exemplified by the case studies included in the book. We conclude with a call for sociologists of agriculture and food to engage more strongly with the controversies unfolding in the Anthropocene. Our effort does not just ask sociologists to study these

---

[1]We do acknowledge that our review of the literature is not exhaustive and our vision is of course partial, but we have done our best to engage the core debates that have been taken up by agrifood scholars.

controversies from the comforts of their ivory towers, but we call upon sociologists to also get their hands dirty. A sociology of agriculture and food in the Anthropocene should be an engaged, empirically focused exploration of society as it emerges from the human and non-human relations on Earth. We close with a brief presentation of the organisation of the book.

The Anthropocene as a Modern Construct

A 2015 report by the International Panel on Climate Change (IPCC) indicated that although their 1990 report did not include a quantification of the impact of human activities on climate change, by 2013 it was 'extremely likely' (95 percent chance) that human-emitted GHGs were responsible for more than one-half of the Earth's temperature rise since 1951.[2] In 2019, the Anthropocene Working Group voted to officially designate the Anthropocene Epoch, indicating the evidence is overwhelming that human activity – we, Anthropos – is drastically affecting the Earth's climate in the atmosphere, biosphere, and hydrosphere.[3] Humans have become a geologic force, joining volcanism and glacial cycles in changing the functions of the Earth systems. The 'golden spike' – required by the stratigraphers to separate and classify historical periods - is the layer of radioactive nuclear fallout from the 1940s and 1950s. Although the Anthropocene can be traced to the Neolithic Revolution and the origins of agriculture some 10K years ago, the Industrial Revolution based on burning fossil fuels, followed by national and global capitalism, institutionalised the carbon-based development model (Hamilton et al., 2015). After World War II the 'Great Acceleration' pushed the Earth past its planetary climatological and ecological boundaries (Rockstrom et al., 2009). In 2000, the term Anthropocene – originally coined in 1833 by Sir Charles Lyell – entered the scientific discourse (Crutzen, 2002; Crutzen and Stoermer, 2000), and it still occupies centre stage some twenty years later.

The implications of the Anthropocene go well beyond the stratigrapher's narrow geologic concerns. This convergence of human and

---

[2]IPCC Report (https://www.ipcc.ch/report/ar5/syr/), accessed 29/07/2022
[3]Anthropocene Working Group (http://quaternary.stratigraphy.org/working-groups/anthropocene/), accessed 29/07/2022

geologic history – of the human species as a 'telluric force' - calls into question the assumptions of Holocene[4] thinking, of Cartesian dualism, of the received modernist view of the clear separation of humans and nature; it raises to prominence 'the politics of unsustainability' (Hamilton et al., 2015). It requires a new way of thinking in the natural and social sciences; it requires exploring new ontological assumptions about the human/nature relationship.

For Earth System scientists,[5] the alarming data regarding the Earth's spheres indicate a major departure from the stability of the Holocene and the breaching of the 'planetary boundaries' regarding greenhouse gas emissions, species extinction, sea-level rise, ocean acidification, nitrogen/phosphorous cycles, synthetic chemical pollution, and other Earth processes (see Rockström et al., 2017). '[E]verything is in play now. Every cubic metre of air and water, and every hectare of land, now has a human imprint' (Hamilton et al., 2015: 34). According to these scientists, the tipping point has been reached whereby human influence has moved well beyond the geologic and even climatological arenas, deeper into impacting the entire Earth system – a scientific concept that was not articulated until the 2000s (Hamilton and Grinevald, 2015).

The 'noösphere' – the world of thought – was the 1924 proposition to explain this recognisable role of 'mankind's brainpower and technological talents in shaping its own future and environment' (Crutzen and Stoermer, 2000: 17). Sociologists have long referred to this as the modernist vision – a techno optimist one in fact – that asserts an empire of man over nature where science and technology create a technical paradise where all things are possible. This vision was first applied to English agriculture, then to the ideology of manifest destiny in the American West and colonialism globally, and finally to the post-World War II techno-engineered utopia. Today, the battle lines are drawn between those who plan to force the Earth into submission and those who see this as ultimate folly (Hamilton et al., 2015).

Social scientists have thus argued that this new epoch requires a drastic rethinking of modernity's assumptions about the relationships between nature and humans, between the boundaries of the natural

---

[4]The Holocene is the epoch that began 12K years ago at the end of the last ice age, which stabilised global temperatures and supported the development of agriculture.
[5]Climatology, global ecology, geochemistry, atmospheric chemistry, oceanography, geology, etc.

and social sciences, and calls for a deliberate deconstruction and reconsideration of the types of knowledge that should be prioritised (Bowden, 2017; Hamilton and Grinevald, 2015). The social science debates about the Anthropocene are varied, with numerous sub-camps that can be generally grouped within the 'Bad Anthropocene' (global ecological, social and economic disaster) and 'Good Anthropocene' (humans achieve total control over the Earth) camps, and then the climate change deniers (Turnheim and Geels, 2013). The optimistic eco-pragmatists and eco-modernists continue to trust in human reason and technology. The eco-modernists build on reflexive modernisation perspectives to advance a model of green capitalism and technical stewardship of the planet (Mol, 1997). The eco-modernist trope that 'Nature no longer runs the Earth. We do'. (Lynas, 2011: 8 as cited in Bonneuil, 2015: 25) has been critiqued as not only unrealistic but dangerous (Pavesich, 2022). Unsurprisingly, it has received a lot of attention by policymakers and promotors of evolutionary 'transitions' rather than system transformations, particularly in the energy sector (Szarka, 2016).

The pessimistic eco-catastrophists and eco-Marxists warn that modernity's project has hit the wall of planetary finitude. For eco-catastrophists, the tipping point is surpassed as we need to acknowledge the imminent collapse of industrial society and prepare for a new 'post-growth resilient society' in the *Small is Beautiful* model of E.F. Schumacher (Schumacher, 1989; Semal, 2015). Eco-Marxists prefer the term 'Capitalocene' (Moore, 2017, 2018), grounded in the metabolic rift and second contradiction of capitalism. For them, capitalism – specifically capitalists in core countries – and its world system of colonial expansion are the true culprits in the Anthropocene, rather than the species Anthropos. The Core has externalised its ecological and social debt into the Periphery through imperialism, cultural genocide, large-scale agriculture for cash/luxury crops, slave-based agriculture, large-scale deforestation, rare mineral plunder, mining for industrial processes, and species depletion for food provisioning and predator control. Sociologists are thus suggesting that Wallerstein's (1975) concept of the 'World System' is far more valuable than the concept of 'Species' to understand the drivers of the conditions that are now characterised as the Anthropocene.

This specific kind of social order grounded in power asymmetries was created by a small percentage of humans in a few countries and a few companies (Bonneuil, 2015). This reading of the has been coined by anthropologists and feminist scholars of science as the 'Plantationo-cene' (Haraway et al., 2016). Wolford (2021) argues – and we agree – that the power of this term lies in the way this form of social order encapsulates the historical path towards the agrifood systems and societies that we know today. 'Plantations are inherently power-laden social structures found in every modern economic system. They embody both racial violence and resistance, straddling or bridging the divide between rural and urban, agriculture and industry, town and country, and local and global' (Wolford, 2021: 1624). The emancipa-tory power of using the plantation as a metaphor for capitalist modernity is that the resistances that have been traced over the cen-turies have been against the notion of large-scale that characterises a plantation economy. It avoids romanticising the small-scale farmer, but it does offer an analytical tool to identify this scale that is within the limits of agro-ecosystems as a form of resistance to the social order that has come to characterise the Anthropocene.

Nonetheless, even in the face of undeniable atmospheric, geologic and social science, the 'politics of unsustainability' is the 'condition and predicament of eco-politics in the Anthropocene' (Bluhdorn, 2015: 157). After many conferences diagnosing the problem and prescribing solutions, political leaders have little appetite for the needed sweeping changes to neoliberal consumer capitalism. The enthusiasm and hope for the Sustainable Devel-opment Goals of the Rio Summit have dissipated in the face of eco-politics. Ecological modernisation utilising a technology-based and policy-oriented approach became the dominant model for increasing the efficient use of natural resources and providing co-benefits for both ecology and economy. The empirical facts got enmeshed in eco-politics powered by concerns and values, where politics trump science. The science was not politically palatable, so eco-modernism manoeuvred it into the safe territory of metrics and standards and multi-stakeholder coalitions – the world of certified sustainability (Loconto and Barbier, 2014) – where the radicals were purged and the politics of the possible was elevated, thereby extending the life expectancy of the unsustainable system (Constance et al., 2018).

Although the warnings are not new, through 'Agnotology' – the purposeful creation of ignorance by the 'merchants of doubt' (see Latour, 2015) – the scientific knowledge has been managed deliberately through a 'history of political and techno-scientific strategies to govern and channel fears and opposition, and to disinhibit Anthropocene agency from initial environmental cautiousness' (Bonneuil, 2015: 22–23). 'Sustaining the established socio-economic order has itself evolved into a categorical imperative' (Blühdorn, 2015: 164). The politics of unsustainability has abandoned any attempt to change individual lifestyles and society structures to comply with the eco-imperative of the Anthropocene. Instead, it focuses on managing the inevitable social, economic, and ecological consequences. Rather than trying to reverse the prevailing trends towards catastrophe, it promotes societal adaption and resilience to sustained unsustainability.

What Then, Can We Say About Transitions Within Such an Epoch?

Blanchette (2018) opens his article on industrial meat production with the story of one of the possible indicators of the Anthropocene that was debated by the Working Group on the Anthropocene – the enlarged skeleton of the post-WWII chicken. This particular fossil record was remarkable in that not only was there a massive increase in the numbers of bones discovered over such a short period of time, but in that the human influence in this form of material accumulation was clear: the carcasses were significantly larger, but the lifetimes of the animals were much shorter. This 'chickenised stratigraphic record' offers a prescient vision of what the global agrifood system looked like in 2015[6]: a system where the bodies of animals and the humans who slaughter them are reciprocally shaped according to unfair working and living conditions, while the chemical and biological compositions of the air, water, land and microbial communities within which they live are likewise irreversibly altered. Blanchette argues that unless agrifood systems change, 'the future stratigraphic record may come to read as a branded reflection of a moment in time when a few corporations had nearly monopolised the killing of a species' (Blanchette (2018): 186). Since the turn of the 21st century, such changes have been referred to in agrifood studies as transitions.

---

[6]The date of 2015 is important here as it marks the pivot point between the eight Millennium Development Goals that were not achieved by this date and the 17 Sustainable Development Goals that are supposed to be achieved by 2030. All indicators point to the fact that these goals will most likely not be met either.

Transitions is a concept that is subject to constant innovation in sociology (cf. Lidskog and Waterton, 2016b). A concept from chemistry that was applied originally to large-scale societal change like the demographic and nutrition transitions, it has been picked up by social scientists to describe the ongoing co-production (Jasanoff, 2004) of societies and environments. Transitions are at once a political imperative of the early 21st century that is analysed by political scientists and sociologists as public policy rhetoric (Aykut and Evrard, 2017), and an emerging epistemic community in STS (Köhler et al., 2019). In line with the notion of the Anthropocene, which stresses the need for systems perspectives, the Transitions Studies community has created, and continuously improves upon, approaches to studying transitions as interactions within socio-technical systems that can profoundly affect their governance. Studies of social innovations explore the changing socio-political roles and routines, beliefs and justifications, knowledge, power and material flows among actors within systems (McGowan and Westley, 2015; Moulaert et al., 2005). Other approaches examine how the socio-technical system and its constituent actors can learn to adapt and bounce forward (Davoudi et al., 2012), or backward through detachment (Goulet and Vinck, 2012) or be completely reconfigured (or not) (Turnheim and Geels, 2013).

As the pioneering approach in this field, the multilevel perspective (MLP) of technological innovation (Geels, 2002, 2010; Geels et al., 2008; Hillman et al., 2009; Rip and Kemp, 1998) theorises that it is the way niches, regimes and landscape processes interact that determines a specific transition. This framework is helpful for conceptualising shifts in socio-technical paradigms over the 'longue durée', particularly when one can examine technological development retrospectively, like the shift from sailing to steam ships (Geels, 2002). Recent advances in this theory have focused on whole system reconfiguration that pays attention to techno-economic developments and changes in actor networks, rules and modes of governing (Geels and Turnheim, 2022). This theory places the analyst in a position to look in from the outside and characterise how multiple, interacting systems and their actors produce and use technical artefacts in attempts to render modern society more sustainable. Their focus on the urgency of whole system change is in line with systems focus that is also found in the concept of the Anthropocene and promoted by Earth System scientists.

If the urgency of the Anthropocene is to be taken seriously in the sociology of agriculture and food, we must acknowledge that we are already within the midst of transitions towards agrifood systems that value sustainability differently from the those of the past. For example, a February 2022 press release on the IPCC's Sixth Assessment Report notes that progress on adaptation is uneven and there are increasing gaps between action taken and what is needed to deal with the increasing risks. The report re-emphasises the 'urgency of immediate and more ambitious action to address climate risks. Half measures are no longer an option'.[7] The report is emblematic of the increasing pressures at a landscape level to change practices at a global scale, and there is significant mobilisation from the bottom-up to propose alternative means to govern and practice this transition (Elzen et al., 2012; Grin, 2006). However, what this approach to transitions seems to forget about working within the Anthropocene is that we – the analysts – cannot be removed from the systems that we analyse. We are at once both producing and using the knowledge about change, which needs to be included in our analyses, our own actions within nature and in our reactions to societal change.

Put differently, the Anthropocene (in all of its different definitions), if understood as a crisis, should reveal the persistent problems in the current agrifood system and offer opportunities for change. Grin et al. (2010) argue that crises are symptomatic of illness in current socio-technical landscapes and push existing institutions to the limits of their current normative frameworks. This can bring both disaster like that seen with Hurricane Katrina (Freudenburg, 2009) and opportunities to seek-out alternative values and norms that may govern a transition to a different socio-technical reality – transformed agrifood systems (Kropp et al., 2020). Thus, the transitions that are explored in this book are understood as changes in the relationships between public, civic and private actors who know and value sustainability differently (see Grin et al., 2010).

In the chapters that are included in this book, we see hints of crises, hints of change and numerous controversies that cut across food systems. But we are also sympathetic to Lockie's (2017) point that 'pre-existing frameworks and questions do not need to be re-packaged

---

[7]IPCC Sixth Assessment Report. Press release. (https://www.ipcc.ch/report/ar6/wg2/resour ces/press/press-release/), accessed 21/07/2022

in the language of the Anthropocene to establish their validity or importance'. For this reason, the authors contributing to this volume are not all drawing upon the Anthropocene as the language for their studies – but rather the context within which the controversies they explore are embedded. In the cases included in this book, the authors' draw upon a range of classic and emergent theories in the sociology of agriculture and food that highlight the relational ontologies that are at the core of the scientific debates over when, where, and how the Anthropocene emerged (Head, 2014). They also all examine the agrifood transitions that are underway and the processes of learning, interaction and transformations that constitute them (Elzen et al., 2017).

A Relational, Sociological Imagination for Agrifood Transitions in the Anthropocene

Sklair (2017) claims that rarely has a scientific term – the Anthropocene – moved so quickly into wide acceptance and general use. She suggests that part of the reason for this is that most scholars agree that scientists can no longer justifiably argue that there is a Cartesian binary between humans and nature. Humans are part of nature and nature is part of humans – they are related, they interact to co-produce each other (Lidskog and Waterton, 2016a). Relational ontologies are not new in sociology; however, they are far from being accepted as the main ontological approach to understanding the social (see Latour, 2005). Emerging as a response to a functionalist vision of social structures and agency, interactionists have long argued that a social fact is not a static, predetermined reality of society but rather a process that is constructed within the framework of concrete situations that have a range of institutions (understood as discourses and rules) that frame the possible range of actions (Carr, 1945; Znaniecki, 1963).

This interactionist approach emerged first from the social psychological philosophy of George Herbert Mead (Mead, [1934] 1962) in the American tradition, but also from Gabriel Tarde (Tarde and Parsons, 1903; Toews, 2003) in the French tradition who argued that actors cannot be recognised other than through their relational contexts (i.e., the theory of imitation-suggestion). It is thus in the dynamics of exchanges between people (interactions), and through the meaning that individuals give to their actions (picked up in both symbolic interactionism, as well as the practice theories (Schatzki et al., 2001; Shove and Spurling, 2013), that the essence of social action can be understood. Interactionist approaches thus consist of the 'study of developmental interaction process – interaction that changes as it continues – as distinct from the relatively static study of the rules that govern interaction' (Glaser and Strauss, 1964: 671). The social order emerging from situations is thus a constitutional process (Hurlbut et al., 2020) where the understandings and orders emerge from social construction, negotiated orders, unintended consequences, and contingent developments (Weik, 2012).

This basic interactionist understanding has been further developed in relational theories of social action where the relations are themselves the results of the interactions. The conceptual innovation of actor-network theory (ANT) is that non-humans are also active participants in the creation of the associations that constitute society (Latour, 2005). Thinking of society in this way means that society is not an infrastructure of objects or signs, but an assemblage of humans and non-humans that maintain relations (Molénat, 2009). Latour proposed 'actant' as a means to capture the fact that interactions are not only the raising of consciousness or simple transactions or exchanges of materials and meanings, but they are also the actions that generate the relations that make up our world. The feminist STS tendency to eliminate fundamental binaries – like human/ non-human, nature/society, knowledge/power or structure/agency – offers an approach to understanding change that embraces the complexity of social relations and seeks to breakdown the reproduction of the above and other binaries in society (Haraway, 1988, 2008).

Adopting such a relational ontology in our studies requires that we rethink the relationships among knowledge, environment and governance, which constitute classic objects of study in the sociology of agriculture and food. The literature that we reviewed above about the Anthropocene have all touched upon the threats of this Epoch to current modes of knowledge making, the human–nature relationship that constitutes the environment of planet Earth, and current forms of governance in agrifood systems. Thus, the focus on knowledge and artefacts in ANT and STS theories offer means to trace the outcomes of interactions, particularly when those interactions produce new meanings, values and differences between actors – like what is observed in agrifood transitions in the Anthropocene. Change (or resistance to change) in the relationships among these three constitutive elements of society is what is empirically illustrated by the contributions to this volume.

De-institutionalising Knowledge in the Anthropocene

At the core of the Anthropocene narrative is the idea of transitioning from a broadly 'ecological' perspective to one that defines thinking at the level of the entire Earth System, which requires different forms of knowledge. Who knows? Who can know? How can we know? How must we know to live and survive in the Anthropocene? These are the types of questions that are addressed in this volume.

Earth System scientists have begun to question the primacy of institutionalised and disciplinary knowledge. In particular, the importance of the social sciences in understanding the Anthropocene has been recognised by natural scientists who claim that capturing the qualitative changes in human–nature relations in predictive, quantitative models will be a challenge (Ellis and Trachtenberg, 2014). Thompson (this volume) picks up on this 'moral imperative' of better understanding the actions of humans within the Earth System through a strong critique of institutionalised knowledge. Using Nietzsche's God metaphor, Thompson argues that knowledge construction and meaning fundamentally shape the possibilities for future action. Thus, despite these well-intentioned calls for expanding the 'legitimate' knowledge base needed to change agrifood systems, the institutions that govern research and education for agricultural and food sciences are not yet prepared for this transition. Indeed, the insistence that we must still rely upon quantitative models in order to know in the Anthropocene illustrates how deep particular ways of knowing are engrained in our disciplinary biases.

As with all knowledge, even these disciplinary biases are co-created through interactions over time. Constance and Loconto (this volume) trace how the modern vision of agriculture was inscribed into global agrifood systems via the Consortium of International Agricultural Research Centres (CGIAR). The CGIAR system is both a microcosm of the global knowledge politics of industrial agriculture and an example of how a particular form of knowledge – chemistry-driven knowledge focused on plant yields – was able to generalise to all corners of the earth. The promotion of standardised technical packages that could be applied pretty much anywhere on Earth is one of the reasons why industrial agriculture is indeed one of the key indicators of the Anthropocene. This approach treated knowledge as something held by scientists and experts in formal organisations who can legitimately know when, how and where to apply it.

Rozas (this volume) explores in detail how this model is reproduced even within those scientific communities who are seeking to reduce the human-induced changes on Earth. By exploring the role of 'verified science' as a component of the social order, she demonstrates why scientific actors can argue for carbon neutrality as the best strategy to achieve the global climate goals. Her chapter, as well as that by Fortané et al. (this volume), demonstrate how institutionalised scientific knowledge reinforces the dominance of industrial meat production models that mark the Anthropocene. They detail how the dominance of scientific knowledge and use of consumer-facing labels on food incentivise companies to reinvest in their industrial approaches that can now be called 'sustainable', rather than reconfiguring their systems towards alternative, non-industrial models.

Blancha (this volume) takes up the concern about the disconnect between what has already been proven in scientific knowledge and the practices by agribusinesses in Argentina. He questions why, if we know that the current agrifood systems are unhealthy for humans and nature, does agribusiness continue to promote high-input intensive agriculture? Blancha's analysis offers evidence of the Capitolocene – and the Plantationocene – in action. The institutionalised ignorance that he explores is linked to how scientific and practitioner knowledge is produced not just in the public sector research, but also in the private sector research that dominates the production of knowledge about agriculture and food.

Loconto (this volume) demonstrates the persistence of the Plantationocene by exploring the trend towards responsible research and innovation that has emerged as the new mantra of the multinational companies who drive plant production and protection. In response to interactions with civic and public actors, these companies are leading the much-critiqued, policy-led transitions. However, she shows that these companies limit their responsibility to reducing the harm of their products on humans; they do not take on the responsibility of protecting the environment. The most hazardous forms of agriculture, which have been proven by scientific evidence, are indeed being reduced. Yet, the companies are not changing their research programs – they still pursue incremental innovation around the 20th century technologies that contributed to the identification of 1950 as a key marker of the Anthropocene.

The chapter by Barbier et al. (this volume) shows that in the historical centres of the Anthropocenic World System, political projects can emerge that place local and situated knowledge at the centre of agroecological transitions. However, their analysis reveals the paradox between discursive and material (e.g., financing, training, local experiments) commitments to the co-production of local knowledge and the difficulty of sharing this knowledge in an agricultural knowledge and innovation system (AKIS) that is deeply institutionalised to be top-down. Alkatiri (this volume) adds an additional nuance to this discussion by problematising the dominant regime in the Indonesian agrifood system that legitimises international scientific knowledge while ignoring local scientific knowledge regarding marine pollution when it is published in the Indonesian language. She shows that even within the official institutions of research and education, not all scientific knowledge is treated equally. Her analysis reminds us that knowledge production in the Anthropocene is thus also part of the World System.

Nonetheless, as in all relations on Earth, the research presented in this book demonstrates that there is also space for valuing alternative knowledges within the Anthropocene. One interesting aspect about the conceptualisation of the Earth as Gaia, which is the original, creative theory used to describe what has become institutionalised as Earth Systems science, is that it was developed by the independent British scientist James Lovelock. Lovelock conducted all of his experiments outside of the formal institutions of science (Latour, 2015; Poole, 2014) and vocally supported what is referred to as the 'third space of research' or citizen science (Joly, 2020; Lhoste, 2020, 2022).

Kilham (this volume) extends the ring of knowledge to include farmers. She interrogates the modernist assumption that farmers who don't adopt new technology lack knowledge and need a 'mindset shift'. She explores the phenomenon of 'opting out' and presents evidence of why we should trust the farmers who don't want to adopt an industrial approach. They have very valid reasons, Kilham argues, particularly given the conditions of the Anthropocene. Her analysis contributes to the calls for epistemic justice in research and innovation processes, particularly in agrifood systems (Peddi et al., 2022), that are increasingly emerging in response to the acknowledgement of the Anthropocene. Ransom and Raymond (this volume) explore an emerging topic in the sociology of knowledge: the recognition that thinking also requires feeling (see Escobar, 2016). They argue that as part of the opening up of knowing to include knowledge from the margins and peripheries, we also need to recognise that knowing is tied to the emotions that are also produced through social relations. The concern for the future of Earth can be a source of new or more appropriate knowledge.

van Dis (this volume) demonstrates that policies that value farmers' knowledge can be developed in the Anthropocene, particularly when policy makers operationalise the results from social science research. The notion of interactive innovation, which is the basis of a European funding program, emerged from qualitative research in the social sciences that proved that innovation is not the sole domain of researchers but emerges from interactions among farmers and researchers. Freyer et al. (this volume) follow this line of thinking when they interrogate what transformative knowledge means in the context of the Anthropocene. What, who, and how must we know if we are serious about changing our agrifood systems? This line of questioning brings us back to the questions posed at the beginning of this section and the disciplinary biases that still exist in institutionalised knowledge. Freyer et al. (this volume) join the Earth System scientists in their calls for disciplined interdisciplinarity. They argue, however, that these disciplines must also open themselves up to include the knowledge that is circulating outside of the formal institutions of research.

A Non-binary Environment in the Anthropocene

This relational ontology is not new to the sociologists who have been long arguing that the human–nature binary is a false one (Buttel, 1987; Catton and Dunlap, 1978; Haraway, 1989). In the sociology of agriculture and food, Carolan and Stuart (2016) have brought forward an important critique of the nature-society binary by explaining how Things – in the Latourian sense – are part of an intermediary layer of 'doing' between social and material worlds. Fox and Alldred (2020) call this layer the 'intricate web of interrelations'. In his original article, Carolan (2005) argued that rather than a nature-society divide, we are actually talking about three natures (i.e., nature as socially understood, nature as socio-technical experience and nature as ecosystem processes). The 2016 update reformulates these layers into what they call 'relational realism', which claims that 'the world is not constituted only of experiences, but also for causally efficacious and afficacious processes and virtual potentials that exist even when not active/enactive' (Carolyn and Stuart, 2016: 77). This idea of 'virtual potentials' is emblematic of agrifood transitions in the Anthropocene as the decisions that we must make in the present determine the direction of agrifood system sustainability in the future. This type of thinking pushes us to ask what notion of nature makes the agriculture of the present and that of the future? The empirical cases in this book ask what inequalities, risks and safety concerns emerge with and against environmental change.

Friedmann (this volume) opens up reflections about the time and timing of the Anthropocene. She suggests that the French word *durabilité* should guide the human–nature relations around agrifood. She argues that the idea of enduring 'as a coherent, evolving, adapting community of relations over centuries and even millennia' is what is required for sustainability. She also proposes that in order to collapse the human–nature boundary, we should emulate ecosystems in the relations that we create. She points out that 'every drop of water is in one place and at the same time in movement across space and time'. This metaphor is meant to encourage us to value the finite and relational nature of life on Earth, before it is no longer.

The empirical chapters in this book take up Head's (2014) suggestion that sociologists do not accept at face value that the Cartesian dualism of human–nature relations is collapsed, but that they explore when, where, and how this binary is or not at play in the relations that constitute the societies in emergence through transitions. Ransom and Raymond (this volume) are perhaps the most straightforward in addressing this supposition. They ask point blank if we are prepared to deal with the impeding crises and catastrophes that are undoubtably part of the future life on Earth. Emotionally and socially, they argue that we are not! Barbier et al. (this volume) are not much more optimistic. Even when the State launches a large programme to incentivise an agroecological transition, the actors who are part of this transition have developed 'modernising' reference systems that box them into the industrial paradigm. In this case, the 'Let's produce differently' plan became the 'Let's evaluate the same', as these modern tools produced counter-intuitive effects that lead to the decoupling of work and resources, and thus little tangible transition.

Constance and Loconto (this volume) explain how the industrial agriculture paradigm created vast environmental damage – and that the modernist desire to control nature remains, despite good intentions to shift research foci towards food systems and agroecology. They argue that the way in which the CGIAR system itself is set up – separate research institutes in different parts of the world focused on single crops – cannot escape binary thinking or disciplinary silos. We note a comfortable shift in the timeline of CGIAR from modernist binaries to modern systems thinking, which itself has 'proven unable to think well about sympoiesis, symbiosis, symbiogenesis, development, webbed ecologies, and microbes' (Haraway, 2016: 49).

Fortané et al. (this volume) provide an excellent example of how the current conditions of industrial animal husbandry are not healthy for the animals. However, when we use market-based instruments (like certification labels) to try to transition, the interdependencies of the model just reinforce each other. The risks associated with the model that required an increase in the use of antibiotics are not eliminated, instead they are now simply fetishised. Alkatiri (this volume) poses a similar question with regards to the direct links between water pollution and food safety. Evidence is accumulating and it suggests that it is increasingly unsafe to eat from the oceans. As Friedmann (this volume) notes, the hydrological cycle is contained on Earth and the pollution can only continue to circulate among humans, plants and fish.

On the other side of the spectrum of animal production, Rozas (this volume) documents how Brazil has massive GHG emissions due to land use change linked to livestock production. Pastureland restoration could mitigate GHG, but the policy trend has been to push Brazil away from free range to confined feeding of animals in order to meet targets for GHG emissions. These targets favour intensive production over extensive production, thus reinforcing a separation between humans, their domesticated livestock, and nature. These results resonate with the chapter by Loconto (this volume), where she explains that the recourse to metrics as the means to know sustainability tend to be reductionist.

In this context, the reductionist approach reduces our options to the least radical and most supporting of large-scale monocultures – which reinforce the inequalities of the Plantationocene around the world.

Blancha (this volume) demonstrates that the consequences of soy monoculture include a simplification of ecosystems. Since human health and society are intricately linked to the health of ecosystems, such simplification is leading to obesity and other diseases. This vicious circle is also part of the cycle of social inequalities that are likewise produced in the communities of soy monoculture. Attempts to curb these negative effects of simplification are emerging, as we learn from van Dis (this volume). There are attempts to paint farmers as good environmental stewards to justify the link between farmer-led innovation and the provision of ecosystem services. However, current policies remain largely inadequate as they pursue an approach that continues to separate humans from nature (see Loconto et al., 2020).

In the case of biofuels production (Kilham, this volume) and organic agriculture (Freyer et al., this volume), the notion of 'virtual potentials' characterises how the authors treat the question at the heart of human–nature relations. Kilham asks if the biofuel industry is really sustainable and is it a viable option for replacing future fossil fuels use. Freyer et al. ask if organic agriculture can truly feed the future population of the Anthropocene. Both chapters present evidence of the potentiality of the two models, based on the emergent relations of re-attached humans and nature, but only Freyer et al. offers optimism in response to their question by arguing policymakers need to pay more attention to social practices in order to develop socially just and ecologically embedded guides for transforming food systems. Nonetheless, it seems that despite the many transition efforts, the potentialities remain 'virtual' rather than 'actual'.

New Forms of Agrifood Governance for the Anthropocene

Underlining the spatial and temporal difficulties that the notion of the Anthropocene pose to scholarship, Chakrabarty (2009) argues the scale of our thinking now needs to encompass a planetary dimension. We now inhabit a hybrid Earth where the human–nature binary is not just deflated, but nature has been injected with human will, 'however responsibly or irresponsibly that will may have been exercised' (Hamilton and Grinevald, 2015). Building on this thinking, Braidotti

(2013) suggests that 'the change of location of humans from mere biological to geological agents calls for recompositions of both subjectivity and community'. She also reminds us that the spectre of human extinction requires us to rethink the institutions that govern humans in nature as 'the future is nothing more and nothing less than inter-generational solidarity, responsibility for posterity, but it is also our shared dream, or a consensual hallucination' (Braidotti, 2013). Scott (2017) argues that agriculture was fundamental to the creation of the concept of the State itself – thus food and agriculture have always been at the core of societal questions of governance, particularly of how we organise our societies within the limits of the planet. These considerations push us agrifood sociologists to continue our reflections about the power and the responsibilities of actors in governing the problems and proposed solutions for change (see Arnold et al., 2022). This volume thus also addresses the question of how we might govern transitions to sustainable, equitable and healthy agrifood systems in the Anthropocene.

In the sociology of agriculture and food, the concept of food regimes (Friedmann and McMichael, 1989) introduced the global scale to our conceptualisation of agrifood systems. The contributions from Friedmann (this volume) and McKeon (this volume) continue in this tradition by bringing strong critiques of the governance models that have fostered the unequal development, exploitation and inequities in the current agrifood system. For example, the food, energy and financial crises of 2007–2008 triggered a re-evaluation of the sustainability of the global agrifood system and the restructuring of the Committee on World Food Security has created a political space for these types of evaluations and debates to take place (Duncan, 2015; McKeon, 2017a, 2017b). Yet, despite this reform, the United Nations Secretary General Antonio Guterres convened a Food Systems Summit (UNFSS) in September 2021 that has since put into place a 'multistakeholderist' institutional structure based on multi-stakeholder coalitions, expert committees, and national focal points that sacrifices 'human rights' for an 'inclusiveness' framework that has only served to reproduce the problematic relations among humans and with nature (McKeon this volume). Friedmann (this volume) goes one step further by questioning the fitness to purpose of the Nation-State model for governing both transitions and future societies.

Based on their analysis of the dynamics in industrial meat production in France, Fortané et al. (this volume) argue that the very notion of transitions in the age of Capitalocene must be challenged. While there is no doubt that antibiotic use is going down, there is no change in the rules or actors who govern the agrifood system. Loconto (this volume) continues in this vein by illustrating how the multinational companies are fast to adapt their strategies to the changing regulatory environments, but both the upcoming regulations and the identification of multinational organisations as the actors responsible for ensuring the sustainability of agrifood systems fall short. As Latour (1993) has claimed, we still are not modern and despite our best intentions cannot dominate nature. Indeed, we are working within the limits of our natures.

Blancha (this volume) echoes this refrain. He argues that the prevailing power relations prevent transforming the agrifood system. His point is that the distance of consumers from producers is on a steady rise and there is no sign that even planetary boundaries will limit this movement. He questions if we – as humans – will survive the Anthropocene if our governance mechanisms do not prioritise health over all other values. Ransom and Raymond (this volume) suggest that we will be destined to be governed by catastrophes as there is no indication that the current forms of governing disasters are proposing system reconfigurations that could counter the fears of collapse that the notion of the Anthropocene has introduced into popular debate (Charbonnier, 2019). Yet they do offer ideas for how to deal with the question of time. Particularly, there is a need to learn from the past and act in the present with an eye to strengthening the resilience of agrifood systems to adapt to change.

Beyond the question of time, scholars of the Anthropocene (Hamilton and Grinevald, 2015) and of transitions (Barbier, 2010; Voß et al., 2006) claim that new forms of governance are needed that rely upon ongoing reflexivity since 'certain governance patterns undermine themselves by inducing changes in the world that then affect their own working' (Voß and Kemp, 2006: 4). One of the new forms that has gained traction is the Hobbesian ideal that responsible scientists should be identifying, diagnosing, warning the public and then solving the societal problems that emerge (Bonneuil, 2015). This narrative is still popular, despite the growing resistance by a number of 'post-truth' movements in the 2000s (Sismondo, 2017). The quote from the IPCC that we cited earlier in this chapter is emblematic of this narrative of the Anthropocene. Moreover, the Scientific Group formed as part of the UNFSS reiterated this narrative in their policy proposal to create an IPCC for Food Systems. While there is nothing inherently insidious about increasing the role of scientists in governing, Rozas' (this volume) examination of 'verified science' shows how scientific actors who argue for carbon neutrality as the best strategy to achieve internationally signed agreements allow policymakers to continue to leave their governance arrangements un-reflexive and non-transformative.

The tensions that Alkatiri (this volume) explores between the positive health benefits that humans can derive from eating fish and the negative health benefits that come from eating fish from polluted waters exemplifies the types of challenges that the Anthropocene poses to modern ways of governing. Thus, rather than just enlarging the governance circle to include scientific knowledge, she argues that governance of agrifood transitions requires holistic, integrated, and coordinated actions across a wide range of actors, rather than the piecemeal and partial approach to poverty eradication, environmental protection, and health improvement that relies only on the scientific evidence produced by international research that is conducted in silos. Freyer et al. (this volume) question whether as a global community we are on the right policy trajectories (e.g., the European Union farm to fork strategy) with sufficient global commitments (e.g., SDGs; EU Biodiversity Strategy for 2030). These policy approaches are using rhetoric that sounds like they support agrifood system transformations, but as we write, these policies are still promises that risk not being realised due to recent geopolitics in Europe and Africa that effect the entire global food system.

Constance and Loconto (this volume) try to understand if a transformative reform is underway within the CGIAR system of international research where it appears that the promise of agroecology is gathering momentum. However, they show that agroecology is just the most recent attempt to keep the modern agriculture research agenda pertinent in an Epoch 'when the best biologies of the twenty-first century cannot do their job with bounded individuals plus contexts, when organisms plus environments, or genes plus whatever they need, no longer sustain the overflowing richness of biological knowledges, if they ever did?' (Haraway, 2016: 30). Despite rather convincing rhetoric, the reflexive approaches to the governing of research, such as the valuing of qualitative, indigenous or farmer knowledge in the research and innovation processes themselves are not widely translated into functioning policies that govern agricultural and food research and innovation programmes around the world (van Dis et al., this volume). Both articles demonstrate just how deeply disciplined knowledge is institutionalised in agrifood research and innovation.

Kilham (this volume) challenges the sociology of agriculture and food community to continue to push for a greater inclusion of these ways of knowing nature and society. Building on a renewed narrative of traditional knowledge, she argues that past-present-future timing of transitions need to start from a new starting point – the privileging of the *autonomy* of smallholder farmers to co-produce knowledge, environment and governance (van der Ploeg and Schneider, 2022). Barbier et al. (this volume) echo this call in their proposal for a sociological observatory of agroecological transitions. In order to be able to value different ways of knowing and doing, as sociologists, we must develop different methods and tools that facilitate this process. If we think that counting resources is sufficient without accounting for how and why they are used by different types of actors, we will not be true to our ethical and epistemic values. Identifying and legitimising situations where farmers come to know their environments in ways that do not privilege humans or individuals and develop forms of governance where decision-making processes are counter-hegemonic is part of the type of scholarship that the recognition of the Anthropocene inspires among sociologists of agriculture and food.

While the term 'Chthulucene' (Haraway, 2016) is both difficult to pronounce and for many even more difficult to comprehend, we want to conclude this introduction with a nod to Haraway's new concept for the simple reason that she calls upon us to think – particularly about how to change the relations that will enable humans to survive on Earth. Escobar (2016) claims that 'we are facing modern problems for which there are no longer modern solutions', a situation that demands a transition to a world that is not modern (i.e., the pluriverse). But to transition, we cannot use the master's tools to dismantle the master's house (Lorde, 1984), we must think, feel, and do differently. Among the alternatives that have enacted to date, there is a growing trend in civil disobedience by scientists. While this approach is increasingly being considered justifiable as a response to the ethical crisis (Capstick et al., 2022), it remains a risky option for scientists in countries where such types of protest remain severely punished.

We return here to one of the founding principles of the sociology of agriculture and food, which echoes Buroway's (2005) call for public sociology: agrifood activists and agrifood researchers must work and organise together in order to change agrifood systems (Friedland, 2010). Friedland called not just for greater communication from sociologists to publics, he called for participatory action research and an opening up of the scholarly process to the activists who are in the farms and in the streets. In the sociology of agriculture and food, we have been seeking to forward this call to action as we push the boundaries of the theories of how society emerges through interactions and in our treatment of humans and non-humans in our studies. For example, the contributors to this volume have been extremely active in this area. Some of our authors are currently activists, others have been in the past. We have institutional entrepreneurs who have observed the seeds of transition within international organisations, pushed those seeds to sprout and continue to cultivate them in both their theories and their practices. Others still are academics who have played key roles in alternative agrifood movements, expert committees and the creation of food policy councils, while also theorising their importance for sociology. Their contributions inspire us to propose that the sociological imagination for the Anthropocene must be closer to the empirics, closer to the humans and non-humans, and closer to the politics. Without this shift in our imagination, we will not succeed in shifting the agrifood systems.

The Organisation of the Book

This book is organised in two sections. The first section includes three short essays from thought leaders in the sociology of agriculture and food, while the second section includes original research from scholars from around the world.

In Chapter 2, Paul Thompson discusses the agricultural and food sciences, philosophy and the reckoning that is still needed for future agrifood research to meet the challenges posed by the Anthropocene. Chapter 3 is a beautiful reflection by Harriet Friedmann, originator with Phil McMichael of the notion of food regimes, about how agrifood scholars could usefully engage with the concept of Gaia. Chapter 4, written by Nora McKeon, brings us the strong critique from practitioners regarding the governance of the modern global food system and how we must do better in order to survive in the Anthropocene.

We then move on to the original research on agrifood transitions. Nicolas Fortané and collegues look at the transition towards an antibiotic free meat production system in France (Chapter 4), while Thais Rozas explores a transition in the meat sector by looking at the role of pastureland in producing climate neutrality in Brazil (Chapter 6). We close up our discussions about animal protein transitions with Wardah Alkatiri's exposé on water pollution and its effects on Indonesian fisheries (Chapter 7).

Agrifood transitions are also occurring through the changing nature of relations between plants and the humans and machines that consume them. Luis Blacha explores the tensions between obesity and soy monocultures in Argentina (Chapter 8), while Sarina Kilham studies farmer resistance to producing biofuels in Brazil (Chapter 9). Elizabeth Ransom and Hope Raymond (Chapter 10) look at when the Earth acts against humans and their machines producing different emotions that change how the humans live with nature. Bernhard Freyer and colleagues (Chapter 11) explore how viewing these human–nature relations as ecosystems services might transform food systems in Africa and Europe.

The final set of empirical studies focus on public, private and civic ways of knowing current and future agrifood systems for the Anthropocene. Allison Loconto explores this topic from the perspective of multinational corporations who are in dialogue with civil society (Chapter 12), Renée van Dis (Chapter 13) looks at the science-policy interface in Europe, while Barbier and colleagues (Chapter 14) propose a new approach to studying agroecological transitions in France. Douglas Constance and Allison Loconto (Chapter 15) close the book with an analysis of transitions within the international research networks. These three chapters are particularly good in highlighting how closely governance, environment and knowledge are connected.

While the chapters in this book most often show that current agrifood transitions are not dealing with the challenges posed to them by the conditions of the Anthropocene, this evidence should be a warning to scientists and policymakers alike that the current approaches and even the current terminology is insufficient for the threat that the Anthropocene poses to societies as we know them. Some of the innovations and future-oriented pieces in this book do offer some glimmer of hope. But it would require that we – as sociologists, citizens, readers and eaters on Earth – take up the challenge posed by the Anthropocene to be more engaged in documenting, studying and challenging the dominant knowledge, environmental and governance regimes.

References

Arnold, N., Brunori, G., Dessein, J., et al. (2022) 'Governing food futures: Towards a "responsibility turn" in food and agriculture'. *Journal of Rural Studies, 89*: 82–6.

Aykut, S.C. and Evrard, A. (2017) 'A transition so that everything can stay the same? Institutional change and path dependence in French and German energy transitions'. *Revue internationale de politique comparée, 24*(1): 17–49.

Barbier, M. (2010) 'The ecologization of agricultural development and the treadmill of sustainable development. A critique in a state of transition'. *Przegląd Socjologiczny (Sociological Review), 59*(October): 9–28.

Blanchette, A. (2018) 'Industrial meat production'. *Annual Review of Anthropology, 47*(1): 185–99.

Blühdorn, I. (2015) 'A much needed renewal of environmentalism? Eco-politics in the Anthropocene'. In C. Hamilton, F. Gemenne and C. Bonneuil (eds), *The Anthropocene and the Global Environmental Crisis*. London: Routledge, pp. 156–67.

Bonanno, A., Busch, L., Friedland, W.H., et al. (1994) *From Columbus to ConAgra: The Globalization of Agriculture and Food*. Lawrence, KS: University Press of Kansas, pp. viii, 294.

Bonneuil, C. (2015) 'The geological turn: Narratives of the Anthropocene'. In C. Hamilton, F. Gemenne and C. Bonneuil (eds), *The Anthropocene and the Global Environmental Crisis*. London: Routledge, pp. 17–31.

Bowden, G. (2017) 'An environmental sociology for the Anthropocene'. *Canadian Review of Sociology/Revue canadienne de sociologie, 54*(1): 48–68.

Braidotti, R. (2013) 'Posthuman Humanities'. *European Educational Research Journal, 12*(1): 1–19.

Burawoy, M. (2005) '2004 ASA presidential address: For public sociology'. *American Sociological Review, 70*(1): 4–28.

Busch, L. and Lacy, W.B. (1983) *Science, Agriculture, and the Politics of Research*. Boulder: Westview Press.

Buttel, F.H. (1987) 'New directions in environmental sociology'. *Annual Review of Sociology, 13*: 465–88.

Buttel, F.H., Larson, O. and Gillespie, G.W. (1990) *The Sociology of Agriculture*. New York, NY: Greenwood Press.

Capstick, S., Thierry, A., Cox, E., et al. (2022) 'Civil disobedience by scientists helps press for urgent climate action'. *Nature Climate Change*. (https://doi.org/10.1038/s41558-022-01461-y)

Carolan, M. (2021) *The Sociology of Food and Agriculture*. Milton Park: Taylor & Francis.

Carolan, M. and Stuart, D. (2016) 'Get real: Climate change and all that 'it' entails'. *Sociologia Ruralis*, *56*(1): 74–95.

Carolan, M.S. (2005) 'Society, biology, and ecology: Bringing nature back into sociology's disciplinary narrative through critical realism'. *Organization & Environment*, *18*(4): 393–421.

Carr, L.J. (1945) 'Situational sociology'. *American Journal of Sociology*, *51*(2): 136–41.

Catton, W.R. and Dunlap, R.E. (1978) 'Environmental sociology: A new paradigm'. *The American Sociologist*, *13*(1): 41–9.

Chakrabarty, D. (2009) 'The climate of history: Four theses'. *Critical Inquiry*, *35*(2): 197–222.

Charbonnier, P. (2019) 'The splendor and squalor of collapsology. What the survivalists of the left fail to consider'. *Revue du Crieur Selected Articles*, (2): 88–95.

Constance, D.H. and Bonanno, A. (2000) 'Regulating the global fisheries: The World Wildlife Fund, Unilever, and the Marine Stewardship Council'. *Agriculture and Human Values*, *17*(2): 125–39.

Constance, D.H., Konefal, J. and Hatanaka, M. (2018) *Contested Sustainability Discourses in the Agrifood System*. London: Routledge, p. 314.

Crippa, M., Solazzo, E., Guizzardi, D., et al. (2021) 'Food systems are responsible for a third of global anthropogenic GHG emissions'. *Nature Food*, *2*(3): 198–209.

Crutzen, P.J. (2002) 'The "Anthropocene"'. *Journal de Physique IV France*, *12*(10): 1–5.

Crutzen, P.J. (2006) 'The "Anthropocene"'. In E.Ehlers and T. Krafft (eds), *Earth System Science in the Anthropocene*. Berlin and Heidelberg: Springer Berlin Heidelberg, pp. 13–8.

Crutzen, P.J. and Stoermer, E.F. (2000) The "Anthropocene"'. *IGBP Newsletter*, 41.

Cucco, I. and Fonte, M. (2015) Local food and civic food networks as a real utopias project. *Socio.hu*, *2015*(3): 22–36.

Davoudi, S., Shaw, K., Haider, L.J., et al. (2012) 'Resilience: A bridging concept or a dead end? "Reframing" resilience: Challenges for planning theory and practice interacting traps: Resilience assessment of a pasture management system in Northern Afghanistan urban resilience: What does it mean in planning practice? Resilience as a useful concept for climate change adaptation? The politics of resilience for planning: A cautionary note'. *Planning Theory & Practice*, *13*(2): 299–333.

Duncan, J. (2015) *Global Food Security Governance: Civil Society Engagement in the Reformed Committee on World Food Security*. Abingdon, Oxon, and New York, NY: Routledge.

Ellis, M.A. and Trachtenberg, Z. (2014) 'Which Anthropocene is it to be? Beyond geology to a moral and public discourse'. *Earth's Future*, *2*(2): 122–5.

Elzen, B., Augustyn, A., Barbier, M., et al. (2017) *AgroEcological Transitions: Changes and Breakthroughs in the Making.* Wageningen, NL: Wageningen University & Research, p. 302.

Elzen, B., Barbier, M., Cerf, M., et al. (2012) 'Stimulating transitions towards sustainable farming systems'. In I. Darnhofer and D. Benoit (eds), *Farming System Research.* Montpellier: Editions QUAE.

Escobar, A. (2016) 'Thinking-feeling with the Earth: Territorial struggles and the ontological dimension of the Epistemologies of the South'. *AIBR, Revista de Antropología Iberoamericana, 11*(01): 11–32.

FAO (2020) *FAO COVID-19 Response and Recovery Programme: Food Systems Transformation: Building to Transform during Response and Recovery.* Rome: Food and Agriculture Organization of the United Nations.

FAO, IFAD, UNICEF, et al. (2017) *The State of Food Security and Nutrition in the World. Building Resilience for Peace and Food Security.* Rome: Food and Agriculture Organization of the United Nations.

Fouilleux, E., Bricas, N. and Alpha, A. (2017) '"Feeding 9 billion people": Global food security debates and the productionist trap'. *Journal of European Public Policy, 24*(11): 1658–77.

Fox, N.J. and Alldred, P. (2020) 'Re-assembling climate change policy: Materialism, posthumanism, and the policy assemblage'. *British Journal of Sociology, 71*(2): 269–83.

Freudenburg, W.R. (2009) *Catastrophe in the Making: The Engineering of Katrina and the Disasters of Tomorrow.* Washington, DC: Island Press/Shearwater Books.

Friedland, W., Barton, A.E. and Thomas, R.J. (1981) *Manufacturing Green Gold: Capital, Labor and Technology in the Lettuce Industry.* Cambridge: Cambridge University Press.

Friedland, W.H. (1984) 'Commodity systems analysis: An approach to the sociology of agriculture'. In H.K. Schwarzweller (ed), *Research in Rural Sociology and Development.* Greenwich, CT: JAI Press, pp. 221–35.

Friedland, W.H. (2010) 'New ways of working and organization: Alternative agrifood movements and agrifood researchers'. *Rural Sociology, 75*(4): 601–27.

Friedmann, H. and McMichael, P. (1989) 'Agriculture and the state system: The rise and decline of national agricultures, 1870 to the present'. *Sociologia Ruralis, 29*: 93–117.

Geels, F.W. (2002) 'Technological transitions as evolutionary reconfiguration processes: A multi-level perspective and a case-study'. *Research Policy, 31*(8–9): 1257–74.

Geels, F.W. (2010) 'Ontologies, socio-technical transitions (to sustainability), and the multi-level perspective'. *Research Policy, 39*(4): 495–510.

Geels, F.W., Hekkert, M.P. and Jacobsson, S. (2008) 'The dynamics of sustainable innovation journeys'. *Technology Analysis & Strategic Management, 20*(5): 521–36.

Geels, F.W. and Turnheim, B. (2022) *The Great Reconfiguration: A Socio-Technical Analysis of Low-Carbon Transitions in UK Electricity, Heat, and Mobility Systems.* Cambridge: Cambridge University Press.

Glaser, B.G. and Strauss, A.L. (1964) 'Awareness contexts and social interaction'. *American Sociological Review, 29*(5): 669–79.

Goodman, D., DuPuis, E.M. and Goodman, M.K. (2012) *Alternative Food Networks: Knowledge, Practice, and Politics.* Abingdon, Oxon; New York, NY: Routledge.

Goulet, F. and Vinck, D. (2012) 'L'innovation par retrait. Contribution à une sociologie du détachement'. *Revue française de sociologie 53*(2): 195–224.

Grin, J. (2006) 'Reflexive modernization as a governance issue-or: Designing and shaping re-structuration'. In J.-P. Voß, D. Bauknect and R. Kemp (eds), *Reflexive Governance for Sustainable Development.* Cheltenham: Edward Elgar, pp. 54–81.

Grin, J., Rotmans, J. and Schot, J.W. (2010) *Transitions to Sustainable Development: New Directions in the Study of Long Term Transformative Change.* New York, NY: Routledge.

Hamilton, C., Gemenne, F. and Bonneuil, C. (2015) *The Anthropocene and the Global Environmental Crisis: Rethinking Modernity in a New Epoch.* Milton Park: Taylor & Francis.

Hamilton, C. and Grinevald, J. (2015) 'Was the Anthropocene anticipated?' *The Anthropocene Review, 2*(1): 59–72.

Haraway, D. (1988) 'Situated knowledges: The science question in feminism and the privilege of partial perspective'. *Feminist Studies, 14*(3): 575–99.

Haraway, D. (2008) *When Species Meet.* Minneapolis, MN: University of Minnesota Press.

Haraway, D., Ishikawa, N., Gilbert, S.F., et al. (2016) 'Anthropologists are talking – About the Anthropocene'. *Ethnos, 81*(3): 535–64.

Haraway, D.J. (1989) *Primate Visions: Gender, Race, and Nature in the World of Modern Science.* New York, NY: Routledge.

Haraway, D.J. (2016) *Staying with the Trouble: Making Kin in the Chthulucene.* Durham: Duke University Press.

Head, L. (2014) 'Contingencies of the Anthropocene: Lessons from the "Neolithic"'. *The Anthropocene Review, 1*(2): 113–25.

Hillman, K., Nilsson, M., Rickne, A., et al. (2009) 'Fostering sustainable technologies – A framework for analysing the governance of innovation systems'. In *First European Conference on Sustainability Transitions.* Amsterdam, pp. 4–6, June.

Hurlbut, J.B., Jasanoff, S. and Saha, K. (2020) 'Constitutionalism at the nexus of life and law'. *Science, Technology & Human Values, 45*(6): 979–1000.

Jasanoff, S. (2004) 'The idiom of co-production'. In S. Jasanoff (ed), *States of Knowledge: The Co-production of Science and Social Order.* London: Routledge.

Joly, P.-B. (2020) 'Les formes multiples de la recherche: Scientifique, industrielle et citoyenne'. *Cahiers de l'action, 55*(1): 47–54.

Köhler, J., Geels, F.W., Kern, F., et al. (2019) 'An agenda for sustainability transitions research: State of the art and future directions'. *Environmental Innovation and Societal Transitions, 31*: 1–32.

Kropp, C., Antoni-Komar, I. and Sage, C. (2020) *Food System Transformations: Social Movements, Local Economies, Collaborative Networks.* Milton Park: Taylor & Francis.

Latour, B. (1993) *We Have Never Been Modern*. Cambridge, MA: Harvard University Press.

Latour, B. (2005) *Reassembling the Social: An Introduction to Actor-Network-Theory*. Oxford and New York, NY: Oxford University Press.

Latour, B. (2015) 'Telling friends from foes in the time of the Anthropocene'. In C. Hamilton, F. Gemenne and C. Bonneuil (eds), *The Anthropocene and the Global Environmental Crisis*. London: Routledge, pp. 145–55.

Lhoste, É. (2020) 'Les tiers-lieux peuvent-ils ouvrir la recherche à la société civile?' *Cahiers de l'action*, 55(1): 13–9.

Lhoste, E.F. (2022) *Trajectoire d'un champ d'action stratégique: les recherches participatives sont-elles solubles dans la science?* Technologie et innovation, p. 7 (Recherche responsable et responsabilité académique).

Lidskog, R. and Waterton, C. (2016a) 'Anthropocene – A cautious welcome from environmental sociology?' *Environmental Sociology*, 2(4): 395–406.

Lidskog, R. and Waterton, C. (2016b) 'Conceptual innovation in environmental sociology'. *Environmental Sociology*, 2(4): 307–11.

Lockie, S. (2017) 'A better Anthropocene?' *Environmental Sociology*, 3(3): 167–72.

Loconto, A. (2022) 'Gouverner par les métriques: Un exercice dans l'intermédiation des connaissances'. In F. Goulet, P. Caron, B. Hubert, et al. (eds), *Sciences Techniques et Agricultures. L'impératif de la transition*. Paris: Presses des Mines.

Loconto, A. and Barbier, M. (2014) Transitioning sustainability: Performing 'governing by standards'. In S. Borrás and J. Edler (eds), *The Governance of Socio-technical Systems: Theorising and Explaining Change*. Cheltenham: Edward Edgar, pp. 70–95.

Loconto, A., Desquilbet, M., Moreau, T., et al. (2020) 'The land sparing – Land sharing controversy: Tracing the politics of knowledge'. *Land Use Policy*, 96: 103610.

Loconto, A. and Fouillieux, E. (2019) 'Defining agroecology: Exploring the circulation of knowledge in FAO's Global Dialogue'. *International Journal of Sociology of Agriculture and Food*, 25(2): 116–37.

Lorde, A. (1984) *Sister Outsider: Essays and Speeches*. Trumansburg, NY: Crossing Press.

McGowan, K. and Westley, F. (2015) 'At the root of change: The history of social innovation'. In A. Nicholls, J. Simon and M. Gabriel (eds), *New Frontiers in Social Innovation Research*. London: Palgrave Macmillan, pp. 52–68.

McGreevy, S.R., Rupprecht, C.D.D., Niles, D., et al. (2022) 'Sustainable agrifood systems for a post-growth world'. *Nature Sustainability*. (https://doi.org/10.1038/s41893-022-00933-5)

McKeon, N. (2017a) 'Are equity and sustainability a likely outcome when foxes and chickens share the same coop? Critiquing the concept of multistakeholder governance of food security'. *Globalizations*, 14(3): 379–98.

McKeon, N. (2017b) 'Transforming global governance in the post-2015 era: Towards an equitable and sustainable world'. *Globalizations*, 14(4): 487–503.

Mead, G.H. ([1934] 1962) *Mind, Self and Society*. Chicago, IL: University of Chicago Press.

Mol, A. (1997) 'Ecological modernization: Industrial transformations and environmental reform'. In M. Redclift and G. Woodgate (eds), *International Handbook of
Environmental Sociology*. London: Elgar, pp. 138–49.

Molénat, X. (2009) *Bruno Latour, du laboratoire à la société. La sociologie*. Auxerre:
Éditions Sciences Humaines, p. 220.

Moore, J.W. (2017) 'The Capitalocene, Part I: On the nature and origins of our
ecological crisis'. *Journal of Peasant Studies*, *44*(3): 594–630.

Moore, J.W. (2018) 'The Capitalocene Part II: Accumulation by appropriation and
the centrality of unpaid work/energy'. *Journal of Peasant Studies*, *45*(2): 237–79.

Moulaert, F., Martinelli, F., Swyngedouw, E., et al. (2005) 'Towards alternative
model (s) of local innovation'. *Urban Studies*, *42*(11): 1969–90.

Pavesich, V. (2022) 'Working on the myth of the Anthropocene: Blumenberg and the
need for philosophical anthropology'. *New German Critique*, *49*(1 (145)): 97–130.

Peddi, B., Ludwig, D. and Dessein, J. (2022) 'Relating inclusive innovations to
Indigenous and local knowledge: A conceptual framework'. *Agriculture and
Human Values*. (https://doi.org/10.1007/s10460-022-10344-z)

Poole, S. (2014) 'The Gaia guy: How James Lovelock struggled to be taken seriously'.
The New Statesman.

Rip, A. and Kemp, R. (1998) 'Technological change'. In S. Rayner and E.L. Malone
(eds), *Human Choice and Climate Change*. Columbus, OH: Battelle Press, pp.
327–99.

Rockström, J., Gaffney, O., Rogelj, J., et al. (2017) A roadmap for rapid decar-
bonization. *Science*, *355*(6331): 1269–71.

Rockstrom, J., Steffen, W., Noone, K., et al. (2009) 'A safe operating space for
humanity'. *Nature*, *461*(7263): 472–75.

Schatzki, T.R., Cetina, K.D.K. and Von Savigny, E. (2001) *The Pratice Turn in
Contemporary Theory*. Milton Park: Taylor & Francis Group.

Schumacher, E.F. (1989) *Small Is Beautiful: Economics as if People Mattered*. New
York, NY: Perennial Library.

Scott, J.C. (2017) *Against the Grain: A Deep History of the Earliest States*. New
Haven, CT: Yale University Press.

Semal, L. (2015) 'Anthropocene, catastrophism and green political theory'. In C.
Hamilton, F. Gemenne and C. Bonneuil (eds), *The Anthropocene and the global
Environmental Crisis*. London: Routledge, pp. 87–99.

Shove, E. and Spurling, N. (2013) *Sustainable Practices: Social Theory and Climate
Change*. New York, NY: Taylor & Francis.

Shukla, P.R., Skea, J., Calvo Buendia, E., et al. (2019) *Climate Change and Land: An
IPCC Special Report on Climate Change, Desertification, Land Degradation,
Sustainable Land Management, Food Security, and Greenhouse Gas Fluxes in
Terrestrial Ecosystems*. New York, NY: Intergovernmental Panel on Climate
Change (IPPC).

Sismondo, S. (2017) 'Post-truth?' *Social Studies of Science*, *47*(1): 3–6.

Sklair, L. (2017) 'Sleepwalking through the Anthropocene'. *British Journal of Sociology*, *68*(4): 775–84.

Szarka, J. (2016) 'Towards an evolutionary or a transformational energy transition? Transition concepts and roadmaps in European Union policy discourse'. *Innovation: The European Journal of Social Science Research*, *29*(3): 222–42.

Tarde, G. and Parsons, E.W.C. (1903) *The Laws of Imitation*. New York, NY: H. Holt and Company.

Toews, D. (2003) 'The new tarde: Sociology after the end of the social'. *Theory, Culture & Society*, *20*(5): 81–98.

Turnheim, B. and Geels, F.W. (2013) 'The destabilisation of existing regimes: Confronting a multi-dimensional framework with a case study of the British coal industry (1913–1967)'. *Research Policy*, *42*(10): 1749–67.

van der Ploeg, J.D. and Schneider, S. (2022) 'Autonomy as a politico-economic concept: Peasant practices and nested markets'. *Journal of Agrarian Change*, *22*(3): 529–46.

Venturini, T. (2010) 'Diving in magma: How to explore controversies with actor-network theory'. *Public Understanding of Science*, *19*(3): 258–73.

Voß, J.-P., Bauknecht, D. and Kemp, R. (2006) *Reflexive Governance for Sustainable Development*. Cheltenham: Edward Elgar.

Voß, J.-P. and Kemp, R. (2006) Sustainability and reflexive governance: Introduction. In: J.-P. Voß, D. Bauknecht and R. Kemp (eds), *Reflexive governance for Sustainable Development*. Cheltenham: Edward Elgar, pp. 3–28.

Wallerstein, I. (1975) *World Inequality: Origins and Perspectives on the World System*. Montreal: Black Rose Books.

Weik, E. (2012) 'Introducing "the creativity of action" into institutionalist theory'. *M@n@gement*, *15*(5): 564–81.

Wolford, W. (2021) 'The Plantationocene: A lusotropical contribution to the theory'. *Annals of the American Association of Geographers*, *111*(6): 1622–39.

Wright, E.O. (2010) *Envisioning Real Utopias*. London: Verso .

Znaniecki, F. (1963) *Cultural Sciences, Their Origin and Development*. Urbana: University of Illinois Press.

Part I

(Agri)Food for Thought on the Anthropocene

2

Food Systems in the Anthropocene: Some Philosophical Reflections

Paul B. Thompson

The Anthropocene is a classificatory term, and classification is of enduring interest to philosophers. I am not entirely sure how geologists distinguish epochs, though I presume it has something to do with characteristic terraforms, populations of flora and fauna and climate regimes. The Anthropocene was a classification popularised by atmospheric scientist Paul Crutzen (1933–2021). It marks a new epoch following the Holocene in which human beings have become drivers for all three of these characteristic markers. Seen from a planetary perspective, agriculture is a terraform serving as a key marker for the transition from Holocene to Anthropocene (see Scott, 2018). About 20 percent of the Earth's land mass is now under cultivation or in pasture. The impact of food production also extends to the seas, as fishing has altered the composition of ocean species. Forests are also increasingly under human management, though their link to the food system could be contested.

Nature is also a classificatory term, often conceptualised as that domain in which human influence is negligible or nonexistent. The Romantic era of European history launched aesthetic and moral appreciation of this nature. 19th century Romanticism transitioned to 20th century social movements for outdoor recreation, wilderness preservation and, following *Silent Spring* in 1962 by Rachel Carson (1907–1964), environmental protection. To the extent that the Anthropocene represents the end of nature in the popular imagination, I say good riddance. As an environmental philosopher, I follow historian William Cronon, who argued that these social movements ignored and marginalised the role of indigenous people in shaping the terraforms of colonised territory (Cronon, 1996). The dichotomisation of nature and society also left food production in an ontological nether zone, a form and set of practices that did not count in the dominant cultural categories of the modern era. If 21st century society is urban and nature is untrammeled by human use, agriculture does not exist.

Whatever geological and atmospheric scientists are saying about the Anthropocene, the term is having a cultural impact akin to the one Friedrich Nietzsche (1844–1900) put in the mouth of his fictional prophet *Zarathustra*: God is dead. 'The Anthropocene' functions less as descriptively classificatory terminology than as proclamation of a cultural era. In this era, no one any longer believes in the presumptive categories that shaped social interaction in ages past. Prophets of the Anthropocene announce a new kind of human being. Nietzsche called it the *Übermensch* (and we would be advised to note the gender neutrality of the original German). As Zarathustra announces that the humanity of the late 19th century must revalue all values, today's new persona must mindfully undertake the tasks that previous generations left to nature. Although science (including social science) is critical for both the conceptualisation and the execution of these tasks, it is unable to account for the prescriptive dimension of the word 'must' in the previous sentence. Neither God nor nature is capable of supplying direction or telos for the future transit of humanity any longer. In the Anthropocene this extends to what we now call the ecosystem services. These ecosystem services deliver benefits that a 19th century *Übermensch* might have relied upon implicitly.

If I were to speculate on what William James (1842–1910) might have called the cash value of this shift in humanity's 'to do' list, I would start by noting the scientific predictions of coming change. A list of them would exceed my word limit, even if we ignore those that seem less relevant to food systems. The projections of the Intergovernmental Panel on Climate Change (IPCC) are a prominent example. In sum, we can expect as much as a 50 percent loss in farm and pasture land by the end of the century owing to climate shifts and rising sea levels. These losses will be heaviest in areas where smallholders are already impoverished, triggering migration and warfare over remaining food system resources. Agricultural scientists have internalised one of two competing normative standpoints in response to these projections. Most have adopted the perspective that all scientific and technological resources should be deployed towards making up the loss in global food production through gene editing and precision agriculture. The other view prioritises the interests of actually existing smallholders, calling for measures that do not force them to bear the brunt of socio-economic forces accompanying a techno-logical revolution (Thompson, 2019).

My reference to Nietzsche marks my belief that although reflection on the Anthropocene's significance for food systems must start with scientific projections, it should not end there. I can pursue my point by noting the social impact of Zarathustra's announcement in 1885. While this could prove to be a convoluted topic in itself, very few human beings living in the third decade of the 21st century think that God is dead. Religion continues to be a potent source of moral direction everywhere, so much so that many if not most recent instances of organised warfare have some theological sanction or underpinning. The combatants imagine a justification for their action in religious terms, even if social theorists would point to material causes. It is hardly the case that they 'no longer believe' in the pre-sumptive categories of their respective faiths. Even many putatively secular motivations are grounded in the Judeo-Christian worldview, and the political or military leaders of these conflicts dare not deny the religious orientation of the masses that must be enlisted to support them.

I do not think this would surprise Nietzsche, for Zarathustra was not a scientific prediction, in the first place. Indeed, although the death of God was meant to mark an epochal transition in cultural history, the important philosophical action in Nietzsche's novel occurs after the prophet has failed to enlighten the masses and must confront the deeper philosophical implications of his thought that God is dead. Now, Doug Constance has not invited me to contribute to this volume on the Anthropocene in order to engage in lengthy Nietzsche inter-pretation, so I will abjure further speculation on the death of God. My point is much simpler, in any case. It is that we cannot expect very many people to follow the Anthropocene's announcement that nature has reached its end. We cannot expect people to accept the idea that we must now do what nature did for us in eons past. The sociological implication is that we will increasingly experience a rift between self-styled *Übermenschen* who see the future food system that the sciences have revealed and the ordinary *Volk* who just want their cheeseburgers.

At the same time, there are real changes afoot among people who do not want to be overly troubled about their food. We have seen dramatic increase in market demand for organic foods, an uptick of concerns about the safety of food ingredients and chemical residues, the re-emergence of farmer's markets and a rise in vegetarianism. I would not want to overstate the role of ethics in accounting for these trends, but neither would I discount it entirely. The idea of food ethics that is most prominent among philosophy professors is derived from Peter Singer. Singer has argued that we should recognise that our food purchases incentivise behaviour back up the value chain, encouraging retailers to offer products that meet standards of fair trade, environmental quality and humane treatment of animals (Singer and Mason, 2006). My interactions with college undergraduates suggest that quite a few of them think this way, even if they have never encountered any of Singer's texts. Breeze Harper's entry into this literature *Sistah Vegan* explores ethical rationales for going vegan that speak directly to the social identity of black women (Harper, 2010). For Singer, food ethics means making consumption decisions that, through the magic of markets, incentivise more socially and environmentally friendly behaviour among farmers and food industry firms. Harper adds that food ethics can also incorporate an ethic of resistance and identity construction. While those who are or once were college undergraduates still represent a minority of the population in industrialised countries, they are large enough to have real impact on the demand curve. Their preferences—at least partially driven by ethical concerns—are shaping food systems even beyond what might be expected by their numbers.

Does the announcement of the Anthropocene have anything to do with the prescriptions of food ethics? My answer to this question starts (again) with scientific predictions about the future food system, such as those made by the IPCC or the more frequent analyses done by the Food and Agriculture Organization of the United Nations (FAO) or the United States Department of Agriculture (USDA). One can certainly see how a consumption ethic might be mobilised by the thought that climate change burdens smallholders disproportionately, for example. However, FAO and USDA have used data and models to predict food system trends wholly apart from the announcement of a transition from the Holocene to the Anthropocene. These predictions take on ethical significance in the tension between world-feeders and farmer-boosters noted already. I can see why someone urging either response might call upon the rhetorical force of the Anthropocene to put an exclamation point on moral arguments that they have been making for decades. Yet I urge readers to ask whether these exclamation points ignore the announcement of the Anthropocene in much the same way that unreflective recitation of religious dogma avoids Zarathustra's announcement of the death of God. One could say all the same things in favour of increasing global productive capacity, on the one hand, or protecting smallholders, on the other, whether or not one recognises the moral imperatives of a world in which faith in a provisioning nature is no longer plausible. Indeed, both perspectives would appear to presume continuities that are deaf to the announcement of the Anthropocene.

The forward-looking nature of predictive models may be part of the problem, but food system professionals come by their devotion to prediction honestly. Farmers themselves have displayed keen interest in the long-range weather forecasts of farmer's almanacs for at least 200 years. A predictive standpoint becomes problematic when it cuts off inquiries couched within a historical appreciation of whence the community of inquirers has come. At such moments, the interest in prediction is ineluctably shaped by whatever habits and institutional practices happen to be in place at the moment. In contrast to this unreflective 'whatever prevails' stance, a historically informed stance can query the assumptions and forces that have brought an individual, a social group or a culture to that point. It is very likely that Western ways of thinking and acting in food systems have incorporated assumptions that privilege the conceptualisations of nature that penetrate the symbolic apparatus of contemporary food systems. We (and by *we* I mean anyone who cares to join me in inquiry) will not illuminate these assumptions by running surveys, or focus groups. We will not understand them through community engaged research or studies on consumer willingness to pay. We are asking questions about ourselves when we undertake such questions, not describing socio-economic entities revealed through data collection.

The Anthropocene announces that all assumptions about nature's efficaciousness, value, function and disposition (if it has one) must be re-examined. They must be re-examined in light of the recognition that an era is dawning—may in fact have dawned some time ago—in which humanity cannot rely on nature anymore. Humans must now rethink the place they inhabit, be it nature *or* society, and ask how notions of responsibility must be recast. This thought on responsibility must move in multiple directions. It must consider the sense in which humanity is responsible for the damage that has already been done to ecosystems and their capacity for delivering provisioning, regulatory and cultural services. It must ask whether reparations are due to the human beings (often marginalised by gender or race) who have withstood the worst of these damages. Yet it must also consider how a forward-looking notion of responsibility can place human intention in the role of steering planetary systems without also succumbing to the vices of arrogance, pride and a domineering attitude.

I am suggesting that the Anthropocene has not been and is not likely to be taken very seriously among most food system insiders, not to mention those who just want their cheeseburgers. When I said that the Anthropocene's cultural impact is like the death of God, I meant that, in sociological terms, it may not be very much impact at all. Those under the sway of the idea of an Anthropocene may perceive themselves to be in the position to prognosticate and pre-scribe, but to the extent that they muster a multitude of pre-existing cultural forms to populate their prognostications and prescriptions, they are shirking the ontological demand the Anthropocene makes on the human condition. They are all too much like the Faux-Nietzschean who interpreted his work as validation for moralities of eugenics and racial cleansing during the first half of the 20th century. They have the answers to the problems of the Anthropocene before they ever encounter them. They do not see the Anthropocene as a call to stand, once again like men and women of past ages have stood, on a precipice where questioning the fundamental categories we use to understand ourselves becomes necessary.

As I have written elsewhere, I launched my work in the ethics of agriculture and food systems at the behest of leading voices from the previous generation. These men (and they were mostly men) saw the branches of the agricultural sciences as lacking a capacity for collaborative reflection on the purposes and significance of food sys-tems. They hoped that the disciplines of philosophical thinking could help. Yet they underestimated the resistance to philosophical discourse that would emerge from social scientists already ensconced in the research and education organisations dedicated to agricultural and food science (Thompson, 2015). The Anthropocene calls humanity at large to ask how loss of faith in nature resonates throughout every pore, every nook and cranny, of biophysical process and the social forms of living beings. It is a monumental task, but I do not hold out much hope that it will be undertaken by people who work in food systems; however, much our food system reproduces the quotidian reality that shapes a generation's imagination and fate.

Of course, I could be wrong about all of this. I am a pragmatist, after all, and fallibilism is the pragmatists' creed. Perhaps the Anthropocene will look very much like the Holocene in terms of what it asks from humanity, and perhaps God isn't dead, after all. My gut as well as my scholarship tells me that it would be unwise to place too many chips on such types of optimism. Nietzsche's deeper hope lay in thinking that one could face the precipice and yet muster the will to persevere in a joyful, playful manner. But that form of optimism takes work. It is with respect to my pessimism about future food scholar's willingness to undertake that work that I most hope to be wrong.

References

Carson, R. (1962) *Silent Spring*. Boston, MA: Houghton Mifflin.

Cronon, W. (1996) 'The trouble with wilderness, or getting back to the wrong nature'. *Environmental History*, 1: 7–28.

Harper, A.B. (ed.) (2010) *Sistah Vegan: Black Female Vegans Speak on Food, Identity, Health and Society*. Brooklyn, NY: Lantern Books.

Scott, N.D. (2018) *Food, Genetic Engineering and Philosophy of Technology*. New York, NY: Springer.

Singer, P. and Mason, J. (2006) *The Way We Eat: Why Our Food Choices Matter*. Emmaus, PA: The Rodale Press.

Thompson, P.B. (2015) 'Agricultural ethics – Then and now'. *Agriculture and Human Values*, 32: 77–85.

Thompson, P.B. (2019) 'Emerging (food) technology as an environmental and philosophical issue in the era of climate change'. In E. Gilson and S. Kenehan (eds), *Food, Environment and Climate Change: Justice at the Intersections*, Lanham, MD: Rowman and Littlefield, pp. 195–212.

3

The Invitation of the Anthropocene: Towards a New Way of Living With All Our Relations

Harriet Friedmann

Together, the human species is invited by the Anthropocene to take the archetypal hero's journey described by Joseph Campbell: Departure, Initiation, Return (Campbell, 2008). Humans departed from close relations with all of nature, in many phases even before recorded history, and most dramatically in ongoing colonial integration and simplification of places and peoples. We have had recurrent initiations through war, enslavement, genocide and degraded life in all its forms, which accompanied much learning and creativity. If we accept the invitation of the Anthropocene, we can learn to return, to combine science with ancient wisdom and to recover what was lost through the experiences we have gained. In this place and in all places, we can fall in love with Earth.

My Journey With the Anthropocene Idea

My journey began with an invitation to write a personal reflection as an elder of food and agrarian studies. Having never engaged with the idea of Anthropocene, I dipped my toes into the waters of far-flung debates, ranging from specific decisions by Earth Scientists about dating the geological periods of Earth history to media and popular awareness, ignorance or denial of its various aspects – climate change, species death and ecocide. I began with the idea that too much of the popular discussion was fear based and led to panic or avoidance; much energy seemed to come from climate's Joan of Arc, Greta Thunberg, who proclaims *the house is on fire*, and from social movements that, despite the often-fine analyses of leaders, seem to reduce action to single issues, such as sequestering carbon or abstaining from eating meat.

Scientists understandably sound ever more shrill alarms. According to an insightful analysis by Clark and Gunaratnam, the very idea of the Anthropocene emerged as a cry of alarm and frustration by geoscientists who faced what they believe to be a looming planetary crisis. The science of the Anthropocene might best be viewed as the public-facing and explicitly politicised outcrop of a much deeper and heftier body of work. And this very lack of disinterestedness, it should be added, has earned Anthropocene scientists considerable opprobrium from their geoscience peers (Clark and Gunaratnam, 2017: 152).

The alarm stems from renewed insight into the unified, dramatically changing history of Earth. After several decades of specialised disciplinary research and theories, Earth Science is helping all of us to understand the unified and dramatic history of Earth, with mutually evolving (and sometimes transforming) spheres of air, water, rocks, soils and living beings. In this light, the question arises: what emotions and other human attributes are at play in embracing or resisting recognition of the current choices facing humankind? Discussions of climate, atmospheric gases and diversity of life, even more of environmental (in)justice, are possible without naming Anthropocene, indeed are far more frequent than use of the term in public discourse (Sklair, 2021). Perhaps engagement is better off without it.

My argument is that history matters more than anything, but that the focus on dating Anthropocene may be a snare and a delusion. Each of the dates proposed is important since problems cumulate over the millennia of human life on Earth. The earliest proposed date is killing of large animals such as mammoths. That continues, from wolves to polar bears, and must stop. Next is agriculture. Industrial agriculture, including confined livestock, are (finally) recognised in climate and biodiversity models; it is a revival and deepening of latifundia from ancient civilisations, now governed not by slave owning Romans or Spanish colonial landlords, but by corporations imposing chemical substitutes for nutrient cycling. This too must stop. The next date is most familiar – although fossil energy also stretches deep into human prehistory, it was brought to the centre of capitalist production and transport in the 19th century. Digging up fossils and burning them must stop. The last and most recent date – the one accepted by the formal committee of Earth Scientists tasked with deciding it – is based on evidence in rock and ice since 1950 of radioactive particles, plastics and novel chemicals which deepened the ruptures of Earthly metabolisms to the point we are now. These substances were created or vastly expanded by warring governments in the 20th century. After World War II, the United States continued nuclear explosions despite the extraordinary harm from the first ones deployed by the United States against Japanese civilians. Chemicals to enhance fertility of depleted soils and to kill competing plants and animals were deployed as substitutes for natural materials by transnational corporations, and plastics became ubiquitous. At the time, they were sources of renewal of accumulation, imagined by the dominant narrative as conversion of weapons into peaceful sources of prosperity.

Yet, Anthropocene has served a purpose by opening spaces for wider and deeper understanding of human history as part of Earth history. Whether the idea's usefulness has passed remains to be discovered. Partly this depends on whether and how relations between humans and the rest of nature can be integrated with relations among humans. The latter are now organised into deepening class relations, with ever more concentration of power and riches on one side and poverty on the other. Class relations have been for several centuries inflected with modernist categories of race and gender and located within widening political histories of state-making, war and conquest.

As I write, war is beginning in Ukraine. War making has been the historical basis of technical innovation, especially in recent centuries. Yet military emissions aren't counted in climate models![1] Are we thinking? More importantly perhaps, are we finding the emotional and spiritual approach to shift from narrow carbon politics – too much out to the atmosphere, not enough into the ground – to one centred on life in all its glorious complexity? For me, the starting point is to understand the awe-inspiring history of Earth and the terrifying history of human conquest and exploitation, which is far older than 1500 but took on new depth and intensity with colonial integration of all places and peoples in Earth.

Earth History and Human History

For any subject, it is a good idea to ask when it began. This invites three further questions. First, how did its founding principles emerge from what went before? These principles emerge only as it unfolds;

---

[1] At the insistence of the US since 1997.

capitalism couldn't be named until after three centuries the new discipline of political economy named its categories, just as the imbalance of atmospheric gases couldn't be studied without the new discipline of Earth Sciences. Second, what were the distinct principles or logics of the prior context? To continue the example, capitalism emerged from feudalism through tensions within specific European places, just as oxygen emerged from a prior period when it was absent. Third, the intertwined unfolding of principles of geological-hydrological-atmospheric-biological dynamics, and of social-political relations, opens to the question of naming possible trajectories towards distinct futures.

Human history can now take its place within Earth history, which is vastly older and even more eventful. Eventually human histories must include the origins of Earth itself in the unfolding of the cosmos since the Primordial Flaring Forth – a name proposed by evolutionary cosmologists Berry and Swimme (1992) in place of the military metaphor Big Bang. It is now possible through the renewal of geological and biological sciences to understand the volatile history of Earth, its tectonic movements of rocks and waters, its dramatic changes in the composition of gases in the atmosphere and the eventual appearance and unfolding of living beings. The Great Oxidation Event, which made it possible for terrestrial beings to exist at all, took half a billion years to emerge and began two and a half billion years ago. It was the waste product of the first dominant life form, anaerobic bacteria (which must live outside an oxygen environment). Once Earth's atmosphere tipped into an oxygen-rich mix of gases, those bacteria surviving Earth's first mass extinction evolved over hundreds of millions of years in several ways: some multiplied in oceans, which became rich in oxygen and supported complex aquatic life; some found new ways to live with emerging terrestrial life forms, including in soils – where they break down organic matter – and in the guts of complex animals – where they digest our food.

The potential disaster for life of being consumed by oxidation – fire – was prevented by circulation of atmospheric gases through the bodies of living beings. This was the insight that led atmospheric scientist James Lovelock to propose the Gaia hypothesis and develop it together with biologist Lynn Margulis in the 1970s (Lovelock and Margulis, 1974). Margulis is responsible for a profound rethinking of evolution to centre on bacteria and on symbiosis, ideas first resisted but ultimately embraced by biologists. It has begun to enter popular consciousness in the idea of the microbiome that humans and all animals remain constituted by symbiotic relations with a multitude of microscopic organisms from which we originally evolved. Although some reject the name Gaia – the ancient Greek Earth Goddess – as mythological, Earth Science itself is now founded on the idea that our planet is a self-regulating, complex system, which supports life and is in turn regulated by life. This idea is not so difficult to grasp for anyone already aware that animals exchange gases with plants, oxygen for carbon dioxide. In the climate policy world, even this simple dynamic vision has been reduced to the static idea of trees and soils as carbon sinks, as if carbon were a pollutant in need of burial, as if policy wonks were not themselves composed of carbon.

By inviting us imaginatively to adopt the perspective of bacteria and other microbes, Margulis has helped to redefine consciousness in ways that resonate with much older cosmologies. At its most visionary, convergence of scientific disciplines points to a contested but compelling vision of a living Earth. Gaia co-creators, Margulis and Lovelock, see life in Earth as self-organising. Atmosphere, hydrosphere and lithosphere (cycles of air, water and minerals) continuously pass through the bodies of living beings, the biosphere. Berry and Swimme interpret this science as offering a new mythology to help humans once again live well in Earth.

The scientific vision is new and revolutionary. Humans, like all living beings, change our environment. Plants change acidity of soils, sometimes to the point of giving way to other species. Animals build dams and change landscapes on a large scale. What is unique to humans is that we are conscious, or can be if we choose to use what novelist Kurt Vonnegut (1985) called our 'Big Brains', the same arguably oversized organ that got us to the point of changing Earth so much that our survival is in doubt.

Those Earth Scientists who publicly state that human survival now depends on fundamental transformations in human institutions rarely name capitalism. They often name the imperative to constant growth, without naming the foundation of that imperative. Even though accumulation and enclosure began to dominate human societies only around 1500 – the blink of a cosmic eye – with the emergence of a capitalist world-economy (Wallerstein, 1974), now understandable as capitalist world-ecology (Moore, 2003), these scientists, like policy officials, usually accept the (impossible) permanence of states and corporations. This is madness. Everything has a beginning and an end. Our task is to understand the origins of ruling institutions and ideas in order to guide the end of capitalism away from disaster and towards thriving of the web of life, and of humans as the reflective, conscious part of it.

Colonial history, in my view, is a key to both the most recent and comprehensive changes in Earth, ones that we stand a chance of changing. Although it was rejected by the official Anthropocene Working Group, I draw on a hugely important intervention in the debate about dating the Anthropocene, which brought together 'natural' and 'social' sciences. Two Earth System scientists proposed to connect a specific 'spike' showing 'anthropogenic signatures in the geological record' to the origins and unfolding of colonial conquest of the Americas. Lewis and Maslin (2015) argued for the date 1610, when there was a downward spike in atmospheric carbon dioxide. They connected this geological marker with the now widely accepted early date for the origins of capitalism.

Why would carbon dioxide dip at that date – upending the usual assumption that human activities have led to consistent if uneven rises in atmospheric carbon? Their explanation is based in world-systems analysis and challenges the prevailing assumption that forests in the Americas were primeval before 1500. Instead, American forests were hiding the ruins of ancient civilisations. In a later co-authored analysis of data on population and land use (Koch et al., 2019: 24) they conclude that deaths of 55 million indigenous peoples in the Americas over the century after 1492 led to abandonment of about 56 million hectares of agricultural area and consequent growth of forests that sequester about 15 times more carbon. Recently – asking related questions – archaeologists have discovered remains of societies whose inhabitants died or fled, from the Amazon through present Mexico to the Mississippian cultures of North America.

Lewis and Maslin (2015: 175) call 1610 the Orbis Hypothesis 'from the Latin for world, because post-1492 humans on the two hemispheres were connected, trade became global'. The century between 1492 and 1610 not only decimated indigenous peoples but also redistributed plants and animals in ways that transformed landscapes across the world. What Crosby (1972) named the Columbian Exchange shifted the balance of living beings in 'old' and 'new' worlds (in inherited

Eurocentric terms) and transplanted not only encultured humans, but also plants and animals from one continent to another. Sugar, a plant of Asian origin, was one of the first intentional transplants; it could thrive in such magnitude because of genocide of indigenous Arawak in the Caribbean, the cutting of their forest habitats to create monocultures, and the forced relocation of differently encultured Africans to work the land appropriated by European elites who called themselves 'planters'. This reorganisation was at once a drastic simplification of biocultural landscapes and reorganisation of historical social hierarchies; it set in motion dynamics that constantly recur over the centuries until today, unifying ever more places and peoples subject capitalist accumulation and geopolitical rivalries. As Cedric Robinson puts it, even as transplants simplified biocultural landscapes, 'The tendency of European civilization through capitalism was. . .not to homogenize but to differentiate — to exaggerate regional, subcultural, and dialectical differences into "racial" ones' (Robinson, 2000, cited in Murphy and Schroering, 2020: 407).

Other reorganisations of biocultural landscapes were unintentional: except for the high Andes, there were no precolonial grazing animals in South America. European cattle and horses used their feet to leave their European masters and grazed their way across the continent, undermining the conditions of life of indigenous peoples (Crosby, 1986). Still other biocultural transformations came from below, as African, Asian and European newcomers carried familiar plants and animals, even in the most difficult conditions. They created diasporic agronomies and cuisines; for example, the national dish of Jamaica consists of *akee* (African), salt fish (imported from the North Atlantic by planters as food for enslaved workers) and rice (either of African or Asian origin). In the other direction, maize was introduced from America to Africa and beyond, as were tomatoes, potatoes and many more ingredients that now seem 'traditional' to 'old world' cuisines. To anticipate implications for the future, biocultural reorganisations from above brought together people whose creativity made for great and continuing diversity of agronomies, cuisines and more in the 'shadow of slavery' and genocide (Carney and Rosomoff, 2011).

To connect the dip in carbon dioxide in 1610 to the history of colonisation of the Americas is a remarkable scientific synthesis with enormous political implications. Transforming Earth was the intent and practice of colonisation, as it had already been of cutting Europe's forests. Following Lewis and Maslin, colonial reshaping of foodways and landscapes across the world was central to the deep, violent history of colonial transformations of places and cultures. Biocultural landscapes in North America, at the centre of accumulation and power in the food system since 1945, created fossil-intensive agriculture on the foundation of the earlier food regime dominated by Great Britain. That earlier colonial regime had displaced native perennial grasses, bison and indigenous people who managed them on a vast scale as a complex biocultural prairie landscape – by an introduced and simplified triad of wheat, cattle and European settler farmers and herders (Cronon, 1991).

We now call taking whatever makes profit and brings power *extractivism*, whether of minerals or forests or soils or 'hypertrophic cities' (Ajl, 2014). Extraction – making all the changes required to take what is profitable – has been the defining principle of world-ecology since colonial reshaping of biocultural landscapes began. Even in 1931, settler agriculture in the American plains was called 'soil mining' (Webb, 1931). Commodity frontiers, which are more complex than the westward movement of European wheat, cattle, farmers and farming techniques, have from the beginning been central to colonial integration of the planet (Beckert, 2015; Moore, 2003). In a mere five centuries, biocultural landscapes have been simplified by marginalising indigenous peoples (including those living as 'peasants' in Europe) and making them dependent on the extracting powers of corporations and states. The implications of dating the Anthropocene from 1610 makes clear 'how rock and climate are bound to flesh' and how a liveable future lies in 'decolonizing the Anthropocene' (Davis and Todd, 2017: 769).

Evolutionary Possibilities of Human Consciousness

In a recent argument for understanding Anthropocene as invitation, Foster and Clark (2021) offer a vision of a Communian Age, which they hope will follow the present Capitalinian Age within the Anthropocene Epoch. They extend Marx's view that '… the private property of particular individuals in the earth will appear just as absurd as the private property of one man in other men [slavery]', to include a vision in which humanity 'reaffirm[s], at a higher level, its communal relations with the earth: the dawn of another age'. Foster and Clark draw on the idea of noosphere postulated in the 1920s by French paleontologist and theologian Teilhard de Chardin and Soviet biogeochemist Vernadsky. The noosphere was to be the third phase in Earth history; first was the geosphere, followed by the biosphere, in which life emerged in intimate relation with flows of air, water and minerals; finally, out of life emerges human consciousness – the noosphere – which again transforms earth. Yet the two originators of noosphere departed in other respects. Foster and Clark draw on the path of Vernadsky,[2] who centred his idea of noosphere on reason and the reach of technology into the nuclear (now we could add the genetic and informatic) as ways that human consciousness reshapes Earth. By envisioning the capacity of humans to use technologies responsibly (an excellent idea), within the context of the early creative days of the Soviet Union, Vernadsky participated in its still undimmed hope to replace chaotic, destructive capitalism with state planning. Although they understand planning to be different from the later Soviet Union, Foster and Clark also conclude that 'the necessary reversal of existing trends and the stabilisation of the human relation to the earth...can only occur through social, economic, and ecological planning'.

Teilhard had a different view of the noosphere, which could lead to a different view of the principles and politics of a Communian Age. While emergence is key to both Teilhard and Vernadsky – consciousness emerges within life, just as life emerged within inanimate rock – Christian theologian Teilhard understands the direction to be increasing differentiation and individualisation, always forming a more complex unity. The noosphere emerges from human minds, which emerge through evolution of life. Still, it is not minds that drive the transformation. It is love.

One does not have to read this through a Christian lens but can accept a wider framework embracing heart and spirit. It can embrace what Wade Davis (2014) calls the ethnosphere:

> the myriad cultures of the world that make up an intellectual, spiritual, and social web of life that envelopes the planet and is as important to its well-being as is the biological web-of-life that we know as the biosphere.

---

[2]Vernadsky was an atheist, from Wikipedia, reference (oddly): Margulis, Lynn; Sagan, Dorion (2000). *What Is Life?* University of California Press. p. 170. ISBN 978-0-520-22021-8. Both the French paleontologist-priest Pierre Teilhard de Chardin and the Russian atheist Vladimir Vernadsky agreed that Earth is developing a global mind.

You might think of this cultural web-of-life as being an ethnosphere. And you might define the ethnosphere as being the sum total of all the thoughts, dreams, ideals, myths, intuitions, and inspirations brought into being by the imagination since the dawn of consciousness. The ethnosphere is humanity's great legacy. It's a symbol of all that we've achieved and the promise of all that we can achieve as the wildly curious and adaptive species we are.

My passing familiarity with planning as a practice in Western cities and national states makes me sceptical that it can be democratic, much less invite heart and spirit; even experiments like popular budgeting pioneered in Porto Alegre, Brazil, work only at the margins of government policy, and even newly created environmental institutions committed to civic participation fall to bureaucratic inertia, commitment to narrow rationality and delimited objectivity (Quinn, 2022). Not only intrinsically hierarchical states, but the system of states whose borders are defined and redefined only through wars and treaties, are a form of governance that must be superseded by something ecological, let us say bioregions, and cultural, let us say ethnosphere.

The still unfolding simplification that began in 1500 continues into the present the reshaping of biocultural landscapes by reducing the number of species, transplanting plants and animals and reorganising encultured humans into hierarchical categories of cultures, languages and (re)constructed races and genders. In place of simplification, the aim can be to restore complex and diverse biocultural landscapes. To accept the invitation of the Anthropocene, I think, suggests paths towards an Age of human responsibility based in diversity and relationship, indeed deep transformations in thought, knowledge and practice – partly decolonising ideas and practices, partly recovering lost cosmologies and ways that humans over centuries and millennia have experimented in living in mutual respect with all beings.

I suggest that a good working definition of sustainability might be to adapt the French word, *durabilité*; to endure as a coherent, evolving, adapting community of relations over centuries and even millennia. In her scientific research, Professor of Forest Ecology Suzanne Simard observed that the forest science she was taught fails to support enduring life by selecting trees desired as raw materials and removing those perceived to be their competitors. Her research (and she is not alone) shows that far from competing, individuals and species live in collaborative communities in which they nourish, warn and in other ways support each other. She concludes in her scientifically based popular book *Finding the Mother Tree: Discovering the Wisdom of the Forest* (Simard, 2021), that North American West Coast indigenous peoples have acted as conscious members of these enduring communities. Even in disrupted habitats, even when their knowledge is ignored or disdained, they sustainably manage the invisible connections among many beings – cedars and birch, salmon and bears, waters and the many plants of the forest. Simard concludes that their practices of experimentation, observation and adaptation – changing course when something doesn't work – is in reality better science than supposedly scientific forest management – which clears and replants to maximise a desired 'resource'. The same is increasingly understood for agriculture in which adaptive practices based on experiment and observation – often called agroecological or regenerative farming – favour diversity and complex interrelations among plants, animals, fungi and bacteria. The link between habitats for sustainable human foodgetting – forest, grassland, wetland, ocean and river – is healthy soil, itself based on underground networks of organisms of almost unimaginable complexity (Montgomery, 2012; Sheldrake, 2021).

The implication for sustainably getting food and all else that we need is to begin with soil. For Earth Sciences, the pedosphere is the outermost layer of the Earth, the thin skin supporting earthly life, and consisting of dynamic interactions among air, water, minerals and living organisms. Farmers have understood soil as the foundation of food and life, even when debt and other social obligations forced them to extract its fertility (Montgomery, 2012). Even pioneers of capitalist agriculture in 18th century England, who reorganised land and labour to maximise commercial grains and livestock, focused on what they called the 'heart of the soil'. Soil is at the heart of earliest criticisms of industrial agriculture: the Soil Association in England (1946) and Rodale in the United States (1930).

Appreciation of soil as the complex foundation of terrestrial plant and therefore animal life is part of a wider reinterpretation of evolution; in place of the narrow understanding of evolution as competition, which has dominated interpretations of Darwin since the 'social Darwinism' of the 19th century, Lynn Margulis (Margulis and Sagan, 2002) pioneered a reinterpretation based on symbiosis. This looks at evolution forwards from bacteria rather than retrospectively from a human point of view. It considers merger to be the origin of complex organisms from those with only a single cell, and speciation to arise through symbiosis of genetically distinct organisms. Life unfolds through the mutual bonds within and among organisms. Symbiosis leads in many directions, from understanding the human body as consisting of communities of bacteria (the human biome) and genetically distinct mitochondria in every living human cell, to a new appreciation of the complex earth-spanning networks of fungi and other organisms sustaining life of larger beings and their habitats. Such ideas are part of a re-emerging unity of scientific disciplines called Earth Sciences. At the same time, paradoxically, Earth Sciences are making crucial discoveries by deepening specialisation of disciplines, which are increasingly difficult for ordinary intelligent, curious people to follow. As a result, like founders of 19th century evolutionary theory, the boundary between amateur and professional scientists is again getting fuzzy; for instance, miners or farmers still discover many fossils. At the same time, in order to gather data on a scale that technology now makes it possible to analyse, professional scientists sometimes rely on a new category of *citizen scientists* to collect observations from stars to dolphins. The earliest I know of, before the internet, was continental observation and reporting of migration paths of Monarch butterflies.

In practical disciplines of agroecology and selective forestry, integrative science converges with indigenous wisdom, not only among Pacific Northwest indigenous peoples appreciated by Simard. Within the framework of the 2007 United Nations Declaration on the Rights of Indigenous Peoples, a network of indigenous peoples agreed to a common approach to life that unifies diverse biocultures embedded in specific territories. Since each territory is unique, the approach to human survival is earthly unity based on biocultural diversity. Their principles are a starting point for how humans can realise our species being within Gaia: view the world holistically, respect interconnected physical, biological, cultural and spiritual spheres of life; understand territory as fundamental; focus on relationships and processes in engaging reciprocally with the cosmos. These principles lead to actions to encourage liveliness: take only what we need; take only what is freely given; give back to renew and restore lives and relationships

(Kimmerer, 2015). Even in territories/ecosystems drastically changed by colonial expropriation and continuing displacements, peoples with varied cultural heritage who encounter each other in a territory can 'become native to [each] place' (Jackson, 1996). These principles can shape responsible governance across territories. Managing scales, not with a hierarchy of city, nation and international institutions, but as nested and overlapping jurisdictions that mimic natural systems; for instance, nutrient and material cycling must be managed close by to prevent sending 'waste' to an unknown place called 'away'. At the widest scale, even though every atom of carbon or oxygen is created in a specific place, responsibility for sustaining the balance of atmospheric gases requires coordination across all places. These principles are already part of contemporary environmental thought (Commoner, 1971) to close broken social and ecological circles if human life is to endure.

Most of the languages through which peoples know the territories of Earth are lost or in grave danger. Latin categories unify the words for plants, and at the same time displace vernacular terms – in England as well as California or New Zealand – that describe appearance, function or other features. Scientific nomenclature allows for sharing across the globe, but also hides the indigenous names of plants and the knowledge of how to use them, which are the source of many useful foods and drugs. English, which has so far displaced even rival colonial languages as the universal language of commerce and governance, is a dominating as well as unifying force. Yet lost and endangered languages carry the knowledge of peoples who once lived in far better harmony with all beings in their habitats, and often still do. These languages, cultures and place-based knowledges have been suppressed and marginalised at great cost to our collective capacity to live as embodied and encultured beings.

What might a new Age respecting the ethnosphere and biosphere look like? For one thing, it cannot assume endurance of crumbling states, with their internal hierarchies, or of the interstate system based on the modern notion of national sovereignty (Ruggie, 1993). Even younger than capitalism, the state system and all its members show signs of sclerosis. The modern interstate system was launched by the Treaty of Westphalia in 1648, which ended religious wars in Europe by allowing each monarch to name a national religion and language and repress all dissidents. It created uniform borders containing everything inside, which defined the authority of the national state and its instruments – passports, customs and police – to control movements of people, other beings and goods. It emerged in early days of colonial conquest, extermination of indigenous peoples and enslavement and transport of Africans. It was completed in the 20th century as colony by colony gained formal independence from empires, then adapted their inherited internal hierarchies within the borders created, fought over and negotiated by those same empires. The implications are profound: borders turn people, who have moved across Earth since our origins in Africa, into *migrants* whom states can admit or refuse; borders turn goods, which humans have exchanged over long distances for as long as we can know, into *trade*, which can be taxed or excluded. The interstate system shows little prospect of agreeing to stabilise the atmosphere, revive the diversity of life or accommodate people on the move. It finally resolves disputes through ever more deadly wars.

What forms might governance take in an Age based on the noosphere? Since the early 19th century some anthropologists, political economists (especially Marx) and even colonial officials have understood the virtues of indigenous forms of governance. Early feminists in North America were deeply influenced by friendships and what they learned from indigenous women (Wagner, 2001). It is likely that Canadian government was influenced for the better by familiarity with the Iroquois Federation, despite its later land thefts, repression of uprisings and forced separation of children from parents as part of brutal cultural assimilation (Saul, 2009). Recovery of these legacies in all parts of the world can support reframing institutions. But most important is to build up from below (Sklair, 2019), to gain control over territory, to understand that the land is the third element in conflicts over land use between indigenous and newcomers, to respect the land as a common home, to regenerate its life, its liveliness, for our children and our children's children – to support all our relations, as Haudenosaunee principles teach, seven generations into the future, guided by wisdom from the past.

I propose that governance of human societies adopt the model of ecosystems. The hydrological cycle is above and below ground as liquid and ice, and in the atmosphere as vapour. Every drop of water is in one place and at the same time in movement across space and time. All the water in Earth is all we have, a precious basis for enduring life and a basis for humans to understand and guide all our relations from the smallest to the largest, the nearest to the farthest. I live in Toronto and my family lives in Michigan. We are fortunate to live in the same Great Lakes Territory or Bioregion, together the largest body of fresh water in Earth. Yet we are separated by a national border. Remembering that the map is not the territory, I like to compare two images of the Great Lakes. The image from space shows beautiful, interlinked blue bodies of water below clouds surrounded by green. The map governments use to control border crossings or to regulate pollution or fishing or shipping has a dotted red line through the middle of the lakes. Fish don't have passports, but they do die from human actions. They can be revived by coordination between Canada and the United States but new threats emerge constantly requiring (but not necessarily calling forth) ever new interstate, bureaucratic regulatory bodies. Bioregional reshaping begins with foodgetting, the continuing basis of human existence, and so basic to moving towards a new Age of relationship, respect and reciprocity for all beings. We don't know in advance what to do with our overgrown cities and degraded countrysides and dying forests. Unless inherited planning can be completely reimagined, it seems to me that the way to a new era of thriving, is to work collectively within and across places, from below, to renew our necessary relation to earthly flows and all beings as foodgetters.

An example from my bioregion is a vision of the Great Lakes Commons, linking indigenous and settlers throughout the territory, to revive and share the life of the lands and waters and beings, by 'becoming a great ancestor'. From the website (www.greatlakescommons.org): 'The Great Lakes Commons is a grassroots effort to establish the Great Lakes as a thriving, living commons — shared and sacred waters that we all protect in perpetuity'. Its Charter is in five languages: Mohawk, Anishinaabemowin, Spanish, French and English. By walking and talking together, we can loosen our machine metaphors for nature and return to appreciate cycles of sun and moon, of seasons and tides. We can learn to live together by sharing a love for the lands and waters here, and for all they are connected to in Earth.

References

Ajl, M. (2014) 'The hypertrophic city versus the planet off fields'. In N. Brenner (ed), *Implosions/Explosions: Towards a Study of Planetary Urbanization*. Berlin: Jovis Verlag, pp. 533–50.

Beckert, S. (2015) *Empire of Cotton: A Global History*. New York, NY: Vintage Books.

Berry, T. and Swimme, B. (1992) *The Universe Story*. San Francisco, CA: Harper.

Campbell, J. (2008) *The Hero with a Thousand Faces (Vol. 17)*. Novato, CA: New World Library.

Carney, J.A. and Rosomoff. R.N. (2011) *In the Shadow of Slavery: Africa's Botanical Legacy in the Atlantic World*. Berkeley, CA: University of California.

Clark, N. and Gunaratnam, Y. (2017) 'Earthing the Anthropos? From 'socializing the Anthropocene' to geologizing the social'. *European Journal of Social Theory*, *20*(1): 146–63.

Commoner, B. (1971) *The Closing Circle*. Cambridge, MA: MIT Press.

Cronon, W. (1991) *Nature's Metropolis: Chicago and the Great West*. New York, NY: W. W. Norton.

Crosby, A.C. (1972) *The Columbian Exchange: Biological and Cultural Consequences of 1492*. Westport, CT: Praeger.

Crosby, A.C. (1986) *Ecological Imperialism: The Biological Expansion of Europe, 900–1900*. Cambridge and New York, NY: Cambridge University Press.

Davis, W. (2014) *Keynote Speech: The Ethnosphere and the Academy*. (https://www.wheretherebedragons.com/wp-content/uploads/2014/09/DavisEthnosphereAcademy.pdf)

Davis, H. and Todd, Z. (2017) 'On the importance of a date, or, decolonizing the Anthropocene'. *ACME: An International Journal for Critical Geographies*, *16*(4): 761–80.

Foster, J.B. and Clark, B. (2021) 'The Capitalinian: The first geological age of the Anthropocene'. *Monthly Review*, *73*(4): 1–16.

Jackson, W. (1996) *Becoming Native to this Place*. Berkeley, CA: Counterpoint.

Kimmerer, R.W. (2015) *Braiding Sweetgrass: Indigenous Wisdom, Scientific Knowledge and the Teachings of Plants*. Minneapolis, MN: Milkweed Press. (www.milkweed.org)

Koch, A., Brierley, C., Maslin, M.M. and Lewis. S.L. (2019)'Earth system impacts of the European arrival and Great Dying in the Americas after 1492'. *Quaternary Science Reviews*, *207*(1): 13–36.

Lewis, S.L. and Maslin, M.A. (2015) 'Defining the Anthropocene'. *Nature*, *519*(7542): 171–9.

Lovelock, J.E. and Margulis, L. (1974)'Atmospheric homeostasis by and for the biosphere: The Gaia hypothesis'. *Tellus*, *26*(1–2): 2–10.

Margulis, L. and Sagan, D. (2002) *Acquiring Genomes: A Theory of the Origins of Species*. New York, NY: Basic Books.

Montgomery, D.R. (2012) *Dirt: The Erosion of Civilizations*. Berkeley, CA: University of California Press.

Moore, J.W. (2003) 'Capitalism as world-ecology: Braudel and Marx on environmental history'. *Organization & Environment*, 16(4): 514–17.

Murphy, M.W. and Schroering, C. (2020) 'Refiguring the Plantationocene: Racial capitalism, World-systems analysis, and global socioecological transformation'. *Journal of World-Systems Research*, 26(2): 372–99.

Quinn, M. (2022) *Towards a New Civic Bureaucracy: Lessons from Sustainable Development for the Crisis of Governance*. Bristol: Policy Press.

Robinson, C.J. (2000) *Black Marxism: The Making of the Black Radical Tradition*. Chapel Hill, NC: University of North Carolina Press.

Ruggie, J.G. (1993) 'Territoriality and beyond: Problematizing modernity in international relations'. *International Organization*, 47(1): 139–74.

Saul, J.R. (2009) *A Fair Country: Telling Truths about Canada*. Toronto: Viking Canada.

Sheldrake, M. (2021) *Entangled Life: How Fungi Make Our Worlds, Change Our Minds & Shape Our Futures*. New York, NY: Penguin.

Simard, S. (2021) *Finding the Mother Tree: Discovering the Wisdom of the Forest*. Toronto: Allen Lane.

Sklair, L. (2019) 'World revolution or socialism, community by community, in the Anthropocene?' *Globalizations*, 16(7): 1012–19.

Sklair, L. (2021) 'Geoethics: A reality check from media coverage of the Anthropocene'. In *Geo-societal Narratives*. London and Cham: Palgrave Macmillan, pp. 127–34.

Vonnegut, K. (1985) *Galapagos: A Novel*. New York, NY: Delacorte Press/Seymour Lawrence.

Wagner, S.R. (2001) *Sisters in Spirit: Haudenosaunee (Iroquois) Influence on Early American Feminists*. Summertown, TN: Native Voices.

Wallerstein, I. (1974) *The Modern World-System: Capitalist Agriculture and the Origins of the European World-Economy in the Sixteenth Century*. New York, NY: Academic Press.

Webb, W.P. (1931) *The Great Plains*. Boston, MA: Ginn and Co.

4

Governing the Agrifood Transition in the Capital-Driven Anthropocene

Nora McKeon

Introduction

In the highly contested realm of food discourse, there is a rare point of practically universal consensus: the current modalities of global food provisioning are not performing satisfactorily. To begin with, they are not effectively addressing food insecurity and malnutrition. According to the latest editions of the authoritative State of Food Security and Nutrition in the World by 2020 the number of people who did not have access to adequate food had risen to 2.4 billion, nearly a third of the world's population, while 46 million joined the ranks of those facing hunger in 2021 alone (FAO et al., 2021, 2022a, 2023). Covid-19 has had a significant impact in determining this dismal trend, but it is widely acknowledged that the pandemic has merely unveiled and exacerbated existing fragilities in global food provisioning and that the spread of industrial agriculture is a contributing factor to diffusion of viruses (CSIPM, 2020; IPES-Food, 2020). The human health impacts of growing consumption of highly processed foods and unhealthy diets is another area of concern, with obesity and diet-related illness on the rise. The global food system has been identified as the primary driver of the alarming rate of biodiversity loss we are experiencing (UNEP, 2021). Its contribution to greenhouse gas emissions has been highlighted for years and the link between agriculture and climate change has finally been inserted in the Climate Change COP agenda.

The war in Ukraine has added a new layer to today's multiple food crises. The widely contrasting narratives surrounding it underscore, as in a mediaeval morality play, the dramatic nature of the issues before us. Powerful geopolitical and economic interests, backed by some UN institutions, call for entrenching the status quo by keeping global trade and supply chains open, ensuring smallholders' access to chemical fertilisers and corporate seeds, and boosting production through 'climate-smart technologies' (FAO et al., 2022). Social movements, civil society actors, many academics and some governments, on the contrary, call for a radical transformation and delocalisation of food systems, helping low and middle-income countries to break their dependence on food and input imports and operating a decisive agroecological transition. They point to the decades of reiterated neoliberal policy responses to food crises which have created vulnerabilities in global food systems (Clapp and Moseley, 2020), outline the structural flaws that must be addressed to prevent future crises Clapp 2023b; (IPES-Food, 2022) and call for global policy coordination anchored in a human rights approach with priority voice for most affected countries and constituencies (CSIPM, 2020, 2022). In short, an agrifood transition is indispensable, and it has to be governed.

Global food governance, however, is also in a fairly bleak condition. Multilateral governance based on sovereign states, which are expected to represent the interests of their people under the principles of Western representative democracy, appears increasingly unable to address the challenges the world is facing. Already at its post-WWII birth the authority of the UN system was diminished by failure to win the agreement to include finance and trade under its umbrella, giving rise to a separate sphere inhabited by the World Bank (WB) and the International Monetary Fund (IMF), accompanied by the GATT, subsequently englobed into the World Trade Organization (WTO). The coming to independence of former colonies in the 1960s–1970s placed in evidence the limitations of the one country one vote rule in a world system in which some votes are incommensurably weightier than others. The efforts of the G77 to construct a New Economic Order, with UNCTAD and the UN Centre on Transnational Corporations as institutional underpinnings and FAO as a reference point for the largely raw commodity exporting countries of the Global South, clashed with the interests of the rich countries. FAO's authority as the UN's 'Ministry of Food and Agriculture' was weakened by the outcomes of the World Food Conference, called by the UN in 1974[1] in response to a major food crisis, which hived off

---

[1] The first instance of use of term 'food security', defined in relation to food availability and hence productivity.

various of its functions contributing to the fragmentation of food governance. The rising waves of neoliberalism adopted the agency of the WB and the IMF to impose structural adjustment policies from the mid-1980s on. In the same period the most powerful economies grouped together in the G7/8, a multilateral setting totally separate from the UN, to get on with the job without the hindrance of lengthy negotiations among parties with widely different objectives.

With all of its inadequacies, however, the UN is the primary global governance space in which weaker countries are present and can group together to defend their interests. Moreover, it is distinguished by the fact that it operates under the framework of Human Rights, according to the Universal Declaration adopted in 1948, which holds governments, as duty bearers, accountable to the people, as rights-holders (UN, 1948). It is this link with 'we, the peoples'[2] that legitimates the power of states acting within the UN system.

Institutionally speaking this connection was tenuous up until the end of the 1980s, with access to UN debates limited to a restricted number of International Non-Governmental Organisations (INGOs) that were granted consultative status through cumbersome procedures. As the 1980s drew to a close, however, awareness of the need to re-examine the architecture of world governance grew. The year 1992 marked the establishment of the Commission on World Governance under the auspices of UN Secretary-General Boutros-Ghali and the first of a decade of UN Summits, the UN Conference on Environment and Development, in which the system opened up to a bewildering array of civil society organisations of various types and scales (McKeon, 2009). The World Food Summits convened by the FAO in 1996 and 2002 proved to have a particularly strong democrat-ising impact, for reasons that we will explore in the first section of this chapter. The second section will contrast this approach to enhancing multilateralism in global food governance with that proposed by the UN Food Systems Summit (UNFSS) held on 23 September 2021, strongly supported by multinational agribusiness corporations. The concluding section will trace the way forward as foreseen both by the proponents of the Food Systems Summit and by what has come to be known as the food sovereignty movement,

---

[2]The opening line of the UN Charter.

delineating the terms of the current struggle to define the principles and practices of food governance.

Beyond Multilateralism in Global Food Governance: The Reformed UN Committee on World Food Security and Inclusive Multilateralism

The introduction of neoliberal structural adjustment policies greatly
reduced developing country governments' policy space and support
services for agriculture. At the same time, the markets of these
countries were opened up and peasant producers' products were
placed into unfair competition with subsidised products from abroad.
The advent of the World Trade Organization in 1995 added the final
touch. Globalisation has systematically undermined the livelihoods of
peasants while promoting market penetration and concentration on
the part of the agribusiness and retail corporations that control the
world's food system.[3] The 'solution' foreseen for 'redundant' peasants
in this logic is either to leave the land altogether – often forcibly – or
to 'modernise' their production and link into the global food market
as subordinate actors at the weak end of the chain. The phenomenon
of peasant organisation for engagement in global politics has emerged
in direct reaction to these developments, starting locally and subsequently reaching the national, regional and global levels as policy
decision-making began to shift upwards.

The civil society forums held in parallel to the FAO-sponsored
World Food Summits of 1996 and 2002 gave a strong impetus to
global networking by rural social movements. The organisers of
these forums, unlike those of the NGO-dominated meetings that
accompanied other UN summits, made a deliberate effort to ensure
that small-scale food producers and Indigenous Peoples were in the
majority by applying a quota system for delegates and mobilising
resources to cover their travel costs. Introduced by the newborn
global peasant network La Via Campesina (LVC) in the 1996 forum,
the principle of food sovereignty – 'the right of peoples to healthy
and culturally appropriate food produced through ecologically

---

[3]Already, by 2007, 10 corporations controlled 67 percent of the global commercial seed
market while the top 10 giant grocery retailers, the most powerful actors in the
agro-industrial food chain, accounted for 40 percent of the retail sales of the top 100
world-wide (ETC, 2008).

sound and sustainable methods, and their right to define their own food and agriculture systems' – had become the civil society rallying point by 2002. The Forum mandated the network that had emerged from the preparatory work, the International Planning Committee for Food Sovereignty (IPC),[4] to carry forward the Action Agenda it adopted, based on four pillars: the right to food and food sovereignty, mainstreaming agroecological family farming, defending people's access to and control of natural resources and trade and food sovereignty.

This mounting movement – the other side of the globalisation coin – expressed a politicisation and deep questioning of the dominant food regime and, progressively, a capacity to propose alternative approaches to addressing the food needs of the world. It signalled a contestation of the corporate food regime (McMichael, 2013), which was clamorously proving incapable of ensuring world food security in a sustainable and equitable fashion. Over the succeeding years, under the terms of an agreement signed with the then Director General of FAO, Jacques Diouf, the IPC and its rural social movement members invested considerable energy in opening up meaningful political space within FAO. From 2003 to 2007, over 2000 representatives of small-scale food producers' organisations participated in FAO policy forums where they had never set foot before, championing the right to food, food sovereignty and agroecological food production as an alternative paradigm to free trade and green revolution technology. The thematic advocacy work was underpinned by an insistence on recognition of civil society's right to autonomy and self-organisation in its interaction with intergovernmental policy forums. This global policy space, and almost a decade of experience in occupying it, was ready to be exploited by the food sovereignty movement when the food crisis hit the headlines in late 2007.

The eruption of the food crisis unveiled a vacuum in global governance. In the absence of an authoritative and inclusive global body deliberating on food issues, decision-making in this vital field was being carried out – by default – by international institutions like the WTO and the World Bank for whom food security is hardly core

---

[4]The IPC defines itself as an autonomous and self-organised global platform of small-scale food producers and rural workers organisations and grassroots/community-based social movements whose goal is to advance the Food Sovereignty agenda at the global and regional level (see https://www.foodsovereignty.org/the-ipc/).

business, by groups of the most powerful economies like the G8, and by economic actors like transnational corporations and financial speculators subject to no political oversight whatsoever. The food crisis sparked a range of international institutional initiatives, of which the only one that sought policy responses to the causes of the food price crisis was a proposal to reform the existing but ineffectual UN Committee on World Food Security (CFS) housed in the FAO. The proposal was opposed by the G8, which preferred an investment-led approach. Nonetheless, it was successfully advocated by a number of G77 countries led by Brazil and Argentina, the FAO and the movement of small-scale producers and civil society organisations that had built up the strength of its global advocacy under the food sovereignty banner.

In this political context the reform process, conducted during 2009, transformed the Committee into a highly innovative global policy forum. The CFS is rooted in a human rights framework in which governments take the final decisions and can hence be held accountable. At the same time, it is open to the full participation of other actors. Priority voice is accorded to organisations representing those sectors of the population most affected by food insecurity, operating in an autonomous, self-organised mechanism[5], making it the most advanced example of what could be called 'inclusive multilateralism'. Equally innovative is the science-policy interface introduced by the CFS reform. The reports of the High-Level Panel of Experts (HLPE) address topics on which the CFS requests it to prepare an evidence base, but they do so in an autonomous fashion (McKeon, 2015; Clapp, 2023a). The multidisciplinary and gender/regionally balanced teams recognise the validity of different forms of knowledge, including traditional and practitioner experience, and consult broadly on the framing and the first draft of their research.

In its first decade of operations, the CFS proved to be an effective forum for negotiating progressive global guidelines on delicate issues such as land tenure, where determined and skillful social movement and CSO engagement won recognition of important elements such as collective, customary tenure rights and states' obligations to regulate their corporations (FAO & Committee on World Food Security, 2012;

---

[5]The Civil Society and Indigenous Peoples' Mechanism (CSIPM), see https://www.csm4c fs.org/https://www.csm4cfs.org/.

IPC, 2016). Further, the CFS has operated as a forum in which to challenge dominant narratives by bringing into the negotiations the lived realities of food insecure communities and small-scale producers. Emblematic in this regard has been recognition by CFS member states that small-scale food producers are responsible for most of the food consumed in the world, 80 percent of which reaches its final destination through local and national markets embedded in territorial food systems and not through global supply chains and supermarkets (CSIPM, 2016; FAO & Committee on World Food Security, 2016). The very success of the CFS has stimulated a push back by powerful economic interests unwilling to countenance any real transformation of food systems, within a severely changed political context characterised by shrinking space for human rights defence, threatened primacy of the public sector and populist nationalism accompanied by attacks against multilateralism (McKeon, 2021).

Side-Stepping Multilateralism in Global Food Governance: Corporate-Led Multistakeholderism and the UN Food Systems Summit

During the same period that has witnessed the rise of the food sovereignty movement and the reform of the CFS corporate concentration in food provisioning chains has continued to grow, with the mega-mergers of key conglomerates, accompanied by broadened financialisation of food and natural resources (Clapp, 2021). For half a century following the founding of the UN corporations were satisfied with influencing the rules of the global game, with the support of complicit governments, without entering overtly into the governance sphere. A prime example is the Trade Related Intellectual Property Rights (TRIPS) agreement,[6] largely drafted by corporation lawyers and pushed through by the US government in 1994 in the context of the nascent WTO (Tansey and Rajotte, 2008). With the turn of the century however, as the UN itself ran up against substantial difficulties in governing globalisation, corporations stepped up more decisively to the decision-making spaces. In this they were aided by a blossoming narrative that characterised the private sector and

---

[6]TRIPS has provided a massive boost to corporate power by extending the protection of 'intellectual property' to cover the products of corporation laboratories.

public–private partnerships as prime movers of development, ignoring the different roles of the two sectors and the conflicts between the interests they promote. The opening up of the UN to the corporate sector was underwritten by powerful Member States, themselves beholden to corporate funding to various degrees, and underpinned by the dominant neoliberal discourse which legitimated the free market, technology-led 'modernisation' and global supply chain efficiency as the way forward. The first overt step in this direction was the establishment of the UN Global Compact – a main conduit for UN-corporate partnerships. It was crafted in the World Economic Forum (WEF)[7] in 1999 and launched by the then UN Secretary-General, Kofi Annan, in 2000, in a period in which the US's refusal to pay its full assessed UN contribution was provoking budgetary stress.

The corporate vision of global governance can be summed up in the term 'multistakeholderism' (Gleckman, 2018; McKeon, 2017). Developed by the WEF in an operation of 'Global Redesign', this approach involves 'redefining the international system as constituting a wider, multifaceted system of global cooperation in which intergovernmental legal frameworks and institutions are embedded as a core, but not the sole and sometimes not the most crucial, component' (WEF, 2010). Instead, self-constituted multistakeholder groups or 'coalitions of the willing and able' take the lead in addressing global issues, with corporations in the forefront along with a sprinkling of governments, civil society organisations, parts of the UN, academic figures and/or institutions. The desired role of the UN, in this scenario, is to provide some form of de facto legitimation for the operations and outcomes of these coalitions.

Essentially, governance is transferred from a wobbling, often ineffective intergovernmental system – intrinsically if insufficiently democratic, legitimate and transparent – to more decisive and proactive self-selected elite bodies that are intrinsically self-interested, undemocratic and illegitimate. Among the victims of this redesign are the human rights framework, governmental accountability and the entire notion of the 'public good', with states mobilising public resources and reframing policies in support of presumably efficient and sustainable

---

[7]The World Economic Forum brings together leading global companies into what is defined as 'the International Organization for Public-Private Cooperation' aimed at to 'ensuring strategic decision-making on the most pressing world issues' (https://www.weforum.org/).

corporate-managed food provisioning (CONCORD, 2017; McKeon, 2014).

Applications of the multistakeholder model in the realm of food security, nutrition and agriculture have multiplied over the past decade (McKeon, 2017). A significant step at the global level was taken in June 2019 with the signature of a special partnership agreement between the WEF and the UN Secretary-General providing the corporate coalition unprecedented access to UN spaces and programs in the name of supporting implementation of the Sustainable Development Goals. This initiative was strongly critiqued in a letter signed by over 500 civil society organisations that remained without response (TNI, 2019). Four months later the Secretary-General announced his intention to organise a UN Food Systems Summit (UNFSS), whose planning had germinated within the WEF–UN partnership. In December 2019, he named Agnes Kalibata, president of the Gates Foundation-funded Alliance for a Green Revolution for Africa (AGRA), as his Special Envoy for the organization of the Summit.

The UN SG's mandate includes the faculty of organising day-long Summits, normally in the ambit of the General Assembly, to draw attention to issues to which he attaches particular importance, as he had done with the Climate Action Summit on 23 September 2019. It is understood, however, that such meetings are once-off affairs with light preparatory processes and no political or normative weight since they are not mandated by an intergovernmental decision and their outcomes are not subject to negotiation. The preparatory process of the UNFSS, in contrast, unfolded over almost two years, giving birth to a bewildering array of bodies constituted under the impulse of the organisers, often in conflict among each other, and an unfathomable process of national and independent and dialogues that did not feed into the thematic outcomes of the FSS in any recognisable way. What got lost in the process – as could be expected in an eminently multistakeholder initiative – included due regard for the human rights framework, respect for civil society self-organisation, assurance of governmental accountability and the authority of the CFS as the foremost, inclusive intergovernmental body mandated to address food issues.

Throughout, the UNFSS organisers have demonstrated an artful capacity for appropriating and deforming concepts expressed by their critics and incorporating them in the Summit narrative. Thus 'agroecology', a taboo word in the Summit's lexicon at the outset, was bundled together with 'regenerative agriculture' into a meaningless 'nature-based solutions' category that risks opening a smooth highway towards the financialisation of nature through net zero and carbon offsetting initiatives (Montenegro de Wit et al., 2021). The very title of the Summit, borrowed from the CFS which has worked on elaborating its meaning since 2014, is a distorted simplification of the civil society's understanding of food systems 'in their multi-dimensionality and circularity, combining and serving multiple public objectives such as the protection and regeneration of nature, health and wellbeing as well as the defense of labor and livelihoods, culture and knowledge, and social relations' (CSIPM, 2021).

Following months of unsuccessful attempts to obtain clear and transparent information regarding the process and the intended outcomes of the Summit, in October 2020 the CFS's autonomous Civil Society and Indigenous People's Mechanism (CSIPM) launched an open call for engagement in response to the Summit.[8] The People's Autonomous Response that resulted organised a counter mobilisation with participation by over 9,000 people around the world in late July 2021, in parallel with the official Pre-Summit, and a political declaration signed by over 1,000 organisations and networks. Strongly rooted in regional mobilisations, the People's Autonomous Response denounced the triple theft that the UNFFS was operating: theft of people's narratives, as illustrated above; theft of science, with the establishment of a narrowly defined, corporate-friendly Science Group poised to unseat the CFS's HLPE (IPES-Food, 2021); and theft of governance, with the substitution of a multistakeholder model for the inclusive multilateralism of the CFS.

The Way Forward

The UNFSS came to a close with a Secretary-General's Statement of Action which delineated the way forward from the viewpoint of the organisers, highlighting the multistakeholder 'coalitions of action' that emerged from the UNFSS global process[9] and the 'national pathways'

---

[8]The open call is available at https://www.csm4cfs.org/wp-content/uploads/2020/10/EN-Open-Call-on-UN-Food-Systems-Summit-12-October-2020-1.pdf.

[9]Nourish All People; Boost Nature-based Solutions; Advance Equitable Livelihoods, Decent Work and Empowered Communities; Build Resilience to Vulnerabilities, Shocks and Stresses; Accelerate the Means of Implementation.

traced by national dialogues held in the run-up to the Summit. In the absence of a collective governance role for governments, the clear intent is to descend to the national level in order to recoup some political legitimacy and to give investors and international agencies a better chance of influencing governmental choices, particularly in the main target of all of this concern, Africa. But the 'national pathways' are the half-baked product of rushed and most often non-inclusive processes, while the coalitions have been designed in a top-down and often opportunistic way, rotating around a set of corporate-friendly key words: 'financing, data, science and innovation, governance and trade'.[10]

The UNFSS organisers had insisted from the outset that no new institutions would be created, as becomes an initiative without an intergovernmental mandate. Quite to the contrary, a global Coordination Hub housed in FAO has been established, accompanied by a Scientific Advisory Group (SAC) that competes with the CFS HLPE and a Stakeholder Engagement and Networking Advisory (SENA) Group whose members are selected by the Hub, contravening the right to self-organisation that protects the autonomy of the CSIPM and the IPC in their interactions with the CFS and the FAO. Reporting flows from the country level, where FAO leads the UN country teams in promoting further development of the 'national pathways', through the Hub to the Secretary-General, by-passing inter-governmental oversight and constituting a competitor to the CFS. The S-G's Statement of Action foresees that he will convene a global stock-taking meeting every two years, with no collective political oversight. The first of these was hosted by FAO on 26–28 July 2023, once again in multistakeholder modality, with no normative outcome, and once again denounced by numerous civil society organisations and social movements (Autonomous Peoples' Response, 2023). What we are witnessing is a shift from an intergovernmental multilateral system to a secretariat-led mechanism, with consequent de-politisation of the entire process and ample space for economic actors to promote their interests.

---

[10]https://www.un.org/en/food-systems-summit/news/making-food-systems-work-people-pla net-and-prosperity For an autonomous assessment by African civil society and producer organizations of what the 'national pathways' look like in a region whose natural resources and markets are the object of considerable attention on the part of economic and geo-political interests, see https://www.csm4cfs.org/they-will-feed-us-a-peoples-route-to-african-food-sovereignty/.

The Russian invasion of Ukraine, as suggested at the outset of this article, has further intensified the narrative warfare surrounding the future of food. Food security has jumped to the top of the international agenda, but it is shrouded in a mantle of geopolitical foot shuffling and great power rivalry that obscures the structural features at play, while allowing agrifood corporations and financial speculators to reap indecent profits from world hunger (Thomas, 2022; IPES Food, 2022). In a scenario in which policy coherence and coordination are of prime importance it has further fragmented political deliberation, opened space for multistakeholderism, and delegated intergovernmental decision-making to groups like the G-7, with its investment-oriented Global Alliance for Food Security, in which most affected countries and constituencies are dispossessed and the fact that farmers are by far the biggest investors in agriculture is ignored (CSIPM, 2022; IPES-Food, 2023).

What does all this translate into in terms of governing the agrifood transition? On the one side multistakeholder governance of pseudo-transformation maintaining the primacy of global trade and advancing solutions of digitalisation and technological innovation to enable corporations to continue to make a mint in the name of defending nature in an overall context of what the founder of the WEF has called stakeholder capitalism (Schwab, 2021). On the other a radical, systemic transformation rooted in defence of indivisible human rights, food sovereignty and a rebuilding of democracy and a solidarity economy operated by people expressing their agency from the territorial level on upwards and outwards. The terms of the struggle insofar as prospects for governance of equitable and sustainable agrifood transitions are concerned could hardly be clearer. What remains to be seen is the ability and force with which the two opposing visions will be defended. On the face of it the multistakeholder vision carries the most economic, political and narrative power, but it is the transformative version that resonates with realities on the ground, nature's needs and the aspirations of the majority of the people in the world who are ill-served by the currently dominant corporate food system.

References

Autonomous Peoples' Response to the UNFSS (2023) 'To overcome the global food crisis, we need real food systems change for people and the planet'. https://

foodsystems4people.org/to-overcome-the-global-food-crisis-we-need-real-food-systems-change-for-people-and-the-planet/

Clapp, J. (2021) 'The problem with growing corporate concentration and power in the global food system'. *Nature Food*, 2(6), 404–08. (https://www.nature.com/articles/s43016-021-00297-7)

Clapp, J. (2023a) 'Shaping Inclusive Science-Based Food Policies'. SIANI, 15 February 2023. (https://www.siani.se/news-story/science-based-food-policies/)

Clapp, J. (2023b) 'Concentration and crises: Exploring the deep roots of vulnerability in the global industrial food system'. *Journal of Peasant Studies*.(https://doi.org/10.1080/03066150.2022.2129013)

Clapp, J. and Moseley, W. G. (2020) 'This food crisis is different: COVID-19 and the fragility of the neoliberal food security order'. *Journal of Peasant Studies*. (https://doi.org/10.1080/03066150.2020.1823838)

Civil Society and Indigenous Peoples' Mechanism (2016) *Connecting Smallholders to Markets. An Analytical Guide.* (https://www.csm4cfs.org/wp-content/uploads/2016/10/English-CONNECTING-SMALLHOLDERS-TO-MARKETS.pdf)

Civil Society and Indigenous Peoples' Mechanism (2020) *Voices from the Ground: From COVID-19 to Radical Transformation of Our Food Systems.* (https://www.csm4cfs.org/csm-global-synthesis-report-covid-19/)

Civil Society and Indigenous Peoples' Mechanism (2021) *CSIPM Vision on Food Systems and Nutrition.* (https://www.csm4cfs.org/csm-vision-on-food-systems-and-nutrition/)

Civil Society and Indigenous Peoples' Mechanism (2022) *Voices from the Ground 2. Transformative Solutions to the Global systemic Food crises. Popular Consultation on Grassroots Impacts of COVID-19, Conflicts and Crises on the Right to Food and Food Sovereignty.* (https://www.csm4cfs.org/wp-content/uploads/2022/09/layout-CSIPM-report-EN.pdf)

CONCORD Europe (2017) *Mixing Ends with Means: What Role for (Which) Private Sector in Agriculture and Food and Nutrition Security.* (https://library.concordeurope.org/record/1902)

ETC Group (2008) 'Who owns nature? Corporate power and the final frontier in the commodification of life'. (https://www.etcgroup.org/content/who-owns-nature)

FAO & Committee on World Food Security (2012) *Voluntary Guidelines on the Responsible Governance of Tenure of Land, Fisheries and Forests in the Context of National Food Security.* (https://www.fao.org/tenure/voluntary-guidelines/en/)

FAO & Committee on World Food Security (2016) *Connecting Smallholders to Markets.* (https://www.fao.org/3/bq853e/bq853e.pdf)

FAO, IFAD, UNICEF, WFP and WHO (2021). *The State of Food Security and Nutrition in the World 2021.* (https://www.fao.org/documents/card/en/c/cb4474en)

FAO, IFAD, UNICEF, WFP and WHO (2022a) *The State of Food Security and Nutrition in the World 2021.* (https://www.fao.org/documents/card/en/c/cc0639en)

FAO, IFAD, UNICEF, WFP and WHO (2023) *The State of Dood Security and Nutrition in the World 2023.* (https://www.fao.org/publications/home/fao-flagship-publications/the-state-of-food-security-and-nutrition-in-the-world)

FAO, IMF, WB and WTO (2022b) 'Joint Statement by the Heads of the Food and Agriculture Organization, International Monetary Fund, World Bank Group, World Food Programme, and World Trade Organization on the Global Food Security Crisis'. 16 July 2022. (https://www.imf.org/en/News/Articles/2022/07/15/pr22259-joint-statement-heads-fao-imf-wbg-wfp-wto-global-food-security-crisis)

Gleckman, H. (2018) *Multistakeholder Governance and Democracy. A Challenge.* London: Routledge.

International Planning Committee for Food Sovereignty (2016) *People's Manuel on the Guidelines on Governance of Land, Fisheries and Forests.* (https://www.foodsovereignty.org/peoples-manual-vggt/)

IPES-Food (2020) *COVID-19 and the Crisis in Food Systems: Symptoms, Causes, and Potential Solutions.* (https://www.ipes-food.org/_img/upload/files/COVID-19_CommuniqueEN.pdf)

IPES-Food (2021) *An IPCC for Food? How the UN Food Systems Summit Is Being Used to Advance a Problematic New Science-Policy Agenda.* (http://www.ipes-food.org/pages/FoodSystemsSummit)

IPES-Food. (2022). *Another Perfect Storm? How the Failure to Reform the Food Systems has Allowed the War in Ukraine to Spark a Third Global Food Crisis in 15 years, and What Can Be Done to Prevent the Next One.* (https://ipes-food.org/pages/foodpricecrisis)

IPES-Food (2023) *Who's Tipping the Scales? The Growing Influence of Corporations on the Governance of Food Systems, and How to Counter It.* (https://www.ipes-food.org/_img/upload/files/tippingthescales.pdf)

McKeon, N. (2009) *The United Nations and Civil Society: Legitimating Global Governance.* London: Zed Books.

McKeon, N. (2014) *The New Alliance for Food Security and Nutrition: A Coup for Corporate Capital?* Transnational Institute and Terra Nuova. (http://www.terranuova.org/publications/the-new-alliance-for-food-security-and-nutrition-a-coup-for-corporate-capital-2014)

McKeon, N. (2015) *Food Security Governance: Regulating Corporations, Empowering Communities.* London and New York, NY: Routledge.

McKeon, N. (2017) Are Equity and sustainability a likely outcome when foxes and chickens share the same coop? Critiquing the concept of multistakeholder governance of food security. *Globalizations, 14*(3): 379–98.

McKeon, N. (2021) 'Global food governance'. *Development, 64*, 48–55. (https://link.springer.com/article/10.1057/s41301-021-00299-9)

McMichael, P. (2013) *Food Regimes and Agrarian Questions.* Halifax: Practical Action & Fernwood.

Montenegro de Wit, M., Canfield, M., Iles, A., Anderson, M., McKeon, N., Guttal, S., Gemmill-Herren, B., Duncan, J., van der Ploeg, J.D. and Prato, S. (2021) 'Resetting power in global food governance: The UN Food Systems Summit'. *Development, (64)*: 153–61.

Schwab, K. with Vanham, P. (2021) *Stakeholder Capitalism: A Global Economy that Works for Progress, People and the Planet.* Hoboken, NJ: Wiley.

Tansey, G. and Rajotte, T. (eds) (2008) *The Future Control of Food: A Guide to International Negotiations and Rules on Intellectual Property, Biodiversity and Food Security*. Oxford: Earthscan.

Thomas, P. (2022) 'Grain Traders' Profits Rise as Ukraine War Tightens Global Food Supply'. *The Wall Street Journal*, 27 April 2022. (https://www.wsj.com/articles/grain-traders-profits-rise-as-ukraine-war-tightens-global-food-supply-11651073868)

Transnational Institute (2019) *Hundreds of Civil Society Organizations Worldwide Denounce World Economic Forum's Takeover of the UN*. (https://www.tni.org/en/article/hundreds-of-civil-society-organizations-worldwide-denounce-world-economic-forums-takeover-of)

United Nations (1948) *Universal Declaration of Human Rights*. (https://www.un.org/en/about-us/universal-declaration-of-human-rights)

UN Environmental Programme (2021) *Food System Impacts on Biodiversity Loss*. (https://www.unep.org/resources/publication/food-system-impacts-biodiversity-loss)

World Economic Forum (2010) *Everybody's Business: Strengthening International Cooperation in a More Interdependent World*. (https://www.weforum.org/reports/everybodys-business-strengthening-international-cooperation-more-interdependent-world)

Part II

Empirical Stories of Transitions in the Anthropocene

5

Does Everything Have to Change for Nothing to Change? Reduced Antibiotic Use in Intensive and Industrial Livestock Farming

Nicolas Fortané, Florence Hellec, Florence Beaugrand, Nathalie Joly and Mathilde Paul

Introduction

For the past decade, resistance to antibiotics [antimicrobial resistance (AMR)] has figured high on the political agenda as a risk to health and the environment posed by agriculture. AMR reduces the overall effectiveness of antibiotics, which are essential drugs in the modern pharmacopoeia, and leads to therapeutic dead-ends. This resistance is largely due to the massive use of antibiotics in human medicine and agriculture for over half a century (Kirchhelle, 2020; Podolsky, 2015). Several attempts at regulation have been made in recent decades. Antibiotic use in livestock farming has been significantly reduced in Europe since the 2010s following the implementation of dedicated action plans.

In France, the policies undertaken have been successful with antibiotic use falling by almost 40 percent during the 2012–17 EcoAntibio plan. This reduction has mainly involved intensive and industrial livestock farms. In fact, half of the reduction in antibiotic consumption was achieved in the pork sector (less than 2 percent of which is engaged in quality assurance schemes or organic production); another third came from the poultry sector (of which only 20 percent is engaged in non-conventional production) (Anses, 2019).[1] In addition, 'antibiotic-free'

---

[1]Between 2011 and 2017, the volume of antibiotic sales fell from 354 to 181 tons in the pig sector, from 202 to 94 tons in the poultry sector, and from 183 to 131 tons in the beef sector, representing a respective decrease in animal exposure to antibiotics of 43 percent, 48 percent and 23 percent. In volume terms, this means that of the overall decrease of 333 tons in these three sectors, 84 percent is attributable to the monogastric sectors (approximately 52 percent for pigs and 32 percent for poultry).

labels for pork and poultry products have been appearing on supermarket shelves. Government authorities and the livestock industry consistently associate reduced antibiotic use with changes in animal husbandry and animal health practices, which they say lead towards more sustainable, agroecological and preventive systems (Fortané, 2019, 2021). Yet what is the actual situation? What are the changes in these intensive and/or industrial farming systems that have allowed this decrease in antibiotic consumption? And ultimately, what can really be called a change (or not) in these antibiotic reduction trajectories?

Antibiotic Transitions in the Anthropocene

The notion of 'agroecological transition' is often used by actors in the agricultural world to describe both the objectives and the means of reducing antibiotic use in livestock production. Transition is seen as a journey of change, without clearly defining what is or should be changed. For example, French AMR control policy, which was managed for over ten years by the Veterinary Pharmacy Office at the French Ministry of Agriculture, has just been transferred to the Agroecological Transition Office. This relates antibiotic reduction to different discourses and symbolic meanings than before, while it has been framed as a professional responsibility (for vets and farmers, mostly) torn between public health and economic issues, the sustainability of agriculture tends to become a more important framework to mobilise actors towards a shared objective of reducing antibiotic use. In European policy, the transition discourse is linked to the notion of innovation and has embraced the 'reduce, replace, rethink' triad, which refers quite explicitly to the old ESR model (efficiency, substitution, redesign) of innovation, and seems to highlight efficiency and substitution tools rather than redesign. This is precisely what this article aims to explore, namely what is change in a system that a priori does not change? In other words, in the age of the Anthropocene or the Capitalocene,[2] is 'transition' actually just an expression of the resilience, or even reinforcement, of the dominant model (in this case,

---

[2]Several authors (see for example Moore, 2016) have chosen to talk about Capitalocene instead of Anthropocene to highlight the fact that only certain societies and production systems are responsible for global warming and other environmental and sanitary issues. According to them, capitalism characterises the type of socio-economic structures and relations that are responsible for such crisis.

intensive and/or industrial), which manages to vary certain formal elements while preserving its fundamental characteristics?

The sociology of innovation through withdrawal, developed by Goulet and Vinck (2012) to analyse innovations that are structured around the subtraction rather than the addition of a technical artefact, offers particularly relevant theoretical and conceptual tools to tackle such questions. Their approach makes it possible to examine the detachment or attachment – to a system (in this case, livestock farming) or to a livestock farming support network – that takes place during the transition process. In their model, withdrawal is achieved not only by the 'detachment' of the farmer or farm from existing socio-technical networks, but also by his or her 'attachment' to alternative networks that include new advisory, mutual aid and support mechanisms. These 'detachment-attachment' processes are not only socio-technical, but also socio-economic, notably through the inclusion of innovative actors in new markets that ensure the supply of inputs and the sale of production.

However, using the case study presented here, we propose the opposite hypothesis, namely that the withdrawal of antibiotics is not part of a detachment from intensive and/or industrial systems, but, on the contrary, is based on the maintenance or reinforcement of attachments to these systems, at least for the livestock farms that have mainly contributed to the drop in antibiotic use in recent years. This article describes the socio-technical and socio-economic dynamics that have accompanied the transitions towards reduced antibiotics use in two different types of sectors, which reflect more or less intensive and/or industrial production methods.[3]

Survey and Methods

A series of surveys were conducted over the past few years by an interdisciplinary group of researchers in sociology, veterinary science and management science to study the forms of transition to reduced

---

[3]We describe intensive livestock production systems as ones based on maximising productivity (of labour or capital) by optimising the means of production, notably by increasing herd sizes, confining the animals, making sustained use of veterinary drugs, rationalising nutrition and breeding techniques and reinforcing biosecurity practices. By industrialisation, we mean systems that promote the concentration and vertical integration of production chains, the Taylorisation and salarisation of work and the standardisation of products and processes (Bowler, 1986; Fraser, 2008).

antibiotic use in different production systems.[4] Our discussion is based on some of this material from the qualitative semi-structured interviews we conducted with farmers. To select the livestock farms visited, we relied on technical and economic support organisations which identified farmers committed to reducing antibiotic use.

The interviews with the farmers focused on the practices implemented on the farms to manage animal health. In this chapter, we compare two livestock systems – conventional industrial pig farming and Label Rouge (a French quality label) chicken farming – to consider their similarities and differences. The contrast allows us to highlight the specificities of each farming system while showing the common dynamics underlying the various forms of innovation associated with antibiotic withdrawal.

First, we strive to characterise the socio-technical dimension of innovation involving the withdrawal of antibiotics at the farm level, highlighting the new entities that appear or disappear due to changes in practices. We then examine whether the transition to less antibiotic use is or is not accompanied by changes in the livestock farmers' socio-professional networks.

Reducing Antibiotic Use in Livestock Farming: A Plurality of Actions

While the livestock farming system is the first level where innovation processes take place, it is not disconnected from its environment. Reduced antibiotic use requires transformations at the level of livestock production practices, in terms of technical tools, knowledge and work organisation. We distinguish three types of action that livestock farmers can take to reduce antibiotic consumption in their herds. The first is to increase the animals' capacity to cope with pathogens. This involves interventions in animal genetics and feed, as well as the use of products designed to strengthen the animals' immune defenses – vaccines and food supplements (particularly plant-based supplements). The second concerns the animals' environment. The task is to control and limit the proliferation of pathogens in their living environment through hygiene and biosecurity techniques.[5]

---

[4]TRAJ project (ten interviews with pig farmers), OMAP project (twelve interviews with Label Rouge broiler farmers).

[5]According to the OIE definition, biosecurity is the set of measures necessary to protect farms from health threats, aimed at preventing the entry and exit of pathogens from farms and their circulation within farms.

The third type concerns antibiotics and what is defined as their legitimate use. Antibiotics are used within a 'rational' or 'prudent' logic, which leads to their being reserved for certain situations that must be objectified by instruments or health risk assessment methods that are used to decide whether or not a treatment is necessary. The prudent use of antibiotics also relies on the possibility of using non-antibiotic treatments – usually referred to as alternatives – as a first line of treatment. We illustrate how these three types of action are employed in each of the livestock systems studied.

Reducing Antibiotics in Industrial Pig Farming

On the pig farms, the reduction of antibiotic use is part of a wider challenge to improve farming practices and better control health risks on farms. Many changes were made in the years prior to the study and involved all three types of action. All of the farmers whom we met agreed that they invested the most – economically, mentally (concerns, thoughts, etc.) and with respect to working time – on the animals and their environment. This means feeding and vaccination on the one hand and building maintenance and biosecurity on the other. The design of buildings appears to be a central element in preventing bacteria from proliferating. For example, one farmer had invested nearly two million euros in a new building equipped with a state-of-the-art air filtration system that was designed so that animals in different stages of production (gestation, maternity, weaning, fattening) could evolve without crossing paths. Like most farmers, he has implemented a vaccination programme against porcine reproductive and respiratory syndrome (PRRS) and piglet wasting disease (PWD).

However, the decisive changes concern nutrition. All of these farmers began to phase out antibiotic supplementation, meaning the systematic addition of antibiotics to the piglets' feed to prevent the development of gastric or respiratory diseases, in the early 2010s. These changes were made progressively, as the other components of the technical system evolved: first for the 'second age' feed (feeding transition starting about 20 days after weaning), then for the 'first age' feed (feeding transition starting at weaning, i.e., 21 or 28 days – weaning at three or four weeks indicating an intensification of the system). The abandonment of this practice led to a massive reduction in antibiotic consumption, including at the industry level, since pig production organisations encouraged this transition within the framework of the EcoAntibio plan. The dosing pump is a technical tool which has been critical to the success of this strategy. All of the farmers whom we met had adopted this system, which allowed them to treat animals only occasionally (rather than systematically, and via drinking water instead of feed), but which requires them to reorganise their work to spend more time with the animals and to adjust their conception of health in order to spot early signs of an infection (Fortané et al., 2015).

All of these elements are essential to the concept of 'good farming' that these farmers emphasise. For them, technicity is a central component of their profession's value, which they associate with a form of quasi-permanent inventiveness that is both constraining (adaptation to administrative rules related to the environment and animal welfare in particular) and satisfying (constant improvement of the livestock production system).

Reducing Antibiotics in Label Rouge Chicken Farming

The Label Rouge chicken farmers whom we met had never used high levels of antibiotics. However, they were proactively implementing techniques and strategies to further reduce their use, or even eliminate it on certain batches. Farmers indeed often evaluated their consumption level by comparing it to two other types of broiler chicken production, which serve as positive and negative references. They claimed that they used far fewer antibiotics than conventional poultry farmers and that their practices were comparable to those of organic farmers.

Mobilising the issue of antibiotics in this way to situate oneself in the world of broiler production – even if it is not necessarily the main working standard or 'quality' indicator – underscores the importance that this issue has assumed in the public space. However, this also shows the difficulty of isolating elements of the 'quality label' technical system to differentiate it from other modes of production, of which it is supposed to embody a compromise (other differentiating elements include notably the presence of a 'free-range' pasture, the density of the animals, the type of stock and the duration of rearing).

Compared to pig farms, the changes implemented on poultry farms to reduce antibiotic use are less dramatic and resemble adjustments. At the forefront is increased rigour in hygiene and biosecurity practices, with an emphasis on cleaning and disinfecting buildings, as well as on respecting the all-in-all-out system involving sanitary breaks between batches of birds. The use of the water acidification technique, initiated through discussions with poultry sector professionals (commercial agents, technicians and veterinarians) or on the recommendation of other farmers, made it possible to reduce the presence of bacteria in drinking water. At the animal level, changes were made in genetics and feeding, as well as by stepping up vaccinations of animals against coccidiosis at the hatchery to stop supplementing feed with coccidiostats. Regarding animal healthcare, the farmers we met had recently turned to alternatives to antibiotics such as probiotics and essential oils, used mainly as prophylaxis and sometimes for treatment. In these cases, they used antibiograms to identify the type of essential oil to use.

Differences in the Use of Technology Depending on the Sector

In the two livestock systems studied, the reduction of antibiotic use is based on the combined implementation of the three types of action defined above. Whether in industrial pork or Label Rouge poultry farming, farmers are taking action at both the level of the animal and of its environment while developing targeted antibiotic treatment strategies. To do this, they learned new methods and they used new tools. They also developed animal observation and monitoring capabilities for the early detection of health problems and preventive intervention. While these changes in animal health management have a positive connotation, this does not mean that the concept of 'good farming' (Burton, 2004), and of the role that antibiotic reduction plays in this, are identical in the two types of livestock systems. Among industrial pig farmers, the decreased use is associated with productivity and profitability values, while among non-conventional, Label Rouge farmers, an ethic of quality prevails. Innovation through withdrawal, which here consists of all of the socio-technical transitions that make it possible to reduce antibiotic use, thus is linked to different value systems and favours the maintenance of attachments to pre-existing conceptions of 'good animal husbandry'. This echoes many research on the social construction of 'quality' in food products, showing that quality is an institution shaped by markets and culture (Allaire, 2010).

Reduced antibiotic use also leads to giving greater visibility to bacteria and antibiotics, which previously had been rendered invisible due to systematic treatments. Indeed, with systematic treatments, for example when piglets are being weaned, antibiotics are part of a routine care protocol. They are associated with other products, like feed, that hide the antibiotics from view. The presence of bacteria is not clearly recognised either. When antibiotic reduction strategies are implemented, antibiotics are only used after clinical signs are identified on the animals, signs perceived as a manifestation of a pathogen's presence, sometimes refined by analyses allowing the type of bacteria involved to be qualified (milk, blood, faeces tests, etc.). As in the case of soil conservation agriculture (Goulet and Vinck, 2012), innovation through withdrawal involves making visible entities (here, biological) that were obscured by the presence of the technical artefact (here, antibiotics). Nevertheless, farmers do not completely detach themselves from antibiotics, which remain an indispensable tool for managing herd health. It is a question of making do *with less;* while 'zero antibiotics' is highlighted, livestock farmers do not wish to do without them completely.

However, differences do appear between production systems in the methods and tools used to reduce antibiotic dependence. The dependence on technologies provided by companies up and down the value chain differentiates the livestock systems. For example, in pig farming, the design of the building is a key and involves high material investments. The feed adapted to each age category are formulated and produced by outside companies, even if the farmer can provide part of the components of this complete feed. The same applies to the dosing pump, which makes it possible to adjust antibiotic treatments according to needs. In the case of Label Rouge poultry, the reduction in antibiotic consumption does not involve increased use of technology, which is already low to begin with. However, buildings and their equipment are key elements in the management of animal health; more rigorous maintenance of them makes it possible to further limit antibiotic therapy.

Overall, the comparison of these case studies highlights two elements. First, it is indeed all of the modifications or adjustments of the livestock system – biosecurity, feed, genetics, building management, vaccination, alternative medicines – that characterise innovation by withdrawal, rather than the withdrawal of antibiotics alone. Moreover, although these changes may lead to a redesign of livestock systems, they do not reflect a change in production methods and associated value systems. Reducing antibiotics is thus part of a continuum rather than a break. This is irrespective of whether the farm in question is one that is intensive and industrial based on the use of technological tools, or one that is extensive, and considered 'alternative' or 'natural'. In this sense, even if changes in practices are needed to foster transitions to reduced use of antibiotics, the maintenance of socio-technical attachments to pre-existing systems remains the norm. In some ways, such transitions could be conceived as part of the 'sustainable intensification' paradigm that characterises farming practices and systems aiming at preserving natural resources while keeping optimising or even increasing production (Garnet and Godfray, 2012).

Socio-Technical and Socio-Economic Networks That Support the Dynamics of Reduced Antibiotic Use

While socio-technical changes at the level of livestock production are essential components of innovation and transition processes, equally decisive is the way in which these changes are embedded in, or made possible by, a web of socio-technical and socio-economic relationships. Although Goulet and Vinck (2012) highlighted mechanisms of detachment and then attachment to new professional networks that would favour the change of practices, our case studies show more varied situations, and even the maintenance or strengthening of attachments to pre-existing networks.

In Integrated Sectors: Strengthening the Links Between Farmers, Veterinarians and Technicians

On intensive pig farms, the role of local technicians and veterinarians is decisive; they work directly with or for the farmers' producers' organisations (POs). The technicians visit the farms regularly to help farmers with the required technical changes. Veterinarians, either independent or contracted by the PO to manage the herd health plan, provide diagnosis, drug supplies and the development of health strategies (Bonnaud and Fortané, 2018). The farmers we met placed considerable trust in their technical and health advisers; they rarely consult technicians or veterinarians who are not their usual contacts. Similarly, exchanges between these farmers about practices or technical and economic results are mainly carried out within the framework of groups set up by the PO or by the veterinary practice.

In the Label Rouge chicken sector, the trajectory of reducing antibiotic use also was initiated through contacts with technical and health advisers from the production organisation (Adam et al., 2017). The veterinarians initiated a process of valorising preventive approaches with the technicians, who then relayed them to the farmers. The veterinarians also are promoting alternatives to antibiotics, even developing partnerships for this purpose, for example with a manufacturer of phytotherapy products, or carrying out their own tests. Farmers also emphasise that mutual trust between themselves and technicians and veterinarians, built on long-term relationships, is an essential element in the transition to reduced antibiotic use.

Traditional production organisations, through their technical and health advisers, thus play a crucial role in the implementation and coordination of antibiotic reduction strategies. In the study of the Label Rouge chicken sector, one PO systematically performs a phytogram in parallel with an antibiogram in order to identify the essential oils to which the pathogens are sensitive, thereby avoiding the use of an antibiotic. One of the POs that we interviewed has a group of farmers auditing its progress, while another has used its network to select farmers likely to produce batches without antibiotics. The quality manager then makes an assessment of the treatments and calculates the usage indicators. In general, a coordinating veterinarian (in this case, the farmers keep their usual veterinarian to monitor the farms individually) or a pair composed of a veterinarian and a technician, plan the production without antibiotics in coordination with the distributor ensuring the marketing of the products. We can thus see, as has been shown in other types of production (Bonnaud et al., 2012), that POs know how to promote and use the social constraints that are exercised within their collective of farmers to build standards of 'good practices' that are shared and partly controlled by the community, strategies that are all the more effective when the farmers have a strong sense of belonging to the collective (Adam et al., 2017).

The Range of Actors Involved in the Reduction of Antibiotics in Livestock

The livestock farmers' attachment to technical and health advisers and their role in reducing the use of antibiotics can be explained by the highly integrated nature of these two sectors. In fact, in the pork and Label Rouge poultry sectors, the entire production chain is committed to reducing the use of antibiotics, from the input supply companies to the animal product marketing channels.

These sectors have developed so-called 'antibiotic-free' products, which does not necessarily mean 'zero antibiotics'; specifications differ from one production or brand to another. In pigs, use is often limited to the pre-weaning period; the timing of weaning thus becoming an issue since it triggers the compliance or not of these specifications. In free-range poultry, if farmers manage to produce antibiotic-free batches, they can still alternate between treated and untreated batches. Although these two sectors are different in terms of livestock systems (intensive on the one hand, alternative on the other), the fact remains that the development of these 'antibiotic-free' labels is part of the same dynamic of maintaining, or even reinforcing, farmers' ties to the pre-existing system. Even if these labels are not standardised and remain privately controlled, their development is related to similar strategies driven by the retailing industry and implemented through POs. These labels enable market segmentation and create an opportunity to value economically products that comply with relatively strict standards regarding antibiotic use. This dynamic also seem to limit the adoption of more restrictive regulation that would constrain the whole sector instead of the sole POs and farms that are willing to get involved in such transitions.

All in all, distributors play a key role in the implementation and monitoring of the specifications ensuring the production of 'antibiotic-free' meat or eggs (and sometimes milk) (Begemann et al., 2020). Through their orders, they trigger the implementation of batches and push the producer groups to improve their quality systems. Distributors often approach producer organisations to ask if they can supply a regular quantity of products that meet certain quality criteria. This dynamic observable in the development of French 'antibiotic-free' labels echoes the work of Burch and Lawrence (2005) on supermarkets' 'own-brands' which rely on just-in-time techniques and flexible production systems to supply a range of innovative food lines defined by certain criteria of 'quality'. Our study thus clearly highlights the role of the retailing industry in transitions towards reduced antibiotic use. They asked the POs to set up monitoring tools to quantitatively assess antibiotic use in order to develop an 'antibiotic-free' label. It is also during negotiations with distributors that production organisations define their in-house specifications to enrol farmers in these quality label programs. In the pork industry, an 'antibiotic-free' ham may thus sometimes come from a pig that was never treated from birth, and sometimes from a pig that was treated only until the end of weaning.

Withdrawal of antibiotics is therefore not only defined by technical production-related criteria, but also integrates market elements. The latter are all the more decisive as they can reinforce the 'integrated' structure of the sector and the livestock farms' ties to their socio-technical and socio-economic networks. Some 'antibiotic-free' specifications, for example, make it compulsory to buy feed from specific suppliers, as this improved animal feed makes it possible to reduce the use of antibiotics. Failure to comply with this component of the standard would result in a farmer losing his or her label (and the associated financial bonus) even if he or she continued to refrain from using antibiotics. Ultimately, the French 'antibiotic-free' landscape is still relatively heterogenous as the various standards remain private initiatives independent from each other and attempts to create a unified label publicly regulated have failed (both the government and the economic operators wanted to avoid the development of a specialised 'quality' sector that would reduce antibiotic use while the rest of the industry wouldn't make any efforts). Further research would be needed to understand such processes at a more political or macroeconomic level. Nonetheless we can see the extent to which certain innovations can reinforce ties to quite integrated sectors whether industrial, as in pork, or 'alternative', as in Label Rouge chicken. Through the dependence that they foster between actors (here, we mostly studied the relationships between farmers and their POs), these innovations can drive large-scale changes in practice but they maintain the socio-technical and socio-economic structures within which these changes take place.

Conclusion

The theory of 'innovation through withdrawal' developed by Goulet and Vinck (2012) emphasises the importance of detachment and reattachment processes in agri-food transitions. However, in the case of the reduction of antibiotic use in intensive and/or industrial livestock farming, the transition takes place in a very different way. Rather than destabilising the dominant system of industrial production as part of the transition, there is a strengthening of relations between farmers and all of the actors involved in providing traditional technical and economic support. This strengthening of ties goes hand in hand with the livestock farmers' significant dependence on technological tools and methods provided by upstream and downstream companies. Production methods, whether intensive or extensive, do not fundamentally change. On the contrary, the antibiotics reduction trajectory can only make sense if the existing model is maintained. Integration, as a means of coordinating actors, is reinforced by technical and contractual mechanisms that further restrict the farmers' autonomy.

Furthermore, in the two sectors studied, the reduction of antibiotics is not the primary focus of the changes observed, even though it is used in marketing strategies through the 'antibiotic-free' label displayed on products. Indeed, the reduced use of antibiotics is a means to several ends – improving product quality and performance, enhancing 'naturalness' – rather than an end in and of itself. Finally, one may ask whether the reduction of antibiotics is really an innovation or even a transition. In public accounts of the fight against AMR, the reduction of antibiotics tends to be associated with forms of transition towards more sustainable, alternative or preventive systems. However, it can be used, as in the case of pig farming or Label Rouge poultry farming, as a resilience strategy for existing production systems, maintaining both a relative intensification of livestock farming and, above all, a strong integration of supply and marketing channels. Moreover, it is the intensive and industrial systems that produce the bulk of antibiotic-free products and encourage, or at least make visible, this so-called transition.

All in all, it is undoubtedly time to question the relevance of the 'reduction' criterion for designing and evaluating our policies to combat AMR, since it conceals from sight the maintenance of intensive and industrial production methods. In this perspective, the very notion of transition can be challenged. In the age of the Anthropocene where, as Fredric Jameson reminds us, it seems easier to imagine the end of the world than the end of capitalism, are we not performing multiple changes so that, in the end, nothing changes? This is, at least, what our study suggests here: there is no doubt that antibiotic use is drastically being reduced in the French pig and poultry sectors (about 45 percent drop in a decade according to recent evaluation of the national action plan against AMR), but it doesn't necessarily means that the production and distribution system has moved towards more sustainable or 'agroecological' structures. This certainly echoes the work of colleagues (Dedieu and Jouzel, 2015) on the 'domestication of critique' which show how certain claims and mobilisations (for the recognition of public health or environmental concerns) could be neutralised through their appropriation by domi- nant actors who take them in charge in a way that doesn't destabilise their socio-economic organisation. This is how we conceive here transitions in the age of Capitalocene, in the sense that the AMR problem is framed and utilised as an opportunity for agricultural capitalism to maintain its roots in the way our daily food is being produced and distributed.

Acknowledgements

This work was supported by INRAE's 'Integrated Animal Health Management' metaprogram (TRAJ project) and the Carnot Institute's France Futur Elevage network (OMAP project).

References

Adam, C., Ducrot, C., Mathilde, P. and Fortané, N. (2017) 'Autonomy under con- tract: The case of traditional free-range poultry farmers'. *Review of Agricultural, Food and Environmental Studies, 98*(1–2): 55–74.

Allaire, G. (2010) 'Applying economic sociology to understand the meaning of "quality" in food markets'. *Agricultural Economics, 41*: 167–80.

Anses (2019) *Suivi des ventes de médicaments vétérinaires contenant des antibiotiques en France en 2018, Rapport annuel.*

Begemann, S., Watkins, F., Van Hoyweghen, I., Vivancos, R., Chrisley, R. and Perkins, E. (2020) 'The governance of UK dairy antibiotic use: Industry-led policy in action'. *Frontiers in Veterinary Science*, 557.

Bonnaud, L., Bouhsina, Z. and Codron, J.M. (2012) 'Le rôle du marché dans le contrôle des traitements phytosanitaires'. *Terrains Travaux, 20*(1): 87–103.

Bonnaud, L. and Fortané, N. (2018) '"L'"État sanitaire de la profession vétérinaire. Action publique et régulation de l'activité professionnelle'. *Sociologie, 9*(3): 253–68.

Bowler, I.R. (1986) 'Intensification, concentration and specialization in agriculture: The case of the European Community'. *Geography, 71*(1): 14–24.

Burch, D. and Lawrence, G. (2005) 'Supermarket own brands, supply chains and the transformation of the agri-food system'. *International Journal of Sociology of Agriculture and Food, 13*(1): 1–18.

Burton, R.J.F. (2004) 'Seeing through the "good farmer's" eyes: Towards developing an understanding of the social symbolic value of "productivist" behaviour'. *Sociologia Ruralis, 44*(2): 195–215.

Dedieu, F. and Jouzel, J.N. (2015) 'How to ignore what one knows: Domesticating uncomfortable knowledge about pesticide poisoning among farmers'. *Revue Française de Sociologie, 56*(1): 105–33.

Fortané, N. (2019) 'Veterinarian "responsibility": Conflicts of definition and appropriation surrounding the public problem of antimicrobial resistance in France'. *Palgrave Communications, 5*(1): 1–12.

Fortané, N. (2021) 'Antimicrobial resistance: Preventive approaches to the rescue? Professional expertise and business model of French "industrial" veterinarians'. *Review of Agricultural, Food and Environmental Studies, 102*(2): 213–38.

Fortané, N., Bonnet-Beaugrand, F., Hémonic, A., Samedi, C., Savy, A. and Belloc, C. (2015) 'Learning processes and trajectories for the reduction of antibiotic use in pig farming: A qualitative approach'. *Antibiotics, 4*(4): 435–54.

Fraser, D. (2008) 'Animal welfare and the intensification of animal production'. In P.B. Thompson (ed), *The Ethics of Intensification: Agricultural Development and Cultural Change.* Dordrecht: Springer Netherlands, pp. 167–89.

Garnett, T. and Godfray, C. (2012) *Sustainable Intensification in Agriculture: Navigating a Course through Competing Food System Objectives.* Oxford: Food Climate Research Network and Oxford Martin School Programme on the Future of Food.

Goulet, F. and Vinck, D. (2012) 'L'innovation par retrait. Contribution à une sociologie du détachement'. *Revue Francaise de Sociologie, 53*(2): 195–224.

Kirchhelle, C. (2020) *Pyrrhic Progress: The History of Antibiotics in Anglo-American Food Production.* New Brunswick: Rutgers University Press.

Moore, J.W. (ed.) (2016) 'Anthropocene or Capitalocene?' In *Nature, History, and the Crisis of Capitalism.* Oakland, CA: PM Press.

Podolsky, S.H. (2015) *The Antibiotic Era: Reform, Resistance, and the Pursuit of a Rational Therapeutics,* 1st edn. Baltimore, MD: Johns Hopkins University Press.

6

Sustainable Transitions for Brazilian Animal Agriculture in the Anthropocene: Scientific Knowledge About Pasture Restoration

Thaís Rozas Teixeira

Introduction

The global animal agriculture industry has been receiving attention because of its environmental consequences and global carbon footprint (Ripple et al., 2014; Steinfeld et al., 2006). When its connections to land-use change, such as deforestation to convert natural coverage areas into pasture lands, are considered, animal grazing impacts increase, including its greenhouse gas emissions (Bustamante et al., 2012; Gerber et al., 2013). This chapter focuses on the connections between land-use change and animal agriculture (land-livestock nexus), given their relevance in both emissions and mitigation alternatives to climate change. In this sense, with high confidence, the recent Climate Change and Land report from the Intergovernmental Panel on Climate Change (IPCC, 2019b: 5) considers the land as 'simultaneously a source and a sink of CO_2 due to both anthropogenic and natural drivers. [...] These net emissions are mostly due to deforestation, partly offset by afforestation/reforestation, and emissions and removals by other land use activities'.

Thus, how can soil act as a source and a sink of greenhouse gas emissions? As the IPCC report indicates, some land-use activities can offset emissions and contribute to climate change removals, such as management production systems and practices. For example, livestock activities, especially cattle-raising, are often based on pasture lands, which result in advanced soil degradation processes. Because of losses in natural coverage and reduction of soil organic matter content, land use contributes to greenhouse gas emissions, including pasture and grasslands (Assad et al., 2013). In particular, 'carbon sequestration potential in pasture lands is directly related to soil management and carbon gain and losses rates, with soils working as drains or sources of CO_2' (Medeiros et al., 2017: 175).[1] Then, it becomes possible to strengthen the soil's potential to sequester and remove carbon by adopting management practices that aim to increase soil carbon content and restore its natural conditions, for example recovery of degraded pastureland and integration with crop-livestock-forest systems. The result of these mitigation strategies 'is an increase in the number of organic compounds preserved from biological action and in the amount formed of total organic carbon and soil organic matter' (Assad et al., 2019: 161), processes that represent removals from land-use changes.

For this reason, considering its climate responsibilities, land use can represent, at the same time, a challenge and an opportunity within the climate change debates. This intersection between emissions and mitigation responsibilities is particularly relevant in Brazil's scientific and political settings. Unlike other countries where most anthropogenic emissions derive from fossil fuel combustion, Brazil's greenhouse gas emissions are singular because land use and farming are its main human driving forces (Brazil, 2012; SEEG, 2020). According to the Greenhouse Gas Emission Estimation System (SEEG), an initiative from the Climate Observatory (OC), both sectors represent more than 70 percent of total net national emissions (SEEG, 2020). Moreover, it is relevant to highlight that cattle-raising in Brazil is traditionally extensively done, where a large portion of land is deforested and converted into pasture. Beyond benefits from natural soil fertility, producers tend to migrate to new areas when these lands reach a low production rate, expanding agricultural frontiers against native forests and abandoning degraded pasture (Cerri and Oliveira, 2017). According to a computer platform entitled 'Digital Atlas of Brazilian Pastures' developed by a university laboratory,[2] more than 32 percent of Brazilian pastures exhibited advanced levels of degradation that directly influence soil organic matter and its carbon sequestration mechanism.

---

[1] All the documents and quotes from Portuguese articles were translated by the author.
[2] Image Processing and Geoprocessing Laboratory of the Federal University of Goiás, translation for Laboratório de Processamento de Imagens e Geoprocessamento da Universidade Federal de Goiás (Lapig/UFG).

The United Nations Framework Convention on Climate Change (UNFCCC) principle of 'common but differentiated responsibilities and respective capabilities' (CBDR/RC), in Article 3, suggests that 'Parties should protect the climate system for the benefit of present and future generations of humankind, on the basis of equity and in accordance with their common but differentiated responsibilities and respective capabilities. Accordingly, the developed country Parties should take the lead in combating climate change and the adverse effects thereof'.[3] That is why, considering the need for adequate mitigation options in each country's context, as the CBDR/RC principle mentions, the intersection between livestock and land-use change represents an important concern for the Brazilian government, in terms of proposing strategies and commitments to reduce climate change. In the scope of UNFCCC, Brazil's Nationally Determined Contributions (NDC) points out commitments to reduce the country's emissions by 37 percent by 2025 (targets that enable better monitoring) and by 43 percent by 2030. Moreover, this communication highlights its compatibility with 'an indicative long-term objective of reaching climate neutrality in 2060' (Brazil, 2020a). Through the Low Agriculture Plan (ABC), the Brazilian government has allocated financial investments 'to a wide range of mitigation measures in the agricultural and animal husbandry sector, such as the recovery of degraded pastures; [...] increased accumulation of organic matter, and therefore carbon, in the soil; [...] crop-livestock-forestry integration' (Brazil, 2020a: 8). Among these mitigation measurements, Brazil is committed to recovering 15 million hectares of degraded pasture and integrating it into 4 million hectares of crop-livestock-forest systems to achieve its climate targets. In this sense, this chapter aims to reflect on Brazilian mitigation strategies adopted to reduce national emissions through removals from carbon accumulation because of soil management techniques, such as recovery and integration of degraded pastures.

These strategies, part of a wide range of technologies designed to tackle climate change that follows international guidelines, are justified by research within soil sciences studies. Such studies demonstrate how regeneration techniques 'provide the system with a more extensive

---

[3]UNFCCC Article 3. Available at https://unfccc.int/files/essential_background/backgr ound_publications_htmlpdf/application/pdf/conveng.pdf. Last access: 06/29/22.

carbon stock when compared to a degraded pasture, as the root system for grasses in that condition is more abundant, and accumulation of organic matter in the soil decreases the loss of CO_2 to the atmosphere' (Assad et al., 2015: 37). Although Brazil's climate policies emphasise these regeneration techniques in their climate commitments and national mitigation future predictions, given its profile emissions and pasture conditions over the territory, climate removals from these managed systems are not fully accounted for in Brazilian contributions because of 'methodological limitations' (Brazil, 2020b: 157). In the 4th Brazilian Communication to the UNFCCC, the report did not include removals from degraded pasture converted to managed pasture systems. This idea aligns with the IPCC uncertainties related to carbon stock dynamics (IPCC, 2006, 2019a). However, despite international guidelines and methodological uncertainties over soil carbon removals, these strategies play a relevant role in the Brazilian political setting regarding climate change mitigation targets. In other words, the doubt in the international scientific community was neither an obstacle to direct investments nor proposed public policies and sustainable transitions to Brazilian animal agriculture. As Science and Technology Studies (STS) have extensively demonstrated, the relationship between science and politics in the modern world is closely related to feedback dynamics between these two dimensions rather than linear processes that *'speak truth to power'* (Duarte, 2019; Jasanoff, 1987, 1998, 2004, 2014; Lahsen, 2009; Miguel, 2021; Miller, 2004a, 2004b).

The controversy over pasture restoration practice to reduce animal agriculture emissions is a relevant subject in the Anthropocene. Initially proposed by Crutzen and Stoermer (2000), this concept refers to a new geological epoch in which humanity has become a predominant influence on biosphere conditions because of a series of anthropogenic effects due to human exploitation of Earth's natural resources, such as increased greenhouse gas emissions in the atmosphere, species extinction and land degradation. Climate change and its driving forces and mitigation mechanisms play a relevant role in this new geological era. More specifically, the land-livestock nexus is central to its climate and environmental impacts since it represents one of the essential sources of greenhouse gas emissions (Ripple et al., 2014). These consequences also extend to issues regarding food security, and it is possible to consider that, along with the need to reduce global emissions to an acceptable rate, 'feeding the world in a sustainable way is one of our most pressing challenges in the coming decades' (Ritchie and Roser, 2017).

In the past fifty years, meat production has tripled, and population growth and economic conditions are some of the many dimensions influencing production and consumption patterns and food security (Ritchie and Roser, 2017; Thornton, 2010). That is why scientists' negotiations around facts, measurements and prediction models related to land management practices in the livestock sector and its mitigation potential are impacting sustainable transitions for the animal agriculture industry. As Brazil has the largest cattle herd in the world and represents a vital beef exporter (ABIEC, 2021[4]; IBGE, 2019[5]), sustainable transitions to food production systems become especially important.

If food production is needed to increase by 70 percent in 2050 (compared to 2017)[6] to feed 9 billion people in that year (Fouilleux et al., 2017), which food systems need to be considered for sustainable goals? Then, along with negotiation processes around climate knowledge and mitigation strategies in Brazils scientific and political settings, these discourses also impact the specific transitions to sustainable futures in the Anthropocene. My argument is that both scientific options to predict future livestock emissions under pasture restoration technologies refer to the same transitions and the same pathways, which is the focus on sustainable development patterns based on increasing production and consumption of animal products.

---

[4]Brazilian Association of Meat Exporting Industries, translation for *Associação Brasileira das Indústrias Exportadoras de Carnes (ABIEC)*, is a Brazilian livestock association that gathers important companies from this economic sector and represents them in international debates such as commercial regulation, sanitary requirements and open markets.

[5]Brazilian Institute of Geography and Statistics, translation for *Instituto Brasileiro de Geografia e Estatística (IBGE)*. This public institution is responsible for many geographic and statistical information about Brazil.

[6]Delivered speech from Alan Bojanic, FAO's representative in Brazil. Available at http://www.fao.org/brasil/noticias/detail-events/pt/c/901168/#:~:text=Representante%20da%20FAO%20Brasil%20apresenta%20cen%C3%A1rio%20da%20demanda%20por%20alimentos,-Foto%3A%20%C2%A9FAO&text=%E2%80%9CPara%20alimentar%20essa%20popula%C3%A7%C3%A3o%20maior,2%2C5%20bilh%C3%B5es%20produzidos%20atualmente. Last access: 06/27/22.

Scientific Climate Knowledge and Its Implications on Sustainable Transitions: Analytical and Theoretical Framework

I collected the data analysed in this chapter in two moments. First, a systematic search of official government documents such as the National Policy to Tackle Climate Change (PNMC),[7] plans to mitigate emissions directed to each sector (as the Low Agriculture Plan, or ABC Plan), Brazilian GHG inventories and Nationally Determined Contributions (NDC), as well as scientific publications related to methods and techniques to measure and predict GHG emissions and carbon stock dynamics under mitigation scenarios. Through these documents and publications, this research aims to understand the scientific knowledge about the relationship between carbon sinks, pasture lands, climate change mitigation, its uncertainties and how it circulates in both scientific and political debates. Second, I conducted interviews (7) with Brazilian head scientists. After defining the 'core-set' of scientists (Collins, 1981, 2011) from publications and articles directly involved in such knowledge claims about pasture restoration as a mitigation strategy for the Brazilian livestock sector, I selected these actors.

Based on this investigation, it became apparent that the scientific studies' results were controversial regarding restoration strategies, specifically recovery and integration of degraded pasture and its potential to achieve nationally determined climate commitments. Therefore, to comprehend the negotiations in these knowledge claims related to the possibility of restored and integrated pasture to mitigate livestock emissions and achieve national climate commitments, the 'core-set' of scientists who 'actively partook' in this controversy through publications and influences on public debates were interviewed (Pinch, 2015). During the interviews, they commented on how they conducted their respective study, which methods and techniques they mobilised to measure soil carbon stock and predict its mitigation potential and how the Brazilian government could achieve climate goals for the livestock sector and national emissions, along with the importance of pasture restoration strategies. Furthermore, when arguing for mitigation strategies to achieve these commitments, the scientists pointed out political directions to food systems configurations, considering that 'the

---

[7]Translation for Política Nacional de Combate à Mudança Climática.

knowledge used to justify action is fundamental to the future of global food and agriculture because it directly shapes and conditions the policies and actions taken' (Loconto and Fouilleux, 2019: 118). Furthermore, these political outlines in scientists' discourses also highlighted which sustainable transitions should be proposed to achieve global and local commitments and mitigation targets.

Analytically, I employ STS contributions related to controversy studies and the science-policy interface to discuss how strategies to tackle climate change are enmeshed in scientific knowledge claims that propose sustainable transitions to different sectors, such as animal agriculture. On the one hand, to understand the controversy, I recognised through those contributions that it is during the contestation and contention moments in science 'that the often invisible processes of the working of science become more visible and hence available to analysis' (Pinch, 2015: 5). In this sense, social dimensions such as discourses, assumptions, negotiations and political struggles embedded in scientific production become more explicit (Collins, 2011; Pinch, 2015). Along such contributions, I mobilised Collins (2011) and Pinch (2015) concepts as 'core-set' of scientists within a controversy, and the idea that only scientific arguments and experiments are not sufficient to close scientific controversies. On the other hand, the controversy discussed in this chapter overflows scientific debates and directly affects climate decision-making and national policies. For this reason, the science-policy interface is relevant, especially the dynamics of regulatory science (Jasanoff, 1987, 1998) and expert scientific advice (Hilgartner, 2000; Miller, 2001; Nelkin, 1975). More directly, from the premise that knowledge and political decisions are intertwined, the need to rethink policymaking strategies to achieve climate commitments and food security issues in an unstable environment (Pereira and Viola, 2022) is not separate from how knowledge is produced, circulates through scientific and political debates, and is used by decision-makers.

Pasture Restoration Controversy: Public Policies, Scientific Publications and Scientists' Discourses

I position my analysis of pasture restoration as a central mitigation option for the livestock sector facing Brazilian climate commitments within the sociological literature around controversies, negotiation processes in scientific and technological production, and regulatory science at public policy interfaces. Even though there is a consensus within the scientific community regarding lands acting as carbon sinks and assumptions that agricultural practices directly affect this mechanism and GHG emissions for the land-use sector (LULUF), controversies remain present in these scientific debates. By describing and analysing government documents, scientific publications and scientists' discourses, the objective is to outline the controversy over pasture restoration, focusing on the recovery and integration with crop-livestock-forest systems of degraded pasture areas. In a few words, although climate public policies to mitigate animal agriculture emissions in Brazil point out these strategies as the best alternatives, scientists are still negotiating methods and techniques to quantify and predict emissions mitigated from these technologies and the outcomes in terms of international commitments and targets.

Brazil's Climate Commitments and Mitigation Initiatives

According to the Minister of Agriculture, Livestock, and Supply (MAPA), Tereza Cristina, the agriculture sector contributes positively to Brazilian commitments to sustainable development and climate change global agreements[8]. As part of mitigation technologies proposed by the Brazilian government, restoration of degraded pastures, through recovery practices and integration with crop-livestock-forest systems, plays a significant role in national strategies, as it represents the best potential for reducing emissions from animal farming activities (Brazil, 2012). The Low Carbon Agriculture Plan (ABC plan), a pioneer and strategic climate initiative, has as its basic principle to achieve low carbon agriculture (including animal farming) through the adoption of technologies that increase resilience, continue economic gains, and still contribute to lower or mitigate emissions as a result of agriculture management practices and soil carbon sinks (Manzatto et al., 2019: 7–8). Especially between 2010 and 2020, among other 'technological processes' to reduce emissions, the ABC Plan proposed to recover 15 million hectares of degraded pasture and integrate it with four million hectares with

---

[8]Delivered speech during the presentation of ABC+, on 10/18/21. Available at https://www.sna.agr.br/plano-abc-pretende-reduzir-emissao-de-carbono-em-mais-de-1-bilhao-de-toneladas/. Last access: 10/20/21.

crop-livestock-forest systems (Brazil, 2012). With the adoption of low carbon technologies, estimated to reduce emissions between 133.9 and 162.9 million tons of CO_2 equivalent based on an average carbon sink rate (3.79 mg of CO_2 equivalent for each hectare recovered or integrated with the crop-livestock-forest system), the two proposed strategies represent approximately 75 percent of total mitigation potential. These commitments are also presented in Brazil's NDC to reach carbon neutrality (Brazil, 2020a). In addition, the 'new' ABC plan (called ABC+), which establishes targets from 2020 to 2030 proposes the 'adoption and maintenance of conservationist and sustainable agricultural production systems', including (but not only) recovery and crop-livestock-forest integration, considered 'science-based' sustainable systems (Brazil, 2021: 17).

In this sense, livestock public policies highlight restoration and grassland management practices to strengthen the soil carbon sequester mechanism, primarily through the recovery and integration of degraded pastures. Nevertheless, producing measurements and accounting for these carbon dynamics and processes requires highly specialised knowledge and investments. The main questions these measurements need to answer are 'how much soil carbon can each restoration technique accumulate, and how much time it takes to achieve a certain amount of removals'. Regarding the problem of mitigating emissions and ensuring national climate commitments, which strategies are the best solution for Brazilian animal agriculture? After all, Brazilian public policies and decision-makers' positions reinforce the idea that recovery and integration of degraded pastures are key strategies to achieve national mitigation commitments, and Low Carbon Agriculture plans (ABC and ABC+) represent one of the most ambitious climates policies for the animal agriculture sector. However, besides considering these sustainable systems proposed as 'science-based' strategies, it does not mean that there is a scientific consensus over their mitigation potential. As presented previously, the national and international scientific community agree on the possibility of reducing livestock emissions through the adoption of land management practices, but the accounting of these mitigated emissions is still in negotiation. More specifically, I indicate a main controversial point: *the average rate for soil carbon accumulation* because of different pasture restoration practices for mitigation predictions over time and the possibility of reducing emissions even with the still increasing cattle herd. This point, interpreted and mobilised in different ways by scientists and their publications, directly affects the climate removal estimates for the livestock sector under those sustainable systems (soil recovery and integration) and the assurance of agreed commitments, which depends on such estimations and impacts calculations.

Average Rates for Carbon Accumulation in Climate Predictions, and How to Estimate Soil Carbon Removal Capacity: Static or Asymptotic Models?

If pasture areas can act as carbon sinks when restoration technologies are adopted, how much carbon accumulates at a specific time? The estimates made by the ABC plan to predict the mitigation potential from sustainable technologies proposed used an average rate (3.79) for soil carbon accumulation on recovered and integrated pasture areas per hectare and per year considered (Brazil, 2012). However, it is worth noting that the quantification of this carbon dynamic and sinks as the result of specific land management strategies is highly complex due to the influence of several factors, both bioclimatic and management related (Alves, 2015; Bernoux et al., 2002; Maia et al., 2009). In this sense, the average rate of carbon sink utilised as the calculation basis for mitigation potential of restoration technologies in Brazilian public policies and nationally determined climate strategies is not agreed upon by all scientific researchers and publications because of external effects such as herd growth. Some scientists agree with this average rate for Brazilian territory, which is mathematically constructed through an average between all carbon accumulation rates, produced by a wide range of scientific publications, on a variety of soil types, vegetation and under the adoption of different technologies, and its mitigation potential under future scenarios (Alves, 2015; Assad et al., 2013, 2015, 2019; Observatorio ABC, 2015, 2017; Silva et al., 2016). For instance, the ABC Observatory, a national initiative that 'monitors the actions of the Plan and the ABC Programme,[9]

---

[9]Program for Reducing Greenhouse Gas Emissions in Agriculture (ABC Program), which finances the proposed actions within ABC Plan to adopt low carbon strategies and reduce greenhouse gas emissions from agriculture activities (Brazil, 2012).

developing technical studies to support and facilitate dialogue with stakeholders'[10] published technical reports on mitigation potential, economic and environmental impacts of low carbon strategies for agriculture. In these reports, the potential of pasture restoration techniques, within nationally determined commitments, is emphasised and recommended as a priority for financial investments, given its possibility to reduce emissions and to spare land for reforestation (Observatorio ABC, 2017). This initiative assumes that recovered and integrated pastures can accumulate 1 and 1.5 tons of carbon per hectare per year, based on carbon stocks surveys throughout Brazilian territory and studies about the impacts of integration techniques. Even with higher animal stock densities per hectare, emissions can be reduced (Observatorio ABC, 2015).

Along with these assumptions by ABC Observatory, other Brazilian scientists also mobilise an average rate measurement to carbon sinks on recovered or integrated pasture areas. For example, regarding improved pastures (under the recovery techniques to restore its natural conditions), Silva et al. (2016: 1) point out other studies that show how it is possible to increase soil carbon stocks with net atmospheric CO_2 removals of almost 1 ton of carbon per hectare per year, by improving tropical grasses productivity. Moreover, Martins and colleagues (2018: 50), by assuming the average rates of 1 and 1.5 tons of carbon accumulated per hectare per year with restoration technologies, argue that Brazilian agriculture mitigation potential 'is more than ten-fold the goal set forth by the ABC Plan. [...] by incorporating the emissions avoided and the carbon stored in the soil through the adoption of three technologies advocated by the ABC Plan (pasture recovery, integrated crop-livestock systems, and the integrated crop-livestock-forest systems)'.

According to a scientist involved in this and other studies related to Brazilian cattle ranching, these calculation bases are within the expected range because they average between the minimum and the maximum value. So, after confirming the credibility of these average rates, this scientist just highlighted the possibility of future adjustments as more data is collected, which does not change the point that Brazilian national strategies for the livestock sector are in the right

[10]Description available at http://observatorioabc.com.br/quem-somos/. Last access: 10/22/21.

direction. This direction is related to mitigation goals determined in national public policies, guided by international agreements, and the capacity of improved and integrated pasture areas to achieve them because of emissions avoided and soil carbon sinks. For these scientists, restoration practices are fundamental to Brazilian strategies to reduce emissions from animal agriculture activities, considering their importance in national estimates. Therefore, despite some adjustments in the average rate for carbon accumulation these measurements can be used to assert that Brazil will ensure its climate commitments to international negotiations when recovering and integrating degraded pasture, even with an increased cattle herd (Silva et al., 2016). These scientists are associated with the Brazilian Agricultural Research Company (Embrapa), a public research institution affiliated with the Ministry of Agriculture, Livestock and Supply (MAPA), and produce scientific knowledge for the Brazilian livestock sector.

However, other Brazilian scientists questioned Embrapa's knowledge claims regarding the carbon accumulation average rate's credibility to support national predictions for livestock mitigation. These scientists are part of a remote monitoring centre from the University of Minas Gerais (CRS/UFMG) and base their arguments on computer platforms and software that simulate future livestock and land-use sector scenarios based on economic impacts, productivity rates and associated emissions. One of the interviewees, unlike the others, argued that those average rates are overestimated because they are based on studies that show the most significant soil accumulation potential; however, some studies demonstrate less potential. Supporting this scientist's critique, Brazilian researchers point out that the Embrapa averages elaborated for carbon stock accumulation cannot circumvent the uncertainties involved in these measurements (Batista, 2016; Batista et al., 2019; Rajão and Soares-Filho, 2015). In other words, this group of scientists indicates that further studies are necessary to understand the soil carbon dynamics under restoration practices. Like one of the interviewed scientists said, it is necessary to invest more in soil carbon sequestration measurements because of still-remaining uncertainties in available and past studies.

Although these models work with data collected and produced by other systems and software, the computer platform allows them to integrate diverse inputs such as different national and international databases, a variety of studies, and information related to land use and land-use change, deforestation rates, future demands for livestock products and expansion of agriculture areas. Furthermore, these models can perform more complex operations and simulate changes in land-use scenarios based on local parameters. For these scientists, the main difference from those other studies that mobilise average rates and support the prominent position of restoration strategies is the given credibility to a static prediction model that disregards other variables like time and spatial variations for such accumulation rates and the number of grazing animals per hectare. Furthermore, the carbon accumulated average resulting from pasture restoration technologies described in the determined national strategies is based on an 'if adopted' assumption that such mitigation technologies can reduce a certain amount of emissions due to a yearly accumulation rate.

On the one hand, for the Embrapa and similar scientists, the use of these average rates is compatible with several studies carried out within the Brazilian context, and it is a valid measurement that indicates how national public policies and scientific research are on 'the right track' to comprehend carbon sinks from restoration techniques. On the other hand, the computer model scientists disagree because although it does not mean that these average rates are scientifically wrong, there are still unresolved uncertainties that can affect the measurement results and do not consider essential variables and aspects of soil carbon dynamics. During the interviews, one of the Embrapa scientists said that through large-scale adoption of an improved pasture system model adopted on 50 to 60 hectares of degraded areas in Brazil, it would be possible to reduce emissions by 30 percent in two years and ensure climate commitments. However, a scientist from the computer model group stated that soil carbon accumulation is not a linear process. He also said that when the soil reaches balanced conditions, the accumulation rate may be zero, impacting the prediction variables for improved pasture mitigation.

In this sense, beyond fighting about removals rates, as an interviewee said, the scientists are negotiating how to predict future emissions under pasture restoration scenarios based on which scientific variables and prediction models are suitable. As a computer model scientist argued, the studies based on average rates for carbon accumulation are founded on a more static climate prediction because the same rate is used as a variable for each modelled year without considering changes in carbon stocks over time. To maintain carbon accumulation rates, Batista (2016) maintains that the pasture needs to remain productive, which requires other practices to balance its conditions and nutrients, but that also impacts climate emissions. Moreover, Batista et al. (2019: 10) state that the carbon sink models in the proposed Brazilian climate policy 'would mitigate only a part of marginal emissions', and restoration practices without a diverse portfolio of mitigation options are not enough to reduce emissions in scenarios of increased beef production. Overall, these scientists propose a wide range of mitigation options for Brazilian animal agriculture, such as 'investments in the enhanced nutritional management of the herd, especially by grain-feed supplementation' (2019: 11), which can produce better outlooks for the cattle sector in Brazil, unlike the restoration strategies proposed in national policies. When pasture technologies gain significant attention in these policies, it is more an economic goal to allocate resources and position Brazil in the climate negotiations than a conservation or climate priority (Merry and Soares-Filho, 2017).

Thus, to predict future emissions for Brazilian animal agriculture under mitigation scenarios proposed through climate national policies and commitments is to discuss which science and policy are more appropriate to achieve agreements made within global climate governance. Assuming average rates for soil carbon accumulation in a more linear prediction model is considered, on the one hand, (1) a reasonable measure, compatible with several studies conducted within the Brazilian territory, and, on the other hand, (2) a limited metric with unresolved uncertainties that do not account for changes in soil carbon stocks over particular time and space. On one hand, mobilising an *asymptotic*[11] *prediction model* for pasture restoration scenarios (because of the nonlinear soil carbon dynamics) can be seen as a complex and more accurate calculation that considers an intertwined net of impacts from the adoption of these mitigation technologies. On the other hand, this model is also considered a case study that has methodological errors and cannot be generalised for national territory, since it demands data that are more specific and most of it is conducted in the Mato Grosso Brazilian state.[12]

---

[11]An asymptotic model, from mathematics and computer science contributions, refers to a variable nonlinear behavior in a specific calculation, in this case, related to carbon accumulation rate that is not linear through time. It depends on other variables and tends to zero rather than stabilise at a specific rate.

[12]Batista's results (2016, 2019) were based on research developed with Mato Grosso's climatic and environmental variables and conditions.

Sustainable Transitions in the Anthropocene: Same Pathways, Same Livestock Systems?

Debates over static and asymptotic prediction models and how to use scientific measurements and rates – understanding the inherent limitations – are linked to political settings because, as Loconto and Rajão (2020: 4) point out, these land-use models are policymaking tools able to shape reality; in this case, the reality of low carbon Brazilian agriculture. If static prediction models are mobilised utilising carbon accumulation average rates for pastures under restoration techniques, this approach provides a significant potential to reduce emissions. In this sense, Brazilian public policies should focus on stimulating the adoption of such technologies, especially with financial incentives. This political setting is similar to the directions from the ABC plan and its investment programs, such as ABC Programme, a credit line to farmers that adopt sustainable technologies proposed on low carbon agriculture guidelines. However, suppose using an asymptotic model to predict reduced emissions, adding time and space variables to carbon accumulation rates. In that case, it will be necessary to diversify the mitigation strategies portfolio to include technologies such as nutritional supplementation to ruminants to facilitate improved digestion that reduces emissions and confinement techniques to spare areas for pasture and intensify its production. However, one of the interviewed scientists said that updates on the ABC Plan would incorporate these strategies that were left out of the original plan as its goal remains to 'recognise the efforts of the productive sector to adopt and maintain sustainable production systems, promoting the conservation and safeguarding of natural resources while guaranteeing the productivity and supply of quality food and other agricultural products' (Brazil, 2021: 20).

As one scientist asked, is improved and integrated pasture systems the best solution to meet national climate commitments, or would it be better to invest financially and politically in an intensification strategy mix? This question further demonstrates the scientific negotiations undertaken and the political implications of each approach. Moreover, within the current ecological crises, climate change occupies a prominent position, as it has become the narrative 'of the modern world that endangers ontological domains of nature and culture, natural variability and cycles and anthropogenic impacts, as well as domains and separations such as local and global, observed present time and modelled future time' (Bailão, 2014: 16). Specifically, since a myriad of human activities is modifying the biosphere, it is worth emphasising the importance assumed by energy (Camelo, 2018) and food issues in these processes. Both activities, especially related to industrial development based on the exploitation of fossil fuels (Artaxo, 2014), and food production by agricultural processes, directly interfere with climatic conditions, as they contribute to greenhouse gas emissions and removals. The climate crisis of the Anthropocene directly impacts the economic, political and social settings as a 'phenomenon that knows no borders and cannot be solved individually' and 'requires systemic reforms to the global order' (Pereira and Viola, 2022: 3).

We usually imagine extreme positions and arguments when we think about controversies or controversial debates. However, I argue that the scientists' research and results are not mutually exclusive regarding a sustainable development pattern based on technologies and high livestock production and consumption levels. The following sections demonstrate how the scientists' positions are similar, based on three dimensions: a linear connection between population growth, increased demand, food security issues; technology-based approaches; and the same production and consumption patterns.

Population Growth and Increased Demand: A Need to Ensure Food Security?

Through an overview of the literature on global food security and governance, Fouilleux et al. (2017: 15) note that increasing production to attend to future consumption demands is the dominant idea, while other dimensions are overlooked. Based on a linear connection between production and food security assurances, the dominant productivist agenda does not account for the asymmetries of power inherent in national and global food security debates. Assuming the imperative of development as growth, increasing food production is fundamental and sufficient to meet the increased demand for food (Porto, 2014).

This productivist approach to food security is a central theme in the Brazilian scientists' discourses when they (1) propose strategies to reduce emissions even with increased herd size and (2) demonstrate how this is an essential element for ensuring the growing demand for livestock production in the context of food security. As a scientist argued, animal agriculture has a 'positive impact on populations with higher food insecurity', and ruminants are extremely important for the survival of some people that depend on these animals for food. Such arguments imply a linear connection between population growth and livestock product demand while relating these products to global food security.

As scientists propose specific mitigation strategies for national public policies, they assume that with high production rates and mitigation technologies, the livestock sector can achieve sustainable transitions and development, besides helping address global food security issues. According to Burns (2016: 8), given the vast literature surrounding 'sustainability' and 'sustainable development', 'these influential concepts emerged from political and administrative processes, not scientific ones. [...] Historically, the linkage of sustainability and development has been, in large part, the result of global political and administrative processes and the diverse interests driving these processes'. In the climate negotiations context, countries follow international guidelines such as the 2030 Agenda, elaborated by the UNFCCC, which sets global objectives to promote sustainable development and eradicate poverty. Thus, it is crucial to notice the normative dimension of the sustainability concept since it also concerns values, interests and how to balance apparent contradictory conditions such as economic growth and environmental protection and conservation (Burns, 2016: 11). To adopt either the mitigation solutions is to agree on the need to propose sustainable transitions for the livestock sector regarding the impacts of increased demand for animal products due to population growth. The strategies are different, but the outcome is the same.

Technology-Based Transitions: A Matter of Choosing the Appropriate Ones

The mitigation technologies presented by the scientists translate into policy recommendations to reduce emissions from activities related to the livestock sector. The elaboration of these recommendations occurs in specific cultural settings, the Brazilian context, and the position of animal agriculture in its economic and environmental dynamics. Along with the sector's importance to national revenue, Brazilian beef production represents a significant part of the international market, approximately 20 percent of global imports (ABIEC, 2021). Accordingly, livestock sustainability issues receive special attention in international negotiations and debates. Scientists recognise the need to elaborate climate strategies to mitigate animal agriculture activities while also highlighting sustainable possibilities for this sector within the national context. Most interviewed scientists emphasised the mitigation opportunity for Brazilian livestock. Only two scientists questioned sustainable transitions for the animal agriculture sector by pointing out how cattle would be environmentally unsustainable. However, both scientists proposed a mix of mitigation strategies to reduce emissions and argued in favour of technologies that could support increased demand for livestock products, farmers' economic feasibility and climate commitments.

In this sense, interviewed scientists agreed upon the need to reconcile the multiple variables in livestock systems, either by improved pasture lands and their carbon accumulation potential or by a wide range of mitigation options such as nutritional supplementation and confinement. For both positions, addressing the climate change mitigation demands on the Brazilian livestock sector is choosing the appropriate technologies to reduce emissions while still growing the cattle herd. On the one hand, some interviewed scientists specifically argued that increasing in animal units (AU) per hectare is inevitable. On the other hand, the idea of reconciling sustainable development and environmental conservation was highlighted. Although the proposition of different strategies as transitions, all the scientists indicated that animal herds would have to increase considering economic demands in future scenarios, and it will be feasible to produce livestock products sustainably by adopting recommended technologies. The pathway remains the same: technology-based options to increase production as a mechanism to deal with Anthropocene crises such as climate change and food insecurity. As Saliba (2020: 336) argues, these statements regarding the need for technological solutions reinforce a techno-enthusiast idea, since they are based on 'an optimistic confidence in science and technology, which can be used to do "good"'.

Production and Consumption Patterns: Maintaining Livestock's Status Quo

Even the scientists who questioned both static prediction models and affirmatives that Brazil could achieve its climate targets by pasture management practices argued that they are trying to reconcile sustainable development with environmental conservation since it is possible to produce beef sustainably. Even though the technologies and prediction models are different, the two groups of scientists agree on the necessity to increase herd and production to ensure food security while proposing sustainable transitions for such food systems. As Michelini (2016) and Porto (2014) indicate, these discourses follow mainstream ideas that point to the national livestock sector as a relevant piece of global food security and environmental sustainability solutions given the increased demand for meat consumption. The maintenance of the beef production chain is necessary given contemporary challenges such as food security and environmental sustainability. In other words, the interviewed scientists align themselves with discourses from the livestock sector's actors that typically underlined increased productivity in the livestock industry and sustainable outcomes by reconciling development with environmental concerns.

However, it is essential to highlight that consumption patterns are not always linear (population growth results in increased demand), especially given recent changes towards plant-based diets and more transformative perspectives on sustainable pathways for the livestock industry. For example, Michelini and Lahsen (2016: 113) present interdisciplinary studies that 'analyse contributions from a possible diet displacement that promotes a decrease in meat consumption as an alternative to face global environmental changes and food insecurity'. Moreover, in its report on land-use and climate change, IPCC (2019b) includes a policy recommendation to reduce meat consumption because it considers plant-based diets as an opportunity to mitigate and adapt to climate change. However, the IPCC recommendation faces significant challenges as it would necessitate a much more profound transformation of the livestock production chain.

Scientists' discourses for both groups contradict such possibilities by sharing normative and mainstream ideas on food security, sustainability and demand for animal products. As Michelini (2016: 120) demonstrates, 'actors [...] performance [are] committed to maintaining the status quo [*business as usual*], which does not produce deep and necessary changes to the current organization of this production chain in Brazil'. Under mitigation strategies predicted by Brazilian scientists based on specific models and variables, future scenarios for the animal agriculture sector point out the same sustainable pathways and livestock systems, with the only difference being which technology to adopt. These scenarios do not propose changes in those systems' organisation, as interviewed scientists' discourses assume the linear connection between population growth, increased demand for livestock production, and, in the end, the need to increase production to meet such demands and promote sustainability along with food security. That is to say that the scientific controversy, though, does not influence the proposed livestock transitions since the sustainable pathways for such food systems are not challenged.

Conclusions

The negotiations between scientists about the valid interpretation of the calculations on carbon stock in different soil types, which variables must be considered, and which instruments are most suitable for making climatic predictions are closely related to how we live in the Anthropocene. Although scientists produce and assume distinct choices for scientific and political directions on livestock mitigation technologies, are their implications different from each other? Even though they differ regarding the specific scientific methods and techniques or which policies should be financially encouraged by the Brazilian government to achieve climate goals, they maintain the livestock production business as usual by arguing for sustainable development, increased productivity and technology-based solutions.

By 'making' science and 'making' politics, scientists propose sustainable transitions for the animal agriculture sector and distinct solutions for its climate responsibility. However, both alternatives for livestock are anchored in productivist approaches to sustainable development and technology-based solutions for producers to reduce emissions, maintain the same systems, production and consumption patterns. In other words, (1) they are based on the linear connection between population growth, demand and consumption of livestock products; (2) they are anchored in a productivist and technology-based approaches to livestock transitions and sustainable development ideas; (3) they do not reflect critically on such patterns for animal husbandry sector, maintaining its production and consumption as 'business as usual'. Facing of global environmental threats in the Anthropocene, sustainable livestock transitions may need to reconsider which pathways will be possible to address the crisis.

This chapter has sought to understand scientific knowledge about pasture restoration techniques to reduce emissions from Brazilian animal agriculture, especially cattle, and its political implications on national climate policies and sustainable transitions in the Anthropocene. I investigated how livestock predictions under mitigation scenarios come to be and how they bring the same (sustainable) world into reality. This research investigated the scientific controversy over quantification measurements of soil carbon accumulation and predictive models for future livestock systems, specially how such negotiations are intertwined with national political settings. In this sense, I conducted interviews with the core-set of scientists involved in this controversy and also employed several STS contributions and the science-policy interface. This analytical framework is useful to highlight how the negotiations related to soil carbon removals, as consequences of distinct mitigations strategies, in transitions' context towards sustainable agrifood systems are connected with more than just scientific negotiations. As decisions are been made, science and politics are also ongoing and mutually constructed processes that need to be considered within this wider context, which is possible from the mentioned contributions. However, it is important to consider that debates over mitigation strategies also occur throughout political processes, at the centre of global and local negotiations and their agreements. This aspect (decision-makers' perspective and how different actors in political arenas negotiate this controversy) was intentionally left out because of the scope of this investigation, but it indicates directions for further research.

References

ABIEC (2021) *Beef Report: Perfil da Pecuária no Brasil*. Relatório Anual. (http://abiec.com.br/publicacoes/beef-report-2021/)

Alves, F. (2015) 'Carne Carbono Neutro: um novo conceito para carne sustentável produzida nos trópicos [recurso eletrônico]'. *Campo Grande: Embrapa Gado de Corte*. (https://ainfo.cnptia.embrapa.br/digital/bitstream/item/158193/1/Carne-carbon-neutro.pdf)

Artaxo, P. (2014) 'Uma nova era geológica em nosso planeta: O Antropoceno?' *Revista USP, 103*: 13–24.

Assad, E.D., Pinto, H.S., Martins, S.C., Groppo, J.D., Salgado, P.R., Evangelista, B., Vasconcellos, E., Sano, E.E., Pavão, E., Luna, R. and Camargo, P.B. (2013) 'Changes in soil carbon stocks in Brazil due to land use: Paired site comparisons and a regional pasture soil survey'. *Biogeosciences, 10*: 6141–60.

Assad, E.D., Cordeiro, L.A.M., Marchão, R.L., Almeida, R.G., Júnior, R.G., Berndt, A., Salton, J.C. and Evangelista, B.A. (2015) 'Potential de mitigação da emissão de gases de efeito estufa por meio da adoção da estratégia de integração lavoura-pecuária-floresta'. In Cordeiro, L. et al. (eds), *Integração lavoura-pecuária-floresta: o produtor pergunta, a Embrapa responde*. Brasília, DF: Embrapa. (https://www. embrapa.br/busca-de-publicacoes/-/publicacao/1023603/potencial-de-mitigacao-da-emissao-de-gases-de-efeito-estufa-por-meio-da-adocao-da-estrategia-de-integracao-lavoura-pecuaria-floresta)

Assad, E.D., Martins, S.C., Cordeiro, L.A.M. and Evangelista, B.A. (2019) 'Sequestro de carbono e mitigação de emissões de gases de efeito estufa pela adoção de sistemas integrados'. In *ILPF: Inovação Com Integração de Lavoura, Pecuária e Floresta*. Brasília: Embrapa, pp. 153–67.

Bailão, A. (2014) *Ciências e mundos aquecidos: narrativas mistas de mudanças climáticas em São Paulo*. PhD dissertation. University of São Paulo, São Paulo.

Batista, E. (2016) *Modeling the Economic and Environmental Impacts of Cattle Ranching Intensification in Mato Grosso*. PhD dissertation. Federal University of Viçosa, Viçosa.

Batista, E., Soares-Filho, B., Barbosa, F., Merry, F., Davis, J., van der Hoff, R. and Rajão, R.G. (2019) 'Large-scale pasture restoration may not be the best option to reduce greenhouse gas emissions in Brazil'. *Environmental Research Letters*, *14*(12): 1–12.

Bernoux, M., Carvalho, M.C.S., Volkoff, B. and Cerri, C.C. (2002) 'Brazil's soil carbon stocks'. *Soil Science Society of America Journal*, *66*(3): 888–96. (https://doi. org/10.2136/sssaj2002.8880)

Brazil (2012) *Plano setorial de mitigação e de adaptação às mudanças climáticas para a consolidação de uma economia de baixa emissão de carbono na agricultura: Plano ABC (Agricultura de Baixa Emissão de Carbono)*. Brasília: Ministério da Agricultura, Pecuária e Abastecimento.

Brazil (2020a) *Nationally Determined Contribution: Towards Achieving the Objective of the United Nations Framework Convention on Climate Change*. Updated submission. (www4.unfccc.int/sites/NDCStaging/Pages/Party.aspx?party=BRA)

Brazil (2020b) *Quarta Comunicação Nacional do Brasil à Convenção-Quadro das Nações Unidas sobre Mudança do Clima, Vol. IV*. Brasília: Ministério da Ciência, Tecnologia e Inovações.

Brazil (2021) *Plano setorial para adaptação à mudança do clima e baixa emissão de carbono na agropecuária com vistas ao desenvolvimento sustentável (2020–2030): visão estratégica para um novo ciclo*. Brasília: Ministério da Agriculture, Pecuária e Abastecimento.

Burns, T. (2016) 'Sustainable development: Agents, systems and the environment'. *Current Sociology*, *64*(6): 875–906.

Bustamante, M. et al. (2012) 'Estimating greenhouse gas emissions from cattle raising in Brazil'. *Climate Change*, *115*: 559–77.

Camelo, A. (2018) 'Futuros energéticos no Antropoceno: trazendo as dimensões sociais para o debate'. *ClimaCom – Diálogos do Antropoceno*, *5*(12). (http:// climacom.mudancasclimaticas.net.br/?p=9296)

Cerri, C. and Oliveira, D. (2017) 'Sequestro de carbono em áreas de pastagem'. In Pedreira, C. (Orgs.), *As Mudanças Climáticas e as Pastagens: desafios e oportunidades. Anais do 28° Simpósio sobre Manejo de Pastagem*. Piracicaba: Fealq, pp. 307–322.

Collins, H. (1981) 'Stages in the empirical programme of relativism'. *Social Studies of Science, 11*(01): 3–10.

Collins, H. (2011) *Mudando a ordem: replicação e indução na prática científica*. Belo Horizonte: Fabrefactum Editora.

Crutzen, P. and Stoermer, E. (2000) 'The "Anthropocene."'. *International Geosphere-Biosphere Programme Newsletter, 41*: 17–18.

Duarte, T. (2019). 'O painel brasileiro de mudanças climáticas na interface entre ciência e políticas públicas: identidades, geopolítica e concepções epistemológicas'. *Sociologias, 21*: 76–101.

Fouilleux, E., Bricas, N. and Alpha, A. (2017) '"Feeding 9 billion people": Global food security debates and the productionist trap'. *Journal of European Public Policy, 24*(11): 1658–77. (https://doi.org/10.1080/13501763.2017.1334084)

Gerber, P.J., Steinfeld, H., Henderson, B., Mottet, A., Opio, C., Dijkman, J., Falcucci, A. and Tempio, G. (2013) *Tackling Climate Change through Livestock – A Global Assessment of Emissions and Mitigation Opportunities*. FAO, Rome. (www.fao.org/3/i3437e/i3437e.pdf)

Hilgartner, S. (2000) *Science on Stage: Expert Advice as Public Drama*. Redwood City, CA: Stanford University Press. (https://books.google.com.br/books/about/Science_on_Stage.html?id=vU8LauawsfkC&redir_esc=y)

IBGE (2019) *Produção da Pecuária Municipal (PPM)*. (https://biblioteca.ibge.gov.br/visualizacao/periodicos/84/ppm_2019_v47_br_informativo.pdf)

IPCC (2006) *Guidelines for Nacional Greenhouse Gas Inventories*. Geneva, p. 104. (https://www.ipcc-nggip.iges.or.jp/public/2006gl/)

IPCC (2019a) *Refinement to the 2006 IPCC Guidelines for National Greenhouse Gas Inventories*. Geneva. (https://www.ipcc.ch/site/assets/uploads/2019/12/19R_V0_01_Overview.pdf)

IPCC (2019b) *Special Report on Climate Change, Desertification, Land Degradation, Sustainable Land Management, Food Security, and Greenhouse Gas Fluxes in Terrestrial Ecosystems*. Summary for Policymakers. (https://www.ipcc.ch/srccl/chapter/summary-for-policymakers/)

Jasanoff, S. (1987) 'Contested boundaries in policy-relevant science'. *Social Studies of Science, 17*: 195–230.

Jasanoff, S. (1998) *The Fifth Branch: Science Advisors as Policymakers*. Cambridge and London: Harvard University Press.

Jasanoff, S. (2004) *States of Knowledge: The Co-production of Science and Social Order*. Nova York: Routledge.

Jasanoff, S. (2014) 'A mirror for science'. *Public Understanding of Science, 23*(1): 21–6.

Lahsen, M. (2009) 'A science-policy interface in the global south: The politics ofcarbon sinks and science in Brazil'. *Climatic Change, 97*: 339–72.

Loconto, A. and Fouilleux, E. (2019) 'Defining agroecology: Exploring the circulation of knowledge in FAO's Global Dialogue'. *International Journal of Sociology of Agriculture and Food*, *25*(2): 116–37.

Loconto, A. and Rajão, R. (2020) 'Governing by models: Exploring the technopolitics of the (in)visilibities of land'. *Land Use Policy*, *96*(104241): 1–5.

Maia, S., Ogle, S.M., Cerri, C.E.P. and Cerri, C.C. (2009) 'Effect on grassland management on soil carbon sequestration in Rondônia and Mato Grosso states, Brazil'. *Geoderma*, *149*(1–2): 84–91.

Manzatto, C.V., Skorupa, L.A., Araújo, L.S., Vicente, L.E. and Assad, E.D. (2019) 'Estimativas de redução de emissões de gases de efeito estufa pela adoção de sistemas ILPF no Brasil'. In Skorupa, L. and Manzatto, C. (eds), *Sistemas de integração lavoura-pecuária-floresta no Brasil: estratégias regionais de transferência de tecnologia, avaliação da adoção e de impactos*. Brasília, DF: Embrapa, pp. 400–24.

Martins, S.C., Assad, E.D., Pavão, E. and Lopes-Assad, M.L.R.C. (2018) 'Inverting the carbon footprint in Brazilian agriculture: An estimates of the effect of ABC Plan'. *Ciência, Tecnologia e Ambiente*, *7*(1): 43–52.

Medeiros, S., Almeida, R.G., and Barioni, L.G. (2017) 'Mitigação da emissão de gases de efeito estufa em sistemas de produção animal em pastagens: Em busca da carne com emissão zero'. In Pedreira, C. et al. (Orgs.) *As Mudanças Climáticas e as Pastagens: desafios e oportunidades. Anais do 28° Simpósio sobre Manejo de Pastagem*. Piracicaba: Fealq, pp. 163–220.

Merry, F. and Soares-Filho, B. (2017) 'Will intensification of beef production deliver conservation outcomes in the Brazilian Amazon?' *Elementa: Science of the Anthropocene*, *5*. (https://doi.org/10.1525/elementa.224s)

Michelini, J. (2016) *A pecuária bovina de corte no Brasil: significados, contradições e desafios em busca da sustentabilidade*. PhD dissertation. National Space Research Agency, São José dos Campos, p. 142.

Michelini, J. and Lahsen, M. (2016) 'Implicações da pecuária brasileira para a segurança alimentar: a ciência e o discurso do setor produtivo'. *Sustentabilidade em Debate*, *7*(3): 112–26.

Miller, C. (2001) 'Challenges in the application of science to global affairs: Contingency, trust and moral order.' In Miller, C. and Edwards, P. (Orgs.) *Changing the Atmosphere: Expert Knowledge and Environmental Governance*. Cambridge, MA and London: The MIT Press, pp. 247–87.

Miller, C. (2004a) 'Climate science and the making of a global political order'. In S. Jasanoff (ed), *States of Knowledge: The Co-production of Science and Social Order*. New York, NY: Routledge, pp. 46–66.

Miller, C. (2004b) 'Resisting empire: Globalism, relocalization, and the politics of knowledge'. In S. Jasanoff and M. Martello (eds), *Earthly Politics, Worldly Knowledge: Local and Global in Environmental Politics*. Cambridge: MIT Press, pp. 81–102.

Miguel, J. (2021) 'Pós-verdade ou produção da ignorância?' *CTS em Foco*, (5): 54–9.

Nelkin, D. (1975) 'The political impact of technical expertise'. *Social Studies of Science*, *5*(1): 35–54.

Observatório ABC. (2015). 'Invertendo o sinal de carbono da agropecuária brasileira: uma estimativa do potencial de mitigação de tecnologias do Plano ABC de 2021 a 2023'. São Paulo: FGV. Observatório ABC. (2017) 'Impactos econômicos e ambientais do Plano ABC'. Relatório Completo. São Paulo: FGV.

Pereira, J.C. and Viola, E. (2022) 'Brazilian climate policy (1992–2019): An exercise in strategic diplomatic failure'. *Contemporary Politics, 28*(1): 55–78. (https://doi.org/10.1080/13569775.2021.1961394)

Pinch, T. (2015) 'Scientific controversies'. *International Encyclopedia of Social and Behavioral Sciences*, 281–286. (https://doi.org/10.1016/B978-0-08-097086-8.85043-6)

Porto, J. (2014) 'O discurso do agronegócio: modernidade, poder e "verdade"'. *Revista Nera, 17*(25): 24–46.

Rajão, R. and Soares-filho, B. (2015) 'Policies undermine Brazil's GHG goals'. *Science, 350*(6260): 519.

Ripple, W.J., Smith, P., Haberl, H., Montzka, S.A., McAlpine, C. and Boucher, D.H. (2014) 'Ruminants, climate change and climate policy'. *Nature Climate Change, 4*: 2–5.

Ritchie, H. and Roser, M. (2017) 'Meat and dairy production'. OurWorldInData.org. (https://ourworldindata.org/meat-production)

Saliba, B. (2020) 'A mineração de urânio em questão: análise da comunicação pública das Indústrias Nucleares do Brasil (INB) em Caetité, Bahia'. *Revista Eletrônica de Comunicação, Informação e Inovação em Saúde, 14*(2): 329–41.

Silva, R., Barioni, L.G., Hall, J.A.J., Folegatti Matsuura, M., Zanett Albertini, T., Fernandes, F.A. and Moran, D. (2016) 'Increasing beef production could lower greenhouse gas emissions in Brazil if decoupled from deforestation'. *Nature Climate Change, 6*(5): 493–7.

SEEG (2020) *Análise das emissões brasileiras de gases de efeito estufa e suas implicações para as metas do Brasil (1970–2019)*. Relatório-síntese. (https://seeg-br.s3.amazonaws.com/Documentos%20Analiticos/SEEG_8/SEEG8_DOC_ANALITICO_SINTESE_1990-2019.pdf)

Steinfeld, H., Gerber, P.J., Wassenaar, T., Castel, V., Rosales, M. and De haan, C. (2006) *Livestock's Long Shadow: Environmental Issues and Options*. Rome: FAO.

Thornton, P. (2010). 'Livestock production: Recent trends, future prospects'. *Philosophical Transactions of the Royal Society B: Biological Sciences, 365*(1554), 2853–67. (https://doi.org/10.1098/rstb.2010.0134)

7

'Anti-fish' Campaign: Food Safety and Ethical Issues of Eating Fish From Indonesia

Wardah Alkatiri

THE OCEANS ARE so vast and deep that until fairly recently, it was widely assumed that no matter how much trash and chemicals humans dumped into them, the effects would be negligible. (Howard, 2019)

Introduction

This chapter highlights the essential role of fisheries for the food security, nutrition and employment of millions of people in the developing world. At the same time, it reveals the not-so promising realities about the environmental dimensions of our contemporary fisheries system and stresses the ever-increasing needs of resources management and pollution monitoring and control.

According to the EAT–Lancet Commission on healthy diets from sustainable food systems (Willet et al., 2019), more than 820 million people still lack sufficient food, and many more consume either low-quality diets or too much food. Moreover, unhealthy diets pose a greater risk to morbidity and mortality than does unsafe sex, alcohol, drug and tobacco use combined (The EAT-Lancet Commission, 2020). Greater public awareness about nutrition is traced to the 19th century, when vitamins were discovered, and the foundations of modern nutrition was then set out. People began to understand what made them healthy was not just how much food they eat and how often, but also what kind. In the 21st century, we are living in the Anthropocene where the human impact on earth has been profoundly noticed. Given the documented health consequences of the environmental destruction that marks the Anthropocene, it is not only a question of how much, how often and what kind of food will make us healthy but also what kind of food to avoid to stay safe. Despite the health benefits associated with eating fish, this chapter contends that wild-caught fish are among the most greatly affected by the deteriorating conditions of the environment that have been introduced during the Anthropocene, particularly so in a developing country like Indonesia.

This chapter draws a picture of water pollution in Indonesia. Heavy metals contamination and plastic waste increase proportionately with the industrialisation and development of the country. It discusses a large number of empirical works that suggest connections between heavy metal toxicity and neurological disorders, hence possible links to the increasing prevalence of Autism in children since researchers first began tracking it in 2000 (e.g., Bernard et al., 2001; Bradstreet et al., 2003). The plastic waste problem is also a public health concern, far larger than the trash we can see. Degraded plastic is broken down into tiny pieces that potentially harm human health. The micro-plastics can be present in fish, mussels and other species. Researchers have found signs that ingested micro-plastics can leach hazardous chemicals added to polymers during production, as well as the environmental pollutants like pesticides that are attracted to the surface of plastic, leading to health effects. In view of this, the public certainly needs to be made aware of the harms associated with fish and seafood contamination from the environment. Assuming the Indonesian government was fully aware about the public health risks at stake, this chapter presents the dilemma of raising such awareness and educating the people: they are doomed if they do, doomed if they do not. As an archipelagic state, such an 'anti-fish' campaign is saddled with ethical considerations. Exposing the health risks in seafood consumption might, in the end, undermine the livelihood of poor fishermen communities. On the contrary, people have, as a matter of fact, been encouraged to consume more fish and seafood to tackle malnutrition and stunting.

Through a postcolonial lens, this chapter takes a critical look at the failure of environmental protection in Indonesia. As a framework, postcolonial theory facilitates an understanding of the consequences of economic development in postcolonial regions whereby investments, and later on the global economy, have tended to take advantage of the country's lack of environmental knowledge and legislations. Building on the intersection between human ecology and postcolonial scholarship, the chapter highlights the prone-to-be-manipulated local culture[1] as a key contributor to the maintenance of the status quo, and the direct linkage it has to the widespread and systemic corruption that exists, and eventually, the poor enforcement of environmental law. Despite the rhetoric of *kearifan lokal* since the 1990s (literally, local wisdom: it refers to the notions that traditional or indigenous knowledge and native science are capable of resolving the environmental ills), the natural environment of Indonesia has continued to degrade at an alarming rate, while the promise of *kearifan lokal* remains elusive. This state of affairs substantiates what is known in postcolonial literature as the return 'not of the repressed' but 'the Same in the guise of the Other' (Moore-Gilbert et al., 2013: 3). Against the tension between health and safety revealed in the Anthropocene, the topic addressed in this chapter at once criticises modernity and rationalises the need for a universal environmental ethics set against the prevailing postmodern mood of the day that often extols local narratives, and ultimately, advocates a more ecologically aware postcolonialism. In addition, I share an insight as a possible intersection between anti-Muslim hatred in the post-colonial literature (such as Meer, 2014) and the feminist critique of power in addressing the inherent inequalities in world structures which permit 'the North to dominate the South, men to dominate women, and the frenetic plunder of ever more resources for ever more unequally distributed economic gain to dominate nature' (Mies and Shiva, 1993: 2).

The Progress Treadmill

Driven perhaps by good intentions, the exponents of modernisation and industrial technologies since the 18th century have not given much thought to the ecological consequences brought by the changes in human reasoning, practices and economic activities incurred by their socio-economic project. The road to hell is paved with good intentions, the saying goes. Humanity has now arrived in an age where they have to take the bull by the horns, dealing with all the challenges

---

[1]Five Indonesian core cultural values are identified by Whitfield III (n.d.): (i) loyalty to a hierarchical structure of authority, (ii) conflict avoidance, (iii) subjugation to nature, (iv) keeping face as a standard social shame and (v) relaxed future time perspective. These are often assumed to be identical with Javanese values.

of feeding people on a hotter, polluted and crowded planet. One way of overcoming these consequences of overpopulation has been to exploit seas and oceans, and this has caused an increase in the consumption of fish and seafood in recent years (Slavka et al., 2012). Alongside Michael Pollan (2006) and Colin Sage (2012) who argue that eating is an 'ecological act', I present public health issues related to fish and seafood consumption against the background of unprecedented marine pollution.

My research was undertaken in Indonesia, at once a developing country and the world's largest archipelagic state with some 17,508 islands, 54, 716 km of coastline and the world's fourth most populous nation (277.4 million in 2021). The seas make up roughly two thirds of the nation's total area. Even though Indonesia has always been plagued by illegal fishing, the country remains the world's second largest fish producer after China (FAO, 2020) and is the world's largest tuna fishing nation. The fisheries sector in Indonesia has played a critical role in providing food security. Fifty-two percent of the animal protein supply for the Indonesian population comes from fish or seafood. In fact, for most native islanders, fish or seafood is the only affordable source. FAO (2016) notes, the countries that rely heavily on fish protein are mostly poor. Indonesian fishery production amounted to 12.642 million tons in 2018. The products include marine and inland catch; aquaculture farms comprise marine, brackish water and freshwater aquaculture; and seaweeds. Forty-six percent of fish is consumed fresh and the rest as dried, salted, smoked, boiled and fermented. Marine fisheries in Indonesia can be grouped into two main segments, small scale and large scale.[2] The small-scale fisheries consist of two major segments, artisanal and commercial, while large-scale fisheries are basically the so-called industrial fisheries. Commercial fisheries are characterised by large vessels that employ medium-size purse seines, Danish seines and gillnets. About 95 percent

---

[2]Fisheries are an open-access resource, freely available to anyone with the means to catch them. The absence of property rights to limit access to the resource is widely considered to be the primary challenge of fisheries management. This calls Hardin's classic statement of the 'tragedy of the commons' to mind (Hardin, 1968). It is, therefore, important to understand the fundamental differences in values and motivations that distinguish these two classes. Both are economically rational individuals who exert heavy pressure on marine resources. The former employed the power of modern technologies to maximize personal gains; the latter, while used less powerful technologies, were posing comparable challenges by the sheer numbers of people involved.

of fishery production comes from artisanal fishermen (FAO, 2014). In 2013, the agricultural/fisheries sector accounted for about 34.9 percent of total employment and 32.8 percent of total female informal employment (USAID, 2017: 62). But for all that, 60 percent of Indonesia's rivers are polluted. While the Citarum was ranked as the world's most polluted river by the World Bank in 2018, the water is dangerous by any standard. It has alarming levels of toxic chemicals, including 1,000 times more lead than the US standard for safe drinking water (Sagita, 2018). In many developing countries, marine products including fresh fish and shellfish are also increasingly important export products used to meet an ever-growing global population's demands for seafood products and contribute to national revenues and foreign direct investments. Thus, a new problem at the intersection between public health, social and ecological issues has emerged in the 21st century.

As the post-development thinkers suggest (e.g., Escobar, 1995), no matter what the outcome of the development project has been, the educated class and the elites in developing countries hold the unwavering belief in the ideal of 'progress'. Their faith in 'progress', succinctly defined by the historian Sydney Pollard (1968: 9ff) as 'the assumption that a pattern of change exists in the history of mankind...that it consists of irreversible changes in one direction only, and that this direction is towards improvement', has ramified and hardened into a nationalist–developmentalist ideology.[3] Accordingly, developing countries have been living in a 'progress treadmill' (cf., 'technology treadmill'), a notion that material progress creates problems that would be soluble only by further and more progress. In *A Short History of Progress*, Ronald Wright (2004: 4) sarcastically likens such a progress-driven ideology to a 'secular religion' which, 'like the religions that progress has challenged, is blind to certain flaws in its credentials'. This chapter will demonstrate post-development issues in Indonesia, which simultaneously fall into the dilemma of food in the Anthropocene. They are: (i) food safety and food borne diseases caused by water pollution from the country's industrialisation, inadequate waste management and its weak legislation; (ii) the 'transition food' issue addressed to the need to feed a growing global

---

[3]Nationalism has been used as an instrument for social and political control in attempts to unify all of a nation's potential towards development programs (Alkatiri, 2018).

population a healthy diet while also defining sustainable food systems that will minimise damage to our planet; and (iii) it touches on the sociology of rural development and poverty in Indonesia's fisheries sector upon the introduction of marine/fishery technologies. This demonstration will be achieved by answering the following research questions:

- How does marine pollution threaten human health through seafood consumption?
- How might the tensions between the health and safety of seafood consumption be addressed through public dialogue and policies?

Given the nature of the research problem, my work belongs to the category of interdisciplinary research – a collaboration between natural science as it is concerned with the industrial pollution and public health issues, and social science in so far as it addresses post-development and postcolonial critiques. This work also highlights a real and verifiable problem of culture that appeared as a hindrance towards transitions to more sustainable development. I utilised secondary data collected from official statistics, news reports, newspaper articles, social media postings and a literature review of empirical reports by Indonesian academics on marine pollution and fish/seafood contamination. My many years of experience as an activist in the sustainable food movement and as an environmental educator in Indonesia since 1998 – and once a chemical engineering intern on a waste water treatment facility in East Java – provide important ethnographic data and experiential understandings to the analysis of the interconnected problems explored in this chapter.

Unattended Oceans: Marine Pollution and Indonesian Sociopolitical Culture

No matter how far from the coast the pollution is produced, the oceans are often the end point for the majority of it. Only in recent decades have some people begun to understand how humans impact this watery habitat. However, many of them continue to believe that 'the solution to pollution is dilution'. Millions of tons of heavy metals and chemical contaminants, along with thousands of containers of radioactive waste, were purposely thrown into the ocean (Howard,

2019: para. 4). Jambeck et al. (2015) and Schmidt et al. (2017) show that the Asian region, especially Southeast Asia, has become an epicentre for plastic discharge into the ocean. Due to fast economic growth, China, Indonesia and the Philippines that already had large coastal populations and lack of management infrastructure became the top three countries regarding mismanaged plastic waste. Six countries in Southeast Asia are listed in the top 20 that mismanage their waste worldwide, with on average 79 percent of waste, primarily plastic, ending up in the ocean (Jambeck et al., 2015). Despite this deplorable state, five out of the ten ASEAN member states (Association of Southeast Asian Nations) have no published studies on the ecological and environmental impacts of marine plastics (Lyons et al., 2019). Indonesia alone produces 3.2 million tons of plastic waste every year, and nearly 1.3 million tons end up in the sea (Ministry of Environment and Forestry, 2020). The country became a dumping ground for the world's plastic waste after China's ban on trash imports (Paulo and Nie, 2020). In 2019, environmental activists called on the Indonesian Trade Ministry to immediately revise its 2016 regulation on waste imports. The regulation contains several loopholes that have turned Indonesia into a dump site for developed countries (The Strait Times, 2016). This brings up the subject that the UN Environmental Programme Basel Convention in 1989 termed 'waste colonialism'.

Cleaning up the garbage patches is complicated. A reminder was voiced by the National Oceanic and Atmospheric Administration (NOAA). Removing the debris is very difficult since it is not only constantly mixing and moving, but it is also extremely small in size (NOAA, 2017). Removal efforts should be focused on shorelines and coastal areas before debris has the chance to make it to the open ocean and before it has broken into microplastic pieces, which are inherently difficult to remove from the environment. Therefore, prevention is critically important (NOAA, 2017: para. 4).

Due to lack of knowledge and inadequate pollution control systems and legislation, low-income and middle-income countries are heavily polluted (Landrigan et al., 2018; Weiss et al., 2016). Worst of all, the elevated release of toxins into the environment is projected to follow the increasing use and production of chemicals that grow proportionately in these countries with population growth, urban development, improvements in living standards and increased pressure to achieve high agricultural yields. Furthermore, chemical production is increasingly moved from high-income to low- and middle-income countries to reduce costs and maintain competitiveness (Weiss et al., 2016: 6). The Lancet Commission on Pollution and Health (Landrigan et al., 2018) reports that pollution is the largest environmental cause of disease and premature death, which disproportionately kills the poor and the vulnerable. More than 70 percent of the diseases caused by pollution are non-communicable diseases. Despite that, in poor and middle-income countries, the health effects of pollution have been underestimated in the calculations of the global burden of disease. Interventions against pollution are barely mentioned in the Global Action Plan for the Prevention and Control of Non-Communicable Diseases (Landrigan et al., 2018: 1, para. 3).

The core problem of marine pollution is the following. First, waterbody contamination generally has been seen as an environmental rather than a public health problem. For that reason, fish contamination and consumer protection have not been a major focus of state efforts to assess waterbodies, and monitoring was not designed to provide the kind of data needed to develop fish consumption guidelines. Second, what makes matters worse is the dominance of the prone-to-be-manipulated Indonesian local culture (see fn #1) as a key contributor to the maintenance of the status quo and the weak enforcement of environmental law at the same time.

Watkins' (1997) comments on this dominance resonates powerfully with my own experience. It is noteworthy to mention, with the rise of the Indonesian version of Islamophobia in the wake of anti-Muslim hatred that swept across the world (UN Human Rights, 2021), as a female scholar who wears the *hijab*, I found the need to borrow a white man's word to express my opinion about the linkage between Indonesian local culture and the widespread and systemic corruption that exists in the country in order not to risk myself for being associated with radical Islamist groups. I am referring in particular to the dismissal of fifty-one employees of the Corruption Eradication Commission (KPK) quite recently, who were dubbed the 'Taliban' (VOI, 2021).[4] Watkins, a

---

[4]It is hard not to see Islamophobia as a 'continuity' of the colonial empire as Meer (2014) argues. Similar reading can be suggested to Indonesia by referring to historian Ricklefs et al. (2010: 220) in regard to the capture of a pious Javanese Muslim Prince, Diponegoro, in 1830 that marked the Dutch's victory that shaped the history of 20th century Indonesia.

master's student in engineering at the University of New South Wales, was suggested by a seemingly frustrated Australian consulting engineer who had an experience of working in a wastewater management in East Java to undertake research in Indonesia. Running counter to the pro-local narratives of the post-modern sentiment, Watkins painted rather unflattering pictures of the local, especially Javanese culture, in the context of the exigency to protect the environment. The cultural factors he exposed were (i) the preeminence of relationships, as opposed to tasks; (ii) a strong desire for consensus and harmony and avoidance of conflict. Besides, Indonesia had a (iii) long history of 'government by man' rather than 'government by law', and accordingly, obedience to a ruler supersedes obedience to a set of laws which are above the ruler. Therefore, the government management practices tend to be patrimonial. In addition, a lasting human consequence of the domination and control practices of the colonial system aggravates the situation further. Having been demoted to powerless bureaucrats, a heavy procedural emphasis for conformity is a hard and fast rule in Indonesian bureaucracy (Blomkamp et al., 2018: 15; Sherlock and Djani, 2015: 1–2),[5] alongside the ceremonial nature of the courtly Javanese culture.

In these circumstances, engineering development to address the environmental concerns is restricted, like everything else, by the emphasis on procedure rather than creativity. Additionally, in my experience a strong desire for consensus and harmony would, on the flipside, make it easier to conveniently loosen the enforcement mechanisms of environmental law, thereby facilitating bribery. In effect, Indonesian tenderness has been manipulated by the industrialists, and now the environment of Indonesia faces a grim future if steps are not taken to protect the natural resources. This should bring to mind the feminists' debates between the 'domination theorists' who concern themselves with male domination and the 'empowerment theorists' who focus on women's empowerment. The 'domination theorists' often criticise the 'empowerment theorists' for glorifying

---

[5]Law making in Indonesia takes a long time. Blomkamp et al. (2015: 15) enumerate the weaknesses in policy capacity. Besides the significant gaps in the capacity of civil servants, the problem is compounded by 'a bureaucratic culture of compliance with the letter of the law, poor staff training, pressure on civil servants to conform to existing practice within their particular ministry, and to obey their superiors'.

practices like mothering, or traits like caring and nurturing, that have themselves been mechanism of women's oppression (Allen, 1998). The same applies to much-lauded Javanese tenderness, which turned out to be manipulated by lingering forms of colonial power.

There has been a long debate whether the Javanese culture has something to do with the culture of corruption in Indonesia (Prabowo and Cooper, 2016: 1040). Prominent anthropologists Benedict Anderson (2006) and Clifford Geertz (1956) are, in a sense, among the participants of the debate. Their main contentions are centred on the Javanese concept of power. In Anderson's view, unity or obsessive concern with oneness is among the cornerstones. For the Javanese leadership, unity over one's political domain should be fought at all costs.

> This unity is in itself a central symbol of Power, and it is this fact as much as the overt goals of statist ideologies that helps to account for the obsessive concern with oneness that suffuses the political thinking of many contemporary Javanese. (Anderson, 2006: 36)

My previous work provides detailed historical accounts of first president Sukarno and the enforcement of unity over diversity (Alkatiri, 2018). Correspondingly, the discussion in this chapter suggests a plausible attribution of clientelism in Indonesian society, its patronage democracy and the corruption that follows, to the obsessive desire for unity in the Javanese polity.

Those who express disagreement in defence of the Javanese culture argue that the culture is in fact full of noble teachings (Irawanto et al., 2011; Sutarto, 2006). Geertz (1956, cited in Prabowo and Cooper, 2016: 1040) too stresses that the ideology of a peaceful life is the core of Javanese values. However, in the quest for a peaceful life, the New Order regime had been proven to curb criticism by unlawful means to create an impression that people were living a peaceful life. As I have argued earlier, the quest for a peaceful life might have equally messed up the necessarily 'strict' laws to protect the environment. Thorburn's (2002) account is appropriate here. He underscores the protean nature of local custom, *adat*, in relation to the devastation of natural resources during the New Order. Suharto's regime uniquely combined 'traditional' Javanese patrimonialism, deference and social stratification with 'unfettered capitalistic acquisition and expansion', and with 'a liberal dose of military power and pomp'. Thorburn notes:

This mixture gave rise to a development juggernaut that undermined existing local social and normative orders as ruthlessly as it depleted forests and other natural riches. Prominent motifs permeating New Order society and governance included frequent references to *adat* and the ubiquitous political mantras *musyawarah* (deliberation) and *mufakat* (consensus). These were invoked as justifications for a range of political measures and economic policies, and to censure anyone who tried to object. (2002: 618)

Interestingly, reflecting postmodern turn towards 'indigenous paradigm', the same 'myth of *adat*' has been conjured as well by the regime's critics, and by local communities attempting to retain or regain some control over the pace or direction of local change.

While there are positive changes that have occurred in Indonesia since the fall of Suharto and his New Order, Aspinall (2010), Blunt et al. (2012) and Warburton (2020) show that contemporary Indonesia remains a patronage society and patronage remains systemic within the government. The power of oligarchy was ascending in the reign of President 'Jokowi' (Asia Sentinel, 2022; Aulia, 2022; Gokkon, 2019). Clientelistic practices, namely jobs or other favours in the bureaucracy in exchange for support at election time, are how elites exercise their influence. Aspinall (2010) contends that clientelistic relationships between politicians and their network of supporters is a fundamental ordering principal of the contemporary Indonesian state. Notably, money politics and corrupt practices continue to constitute and sustain patronage, and the state assets are treated as the private property of the patrons. Blunt et al. (2012: 64) describe plainly in their illustration of clientelistic system where positions were bought and sold, the way state assets turn to be treated as if they were the private property of elected or administrative officials or patrons who are largely unaccountable and rule with the help of networks of clients that are paid off for their support.

According to Blunt et al. (2012: 65), Indonesia is an interesting case of patronage, 'because its development has entailed such long and close collaboration with market-oriented agencies, like the World Bank and the United States Agency for International Development, and because it has been portrayed in the media and in the donor literature as a model of democratic development'. Reinforcing further the postcolonial notion of *'development is colonialism in disguise'*, Blunt et al. presented empirical evidence to suggest that 'whether by design or by default, development assistance has contributed to the spread and consolidation of patronage – by providing resources for predation…, by not knowing how to address questions of patronage or by simply turning a blind eye to it' (2012: 65).

The development assistance has been criticised by many for not giving sufficient attention in practice to the political mediation of state–society interactions, including patronage (Blunt et al., 2012: 66). *Proyek* (Indonesian word for project, denoting development projects) as a source of patronage is widely accepted as it continues to characterise Indonesian politics (Aspinall, 2010). Additionally, Blunt et al. (2012) demonstrate that wherever patronage is systemic, standard technocratic forms of governance reform alone are not likely to succeed and are relatively easily deflected or reconstituted by patronage networks. Predictably, oligarchs in 'dirty energy' have proved to be invincible opponents on low-carbon energy transition (Gokkon, 2019). Notably, the demise of Suharto with the dramatic political turmoil that followed has not ended the patronage system and corruption.

Watkins' identification of the local culture issues has thrown some light on the well-known interrelation between local culture and the colonial legacy, which helps to explain the deep-rooted corruption and 'bribe culture' in Indonesian public services (see Kartika, 2015; Prabowo and Cooper, 2016; Wijayanto, 2011; Windarto, 2019). For that reason, simply providing more education is not going to help because the education system is the grounds for perpetuating the culture, as Bourdieu (1973) posits. Furthermore, Trainer (2012) argues that under the capitalist–development paradigm, education induces acquisitive materialism and carries the promise of material happiness that entails lust and a sense of greed, which results in ever greater demands upon the environment. In advocating the need of universal environmental ethics in the world divided by nation-states' interests, I contend (Alkatiri, 2018: 117) that an Indonesian education imbued with nationalism and developmentalism may have become the main culprit in cultivating sustainability illiteracy. Instrumentalisation of nationalism to pursue development was the defining spirit in so-called Third World countries. Synthesising nationalism as a project of identity and developmentalism cultivates a desire for competition in economic growth and progress, which in turn impairs students' ability to comprehend the ideals of sustainability in the context of a finite earth and inhibits the 'whole-earth one-world family' vision needed to respond to the challenges posed by ecological crises which have reached a global scale. The tension between marine pollution, food safety, food security and health illustrated in this chapter substantiates the call for universal environmental ethics even louder.

I focus on food issues to raise the awareness of the academics and international community about the intractable problems underlying Indonesia's environmental devastation and the supervening health risks associated with fish and seafood consumption. It is worth noting that developing countries' access to food export markets depends so much on their capacity to meet the international regulatory require-ments. The regulatory standards are determined by the Agreement on the Application of Sanitary and Phytosanitary Measures (SPS) of the World Trade Organization (WTO). Unsafe exports can lead to sig-nificant economic losses. Therefore, environmental pollution in developing countries entails both public health and economic conse-quences. With the mounting body of empirical work that shows the links between heavy metal toxicity and neurological disorders pre-sented in the Fish and Health Risks of Environmental Contaminants section, there are compelling reasons to worry and thus call for the local and global environmental governance' attention to the public health consequences of river and marine pollution.

Fish and Health Risks of Environmental Contaminants

Fish is a food of excellent nutritional value, providing high-quality protein rich in essential amino acids and other essential nutrients such as selenium, iodine, vitamin D, choline and taurine (FAO, 2010). The health attributes of fish are most likely due in large part to long chain omega-3 (n-3) polyunsaturated fatty acids (LCn3PUFAs) (FAO, 2010). Depending on their lipid content, fish are classified as lean, semi-fatty and fatty. Fish oils in fatty fish such as salmon, tuna, mackerel and sardine are the richest source of the omega-3. The health effects of fish consumption may be greater than the sum of its individual constituents. Despite these positive attributes, it is important to understand the potential health risks of fish. Researchers who specialise in the impact of ocean contaminants on human health identified persistent organic pollutants (POPs), such as polychlorinated biphenyls (PCBs), dioxin, chlorinated pesticides and heavy metals, especially mercury (Hg), can build up in the fish bodies over time. The amount of these organic pollutants in fish and other seafood depends on the species and the levels of pollution in its environment. These residual chemical hazards potentially harm vital organs and processes, especially in developing human foetuses and infants. The effects of POPs include developmental, immune and/or cognitive deficits in newborns, some lasting into later childhood. In addition, some of these contaminants affect the central nervous system, the reproductive system and the liver and can cause cancer.

Heavy metals are defined as metallic elements that have a relatively high density compared to water (Fergusson, 1990). The atomic weight and density of those at least 5 times greater than that of water. Arsenic (As), Cadmium (Cd), Chromium (Cr), Lead (Pb) and Mercury (Hg) rank among the heavy metals dangerous to public health. They are considered systemic toxicants that are known to induce multiple organ damage, even at lower levels of exposure. Heavy metals are also classified as human carcinogens (known or probable) according to the US Environmental Protection Agency and the International Agency for Research on Cancer (IARC) (Tchounwou et al., 2012). Khoshnood (2016, 2017) examined the bioaccumulation process of these metals in fish organs and Tchounwou et al. (2012) focused on the molecular mechanisms of toxicity, genotoxicity and carcinogenicity. The molecular mechanisms of toxicity of mercury are explained by Takeichi et al. (1962). They concluded that heavy metal–induced toxicity and carcinogenicity involves many mechanistic aspects, some of which are not clearly elucidated or understood. Each metal is known to have unique features and physical–chemical properties that confer to its specific toxicological mechanisms of action (Takeuchi et al., 1962).

Heavy metals are naturally occurring elements that are found throughout the earth crust. Natural phenomena such as weathering and volcanic eruptions significantly contribute to this metallic pollution. Most heavy metals are found in nature in three forms: elemental, inorganic and organic compounds such as methylmercury (MeHg). Each has its own profile of toxicity. Arsenic is also present in fish in the organic compound as 'arsenocholine ($C_5H_{14}AsO+$), tetramethylarsonium and arsenobetaine ($C_5H_{11}AsO_2$) ions' (Hakami, 2016: 345). There is evidence that most of heavy metals' presence as the environmental contaminants result from anthropogenic activities such as mining and smelting operations, refineries, coal burning power plants, petroleum combustion, nuclear power stations, chemical industries, textiles, microelectronics, wood preservation and paper processing plants (Arruti et al., 2010; Pacyna, 1996). As a result of an exponential increase of their use in several industrial and technological applications, the wide distribution in the environment and human exposure of these metals have risen dramatically. The Minamata scandal in Japan in the 1960s is a significant case. In 1956, a neurological syndrome called the 'Minamata disease' was first officially discovered in Minamata city in Kumamoto Prefecture, Japan. The tragedy was caused by the release of MeHg in the industrial wastewater from the Chisso Corporation's chemical factory, which continued from 1932 to 1968. This highly toxic chemical bioaccumulated and biomagnified in fish and shellfish in Minamata Bay and the Shiranui Sea (Harada, 1982). The local population who ingested the contaminated marine products from that area displayed high levels of mercury (Hg) contaminant (5.61–35.7 ppm). The Hg content in the hair of patients, their family and inhabitants of the Shiranui Sea coastline was as high as 705 ppm (Harada, 1995). A similar epidemic occurred in 1965 along the Agano River, Niigata Prefecture, Japan (Eto, 1997). The symptoms of Minamata disease include sensory disturbances (glove and stocking type), ataxia,[6] dysarthria,[7] constriction of the visual field, damage to hearing and speech and tremors (Harada, 1995). There are little or no remarkable changes in organs other than the nervous system, except for an occasional fatty degeneration of the liver and kidney, erosion in the digestive tract and hypoplasia of the bone marrow (Takeuchi et al., 1962). In extreme cases, insanity, paralysis, coma and death follow within weeks of the onset of symptoms. Environmental contamination mostly affects the physiologically weak. The earliest victims of Minamata disease were small children (Harada, 2005). A congenital form of the disease can also affect foetuses (Choi et al., 1978; Eto, 1997; Harada, 1978; Snyder, 1971). The disease caused abnormalities in the foetus due to a toxic agent passing through the placenta. In an attempt to remind the whole world about the Minamata environmental disaster of methyl mercury

---

[6]Ataxia is a degenerative disease of the nervous system.
[7]Dysarthria is a collective name that refers to a group of movement disorders that affect the muscular control of speech, resulting in altered voice quality, speech clarity and intelligibility.

indirect poisoning through the food chain, Masazumi Harada (2005) wrote *The Global Lessons of Minamata Disease.*

It is important to note that fish from deeper waters, like tuna, might be more toxic than from shallow waters due to the presence of an oceanic bacteria in the deep ocean that converts mercury from the atmosphere into monomethyl mercury (Blum et al., 2013). Therefore, as the deep ocean becomes increasingly polluted with mercury emissions, more and more fish will become toxic to humans. Many epidemiological and experimental studies have also shown the association between exposure of heavy metals and cancer incidence in humans and animals. Heavy metals accumulate in different parts of fish organs. Overall, larger and longer lived fish tend to contain the most mercury. Larger fish tend to eat many smaller fish, which contain small amounts of mercury. As it is not easily excreted from their bodies, levels accumulate over time. Notably, shellfish and mussels filter large volumes of water to extract their food and are excellent bio-accumulators.

Notwithstanding these challenges, fish is irreplaceable as a source of omega-3 fatty acids (FAO, n.d.). While there is convincing evidence of adverse neurological/neurodevelopmental outcomes in infants and young children associated with MeHg exposure during foetal development due to maternal fish consumption during pregnancy, there is also convincing evidence of beneficial health outcomes from fish consumption for improved neurodevelopment in infants and young children when fish is consumed by the mother. Thus, fish consumption during pregnancy may be associated with a lower risk of neurodevelopmental disorder (FAO, 2010: 8–9). To address these opposing facts, the FAO report presents a careful risks and benefits evaluation of fish consumption and highlights the following:

(i)   There is convincing evidence of adverse neurological/neurodevelopmental outcomes in infants and young children associated with MeHg exposure during foetal development due to maternal fish consumption during pregnancy.

(ii) In addition, there is possible evidence for cardiovascular harm and for other adverse effects (e.g., immunological and reproductive effects) associated with MeHg exposure.

(iii) There is insufficient evidence for adverse health effects (e.g., endocrine disruption, immunological and neurodevelopmental effects, cancer) associated with exposure to dioxins from fish consumption. The World

Cancer Research Fund and American Institute for Cancer Research (2007) report on diet, nutrition, physical activity, and cancer prevention did not identify fish consumption patterns as being associated with any cancers, nor did it address exposure to specific chemical contaminants from fish consumption. (2010: 5)

Along this line, the conflicting recommendations by anti-fish and pro-fish campaigns have spurred confusion among consumers. The FAO report shows that evaluating and communicating the risks and benefits of fish have become contentious issues. Considering the uniqueness of fish nutrients (FAO, 2010: 8–9), it is generally recommended to maximise the benefits of eating fish while minimising the risks of mercury exposure by choosing low-mercury fish and seafood such as salmon, cod and some others and avoid higher mercury fish such as shark, swordfish, tilefish, marlin, tuna and some others. Pregnant, breastfeeding women and children are considered the group at high risk of mercury toxicity; therefore, they need to follow the recommendations seriously. This suggests that it would be wiser to include women of childbearing age in the high-risk group. The following discussion brings up the tensions between different types of knowledge used to understand marine pollution in Indonesia.

Since the 1990s, several studies have been conducted by Indonesian academics to investigate the environmental pollution in coastal areas (Fajri, 2001; Rahmansyah, 1997; Rochyatun, 1997; Wahyuni and Hartati, 1991). Most of the works focused on heavy metal contamination on fish and seafood (Aris and Tamrin, 2020; Hananingtyas, 2017; Ismarti et al., 2017; Muliani et al., 2018; Murtini et al., 2003a, 2003b, 2005; Murtini and Ariyani, 2005; Murtini and Peranginangin, 2006; Priyanto and Murtini, 2006; Siregar et al., 2020; Suyanto et al., 2010; 2017; Yennie and Murtini, 2005; Yulianto et al., 2018). Some studies report such alarming level of pollutants that they recommend discontinuing fish farming activities in the researched location (Mustafa et al., 2019). A recent study by Amqam et al. (2020) reported the arsenic and mercury content of fish around a gold mine[8] at Kao Bay (North Halmahera) has exceeded the allowable standard for food. The hazard risk quotient based on cancer and non-cancer was more than one, which implies the fish and seafood in that area are not safe for

---

[8]Mercury is used to extract gold from ore.

consumption. Regarding mercury pollution, in 2016, the Indonesian Ministry of Health through the Regulation no. 57 stipulated to implement a national action to alleviate the exposure (Minister Regulation, 2016). The document identified that small-scale industries, including small-scale gold mines dotted around the archipelago in 44 locations shown on a map (2016: 19), were among the major sources of mercury discharge to the seas.

In the light of continuing deterioration of Indonesian waterbodies, it can be assumed that those studies by Indonesian academics have not been heeded by the government authorities. Most of the studies are published in local journals and presented in Indonesian language and therefore might not have been accessible to the international community. There is an acute disjuncture between academic research and policy-making in Indonesia. Prasetiamartati et al. identified this issue: 'there is a marked divide between the political world of policymaking and the intellectual world of research: policymakers' needs and priorities are not well communicated, and academic researchers seldom see policymakers or the public as key audiences for their research' (2018: 13).

Other than what was found on health community websites and social media talks, my search for state-sponsored public health campaigns on the health consequences of marine pollution resulted in close to nil. While this inconvenient truth has certainly been acknowledged and discussed in the academic conferences, such a gloomy prospect of environmental sustainability is largely regarded as 'pessimism' that is not worth considering. To bear out the logic of Foucault's power–knowledge framework, it should come as no surprise that any knowledge that does not bear significance to support the growth ideology of the nationalist–developmentalist regime is deemed totally incompatible.

Concerns about the effects of mercury and other contaminants on fish and seafood have led some medical doctors in the health community websites and newsletters (e.g., Alodokter, 2019; Medcom, 2016; Sindonews, 2017) to give 'stop-fish consumption' advisories, especially for children and women during pregnancy and breastfeeding. Meanwhile, in an attempt to eradicate malnourished and stunting, the government continues to advance the Eat Fish Movement known as 'Gerakan Makan Ikan (GEMARIKAN)' to encourage the Indonesian population to eat more fish. Consumers face a dilemma. They are told that seafood is good for them and should be consumed regularly, yet they are cautioned against consuming fish and seafood.

Different messages from different sources confuse the consumers, who often don't know whom to believe. This is an important dilemma posed by the Anthropocene. As an activist in this field, I believe presenting the reality of a problem would encourage activism, not despair or withdrawal. Therefore, what people need is an overall outlook of Indonesian marine pollution in a comprehensive report from all parts of the country, presented in a single document,[9] on a regular basis. The government needs, accordingly, to develop fish consumption guidelines based on the report on a regular basis. In view of the evidently weak environmental law enforcement, an effort needs to be made on the global environmental governance level to establish a 'marine pollution watch' in Indonesia.

Modern Science. A Double-Edged Sword

The crux of the matter is the conflicting ideals between sustainability-literate education and the one formulated for Indonesian schools with strong nationalist–developmentalist ideological overtones. Throughout what is known today as the Third World or developing countries, the education system has evolved from colonial heritage (Cogan, 1982; Watson, 1982) in which it existed to serve the interests of capitalism and colonialism. Posing a Marxist critique, Ted Trainer, who advocates 'The Simpler Way', has been critical of 'education under consumer capitalism' in which schools and universities teach things that are 'of no apparent relevance to students' (2012: 3) and 'legitimize social position and inequality' (2012: 1). This kind of education, among other things:

Helps to produce enthusiastic consumers, people who are keen to get ahead, succeed and get rich; who identify modernity and progress with affluence and see Western ways as the goal for the Third World; and who accept the market system and think technical wizardry will solve all problems. Just as they have passively consumed the activities, work and decisions presented by their teachers, so they passively consume the products, services and decisions presented to them by government, corporations and professionals (Trainer, 2012: 1).

Providing more of this kind of education is a recipe for disaster. From my experience, the environmental views in Indonesia's

---

[9]An example of a sound report was shown by Othman Hakami (2016) in Saudi Arabia's context.

academic world have been dominated by the shallow ecologist's approach (Alkatiri, 2016). This view can be found among the 'sustainable development' camp which believes that strengthening the economic viability in developing countries is the basis for providing the means of preserving their social and environmental functions – and in return, preserving environmental quality is a precondition for developing economic potentials. The shallow approach can also be found among the 'techno quick-fix' camp who believes in the power of technology to fix all problems. This is the view held by the government and in activities invented by big businesses as part of their corporate 'green-wash'. Their approach never touches the level of fundamental change; it merely promotes technological fixes such as recycling, increased automotive efficiency and even export-driven monocultural, organic agriculture, based on the same consumption-oriented values and methods of the industrial economy. The characteristic of this camp is pragmatic and managerialist attitude to environmental issues, founded on an assumption that technology and sound governance will provide solutions. In their viewpoint, problems in developing countries can be rationalised in terms of poor governance, inefficiency, corruption and a lack of technology and education. A contrast view is posited by the deep ecologist's camp. Deep ecology is a particular school of ecological philosophy that arose from the contemporary planetary crisis and human dilemma which have prompted people to question the validity of the conception of nature held in modern science. The distinguishing and original characteristics of this school recognise the inherent worth of all living beings regardless of their instrumental utility to human needs and the use of this view in shaping environmental policies and education. The word 'deep' in part referred to the level of questioning of human's purposes and values when arguing in environmental conflicts. Deep ecology involves deep questioning right down to fundamental root causes.

In light of the facts about the lack of sustainability-literacy in Indonesia's education system, promoting the 'shallow' approach towards the environmental problems which relies heavily on technological quick-fix, managerialist attitudes and good governance is like building castles in the air (Alkatiri, 2016). What is needed is the new learning paradigm that will address the need to understand the vast network of earth ecology. That same paradigm will enable students to see the world as one, yet complex and interconnected system, and humankind who is the veritable 'sucker', exploiter, as well as manager of the earth also as one – yet complex and interconnected community. In other words, it is an education that is rooted in a holistic worldview and which has the potential to foster a sustainable human culture (Alkatiri, 2016).

In the Ethical Dilemma: Modernisation and Unsustainable Practices section, I will expose the pitfall of modern economic rationality that emphasises production and the consequences to the fishery sector in Indonesia. The modernisation programme resulted in overfishing and created an ethical challenge to discuss scientifically and publicly the health consequences of marine pollution, a discussion that might undermine the livelihood of small-scale fishers.

Ethical Dilemma: Modernisation and Unsustainable Practices

Nearly 95 percent of Indonesian fishers are artisanal, small-scale fishers. Among them are the poorest people in the entire population (Anna, 2019: 5). As has been documented in periods of rapid technological and structural change in developing countries, the benefits of fisheries development in Indonesia have not been equally shared. Bailey's (1988) ethnographic study of Indonesian fisheries as part of the rural development in 1970s–1980s depicted the situation as partly analogous to the impact of the Green Revolution upon which the landless laborers and limited resource farm households often gain relatively little from increased productivity. Sometimes, they even suffered from lost income and declining employment opportunities as a result of new agricultural technologies (Bailey, 1988). Improved technologies in the fisheries sector too have benefitted some at the expense of others. It can be argued that the situation in fisheries is even worse than in agricultures because fishers directly compete with one another over a finite resource in Hardin's (1968) 'tragedy of the commons'. 'Through the promotion of rapid technological change, fisheries development in Indonesia has become a "zero sum game", where those who control the most powerful technologies have a clear competitive advantage and individually prosper, even as others are swept aside and fish stocks depleted' (Bailey, 1988: 26). Driven by national economic priorities that had been consistently supported by external development assistance agencies, Indonesia's policy was developed with emphases on favouring efficiency over quality, exports over domestic fisheries supply and resource exploitation rather than resource management. The result was the creation of 'clearly identifiable dualistic industry structure in the fisheries sector' (Bailey, 1988: 26). The groups are traditional fishers versus modernised entrepreneurs through the supports given to domestic entrepreneurs. The latter invested in powerful new fishing technologies, most notably trawlers and purse seiners, which eventually caused overfishing. More about conflicts in Indonesia's fishers' community is written by Kinseng (2020).

Bailey noted a parallel between Indonesia's Agriculture Ministry's Green Revolution and the Directorate General of Fisheries' Blue Revolution (Bailey, 1988: 30). Given the biological vulnerability to over exploitation of fishery resources, the Blue Revolution policies and allocation of development funds to increase fisheries production through rapid modernisation of the fishery sector was short-sighted. The idea of a Blue Revolution provides an overly positive image of the fisheries sector's future. The efforts have been focused primarily on the introduction of powerful new fishing technologies, and the major infrastructural improvements needed to support this development. To achieve that end, the government provided subsidised credit programs, port development projects and research on the most efficient designs for boats and fishing gears, with the stated goal of 'modernising' the fisheries sector by encouraging the use of more powerful and profitable technologies (Bailey, 1988: 30). External assistance agencies have been very influential in shaping the direction of fisheries policies in Indonesia. For instance, to exploit tuna for export markets, in the 1970s, the Asian Development Bank, World Bank and Japanese Government provided loans to the Indonesian government. External agencies' loans were also provided for construction of new trawlers, improvement of fishing ports, ice plants and other infrastructures. To support these rapidly growing capital-intensive fishing enterprises, the FAO established a school for training captains, mechanics and gear specialists (Bailey, 1988: 31). The use of trawlers led to resource depletion in some parts of Indonesia as soon as the late 1970s (Bailey, 1988: 33). Bailey also identified that a peculiar problem behind the depletion of fisheries resources was rooted in Indonesia statistical inaccuracy, which provided estimates that seriously overstated realistically achievable harvests. These estimates are dangerous in that they encouraged continued emphasis on production-oriented development programs. In the absence of the adequate resource management capacity, these programs threaten to increase overfishing.

'Fully fished' refers to the stock situation when fishing pressure is at the maximum limit of what can be sustained before overfishing, and 'overfishing' means catching too many fish at once, so the breeding population becomes too depleted to recover. The situation often goes hand in hand with 'bycatch', wasteful types of commercial fishing with the help of trawler fishing boats that haul in massive amounts of unwanted fish or other animals, which are then discarded. This practice causes severe depletion of the spawning fish stock. Historical and ongoing overfishing has depleted Indonesia's fish stock, and data from the National Commission on Stock Assessments in 2017 showed that nearly half of the nation's wild fish stocks were overfished – meaning their stocks have been partially depleted, and their current and future productivity has been undermined (California Environmental Associates, 2018: 12; CEA and Green, 2018: 48; Conway, 2018: 104). In the global arena, among the 16 FAO Major Fishing Areas for Statistical Purposes (for the definition, see: FAO 2015), the Mediterranean and Black Sea (Area 37) had the highest percentage (62.2 percent) of unsustainable stocks, closely followed by Southeast Pacific where Indonesian water belongs to (Area 87) has 61.5 percent of unsustainable stocks (FAO, 2018). In 2018, the World Economic Forum highlighted that 90 percent of world fish stocks are either fully fished or overfished (Kituyi and Thomson, 2018). In addition, OCEANA, an international ocean conservation and advocacy organisation, reported overfished and fully fished stocks were at 89.5 percent in 2016 compared to around 62–68 percent in 2000, indicating that stock depletion is accelerating (OCEANA, 2016).

Fish stock depletion is closely linked to the rise of human population alongside the fish per capita consumption (average person consumption of fish) that increased from 22 pounds of fish/year in 1960 to 44 pounds of fish/year in 2016 (FAO, 2016). Due to various reasons, people are now consuming more farmed fish than wild-caught fish for the first time (FAO, 2016, 2018: 7, Figure 1). Most of the growth of fish farming took place in Asia, home to 90 percent of fish farms (Bourne, 2014). Given that wild fish simply cannot reproduce as fast as a 9 billion global population by 2050 can eat them, aquaculture is largely considered as a viable solution to the need for more fish in the Anthropocene. However, while farm-raised fish are generally cheaper, they can be less nutritious. According to the Food and

Drug Administration (FDA), farm-raised salmon has higher fats and less protein than its wild-caught counterparts (Velasco, 2013). Although marine mussel and shellfish are excellent candidates for aquaculture, they accumulate a wide range of metals in their soft tissue. It is also important to note that aquaculture faces risks from contamination of waterways by agriculture and industrial activities. Without sustainable fisheries resources management and stringent water pollution control, our fisheries face collapse – and humanity faces a food crisis (McDermott, 2018).

Indonesia urgently needs a tool for the fisheries management with the primary objectives of bringing economic rationality to commercial fishing and providing a better basis for the conservation and sustainability of fisheries resources. From the sustainability point of view, farming fish is in fact more efficient than raising beef (Goodland, 1997). Fisheries have a much smaller footprint than other main sources of animal protein. Manuel Barange, director of FAO Fisheries and Aquaculture Policy (Kinver, 2016), said that fish is six times more efficient at converting feed than cattle and four times more efficient than pork. Therefore, increasing the consumption of fish is good for food security and the environment. However, as previously noted, Hardin's tragedy of the commons is so evident in the case of capture fisheries. In 2020, the Indonesian government began to contemplate a Quota Management System (QMS) to limit the allowable catch quantity by the Decree of the Director General of Capture Fisheries Number 51 (Director General Decree, 2020). Furthermore, in 2021, the government sought to impose landing tariffs in fishery management through the Minister of Marine Affairs and Fishery Regulation Number 39, 2021 (Minister Regulation, 2021). In an archipelagic country with scarce research resources and 90 percent of its fishers are small-scale and a significant proportion of them being in abject poverty, these approaches, in my view, make little sense. For the sake of comparison, I shall like to show the implausibility to implement such systems in Indonesia's context.

In the Europe Union, The Common Fisheries Policy (CFP) was first formulated in the Treaty of Rome in 1958. In its later development, CFP sets quotas for which member states are allowed to catch each type of fish. Daw and Tim (2005) argue that the system has largely failed to achieve sustainable fisheries management due to inadequate coordination between scientific fisheries researchers and policymaking. New Zealand introduced the QMS in 1986. To a certain degree, the system worked relatively well to a certain degree--the country did not appear to have any spectacular 'collapses' of fisheries as was seen, for example in the cod fishery in the NW Atlantic. However, McKoy (2006) contends that the science effort over the 20 years has not been adequate to improve their confidence towards sustainable fish stocks management. Systems based on total allowable catches and oriented around the concept of maximum sustainable yield needs to be equipped with reliable information systems. McKoy explains how New Zealands's attempt to combat 'the tragedy of the commons' by privatisation through access rights and cost recovery systems turned to be counterproductive. He came up with a set of proposals for proactive management based on the best available information and encourage revamping the cost recovery research funding system to ensure the continuance of necessary research to provide more of that 'best available information'.

Apparently, the precondition that needs to be in place for the quota and landing tax systems to function is not what Indonesia is likely to have in the near future. While the resource management tools to limit the allowable catches is urgently needed for the large-scale fisheries, the proactive approach for the multitude of small-scale fishers, in my opinion, is to gradually transform their livelihoods towards innovative, economically viable and sustainable alternatives. The gravity of these issues is comparable to the urgent needs to address climate migrations where people are forced to flee due to sea-level rise, extreme weather events, draught and water scarcity as the impacts of climate change.

Conclusions: Fish in the Anthropocene

In summary, this research can be considered as a further validation of the widely accepted belief that the real tragedy of food contamination and environmental health issues take place in developing world. Broadly translated in a rank order from the most apparent, my findings indicate the source of the problems:

1. 'Waste colonialism' that turns the Global South countries into dumping grounds for the wealthier Global North;
2. Modern economic rationality that assertively prioritises production over conservation, thus, government policy's emphasis on resource exploitation over resource management;
3. The failure of developmentalist–nationalist education to cultivate sustainability literacy, compounded by the acute disconnection between academic research and policymaking. It is, therefore, difficult to arrive at any conclusions with regards to the way to address the tensions between the health and safety of seafood consumption through public dialogue and policies.

Colonial history shapes what is now motivating the participants of activities related to environmental destruction in developing countries. The postcolonial perspective in this chapter helps to decolonise environmental history of Indonesia's fisheries sector and provides a sharpened understanding of the way the educated class and the elites hold unwavering faith in 'progress' that manifests in the development ideology. Caught between the pincers of, on the one hand, nationalist–developmentalist ideology that practically is synonymous with an extractive economy to engage in growth, expansion and competition – whereby corruption has become part and parcel of the system under the international development aid agencies, and on the other hand, a heavy dependence on the global economic system that rapes the societies and the environment, no changes towards sustainability would be possible without an integrated and interconnected framework within an equitable global cooperation. Besides, the broad implication of this research is that giving more education in its present learning paradigm is a recipe for more disaster.

In view of the evidently weak environmental law enforcement, an effort needs to be made on the global environmental governance level to establish a 'marine pollution watch' in Indonesia. Nevertheless, by the sheer length of Indonesia's coastline as the world' second longest, it would be hard to imagine an effective management of marine resources and water pollution controls without decentralising its environmental governance or splitting the large country into states altogether. Decentralised environmental governance will improve efficiency, equity and accountability. Fractioning into states might moderate the development ideology.

This chapter provides an important insight into the prone-to-be-manipulated Indonesian local culture as a key contributor to the maintenance of the status quo, and the direct linkage it has to the widespread and systemic corruption that exists, and eventually, the poor enforcement of environmental law. Thereby, it offers a provocative twist on traditional analysis of local wisdom (*kearifan lokal*) which has often been used as semantic cover. Against the tension between health and safety revealed in the Anthropocene, this chapter at once criticises modernity and rationalises the need for a universal environmental ethics set against the prevailing postmodern mood of the day that often extols local narratives, and ultimately, advocates a more ecologically-aware postcolonialism.

Finally, this chapter points a way to the needed researches to help Indonesia's government develop fish consumption guidelines. Overall, the work points to the need of holistic, integrated and coordinated actions for public health improvement, poverty eradication and environmental protection towards a more sustainable development in the Global South.

References

Alkatiri, W. (2016) 'Sustainability literacy: Some challenges in education in developing countries'. In *Paper presented at the 9th International Congress of the Asian Philosophical Association, Decolonization, Education, Arts and Humanities, and Higher Education Leadership in the Asian Community*, Kuala Lumpur, Malaysia, July 20–24, 2016.

Alkatiri, W. (2018) 'Reconsidering modern nation-state in the Anthropocene: Muslim's perspective'. *Scripta Instituti Donneriani Aboensis*, 28(4): 116–58. (https://journal.fi/scripta/article/view/70070)

Allen, A. (1998) 'Rethinking power', *Hypatia*, 13(1): 21–40. (http://www.jstor.org/stable/3810605)

Alodokter (2019) *Konsumsi Ikan Tidak Selamanya Sehat, Waspadai Bahaya Merkuri*. (https://www.alodokter.com/konsumsi-ikan-tidak-selamanya-sehat-waspadai-bahaya-merkuri)

Amqam, H., Thalib, D., Anwar, D., Sirajuddin, S. and Mallongi, A. (2020) 'Human health risk assessment of heavy metals via consumption of fish from Kao Bay'. *Reviews on Environmental Health*, 35(3): 257–63.

Anderson, B.R.O.G. (2006) *Language and Power: Exploring Political Cultures in Indonesia*. Jakarta: Equinox Publishing Indonesia.

Anna, Z. (2019) *Pemanfaatan Model Bio-Ekonomi dalam Pengelolaan Sumber Daya Perikanan yang Berkelanjutan*. Inauguration of Professorship, Fishery and Marine Science, Universitas Padjajaran, Indonesia, November 8, 2019.

Aris, M. and Tamrin, T. (2020) 'Heavy metal (Ni, Fe) concentration in water and Histopathological of marine fish in the Obi Island, Indonesia'. *Jurnal Ilmiah Platax*, 8(2): 221–33. (https://ejournal.unsrat.ac.id/index.php/platax/article/view/30673)

Arruti, A., Fernández-Olmo, I., and Irabien, A. (2010) 'Evaluation of the contribution of local sources to trace metals levels in urban PM2.5 and PM10 in the Cantabria region (Northern Spain)'. *Journal of Environmental Monitoring*, 12(7): 1451–58.

Asia Sentinel (2022) *Indonesia's New Oligarchs*. February 11, 2022. (https://www.asiasentinel.com/p/indonesia-new-oligarchs?s=r)

Aspinall, E. (2010) *Assessing Democracy Assistance: Indonesia*. FRIDE Project Report. (https://www.files.ethz.ch/isn/130783/IP_WMD_Indonesia_ENG_jul10.pdf)

Aulia, Y. (2022) *Indonesian Oligarchs Are Defending Their Wealth at the Cost of Democracy*, The University of Melbourne, April 19, 2022. (https://indonesiaatmelbourne.unimelb.edu.au/indonesian-oligarchs-are-defending-their-wealth-at-the-cost-of-democracy/)

Bailey, C. (1988) 'The political economy of marine fisheries development in Indonesia', *Indonesia*, 46: 25–38.

Bernard, S., Enayati, A., Redwood, L., Roger, H. and Binstock, T. (2001) 'Autism: A novel form of mercury poisoning', *Medical Hypotheses*, 56(4): 462–71.

Blomkamp, E., Sholikin, M.N., Nursyamsi, F., Lewis, J.M. and Toumbourou, T. (2018) *Understanding Policymaking in Indonesia: In Search of a Policy Cycle*. The University of Melbourne and the Indonesian Centre for Law and Policy Studies (PSHK), for Knowledge Sector Initiative.

Blum, J., Popp, B., Drazen, J., Choy, C.A. and Johnson, M.W. (2013) 'Methylmercury production below the mixed layer in the North Pacific Ocean'. *Nature Geoscience*, 6(10): 879–84.

Blunt, P., Turner, M. and Lindroth, L. (2012) 'Patronage's progress in post-Soeharto Indonesia'. *Public Administration and Development*, 32(1): 64–81.

Bourdieu, P. (1973) 'Cultural reproduction and social reproduction'. In R. Brown (ed), *Knowledge, Education, and Cultural Change*. London: Tavistock, pp. 71–112.

Bourne, J.K. (2014) 'How to farm a better fish'. *National Geographic Magazine*, 225: 92–111.

Bradstreet J., Geier D.A., Kartzinel J.J., Adams J.B., Geier M.R. (2003). 'A case-control study of mercury burden in children with autistic spectrum disorders'. *Journal of American Physicians and Surgeons*, 8(3): 76–79.

California Environmental Associates (2018) 'Executive summary'. In *Trends in Marine Resources and Fisheries Management in Indonesia. A 2018 Review*, pp. 9–17. (https://www.packard.org/wp-content/uploads/2018/08/Indonesia-Marine-Full-Report-08.07.2018.pdf)

California Environmental Associates and Green, S.J. (2018) 'Wild fisheries and aquaculture'. In *Trends in Marine Resources and Fisheries Management in Indonesia. A 2018 Review*, pp. 42–60. (https://www.packard.org/wp-content/uploads/2018/08/Indonesia-Marine-Full-Report-08.07.2018.pdf)

Choi, B.H., Lapham, L.W., Amin-Zaki, L. and Saleem, T. (1978) 'Abnormal neuronal migration, deranged cerebral cortical organization, and diffuse white matter astrocytosis of human fetal brain: A major effect of methylmercury poisoning in utero'. *Journal of Neuropathology & Experimental Neurology*, 37(6): 719–33.

Cogan, J.J. (1982) 'Education and development in the Third World'. *Educational Leadership*, 39.

Conway, S. (2018) 'Private sectors investment'. In *Trends in Marine Resources and Fisheries Management in Indonesia. A 2018 Review*, pp. 102–9. California Environmental Associates. (https://www.packard.org/wp-content/uploads/2018/08/Indonesia-Marine-Full-Report-08.07.2018.pdf)

Daw, T. and Gray, T. (2005) 'Fisheries science and sustainability in international policy: A study of failure in the European Union's Common Fisheries Policy'. *Marine Policy*, 29(3): 189–97.

Director General Decree (2020) *Directorate General of Capture Fisheries*, No. 26. [Kuota Sumber Daya Ikan Dan Kuota Usaha Penangkapan Ikan Di Wilayah Pengelolaan Perikanan Negara Republik Indonesia 711]

Escobar, A. (1995) *Encountering Development. The Making and Unmaking of the Third World*. Princeton, NJ: Princeton University Press.

Eto, K. (1997) 'Review article: Pathology of Minamata disease'. *Toxicologic Pathology*, 25(6): 614–23.

Fajri, N.E. (2001) *Analisis Kandungan Logam Berat Hg, Cd dan Pb dalam Air Laut, Sedimen dan Tiram (Carassostrea cucullatta) di Perairan Pesisir Kecamatan Pedes, Kabupaten Karawang, Jawa Barat*, Postgraduate Thesis. Institut Pertanian Bogor (IPB), Bogor.

FAO. (n.d.) *The Nutritional Benefits of Fish Are Unique*. Food and Agricultural Organization of the United States. (http://www.fao.org/in-action/globefish/fishery-information/resourcedetail/en/c/338772/)

FAO (2010) *Report of the Joint FAO/WHO Expert Consultation on the Risks and Benefits of Fish Consumption*. Report No. 978. FAO Fisheries and Aquaculture. (http://www.fao.org/3/ba0136e/ba0136e00.pdf)

FAO (2014) *The Republic of Indonesia. Fishery and Aquaculture Country Profiles*. (https://www.fao.org/fishery/facp/IDN/en)

FAO (2015) *FAO Major Fishing Areas for Statistical Purposes*. (https://www.fao.org/publications/card/fr/c/50c441be-a207-4419-91fb-ff6bc7f2945b)

FAO (2016) '*Global Per Capita Fish Consumption Rises above 20 Kilograms a Year*'. (http://www.fao.org/news/story/en/item/421871/icode/)

FAO (2018) *The State of World Fisheries and Aquaculture. Meeting the Sustainable Development Goals*. (https://www.fao.org/3/CA0191EN/CA0191EN.pdf)

FAO (2020) *The State of World Fisheries and Aquaculture*. SOFIA. (https://www.fao.org/state-of-fisheries-aquaculture)

Fergusson J.E. (ed) (1990) *The Heavy Elements: Chemistry, Environmental Impact and Health Effects*. Oxford: Pergamon Press.

Geertz, C. (1956) 'Religious belief and economic behavior in a central Javanese town: Some preliminary considerations'. *Economic Development and Cultural Change*, 4(2): 134–58.

Gokkon, B. (2019) 'Indonesia's new cabinet a 'marriage of oligarchs, environmentalists say'. *Mongabay*, October 23, 2019. (https://news.mongabay.com/2019/10/indonesia-cabinet-jokowi-widodo-oligarchs-environment/)

Goodland, R. (1997) 'Environmental sustainability in agriculture: Diet matters'. *Ecological Economics*, 23(3): 189–200.

Hakami, O.M. (2016) 'Risk assessment of heavy metals in fish in Saudi Arabia'. *American Journal of Environmental Sciences*, 12(6): 341–57.

Hananingtyas, I. (2017) 'Studi Pencemaran Kandungan Logam Berat Timbal (Pb) dan Kadmium (Cd) pada Ikan Tongkol (Euthynnus SP.) di Pantai Utara Jawa'. *BIOTROPIC The Journal of Tropical Biology*, 1(2): 41–50.

Harada, M. (1978) 'Congenital Minamata disease: Intrauterine methylmercury poisoning'. *Teratology*, 18(2): 285–8.

Harada M. (1982) 'Minamata disease'. In E.F.P. Jelliffe and D.B. Jelliffe (eds), *Adverse Effects of Foods*. Boston, MA: Springer, pp. 135–48.

Harada, M. (1995) 'Minamata disease: Methylmercury poisoning in Japan caused by environmental pollution'. *Critical Reviews in Toxicology*, 25(1): 1–24.

Harada, M. (2005) 'The global lessons of Minamata disease: An introduction to Minamata studies'. In T. Takahashi (ed), *Taking Life and Death Seriously – Bioethics from Japan*. Amsterdam and Boston, MA: Elsevier JAI.

Hardin, G. (1968) 'The tragedy of the commons'. *Science*, 162(1): 1243–8.

Howard, J. (2019) 'Marine pollution, explained'. *National Geographic*, August 2, 2019.

Irawanto, D.W., Ramsey, P.L. and Ryan, J.C. (2011) 'Challenge of leading in Javanese culture'. *Asian Ethnicity*, 12(2): 125–39.

Ismarti, I., Ramses, R., Suheryanto, S. and Amelia, F. (2017) 'Heavy Metals (Cu, Pb and Cd) in Water and Angel Fish (Chelmon rostractus) from Batam Coastal, Indonesia', *Omni-Akuatika*, 13(1): 78–84. (https://ojs.omniakuatika.net/index.php/joa/article/view/77)

Jambeck, J.R., Geyer, R., Wilcox, C., Siegler, T.R., Perryman, M., Andrady, A., Narayan, R., and Law, K.L. (2015) 'Plastic waste inputs from land into the ocean', *Science*, 347(6223): 728–71.

Kartika, L. (2015) 'Bribe culture in public services in Indonesia'. *Kompasiana*, June 26, 2015. (https://www.kompasiana.com/luwi.kartika/54fff68da33311c56d50f85a/bribe-culture-in-public-services-in-indonesia)

Khoshnood, Z. (2016) 'Using biomarkers in ecotoxicology: What and why?' *Focus on Sciences*, 2(2): 1–2.

Khoshnood, Z. (2017) 'Effects of environmental pollution on fish: A short review'. *Transylvanian Review of Systematical and Ecological Research*, 19(1): 49–60.

Kinseng, R.A. (2020) *Class and Conflict in the Fishers' Community in Indonesia*. Jakarta: Obor.

Kinver, Mark (2016) *'UN: Global fish consumption per capita hits record high.'* BBC, July 7, 2016. https://www.bbc.com/news/science-environment-36716579/

Kituyi, M. and Thomson, P. (2018) '90% of fish stocks are used up – Fisheries subsidies must stop emptying the ocean'. *World Economic Forum*, July 13, 2018. (https://www.weforum.org/agenda/2018/07/fish-stocks-are-used-up-fisheries-subsidies-muststop/)

Landrigan, P.J., Fuller, R., Acosta, N.J., Adeyi, O., Arnold, R., Balde, A.B., Bertollini, R., Bose-O'Reilly, S., Boufford, J.I., Breysse, P.N. and Chiles, T. et al. (2018) 'The Lancet Commission on pollution and health'. *The Lancet Commissions*, 391(10119): 462–512.

Lyons, Y., Linting, T.S. and Neo, M.L. (2019) *A Review of Research on Marine Plastics in Southeast Asia.* (https://cil.nus.edu.sg/wp-content/uploads/2019/07/A-review-of-research-on-marine-plastics-in-Southeast-Asia_Final28June2019Rev4July2019.pdf)

McDermott, A. (2018) 'Eating seafood can reduce your carbon footprint, but some fish are better than others'. *OCEANA*, February 1. (https://oceana.org/blog/eating-seafood-can-reduce-yourcarbon-footprint-some-fish-are-better-others)

McKoy, J. (2006) 'Fisheries resource knowledge, management, and opportunities: Has the Emperor got no clothes?' In *New Zealand's Ocean and Its Future: Knowledge, Opportunities and Management*, pp. 35–44. NIWA. (https://docs.niwa.co.nz/library/public/1877264229C.pdf)

Medcom (2016) 'Bumil Sebaiknya Batasi Konsumsi Ikan, Ini Alasannya'. (https://www.medcom.id/rona/kesehatan/zNA8LQwK-bumil-sebaiknya-batasi-konsumsi-ikanini-alasannya)

Meer, N. (2014) 'Islamophobia and postcolonialism: Continuity, orientalism and Muslim consciousness'. *Patterns of Prejudice*, 48(5): 500–15.

Mies, M. and Shiva, V. (1993) *Ecofeminism.* London: Zed Books.

Minister Regulation (2016) *Department of Health Republic Indonesia*, No. 57. [Peraturan Menteri Kesehatan Republik Indonesia no. 57 tahun 2016 tentang rencana aksi nasional pengendalian dampak kesehatan akibat pajanan merkuri tahun 2016–2020].

Minister Regulation (2021) *Ministry of Marine Affairs and Fisheries*, No. 39. [Persyaratan dan Tatacara Pengenaan Tarif Yang Berlaku Pada Kementrian Kelautan Dan Perikanan].

Ministry of Environment and Forestry (2020) *National Plastic Waste Reduction Strategic Actions for Indonesia.* Republic of Indonesia. (https://wedocs.unep.org/bitstream/handle/20.500.11822/32898/NPWRSI.pdf?sequence=1&isAllowed=y)

Moore-Gilbert, B., Shanton, G. and Maley, W. (2013) *Postcolonial Criticism.* Oxon and New York, NY: Routledge.

Muliani, R.D.U., Sutrisno, A., Azis, N.B. and Frida P. (2018) 'Water quality and the heavy metal occurrence of fish in polluted watershed'. *Indonesian Food and Nutrition Progress*, 15(1): 21–7. (https://journal.ugm.ac.id/ifnp/article/view/29679/0)

Murtini, J.T., Yennie, Y. and Peranginangin, R. (2003a) 'Kandungan logam berat pada kerang darah (Anadara granosa), air laut dan sedimen di perairan Tanjung Balai dan Bagan Siapi-api'. *Jurnal Penelitian Perikanan Indonesia*, 9(5): 77–84.

Murtini, J.T., Yennie, Y. and Ariyani, F. (2003b) 'Penelitian pencemaran logam berat di Selat Madura dan Selat Bali'. In *Prosiding Seminar Nasional Perikanan Indonesia 2003*. Sekolah Tinggi Perikanan, Jakarta, Vol. 1: pp. 83–93.

Murtini, J.T. and Ariyani, F. (2005) 'Kandungan logam berat kerang darah (Anadara granosa) dan kualitas perairan di Tanjung Pasir, Jawa Barat'. *Jurnal Penelitian Perikanan Indonesia*, 11(8): 39–45.

Murtini, J.T., Heruwati, E.S., Dwiyitno, D. and Aji, N. (2005) *Riset identifikasi residu logam berat dan pestisida pada produk perikanan. Laporan Teknis.* Pusat Riset Pengolahan Produk dan Sosial Ekonomi Kelautan dan Perikanan, Jakarta.

Murtini, J.T. and Peranginangin, R. (2006) 'Kandungan logam berat pada kerang kepah (Meritrix meritrix) dan air laut di Perairan Banjarmasin'. *Jurnal Penelitian Perikanan Indonesia*, 8(2): 177–84.

Mustafa, A., Hasnawi, H., Tarunamulia, T., Banda Selamat, M. and Samawi, M.F. (2019) 'Distribusi Polutan Logam Berat di Perairan Pantai yang Digunakan untuk Memasok Tambak Udang Terdekat dan Mitigasinya di Kecamatan Jabon Provinsi Jawa Timur'. *Jurnal Riset Akuakultur*, 14(2): 127–38.

NOOA (National Oceanic and Atmospheric Administration) (2017) *Debunking the Myths about Garbage Patches.* February 13. (https://response.restoration.noaa.gov/about/media/debunking-myths-about-garbage-patches.html)

OCEANA (2016) 'Future of world fish production depends on urgent action to combat falling fish stocks'. July 7. (https://europe.oceana.org/en/press-center/press-releases/losdatos-de-la-fao-confirman-la-gravedad-de-la-sobrepesca-nivel-mundial?utm_source=Twitter&utm_medium=Social&utm_content=070716PR&utm_campaign=ResponsibleFishing)

Pacyna, J.M. (1996) 'Monitoring and assessment of metal contaminants in the air'. In L.W. Chang, L. Magos and T. Suzuli (eds), *Toxicology of Metals*. Boca Raton, FL: CRC Press, pp. 9–28.

Paulo, D.A. and Nie, H.Y. (2020) 'Indonesia stands at the crossroads of a waste crisis and plastics problem'. *Channel News Asia*, 22 March. (https://www.channelnewsasia.com/news/cnainsider/indonesia-stands-crossroads-waste-crisisplastics-problem-12564234)

Pollan, M. (2006) *The Omnivore's Dilemma. A Natural History of Four Meals.* New York, NY: The Penguin Press.

Pollard, S. (1968) *The Idea of Progress: History and Society*. London: C.A. Watts.

Prabowo, H.Y. and Cooper, K. (2016) 'Re-understanding corruption in the Indonesian public sector through three behavioral lenses'. *Journal of Financial Crime*, 23(4): 1028–62.

Prasetiamartati, B., Carden F., Ruhanawati S., Rakhmani I. and Nugroho Y. (2018) 'Linking academic research and policymaking'. In A. Pellini, B. Prasetiamartati, K. Nugroho, E. Jackson and F. Carden (eds), *Knowledge, Politics and Policymaking in Indonesia*. Singapore: Springer, pp. 13–30.

Priyanto, N. and Murtini, J.T. (2006) 'Kandungan logam berat pada ikan yang ditangkap dari Muara Sungai Kahayan, Kalimantan Tengah'. *Jurnal Papadak Bahari*, 1(2): 135–41.

Rahmansyah (1997) *Akumulasi logam berat (pb) dalam tubuh udang windu (Penaeus monodon) pada kondisi salinitas dan individu yang berbeda – Laporan Hasil Penelitian Perikanan Pantai*. Balai Penelitian Perikanan Pantai, Maros.

Ricklefs, M.C., Lockhart, B., Lau, A., Reyes, P., and Aung-Thwin, M. (2010) *A New History of Southeast Asia*. Basingstoke: Palgrave Macmillan.

Rochyatun, E. (1997) *Pemantauan Kadar Logam Berat (PB, Cd dan Cr) dalam Sedimen di Muara Sungai Dadap (Teluk Jakarta), dalam Inventarisasi dan Evaluasi Potensi Laut Pesisir II. Puslitbang Oseanologi*, Jakarta: LIPI, pp. 25–30.

Sage, C. (2012) *Environment and Food*. Oxon: Routledge.

Sagita, D. (2018) 'Indonesia scrubbing the 'world's dirtiest river'. *The Jakarta Post*, 2 March. (https://www.thejakartapost.com/life/2018/03/02/indonesia-scrubbing-theworlds-dirtiest-river.html)

Schmidt, C., Krauth, T., and Wagner, S. (2017) 'Export of plastic debris by rivers into the sea'. *Environmental Science & Technology*, 51(21): 12246–53.

Sherlock, S. and Djani, L. (2015) *Update on Constraints in the Enabling Environment to the Provision of Knowledge in Executive and Legislative Government*. Diagnostic Study. Jakarta: Knowledge Sector Initiative.

Sindonews (2017) 'Ibu Hamil Sebaiknya Batasi Makan Ikan Laut'. (https://lifestyle.sindonews.com/berita/1200741/155/ibu-hamil-sebaiknya-batasi-makan-ikan-Laut)

Siregar, A.S., Sulistyo, I., and Prayogo, N.A. (2020) 'Heavy metal contamination in water, sediments and Planiliza subviridis tissue in the Donan River, Indonesia'. *Journal of Water and Land Development*, 45: 157–64.

Slavka, S., Jovic, J., Stankovic, A.R. and Katsikas, L. (2012) 'Heavy metals in seafood mussels: Risks for human health'. In E. Lichtfouse, J. Schwarzbauer and D. Robert (eds.) *Environmental Chemistry for a Sustainable World: Vol. 1: Nanotechnology and Health Risk*. Heidelberg, London, New York, NY: Springer, pp. 311–73.

Snyder, R.D. (1971) 'Medical intelligence. Congenital mercury poisoning'. *The New England Journal of Medicine*, 284: 1014–16.

Sutarto, A. (2006) 'Becoming a true Javanese: A Javanese view of attempts at javanisation'. *Indonesia and the Malay World*, 34(98): 39–53.

Suyatna, I., Sulistyawati, Adnan, A., Syahrir, M., Ghitarina, G., Abdunnur, A. and Saleh, S. (2017) 'Heavy metal levels in water and fish samples from coastal waters of Mahakam Delta, Kutai Kartanegara District, East Kalimantan, Indonesia'. *AACL Bioflux*, 10(5): 1319–29. (http://www.bioflux.com.ro/docs/2017.1319-1329.pdf)

Suyanto, A., Kusmiyati, S. and Retnaningsih, C. (2010) 'Residu Logam Berat Ikan dari Perairan Tercemar di Pantai Utara Jawa Tengah (Residual Heavy Metals in Fish from Contaminated Water in North Coast of Central Java)'. *Jurnal Pangan dan Gizi*, 1(2): 33–8.

Takeuchi, T., Morikawa, N., Matsumoto, H. et al. (1962) 'A pathological study of Minamata disease in Japan'. *Acta Neuropathologica*, 2: 40–57.

Tchounwou, P.B. et al. (2012) 'Heavy metal toxicity and the environment'. *Experientia supplementum*, 101: 133–64.

The EAT-Lancet Commission Summary Report (2020). (https://knowledge4policy.ec.europa.eu/publication/eat-lancet-commission-summary-report_en)

The Strait Times (2016) *Policy Loopholes Turn Indonesia into Dumping Site: Environmentalists*. May 13, 2016. (https://www.straitstimes.com/asia/se-asia/policy-loopholesturn-indonesia-into-dumping-site-environmentalists)

Thorburn, C. (2002) 'Regime change: Prospects for community-based resource management in Post-New Order Indonesia'. *Society and Natural Resources*, 15: 617–28.

Trainer, T. (2012) *Education under Consumer-Capitalism and the Simpler Way Alternative*. Simplicity Institute Report 12m, Melbourne: Simplicity Institute.

United Nations – Human Rights (2021) *UN Expert Says Anti-muslim Hatred Rises to Epidemic Proportions, Urges State to Act*. Geneva: Office of the High Commissioner.

(https://www.ohchr.org/EN/NewsEvents/Pages/DisplayNews.aspx?NewsID=26841&LangID=E)

USAID (2017) *Marine Tenure and Small-scale Fisheries: Learning from the Indonesia Experience*. Tenure and Global Climate Change Program. May, 2017.

Velasco, S. (2013) 'Food labeling 101: GMO, organic, and other common grocery labels decoded'. *The Christian Science Monitor*, April 29, 2013. (https://www.csmonitor.com/Business/2013/0429/Food-labeling-101-GMO-organic-and-othercommon-grocery-labels-decoded/Wild-caught-vs.-farm-raised)

VOI (2021) *KPK Taliban Issues: Initiated by Neta S. Pane, Used in the Selection of Independent Investigators 2009, to Present TWK*. June 7, 2021. (https://voi.id/en/memori/57296/kpk-taliban-issues-initiated-by-neta-s-pane-used-in-the-selection-of-independent-investigators-2009-to-present-twk)

Wahyuni, I.S. and Hartati, S.T. (1991) *Penelitian kualitas perairan pantai barat teluk Jakarta. Prosiding Temu Karya Ilmiah Perikanan Rakyat*, Jakarta: Buku II. Jakarta.

Warburton, E. (2020). 'Deepening Polarization and Democratic Decline in Indonesia'. In T. Carothers and A. O'Donohue (eds). *Political Polarization in South and Southeast Asia: Old Divisions, New Dangers*. Washington, DC: Carnegie Endowment for International Peace, pp. 25–40.

Watkins, C. (1997) *Water Management and Culture in Indonesian Cities*. A thesis of the Masters program in Engineering (Public Health) at UNSW. (https://www.appropedia.org/Water_management_and_culture_in_Indonesian_cities#Abstract)

Watson, K. (1982) *Education in the Third World*. Oxon: Routledge.

Weiss, F.T., Leuzinger, M., Zurbrügg, C. and Eggen, R.I.L. (2016) *Chemical Pollution in Low- and Middle-Income Countries*. Dubendorf: Swiss Federal Institute of Aquatic Science and Technology.

Wijayanto (2011) 'New state, old society: The practice of corruption in Indonesian politics in historical comparative perspective'. *Politika: Jurnal Ilmu Politik Undip*, 2(2): 5–17.

Willet, W. et al. (2019) 'Food in the Anthropocene: The EAT–Lancet Commission on healthy diets from sustainable food systems'. *The Lancet Commissions*, 393(10170): 447–92. (https://www.thelancet.com/journals/lancet/article/PIIS0140-6736(18)31788-4/fulltext)

Windarto, D. (2019) 'Getting away with it: Bribery culture in Indonesia'. *Glass Lewis*, March 20, 2019. (https://www.glasslewis.com/getting-away-with-it-bribery-culture-in-indonesia/)

Wright, R. (2004) *Short History of Progress*. Melbourne: Text Publishing.

Whitfield, III, G. (n.d.) 'The Indonesian Big Five Part II: Conflicts of Nature'. *Living in Indonesia. A Site for Expatriates*. (http://www.expat.or.id/business/bigfive-conflictsofnature.html)

Yennie, Y. and Murtini, J.T. (2005) 'Kandungan logam berat air laut, sedimen dan daging kerang darah (Anadara granosa) di perairan Mentok dan Tanjung Jabung Timur'. *Jurnal Ilmu-Ilmu Perairan dan Perikanan. Indonesia*, 12(1): 27–32.

Yulianto, B., Oetari, P.S., Februhardi, S., Putranto, T.W.C. and Soegianto, A. (2018) 'Heavy metals (Cd, Pb, Cu, Zn) concentrations in edible bivalves harvested from Northern Coast of Central Java, Indonesia'. In *IOP Conference Series: Earth and Environmental Science*. (https://iopscience.iop.org/article/10.1088/1755-1315/259/1/012005/meta)

8

Hunger, Obesity and Soy: The Corporate Agribusiness Diet in Argentina

Luis E. Blacha

Introduction

The global agri-food system is a key element for the recognition of the Anthropocene as a new epoch when 'humans have become dominating drivers of change' (Willet et al., 2019: 461). It implicates a climate impact as well as the transformation in the human body. The aim of this research is to analyse the impact on corporate agribusiness in Argentina during the 21st century in which the overproduction of food has generated new ways of hunger and social inequalities that make the original idea of the Anthropocene more complex (Arias-Maldonado, 2016; Barnosky, 2013; Crutzen, 2002; Waters et al., 2014). It is necessary to include this topic in social science studies of the Anthropocene in order to evaluate the real impact (Forrester and Smith, 2018; Hamilton, 2017; Latour, 2017, 2018; Mann and Wainwright, 2018; Purdy, 2015).

Industrial food increases obesity in the world population which results in a central driver in the Anthropocene. It is part of what Otero (2018) defines as the neoliberal diet with a small oligopolistic group of food-manufacturing multinational corporations who globalise an energy-dense diet which drives the obesity crisis and the rise of the industrial diet. Food insecurity also affects the population of food-producing countries such as Argentina.

In the Argentinean case, the consequences of soy monocultures include an important loss of biodiversity and a dramatic increase of the overweight population. This chapter analyses the new social inequalities that are linked to the access to nutrients in a country that produces calories for 400 million human beings. Many of these calories are high-nutritional quality proteins from the soy monoculture for export (Diaz et al., 2017). The access to proteins in the domestic market is ensured by the high consumption of beef. The uncertainties defining Beck's (1998, 2002) risk society and the 'making live' of Foucault's (1999, 2007, 2012) biopower are the conceptual framework of this chapter. The research question is, how does the Anthropocene diet foster nutritional inequalities in a country that includes an important corporate agribusiness?

The highest consumption of vegetable oils stems from the energy-dense foods, which characterises the neoliberal diet. Between 1982 and 2002, vegetable oils 'contributed more than any other food group to the increase of calorie availability worldwide' (Hawkes, 2006: 4). Argentina is the main soy oil exporter worldwide and plays a key role in the global supply of these kinds of oils. The corporate agribusiness encourages the soy monoculture, which negatively affects fresh food production for the domestic market, even beef which is a central focus point in the Argentinean diet. These changes in the Argentinean diet were made possible through a combination of a neoliberal state, corporate agribusiness, biotechnology and the supermarkets, which together lead to malnutrition (Otero, 2018).

The Argentinean case is relevant to the Anthropocene diet since it presents similarities, as well as differences, regarding the neoliberal diet. The early consolidation of a unified dietary pattern in Argentina, in which poor and rich people share a social link to food, is a different starting point in Popkin's et al. (2019) nutritional transition. High beef consumption, which distinguishes the Argentinean diet, remains among the highest ones worldwide. However, one of the consequences of neoliberal policies is the fact that its consumption is reduced by half of 80 kg/year/capita in December 1980 to 40 kg/year/capita in December 2020 (CiCCRA, 2020). The country does not need to import food but the nutritional quality of food is reduced because the consumption of ultra-processed food increases. These were changes that went beyond class components and new social differentiating elements such as excess weight and short stature have emerged as new forms of inequalities (Galicia et al., 2016).

In order to analyze the Argentinean case I use secondary data (FAO-STATS) and national level statistics for health (ENNyS 2), economic indicators (EPH, ENGHO),[1] as well as information provided by

---

[1]ENNyS: National Survey of Nutrition and Health. It is the first national survey that links health indicators with the population eating habits. It includes weight, height and biochemical measurements for nutrient consumption. ENGHo: National Survey of Household Expenditures. It collects data on all household expenses and income at a national level. It allows us to rebuild the social and economic structure of Argentina. It is used to measure the evolution of food consumption – among other variables. EPH: Permanent Household Survey. It is a set of socio-economic indicators of the population. They are updated regularly and it is used to measure the evolution of poverty in Argentina.

private institutions such as 'Cámara de la industria y comercio de carnes y derivados de la República Argentina – the Argentine Republic Chamber of Industry and Commerce of meat and its derivatives' (CICCRA). These sources allow measuring the impact of corporate agribusiness of the Pampa region on the whole Argentinean diet, beyond regional differences and class components. They are the most updated data with greater geographic scope for the case study.

Risk and Biopower in the Anthropocene Diet

In the Anthropocene, hunger acquires new forms since the diets are energy-dense but the nutrients are degraded. The political economy of food security that fosters biopower will not be sufficient to avoid hunger in the 21st century. The corporate agribusiness and biotechnology are 'attempting to recondition human, animal and bacterial life in order to quicken the reproduction of capital' (Nally, 2011: 37). The Anthropocene demonstrates that the strategies for the governing of life are more complex than the theorised by Foucault. The 'making live' (faire vivre) identified by Foucault with human life also allows the birth of agricultural monotony (Foucault, 2007). With biopower it is possible to control the biophysical aspects of production (Nally, 2011: 44). Human health and the environment will interrelate thus turning nature into part of culture (Beck, 2002). The risk is an 'intermediate state between security and destruction, where the perception of threatening risks determines thought and action' (Beck, 2002: 213). Unlike wealth, the risk is more democratic, and due to its equalising effects, it does not alter the pre-existing social inequality, but it changes its logics. Risk consequences, mainly the negative ones, are not distributed in an equal way among people because 'the first law of environmental risks was that the contamination followed poor people' (Beck, 2002: 8).

Risk is a boundary to the transformative capacity of biopower. The production of risk 'becomes endemic to society' (Pascale, 2017: 4). Risk and the neoliberal ideology have several points in common as part of Beck's individualisation thesis, which goes far beyond social classes (Almas, 1999). Food consumption is part of this individualisation process in late modernity (Beck et al., 1994). In the neoliberal diet biopower and risk are important drivers that refer to an individual responsibility for health, which presents itself separate from social changes (Rasborg, 2018). These two frameworks – biopower and risk – emerge from different theoretical traditions; however, they allow the explanation of the inequalities characterising the Anthropocene diet. The anatomo-politics of the human body that maximises its efficiency and the biopolitics of the population are both influenced by risk. The increase in agri-food productivity is not enough for food security and it is part of the uncertainty that characterises the risk society.

Malnutrition is the typical form of the neoliberal diet and it questions the 'making live' from biopower. With biopower in the Anthropocene, a privatisation of nature deepened through the neoliberal politics of the late 20th century, where nature is understood in the risk society as part of culture, which adapts itself to the speed of production of capital. Biopower may establish changes at a molecular level according to the corporate agribusiness interests; it is a corporate biopower (Nally, 2011: 48). The increase of obesity is part of this transition in the link with food as part of the inequalities in the Anthropocene. Access to fruit and vegetables is reduced at the expense of ultra-processed food which leads to an inequal access to nutrients in the industrial diet (Winson, 2013).

Corporate Agribusiness and the Soybean Monocultures

Since the end of the 19th century the differential fertility of the Pampa Region allowed Argentina to enter the international market as a major agricultural commodities producer. Its environmental conditions were reinforced with a sociopolitical and economic organisation that prioritised the foreign market over the domestic one. About 70 percent of its 52,300,000 hectares could alternate between livestock cycles and agricultural ones in a warm and wet climate. It includes most of Buenos Aires and Entre Rios Provinces, the centre and south of Santa Fe Province, the centre and southeast of Córdoba Province and the northeast of La Pampa Province (see Figure 8.1). The very low population density also sped up the transformation of the ecosystems since 1880 after the European immigration to meet large-scale international demands for agricultural commodities.

A conservative political structure promoting a liberal economy is part of biopower, which consolidates a capital production system that facilitates meat (beef) and grains exports. The large landowners, fencing and the railway ensured the consolidation of the extensive production that turned Argentina into the 'Granary of the World' at the end of the 19th century. As a result of the genetic refinement in livestock (Shorthorn, Hereford and Aberdeen Angus cattle breeds), in 1905 Argentina became the main supplier of frozen beef meat to England. This was a type of production characterised by its capitalist practices, but without capitalised small

Figure 8.1 Position of Pampa region

producers as was the case of North American farmers (Shugart, 2015: 268). At the beginning of the 20th century, Argentina was the leading Latin America exporter of beef and grains. It represented 32 percent of the exports produced by only 9.6 percent of the inhabitants of the region. This international success was offset by a small domestic market.

Around 1914, and with a population of almost 8 million inhabitants, in Argentina there were no more lands with sufficient fertility to include in this productive model. This started a strong economic stagnation that was translated into social dissatisfaction and the first activities of the traditional elites who held liberal economic views, but conservative political practices. However, even until 1930 the Argentinean exports represented 80 percent of the global market of flax seeds, 61 percent of meat and 20 percent of wheat (Barsky and Gelman, 2012: 216). The transition from an extensive agriculture to an intensive version was delayed for many decades and it required a series of different political projects for the country: interventionist public policies since 1930s and until the late 1950s; the developmentalism of the Economic Commission for Latin America and the Caribbean (ECLAC-UN); and the Green Revolution in the mid-1960s. At different times, the industrialisation of the Argentinean agriculture was influenced by both, the *Agricultural Technical Studies Centre* originated in France and the North American perspective of agribusiness of John H. Davis and Ray A. Goldberg from Harvard University that took action as leaders for this transition from extensive to intensive practices. The model that they promoted tied the production practices closely together with the rest of the financial activities (Graciano Da Silva, 1994: 211). Foreign Direct Investment (FDI) at the end of the 20th century permitted the implementation of these production changes, which allowed processed food to be available for more and more people (Hawkes, 2006: 7).

Biopower is the key to industrialised agriculture. Food production was at the base of the social order (Douglas, 2003). The increase of fertility at the expense of biodiversity had its correlation in the variety of food in which there were more calories available, but less variety and a micronutrient deficiency (Hawkes, 2006: 2). It is part of the neoliberal diet that combines four key dynamics factors: neoliberal states, agribusiness multinational corporations, biotechnology and supermarkets (Otero, 2018: 61–2). Biotechnology 'is the technology with the fastest adoption rate in the history of modern agriculture' (Otero, 2018: 62). This process leads to a 're-primarisation' of the economies of the Southern Cone where the large multinational corporations like Monsanto, Syngenta, Bayer, Cargill, ADM, Maggi and Bunge had a great influence (Grain, 2013; Manzanal, 2017).

The monoculture that was implemented as a corporate agribusiness model was possible due to biopower which broadens the scope of what Foucault names 'making live'. Industrialised agriculture politicised not only the human being but also other living beings in order to adapt them to the demands of the capitalist production system. The rationality that guided that model changed agricultural production into a corporate agribusiness, i.e., 'a series of operations that started in research and development, went through the agro, the industry, the business and also related services to understand the customers' demands' (Vilela and Senesi, 2009: VII–VIII). Its implementation in Argentina was part of the opening that promoted neoliberal policies in the region during the 1990s and its exports were adapted to satisfy one of the highest consumed components of the neoliberal diet: vegetable oils. There were technical, social and political factors that allowed the Argentinean soy production to expand to higher rates than the global average. The country changed from exporting food for $1,300 million in 1970 to $35,000 million in 2008 (Scheinkerman de Obschatko, 2010: 274). That growth demanded that in the Pampa region 5 million hectares of land changed from livestock to agriculture (Barsky and Gelman, 2012: 300).

The new technologies implementation, such as direct seeding, allowed two crops per year of the same land and expanded, for the first time since 1914, the agricultural frontier outweighing the production of the 'Granary of the World' at the beginning of the 20th century. Between 1996 and 2010 the cultivated surface was tripled, from 10 to 30 million hectares, while its average fertility increased 800 percent, from 12 to 95 million tons (Reca, 2010: 7–8). According to the latest available information, referring to the 2019/2020 campaign, a cultivated hectare produced 2,927 kilograms of soy, 7,554 kilograms of corn and 2,939 kilograms of wheat (Dirección de Estimaciones Agrícolas, 2020). Even though corn efficiency increased the most, the high international prices of soy explain the greater surface in the Pampa region dedicated to this crop: 16,882,238 hectares, while 9,504,473 hectares of corn and 6,951,171 hectares of wheat (Dirección de Estimaciones Agrícolas, 2020). The corn was processed into biofuels and the soy for feedstuffs for livestock and exports to Asia for human food.

Since the neoliberal opening at the end of the 20th century, no Argentinean commodity has increased its production as much as soy,

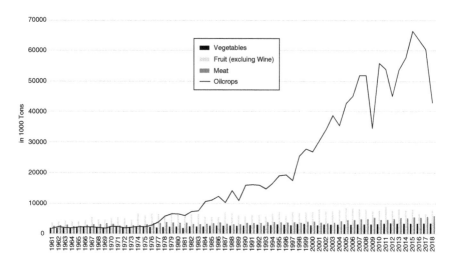

Figure 8.2 Argentina: Food production (1961–2018)
Source: Food-Balance FAO STAT data.

a commodity that is produced almost exclusively for the international market. Figure 8.2 shows the quantitative importance of this increase in oil crops production compared to other traditional foods.

Since the 1990s, soy is what makes possible oil crops growth (Ordo-ñez, 2009). The soy production demanded less investment than other crops in the region such as dairy and livestock. It also reduced the amount of land in crops such as corn and sunflower. Soy monoculture better adapts itself to the needs of the financial capital organised in sowing pools – a form of organisation that facilitates the income of economic actors not related to agricultural production (Murmis and Murmis, 2012). The vast extension of soybeans cultivation is possible due to the financial capital of these sowing pools which allow renting machinery, land and specialised services called 'contratistas' (contrac-tors) (Vértiz, 2015: 23). Argentina became the main oil and soy flour exporter with 56 percent and 48 percent of the global market, respec-tively. Together, Brazil, the United States and Argentina represented 85 percent of the global supply of soy and soy sub-products. These vege-table oils constitute a key component in the neoliberal diet (Otero, 2018).

Unlike the 'Granary of the World' time period, the productive increases in agriculture were not related to cattle production, which remained steady with little change. Argentinean beef production went beyond the Pampa region, where it had always had the best efficiency per hectare. The availability of the total meat in Argentina in 2013 was 2.7 times more than the rest of the world; however; in 1963 it was 4.2 times more (Diaz et al., 2017: 18). Beef consumption in Argentina has decreased in the 21st century, but it continues to be one of the highest worldwide (Ruby et al., 2015). Meat consumption dropped in all the income quintiles while semi-finished products grew 179 percent. It was not only an effect of the agricultural development of the main productive area of the country, but also since 2000 meat processing has consolidated under foreign investment with North American and Brazilian firms controlling 70 percent of cattle slaughtering. The purchase of Quick-Food Company by Brazilian companies Marfig and JBS pushed up the production of hamburgers, sausages and cold meat, which contributed to higher consumption of semi-finished products. These changes in consumption also had another impact on cattle slaughtering. Until the beginning of the 21st century, the average weight of slaughtered cattle was 250 kilograms per animal, but since then it has increased to an average of 320 kilograms, closer to the 400 and 500 kilograms used in the United States or Australia.

The tendency for a higher worldwide consumption of meat (beef) characterises the neoliberal diet, but shows an opposing trend in Argentina. The corporate meat (beef) model contains a higher percentage of fat due to changes in the livestock diet. The feedlot is part of the corporate agribusiness system, especially as land previously grazed for beef goes into row crop production. The agricultural surpluses are then used as livestock feed in the feedlot system (Blacha, 2019). In fact, '36 per cent of the world's crop calories are fed to animals worldwide' (Cassidy et al., 2013: 3). It was part of a productive model that consumes 10 calories to generate 1 calorie of food.

The rapid implementation of the corporate agribusiness model was based on its productive logics with 'the structural forces at work in shaping food production and consumption, driven primarily by agribusiness multinationals (ABMs) originating in the United States' (Otero, 2018: 53). Biotechnology (Monsanto RoundUp Ready Soy in the Argentinean case) and the supermarkets as the main food distribution actors increase inequality regarding access to nutrients. Consumption of sugar, fat and salt increases as the neoliberal diet also seduces the senses and it becomes part of biopower in the 21st century (Moss, 2021). These components are also present in the Argentinean case; in 2003 the government started implementing tax subsidies for soybean exports. There is a substantial difference compared to the subsidies in the United States, but both models foster overproduction of commodities through the expansion of monoculture.

Soybean production in Argentina generates big profits even with high taxes on these crop exports known as 'retenciones' (retentions). It also benefited from the devaluation of Argentine money. It is the opposite scenario of US farm subsidies and even so, it is very profitable. Argentina moved from producing meat (beef) to exporting grains to feed livestock in other countries, a change based on a 'differential profit' with higher returns to the capital (Winson, 2013). As a result, geographical disparities grew when the Global South went from exporting $1,000 million of food per year in 1970 to importing $11,000 million in 2001 (Holt-Gimenez, 2017: 54).

Diet and Body in the Anthropocene

Even in the 21st century, during a time in human history when the least percentage of household income is spent on food, hunger is present because proper nutrition is not guaranteed (Oyhenart et al., 2018: 598). The year 2006 was a key turning event in this history as the percentage of individuals with excess weight outnumbered the malnourished ones (FAO-STATS). Most food available is nutritionally degraded and is characterised by excessive processing. Industrialised food production moved the monotony of monoculture to the daily dish (Fischler, 1995). The excess of low-cost calories in energy-dense food is a risk to consumer's health (Lindeberg, 2010).

This excess of calories does not ensure access to nutrients. Even in countries which are characterised by their abundant food production such as Argentina, only 6 percent of its population fulfils the recommendation of eating at least five servings a day of fruit and vegetables (Indec, 2019: 9). Nutritional degradation and the overproduction of food link the obesity epidemic with the climate change. The commoditisation of food produces more ingredients than food in the strict sense of the word. Malnutrition is part of the risk that characterises agri-food chains in the 21st century. Social relationships which link producers with consumers are lost and economic relationships take their place.

The Argentinean case is part of the global tendency in which obesity is more prevalent than undernourishment as a persistent problem in the country (Oyhenart et al., 2018: 604). As the consolidation of corporate agribusiness spreads from the Global North to the Global South, categories such as farmer or peasant do not have the same features as the traditional Argentinean 'arrendatarios (tenants)' or 'chacareros (farmers)'. A population who at the beginning of the 20th century showed demographic characteristics similar to their European peers and had high levels of literacy exhibited a unified nutritional pattern (Aguirre, 2004: 30). Poor and rich people did not eat the same, but they had a similar link to their food. Beyond the important regional differences, the Argentinean population has been characterised by a high consumption of beef and a wide range of high quality, nutritional foods that ensured a long and persistent reduction in malnutrition rates that extended from the 1880s to the 1950s (Salvatore, 2020: 2). As shown in Figure 8.3, even during one of the worst social crises in the whole Argentinean history – 1989 and 2001 – with hyperinflation and high rates of unemployment, the daily availability per kcal per capita outweighed the minimum requirements recommended by the WHO.

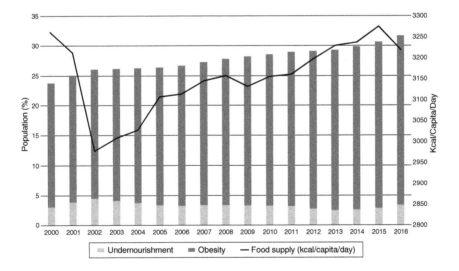

Figure 8.3 Prevalence of undernourishment and obesity in Argentina (2000–2016)

Source: Food-Balance FAO STAT data.

According to FAO-STATS data, the availability of kcal/capita/day in Argentina surpassed the 3,000 mark from 1961 to 2018, with unique exceptions in 1989 and 2001 because of the reasons mentioned above that reduced them to almost 2,900 kcal. Even with corporate agribusiness higher yields crops, hunger is a major problem in Argentina. A considerable calorie offer does not ensure food. There were 18,469 school eateries and 1,165 community eateries operating, according to the estimates of the National State (Salvia et al., 2020: 7).

In Argentina, the great increase in calorie consumption occurred in a context of high availability of proteins, not only because of the usual consumption of red meat, but more so because of soy flour that was used in the cheaper food. This first factor is not usual in the Global South, and it represents a special feature of the case that complicates the impact of malnutrition. The quality of carbohydrates – simple or complex – is a key driver of social inequality. Poor home diet has a lot of low-quality carbs from ultra-processed food, but almost no fruits and vegetables containing complex carbohydrates (ENNyS, 2007). It is part of the neoliberal diet as the nutritional expression of the neoliberal regime. A political regime that imposes 'the international realignments and historically and geographically variegated national and local regulatory trends in global political economy since the 1980s' (Otero, 2018: 158).

In Argentina in early 2020 about 41 percent of the population was under the poverty line with an unemployment rate of 11.7 percent (INDEC, 2020). This occurred as the proportion of income spent on food declined from 28.8 percent in 1996 to 22.6 percent in 2018 (ENGHo, 2019). During this same time period, as the number of poor people increased so did the cost of transport and communication. In these households of the poor, the food expenses represented 36 percent of income while in the highest quintile it was 14.8 percent (ENGHo, 2019: 29). The nutritional quality of food is another indicator of social inequality. There is a strong relationship between the highest consumption of simple carbohydrates that come from ultra-processed food and the decrease in incomes and increase in poverty. The great Argentinean consumption of beef, which differentiates it from other countries of the Global South, shows high inequalities. After cattle slaughtering, meat cuts go to different places. The front part of the animal, with more bones, goes to sectors of low incomes. The hindquarter goes to middle- and high-income sectors.

The consumption of sugary drinks is a huge indicator of these transformations, as it increased by 450 calories daily consumed worldwide between 1965 and 2010. In Argentina, the second highest consuming country in Latin America after Mexico, soda consumption doubled between 1996 and 2013 from daily half a glass to a complete one (Zapata et al., 2016: 54). These consumption changes also showed differences in the inner social framework. Lower incomes were linked to a daily consumption of sugary drinks: 47 percent in homes with lower incomes, while 21 percent in the ones with higher incomes. Something similar happens with industrialised snacks in which the quintile of the lowest income daily consumes 22 percent of the total while the highest one is only 10.5 percent (ENGHo, 2013; Zapata et al., 2016). There is an opposite tendency in fresh food such as fruit and vegetables: less consumption is associated with lower incomes (ENNyS2, 2019).

The food industry is willing to generate and satisfy these caloric needs at a low price (Carolan, 2014). The individual, isolated eater validates this demand with their consumption practices as part of the individual responsibility and concern for the health under neoliberalism. The supermarket contributes to the increased consumption of these foods. It is not only designed to sell food, but also to sell a specific type of food: industrialised foods that are generally classed as ultra-processed. The homogenisation of the food supply is transferred to a standardisation of sales contexts that takes place worldwide. Self-service as a way of buying food was expanded at the end of 1940s. In Argentina, the first supermarkets appeared in mid-1950s, but it was with neoliberal policies of 1990s when the big chains of hypermarkets (i.e., Carrefour, Walmart, Auchan, Cencosur) entered the country and dominated the market (Chiodo, 2010). As part of the neoliberal diet, the supermarket revolution occurred across Latin America in the same period and explains the rise in the consumption of ultra-processed food – from 10 percent of household expenses to 60 percent between 1990 and 2000 (Popkin et al., 2019: 7).

Supermarkets offer the illusion of providing the consumer the power to make a true choice of what to eat: the practices of grabbing the food on your own, minimising the buying time and increasing the privacy of purchases all contribute to this illusion (Warde, 2016: 38). However, the standardisation of the products available ends up increasing the distance that divides the producers and the consumers.

Supermarkets are also designed to promote excessive consumption through frequent price discounts and sales of greater quantities (e.g., buy one, get one free). These promotions are necessary to sell off the excess production of the corporate agribusiness model. There are certain components of the food produced through the industrial food system – such as sugar, fat and salt, which are most often found in supermarkets and generate heightened consumer satisfaction (Willet, 2019). Although meat, fruit and vegetables in Argentina are bought in specialised shops, such as butcheries and greengrocers, the strong presence of supermarket chains that emerged in the 1990s coincides with an increase of the consumption of ultra-processed food (ENGHo, 2019).

Supermarkets contribute to the break of the historical unified nutritional food pattern in Argentina in which fresh food were always included in the diet. Not differentiating between quintiles of income or educational levels that mitigated those transitions, between 1996 and 2013 fruit consumption was reduced by 40 percent and vegetables by 20 percent, respectively (Zapata et al., 2016). In contrast, soda consumption, industrialised bakery products and sweets doubled their sales. The selection capacity is limited and is presented as an individual problem typical of neoliberalism. Nevertheless, it has social reasons based on a standardisation of food production. This energy-dense diet with a low quality of micronutrients incorporates biofortification as part of biopower. It is Gyorgy Scrinis nutritionism (2013) where an individual nutrient is more important than the whole food. It is a strategy 'for transforming nutrients and nutritional knowledge into marketable food products and for further commodifying food production and consumption practices' (Scrinis, 2013: 27). In Argentina, the Law 25.630 of flour fortification requires the addition of ferrous sulfate (30 mg/kg), folic acid (2.2 mg/kg), thiamine mononitrate (B1) (6.3 mg/kg), riboflavin (B2) (1.3 mg/kg) and Nicotinamide (13 mg/kg) in wheat flour. This fortification represents 50 percent of iron consumption in the Argentine population. However, the higher income quintiles obtain 50 percent more iron in their diet from meat, while iron in the poorer quintile comes from this fortified flour.

Biopower in the neoliberal diet explains how nutritionism is a key component to turn health into an individual concern. Nutritionism tries to differentiate the consumption of food from the impact that it has on the body. The changes in the composition of food explain the greater incidence of overweight and obesity in those people with less economic resources (Popkin et al., 2019: 5). Standardisation promoted by nutritionism is complemented with the Body Mass Index (BMI = kg/m^2) as the measure of overweight and obesity. Both compose a biopower in the Anthropocene, in which diet affects individual health as well as society. According to the BMI, 67.9 percent adult Argentineans have excess weight, which includes not only overweight (BMI ≥ 25 y ≤ 30) but also obesity (BMI ≥ 30) (ENNyS 2, 2019). However, this high calorie consumption that promotes the excess weight does not imply that they eat the daily intake of at least five servings of fruit or vegetables, something that is only followed by 5 percent of the adult population (ENNyS2, 2019). Nutritionism does not question why the traditional sources of nutrients disappeared. In the Argentinean case of the 21st century, the main nutritional deficiencies marked are calcium, vitamins A and C, iron and Omega-3 fatty acids (Britos et al., 2015: 6). The main change consists of replacing fresh food with processed food, including replacing beef with hamburger and processed cold cuts. 'Meatification' in the neoliberal diet has distinctive features in the Argentinean case, which manifests as higher BMI levels since more fats are consumed.

Nutritionism is part of productionism where food security is pursued through an increase in production (Fouilleux et al., 2017). Corporate agribusiness obtains a surplus in production; however, hunger increases. Soy monoculture in Argentina constitutes a clear example of these changes. Not even beef consumption manages to remain steady since the focus is placed on soy production, which is used to feed livestock in other parts of the world. Even though the kcal available in the country remains the same, the macronutrient composition is changed to cheaper foods that contain a lot of fat and carbohydrates. It is this energy-dense diet that leads to a very high BMI.

The BMI is often used to measure overweight and obesity in humans, i.e., the result of dividing the weight in kilos by the height in square meters. It is an indicator that does not require complex tools and it is presented as a universal measure. Nevertheless, the BMI cannot distinguish between muscle and fat. It is a tool developed at the end of the 19th century and then popularised by the Metropolitan Life Insurance Company in the 1940s to calculate life insurance rates

(Guthman, 2011). BMI is part of biopower because it measures overweight and obesity in the human body without questioning the food supply. It also reveals a tendency over time for individuals who are overweight (BMI ≥ 25 y ≤ 30) to become obese (BMI ≥ 30) if they continue to consume the same diet. It also allows us to recognise the impact of the nutritional inequalities in the diet. In the Argentinean case, when this classification is split by educational levels, it is possible to identify the impact of nutritional inequality and the excessive consumption of calories as the levels of education lessen (see Figure 8.4).

This tendency is explained, for example in the sense that 58 percent of the women's diet during the reproductive ages (between 10- and 49-years old) of poor households is formed by carbohydrates compared to 50 percent of those who are not poor. Carbohydrate quality is the main indicator of inequalities in the Argentinean diet (ENNyS, 2007). The carbohydrates in cheaper food give a feeling of satiation at a lower cost and promote an excessive consumption because they are digested quickly due to their low content of dietary fibre. The high calorie density of this food creates undernourishment, but the individuals who eat it gain weight fast and they also have high BMI. Malnutrition is a new way of hunger even in countries with high consumption of meat that assures high-quality proteins. The problem itself is not how much food is being produced but what is being

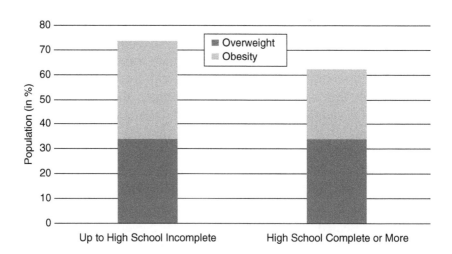

Figure 8.4   Overweight and obesity according to educational level (in %)
Source: ENNyS 2 data.

produced. The Argentinean case reveals that the consequences of Otero's neoliberal diet are even harder to solve. A change in the food supply is not sufficient unless that neoliberal logic of personal responsibility with scarce capacity of change is also transformed. Access to nutrients should come from the relationship between producers and consumers, not as a from the biofortification of corporate agribusiness. This is the main challenge to the Anthropocene diet.

Conclusions

In the Anthropocene humans are dominating drivers of change, especially changes in the human diet. Biopower gains the capacity of 'making live', which goes beyond Foucault's original proposal. Biopower now impacts on human, animal and environmental health. Transformations are so broad that they foster risk, in the sense understood by Ulrich Beck. Risk appears as a limit to biopower because changes in the diet are also changes in the environment. The human body, similar to what happens in the bodies of the animals that feed us, suffers important changes as a result of eating this food. It is also an indicator of profound changes in the way to understand the diet not only at a business scale, but also from the perspective of the individual consumer. The Anthropocene is marked by sociocultural changes that transform the way we understand and interpret the world, and ourselves as social actors. Biopower in the 21st century are radical transformations because 'making live' because it affects/ non-human actors. The risk multiplies the greater capacity to produce changes. The agri-food system is a good example of this link between risk and biopower.

The neoliberal diet creates homogenised food consumptions patterns, even in food-producing countries like Argentina. Corporate agribusiness manages to remain stable even against food sovereignty challenges; the increasing consumption of vegetable oils is a clear example of this. Argentina owns a daily supply of kcal per capita higher than the global average and it does not need to import food. However, the North-South relationship shows a quality degradation of carbohydrates in the Argentinean diet since not all the population can have access to fresh food. Processed food reduces in cost, while the supply of healthy food declines and becomes more expensive. In this way corporate agribusiness encourages unequal access to nutrients in

energy-dense diets. Neoliberal policies turn diet into a personal matter, although the food supply is more and more determined by agribusiness from production to consumption. This results in a more
nutritionally unequal society where energy-dense calories can be
bought at a low-cost. Ultra-processed food increases social inequalities. Argentina produces vegetable oils at the same time it stops
producing fresh food for its population. The neoliberal diet in
Argentina is more complex than in any other country because it is a
problem of social bonds, not production or distribution. The country
had less presence of hunger with lower crop yields. There is a change
in the social relationships between producers and consumers that
explains the changes in the diet. Nutritional inequality is part of the
commoditisation of food; social identity and health of the consumer
appear to be forgotten.

The social relationship between 'the farm and the table became
dark and was disguised' (Belasco, 2008: 15) when large-scale monoculture and supermarkets became the accepted way to feed a mass
society in the 21st century. In the Argentinean case, the productivity
of agribusiness does not take into account the domestic market; record
crop production occurs alongside increased food insecurity for large
sectors of the population. Neither state aid nor conditioned transfers
of incomes (Tarjeta Alimentar, Asignación Universal por Hijo)
manage to provide food security in times of crisis and pandemic. The
challenge to a sustainable diet is to promote social inclusion in the
Global South, but the corporate agribusiness overproduction of low
nutritional quality commodities restricts this goal (Loconto, 2021). It
is necessary to rethink the neoliberal diet because it is a key driver of
social inequalities in the Anthropocene.

References

Aguirre, P. (2004) *Ricos flacos y pobres gordos. La alimentación en crisis.* Buenos
    Aires: Claves para Todos-Capital Intelectual.
Almas, R. (1999) 'Food trust, ethics and safety in Risk Society'. *Sociological Research
    Online*, 4(3): 275–81. (http://www.socresonline.org.uk/4/3/almas.html)
Arias-Maldonado, M. (2016) 'The Anthropocenic turn: Theorizing sustainability in a
    postnatural age'. *Sustainability*, 8(1): 10. (https://doi.org/10.3390/su8010010)
Barnosky, A.D. (2013) 'Palaeontological evidence for defining the Anthropocene'.
    Geological Society, London, Special Publications, 395(1): 149–65. (https://doi.org/
    10.1144/SP395.6)

Barsky, O. and Gelman, J. (2012) *Historia del agro argentino. Desde la conquista hasta comienzos del siglo XXI*. Buenos Aires: Sudamericana.

Beck, U., Giddens, A. and Lash, S. (1994) *Reflexive Modernization*. Cambridge: Polity Press.

Beck, U. (1998) *La sociedad del riesgo. Hacia una nueva modernidad*. Barcelona: Ediciones Paidós Ibérica.

Beck, U. (2002) *La sociedad del riesgo global*. Madrid: Siglo XXI.

Belasco, W. (2008) *Food: The Key Concepts*. Oxford and New York, NY: Berg Publishers.

Blacha, L. (2019) 'La retroalimentación del agronegocio. Dieta, poder y cambio climático en el agro pampeano (1960–2008)'. *Revista Estudios. Revista del Centro de Estudios Avanzados*, 41: 109–28. (https://doi.org/10.31050/1852.1568.n41.23435)

Britos, S., Chichizola, N., Feeney, R., Mac Clay, P. and Villela, F. (2015) *Comer saludable y exportar seguridad alimentaria al mundo. Aportes para una Política Nacional de Seguridad Alimentaria y Nutricional. Documento de Proyecto*. Buenos Aires: Universidad Austral-CEPEA.

Carolan, M. (2014) *Cheaponomics. The High Cost of Low Prices*. New York, NY: Routledge.

Cassidy, E.S., West, P.C., Gerber, J.S. and Foley, J.A. (2013) 'Redefining agricultural yields: From tonnes to people nourished per hectare'. *Environmental Research Letters*, 8(3). (https://doi.org/10.1088/1748-9326/8/3/034015)

CICCRA (2020) *Informe económico mensual. Buenos Aires, cámara de la industria y comercio de carnes y derivados de la República Argentina*. Documento N° 239-Diciembre.

Chiodo, L. (2010) *Hipermercados en América Latina: historia del comercio de alimentos, de los autoservicios hasta el imperio de cinco cadenas multinacionales*. Buenos Aires: Antropofagia.

Crutzen, P.J. (2002) 'Geology of mankind'. *Nature*, 415(23). (https://doi.org/10.1038/415023a)

Diaz, D., Goldberg, A. and Fernandez, R. (2017) *Dimensiones sobre la Seguridad Alimentaria en el Nuevo escenario global: ¿el mito del plato vacío? Evolución de la disponibilidad de alimentos per cápita en Argentina y en el mundo entre 1963 y 2013*. Buenos Aires: Instituto de Estudios Sociales, CICPES.

Dirección de Estimaciones Agrícolas (2020) *Ministerio de Agricultura, Ganadería y Pesca*.

Douglas, M. (2003 [1976]) *Food in the Social Order. Studies of Food and Festivities in Three American Communities. Mary Douglas Collected Works*, Volume IX. London and New York, NY: Routledge – Taylor & Francis Group.

Encuesta Nacional de Gastos de Hogares (ENGHo) (2019) *ENGHo 2017–2018. Informe de gastos*. INDEC.

Encuesta Nacional de Nutrición y Salud (ENNyS) (2007) *Ministerio de Salud: Documento de Resultados*.

Encuesta Nacional de Nutrición y Salud 2 (ENNyS 2) (2019) *Ministerio de Salud y Desarrollo Social. Presidencia de la Nación. Secretaría de Gobierno de salud*. Indicadores Priorizados.

Fischler, C. (1995) *El (h)omnívoro. El gusto, la cocina y el cuerpo.* Barcelona: Editorial Anagrama.

Forrester, K. and Smith, S. (eds) (2018) *Nature, Action, and the Future: Political Thought and the Environment.* Cambridge: Cambridge University Press.

Foucault, M. (1999) *Historia de la sexualidad. 1- la voluntad de saber.* México: Siglo XXI.

Foucault, M. (2007) *Seguridad, territorio, población: curso en el Collage de France: 1977–1978.* Buenos Aires: Siglo XXI.

Foucault, M. (2012) *Nacimiento de la biopolítica. Curso en el Collage de France (1978–1979).* Buenos Aires: FCE.

Fouilleux, E., Bricas, N. and Alpha, A. (2017) 'Feeding 9 billion people': Global food security debates and the productionist trap'. *Journal of European Public Policy*, 24(11): 1658–77. (https://doi.org/10.1080/13501763.2017.1334084)

Galicia, L., López de Romaña. D., Harding, K.B., De-Regil, L.M. and Grajeda, R. (2016) 'Tackling malnutrition in Latin America and the Caribbean: Challenges and opportunities'. *Revista Panamericana de Salud Publica*, 40(2): 138–46.

Graciano Da Silva, J. (1994) 'Complejos agroindustriales y otros complejos'. *Agricultura y Sociedad*, 72: 205–40.

Grain (2013) 'La república unida de la soja recargada'. (http://www.grain.org/es/article/entries/4739-la-republica-unida-de-la-soja-recargada)

Guthman, J. (2011) *Weighing in. Obesity, Food Justice, and the Limits of Capitalism.* Berkeley: University of California Press.

Hamilton, C. (2017) *Defiant Earth: The Fate of Humans in the Anthropocene.* Cambridge: Polity Press.

Hawkes, C. (2006) 'Uneven dietary development: Linking the policies and processes of globalization with the nutrition transition, obesity and diet-related chronic diseases'. *Globalization and Health*, 2:4. (https//:doi.org/10.1186/1744-8603-2-4)

Holt-Giménez, E. (2017) *El capitalismo también entra por la boca: comprendamos la economía política de nuestra comida.* New York, NY: Monthly Review Press-Food First Books.

INDEC (2019) *Cuarta Encuesta Nacional de Factores de Riesgo. Principales resultados.* CABA

INDEC (2020) *Indicadores de pobreza y empleo.* Disponibles en. (https://www.indec.gob.ar/indec/web/Nivel3-Tema-4-46)

Latour, B. (2017) *Facing Gaia: Eight Lectures on the New Climatic Regime.* Cambridge: Polity Press.

Latour, B. (2018) *Down to Earth: Politics in the New Climatic Regime.* Cambridge: Polity Press.

Lindeberg, S. (2010) *Food and Western Disease. Health and Nutrition from an Evolutionary Perspective.* Chichester: John Wiley and Sons.

Loconto, A.M. (2021) 'Innovating locally for global transformation: Intermediating fluid, agroecological solutions. Examples from France, USA, Benin, and South America'. In K. Cordula, I. Antoni-Komar and C. Sage (eds), *Food System Transformations: Social Movements, Local Economies, Collaborative Networks.* London: Routledge, pp. 100–18.

Mann, G., and Wainwright, J. (2018) *Climate Leviathan: A Political Theory of Our Planetary Future*. London: Verso.

Manzanal, M. (2017) 'Territorio, poder y sojización en el Cono Sur latinoamericano. El caso Argentino'. *Mundo Agrario*, 18(37): 1–26. https://doi.org/10.24215/15155994e048

Moss, M. (2021) *Hooked. Food, Free Will and How the Food Giants Exploit Our Addictions*. New York, NY: Random House.

Murmis, M., and Murmis, M.R. (2012) 'El caso de Argentina'. In F. Soto Baquero and S. Gómez (eds), *Dinámicas del mercado de la tierra en América Latina y el Caribe: Concentración y extranjerización*. Santiago de Chile: Organización de las Naciones Unidas para la Alimentación y la Agricultura, pp. 15–57.

Nally, D. (2011) 'The biopolitics of food provisioning'. *Transactions of the Institute of British Geographers*, 36(1): 37–53.

Ordoñez, H.A. (2009) *La nueva economía y negocios agroalimentarios*. Buenos Aires: Editorial Facultad de Agronomía.

Otero, G. (2018) *The Neoliberal Diet: Healthy Profits, Unhealthy People*. Austin: University of Texas Press. (https://doi.org/10.7560/316979)

Oyhenart, E.E., Torres, M.F., Luis, M.A., Luna, M.E., Castro, L.E., Garraza, M., Navazo, B., Fucini, M.C., Quintero, F.A. and Cesani. M.F. (2018) 'Estudio comparativo del estado nutricional de niños y niñas residentes en cuatro partidos de la provincia de Buenos Aires (Argentina), en el marco de la transición nutricional'. *Salud Colectiva*, 14(3): 597–606. (https//:doi.org/10.18294/sc.2018.1576)

Pascale, C.M. (2017) 'Vernacular epistemologies of risk: The crisis in Fukushima'. *Current Sociology*, 65(1): 3–20. (https://doi.org/10.1177/0011392115627284)

Popkin, B., Corvalan, C. and Grummer-Strawn, L. (2019) 'Dynamics of the double burden of malnutrition and the changing nutrition reality'. *The Lancet*, 395(10217): 65–74. (https://doi.org/10.1016/S0140-6736(19)32497-3)

Purdy, J. (2015) *After Nature: A Politics for the Anthropocene*. Cambridge: Harvard University Press.

Rasborg, K. (2018) 'From 'the Bads of Goods' to 'the Goods of Bads': The most recent developments in Ulrich Beck's cosmopolitan sociology'. *Theory, Culture & Society*, 35(7–8): 1–16. (https://doi.org10.1177/0263276418810418)

Reca, L.G. (2010) 'Una agricultura renovada: La producción de cereales y oleaginosas'. In Reca, L.G., Lema, D. and Flood, C. (eds), *El crecimiento de la agricultura argentina. Medio siglo de logros y desafíos*. Buenos Aires: Universidad de Buenos Aires, pp. 1–26.

Ruby, M.B., Alvarenga, M.S., Rozin, P., Kirby, T.A., Richer, E. and Rutsztein, G. (2015) 'Attitudes toward beef and vegetarians in Argentina, Brazil, France, and the USA'. *Appetite* 1(96): 546–54. (https//:doi.org/10.1016/j.appet.2015.10.018)

Salvatore R.D. (2020) 'Stunting rates in a food-rich country: The Argentine Pampas from the 1850s to the 1950s'. *International Journal of Environmental Research and Public Health,* 17(21): 7806. (https//:doi.org/10.3390/ijerph17217806)

Salvia, A., Britos, S. and Díaz-Bonilla, E. (eds) (2020) *Reflexiones sobre las políticas alimentario-nutricionales de la Argentina, antes y durante la pandemia del COVID*. Buenos Aires: ODSA-CEPEA, IFPRI.

Scheinkerman de Obschatko, E. (2010) 'Desarrollo, estructura y posibilidades de la industria de alimentos y bebidas'. In L.G. Reca, D. Lema and C. Flood (eds), *El crecimiento de la agricultura argentina. Medio siglo de logros y desafíos*. Buenos Aires: Universidad de Buenos Aires.

Scrinis, G. (2013) *Nutritionism: The Science and Politics of Dietary Advice*. New York, NY: Columbia University Press.

Shugart, H.A. (2015) 'Food fixations. Reconfiguring class in Contemporary US food discourse'. *Food, Culture and Society* 17(2): 261–81. (https://doi.org/10.2752/175174414X13871910531665)

Vilella, F. and Senesi, S. (2009) 'Prólogo'. In H.A. Ordoñez (ed), *La nueva economía y negocios agroalimentarios*. Buenos Aires: Editorial Facultad de Agronomía.

Vértiz, P. (2015) 'El avance de los agronegocios en regiones marginales del agro pampeano: Concentración de la producción y tensiones entre las fracciones del capital agrario'. *Mundo Agrario*, 16(33): 1–31. (http://www.mundoagrario.unlp.edu.ar/article/view/MAv16n33a05)

Warde, A. (2016) *The Practice of Eating*. Cambridge: Polity Press.

Waters, C.N., Zalasiewicz, J.A., Williams, M., Ellis, M.A. and Snelling, A.M. (2014) 'A stratigraphical basis for the Anthropocene?' *Geological Society, London, Special Publications*, 395(1): 1–21. (http://doi.org/10.1144/SP395.18)

Willett, W. et al (2019) 'Food in the Anthropocene: The EAT–Lancet Commission on healthy diets from sustainable food systems'. *The Lancet*, 393(10170): 447–92. (https://doi.org/10.1016/S0140-6736(18)31788-4)

Winson, A. (2013) *Industrial Diet: The Degradation of Food and the Struggle for Healthy Eating*. Vancouver: UBC Press.

Zapata, M.E., Rovirosa, A. and Carmuega, E. (2016) *La mesa Argentina en las últimas dos décadas: cambios en el patrón de consumo de alimentos y nutrientes (1996–2013)*. CABA: CESNI.

9

Farmers, Autonomy and Biodiesel: What Can We Expect From Brazil's Experiment With Biodiesel for Rural Development Policy?

Sarina Kilham

Introduction

Biofuels have been centre to much of the public debate and controversy about the sustainability of globalised agrifood systems and the balance between food-fuel-fibre production. The promotion of first-generation biofuel production in the Global South was a technological solution to peak fossil fuels that privileged specific Western scientific knowledges about productivity, profit and the need for state intervention in farmer livelihoods. In Brazil, farmer-knowledges were excluded in the development and implementation of the National Biodiesel Production and Use Policy (PNPB). Despite its surface-level focus on social and environmental sustainability, the PNPB adhered to a discourse about rural modernisation and industrial agriculture. This paternalistic state-driven model conceptualises social inclusion and rural development as essentially social welfare policies for the rural poor (specifically farmers and agricultural laborers) and primarily about the provision of public goods as externalities that result from agricultural production, and thus is a state responsibility (Van Der Ploeg et al., 2012).

As with the central tenet of rural modernization theories, family farmers were conceptualized as needing government intervention to provide direction to their livelihoods and in need of state support to move away from the peasantry towards the role of the proletariat; prioritizing income generating activities, market-focused agricultural production, and increasingly linked into globalised agrifood networks (Woods, 2014). The PNPB failed to consider the autonomy of farmers as full citizens and lacked epistemic justice – that is, the right to know and the right to be recognized as a knowledgeable person (Fricker, 2007). This motivates us to ask: what types of conceptual understandings and knowledges might support novel ways of theorizing about farmers in agrifood transitions? One path is to recenter our focus on family farmers themselves and widen the analytical lens to see farmers as actors with autonomy and ways of knowing that contribute to agrifood transitions and policy. In this chapter, I draw on a body of literature applying the philosophical concept of autonomy to rural livelihoods and use concepts of autonomy and epistemic injustice to interpret how family farmers constructed their livelihoods in resistance to exogenous forces of the PNPB.

This chapter is organized as follows, the first section addresses the PNPB and the social inclusion tenets of the policy. I touch briefly on the role of different state actors and their positions concerning rural development and social inclusion policies. The second section proposes autonomy of smallholder farmers and epistemic injustice as key to successful agrifood transitions.

Methods

This chapter is based on qualitative social research undertaken between 2009 and 2017 on biofuel production in Brazil and Timor-Leste. This chapter specifically draws on interviews with 18 smallholder farmers and three rural extension workers in the northeast State of Bahia, Brazil in 2010. The inclusion criteria were broadly defined as smallholder farmers participating, or in the past participated or chosen not to participate in the PNPB. Farmer informants were recruited via word-of-mouth and snowball sampling with a range of gender, age, landownership and crop specialization represented. The study sites were situated within two regions of Bahia, namely the central savanna (Portuguese: Caatinga) region and the coastal Atlantic forest (Portuguese: Mata Atlantica) region. These study sites were within targeted regions under the PNPB due to high indexes of poverty, high concentration of family farmers and regional production of oleaginous feedstock.

Overview of the PNPB

Brazil is a global pioneer in the development and transition towards biofuels as a non-petroleum energy source. Brazil has produced biofuel since the 1970s through the National Fuel Alcohol Programme (Portuguese: Programa Nacional do Álcool – referred to as Proálcool) that was widely considered to be successful in terms of stimulating the Brazilian sugarcane industry and reducing Brazil's dependency on oil exports (Lehtonen, 2009; Manzi, 2013; Pousa et al., 2007). Until 2006, Brazil was both the leading global producer and consumer of biofuels (Johnson and Silveira, 2014; Pousa et al., 2007), and in 2005 Brazil launched the National Biodiesel Production and Use Policy (Portuguese: Programa Nacional de Produção e uso do Biodiesel; PNPB) that had the explicit aim of increasing social inclusion for family farmers located in the north and northeast of the country. The Brazilian National Biodiesel Production and Use Policy (PNPB) was established through Law No. 11.097 in 2005 and prescribed gradual increases in national fuel mixes in order to incorporate locally smallholder, farmer-grown biodiesel feedstock – stimulated through federal government incentives, finance and technology (Colares, 2008). The PNPB was explicitly designed to support smallholder family farmers through rural development and social inclusion outcomes while maintaining core elements of productivist agriculture. In 2011, a peak of over 100,000 family farmers were participating in the PNPB and yet by 2015, this number had dropped to less than half with only 45,000 participants remaining. The demise of the PNPB was rapid – the Brazilian state largely turned away from the biodiesel experiment and the social inclusion goals of the PNPB and by 2018 quietly started the process of the divestment from biodiesel processing and production. Family farmers themselves were opting out, co-opting the resources from the programme and resisting involvement.

The PNPB was promoted as essentially different from Proálcool with policy measures designed to mitigate the negative public perceptions and outcomes of the Proálcool bioethanol programme, notably that Proálcool benefited agro-industry in the southern Brazilian states (Granco et al., 2015), and contributed to the further marginalization of smallholder farmers and ongoing poverty of regions in the north, northeast and central Brazil. The government attempted to differentiate the PNPB through a focus on social inclusion benefits for family farmers, positive environmental outcomes through the promotion of small-scale local crops and an emphasis on regional development (Leite et al., 2014b; Marcossi and Moreno-Pérez, 2017; Ministério do Desenvolvimento Indústria e Comércio Exterior, 2006; Secretaria Da Agricultura Familiar/Ministério do Desenvolvimento Agrário, 2010).

Brazil has strongly promoted its biofuel policies – both bioethanol and biodiesel – as a suitable model for other nations in the Global South. Brazil positioned itself as a knowledge broker in the international discourse on biofuels and a leader in biofuel investment and trade through direct South-South development cooperation (Dauvergne and Neville, 2009). The government-led nature of the Brazilian biofuel policies was identified as key to supporting their fledgling biofuel market while simultaneously investing in research, development and infrastructure (Hira and De Oliveira, 2009). Specifically, the PNPB can be considered a structured market demand that connects smallholder farmers to large, predictable corporate procurement. The government essentially facilitates trade relations, ensures demand via legislation and provides incentives for both smallholder and corporate participation. This model of structured market demand is considered to be a socially efficient way to support rural development and has been relatively successful in other Brazilian National Programs such as the National School Feeding Programme (Portuguese: Programa Nacional de Alimentação Escolar; PNAE) and the Food Procurement Programme (Portuguese: Programa de Aquisição de Alimentos; PAA) (Blesh and Wittman, 2015; Rocha, 2009).

The PNPB Political Narrative

The PNPB was conceptualized and developed into a national policy under the Presidential leadership of Luiz Inacio Lula da Silva (commonly referred to as 'President Lula' or simply 'Lula') – an ex-union leader elected largely on a social welfare platform. Lula's policies were seen to provide macroeconomic stability, increased purchasing power for the middle class and strategic poverty reduction through socioeconomic programmes. A part of his administration's political strategy was to meet internal fuel needs, in part through investment in biofuels (Brands, 2011). The PNPB was a cornerstone policy because it essentially was able to encapture a number of key actors (both state and civil society), meet certain internal and foreign policy objectives and align with the political discourse of Lula's administration (Costa, 2019).

As a federal government multi-ministerial policy, the PNPB attempted to fulfil multiple objectives of the different ministries and other stakeholders *at the same time.* The National Agency for

Petroleum, Natural Gas and Biofuels (Portuguese: Agência Nacional do Petróleo, Gás Natural e Biocombustíveis; ANP) was responsible for organizing the national biodiesel auctions, price regulation and determining quality fuel standards (Azevedo and Müller Pereira, 2013), whereas the Ministry for Agrarian Development (Portuguese: Ministério do Desenvolvimento Agrário; MDA) supplied and monitored the Social Fuel Stamp (Da Silva Júnior et al., 2014). There were significant underlying ideological differences between the different Ministries – most notably between the Ministry of Agrarian Development, formed to support smallholder farmers, and the Ministry of Agriculture, primarily servicing corporate, export-oriented agribusiness (Niederle and Junior, 2021).

Beyond the challenge of meeting the multiple objectives of different ministries, the PNPB attempted to bring together transnational corporations (i.e., biodiesel refinery companies) and social agrarian movements (e.g., The Landless Peasants Movement) – actors who have traditionally been antagonistic and whose philosophies and aims for rural development would seem at odds (Manzi, 2013). The interests of agribusiness quickly superseded the basic environmental, economic and social focus of the PNPB. Notably, the agro-industries successfully advocated for the introduction of mandatory minimum blends, which effectively displaced the social inclusion goals, as large, commercial volumes of feedstock were required to meet the minimum quotas and realistically this could only be provided by agribusiness, rather than scattered, small-scale local producers (Azevedo and Müller Pereira, 2013; Stattman et al., 2013). Family farmers were effectively squeezed out of the policy arena (Mourad and Zylbersztajn, 2012).

Several studies have found that the PNPB has effectively managed to work against its own goals; that is, the more developed regions and agro-industrial firms have benefited the most (Borba and Dias Paes Ferreira, 2019; Conejero et al., 2017; Da Silva Júnior et al., 2014; Da Silva César et al., 2019; Exterckoter et al., 2015; Leite et al., 2014b, 2015; Marcossi and Moreno-Pérez, 2017; Moreno-Pérez et al., 2017; Ribeiro and Dias, 2016; Selfa et al., 2015; Silva et al., 2014b; Vieira, 2015). Indeed, as Selbmann and Ide (2015) note, part of the problem with the PNPB was the idea of a government agricultural value chain programme to overcome social exclusion of family farmers, which could be argued, was primarily caused by the government pursuing international export markets and market-dependent value chains in the first place.

The challenges to meeting the social inclusion and regional development goals of the PNPB in Bahia have been widely acknowledged even by government representatives such as the Secretary for Rural Development in Bahia, Jerônimo Rodrigues:

> In these 10 years of the programme there has been an agreeable partnership between governments, businesses and workers. At this time, the country has matured enough, however we still have some bottlenecks and we still need to pay attention to issues such as land reform, access to land, secure tenure, technical assistance as an element that ensures productivity, increase production, relationship with the environment. (Luiz, 2015: para 2)

During the PNPB's tenure from 2005 to 2011,[1] the policy can clearly be tied to global, political, institutional and fiscal shifts in power and competing political priorities. Notably, internal Brazilian political upheavals during this time included the end of the Lula's presidency in 2010, the impeachment of his protégé President Dilma Rousseff in 2015 and the election of social conservation Jair Bolsonaro in 2018 (Calmon, 2022). These political shifts influenced the scope, focus and implementation of the PNPB. However, this chapter is primarily focused on understanding how a social inclusion paradigm became central to the PNPB and the problems experienced with social inclusion framing by the farmers themselves. Examining the social inclusion rhetoric is important in addressing our understanding of agricultural policies for social inclusion and moves us towards alternative interpretations. I propose that autonomy and epistemic injustice offer an alternate framework for interpreting farmers' actions and decisions vis-à-vis the PNPB.

Social Inclusion Theory

The terms social inclusion and social exclusion emerged in Europe in the latter part of the 20th century in social policy debates that defined poverty as multifaceted and social disadvantage linked to the denial of citizen rights – particularly participation in social, political and economic aspects of society (Shortall, 2008; Wilson, 2006). Social exclusion

---

[1]Noting a policy gap between 2011 and 2017.

referred to poverty in relative rather than absolute terms. It explicitly linked poverty and inequality and it emphasised power and participation: 'Social exclusion... refers not only to the distribution of income and assets (as does poverty analysis) but also to social deprivation and lack of voice and power in society...' (Buvinic, 2004: 5). However, the term social inclusion was co-opted and used in a way that Veit-Wilson (1998) identifies as weak social inclusion – centred on the notion of the excluded as requiring integration into the dominant society. Weak social inclusion obscures inequalities and conflict and fails to consider the historical and social context in which actors are embedded. In comparison, strong social inclusion addresses issues such as who has the power to decide, who is excluded and how the excluded are imagined (Levitas, 1998; Veit-Wilson, 1998). For instance, Veit-Wilson emphasises the centrality of access to power as part of social inclusion:

> The question of power to choose one method of combating poverty and deprivation as against others must be faced openly. Whose definition of the problem is it? ... Are the costs and benefits to them consistent with their own social value system and respectful towards their modes of life and conception of human dignity? (1998: 18)

These theoretical arguments provide an important background to understanding the ways that the terminology of social inclusion has been used within the PNPB. As I demonstrate in this chapter, PNPB's social sustainability goals use the language of social inclusion. While the two terms are not commensurate – the PNPB treats them as such, and in doing so avoids the difficulty of defining either social sustainability or social inclusion.

PNPB and Social Inclusion Discourse

Social inclusion for family farmers was a central ideological tenet of the PNPB – initially incentivised through the use of a policy mechanism titled the Social Fuel Stamp (Portuguese: Selo Combustível Social)[2] that obligated refineries to purchase a percentage of their biodiesel feedstock from family farmers[3] in underdeveloped regions

---

[2]Decree No. 5297.
[3]As legally defined and registered according to the National Policy for Family Farming 11.326, 24 July 2006 (http://www.planalto.gov.br/ccivil_03/_Ato2004-2006/2006/Lei/L11326.htm).

and provide agronomic services such as technical assistance and capacity building[4] (Kilham, 2014; Manzi, 2013). In return, the Social Fuel Stamp certification allowed industry to access tax benefits, finance, subsidies and was a key eligibility criterion to participate in the government-run biodiesel auctions[5] (Silva et al., 2014a). The PNPB originally required that 80 percent of all biodiesel feedstock to come from refineries that have the Social Fuel Stamp (Leite et al., 2014b). However, the percentage was reduced when it became evident that family farmers were not able to consistently meet the demand for high volumes of feedstock. In addition, refineries were purchasing family farmer feedstock only to on-sell to it to other non-biodiesel markets and purchasing agribusiness by-products of soy, cotton and animal tallow as the primary feedstock for biodiesel production. This was due to challenges with poor transport routes between the refineries and dispersed and isolated family farms, technical constraints of the chemical composition of family farmer produced oilseeds (particularly castor bean) making them difficult to process into biodiesel (De Oliveira et al., 2019) and the high commercial value of castor oil feedstock for the established pharmaceutical industry. In this way, very little family farmer feedstock was ever processed into biodiesel, but refineries remained eligible for the Social Fuel Stamp and associated benefits.

Social Inclusion in the PNPB

At a basic level, the PNPB was designed on the idea of achieving social inclusion through the mediated inclusion of smallholder farmers in biodiesel production value chains. The PNPB worked from the premise that a change in farming conditions, such as a link to external markets and access to technological extension services, would result in increased farmer income and ipso facto result in social inclusion of

---

[4]In 2020, The National Energy Policy Council (CNPE Portuguese acronym) passes resolution 14/2020 which replaced public government-controlled auctions with a privatised marketing model and changed the provisions of the Social Fuel Stamp. Due to the significant change in policy direction, this chapter deals only with the policy prior to 2020.

[5]The public auctions were the only channel in Brazil for biodiesel producers to sell to distributors.

smallholder farmers and social sustainability for underdeveloped rural communities (Schaffel et al., 2012).

Early critique (prior to 2009) of the PNPB social inclusion goals focused on the implementation limitations rather than questioning whether social inclusion was an appropriate way to conceptualise rural development and social sustainability for smallholder farms and farmers. This focus reinforced the rhetoric that smallholder farmers are socially excluded because they are materially poor due to lack of integration in commercial and export markets, rather than due to structural power imbalances. In addition, this critique worked from the basis that if implementation and additional enforcement of the policy could be realised, that the social inclusion goals would be met (Geraldes Castanheira et al., 2014). This is a weak social inclusion approach that ignores the social and historical structural power imbalances in Brazil vis-à-vis rural communities and urban elites and positions the state as powerful, knowledgeable and in a patriarchal association with smallholder farmers who are framed as weak and ignorant of their own needs.

In northeast Brazil the implementation limitations to achieving social inclusion in the PNPB can largely be grouped into two main topics. The first is locational and logistical barriers such as dispersed locations of smallholder farms, poor infrastructure for transporting feedstock and difficultly in achieving production at scale (César and Batalha, 2013; Leite et al., 2014a). The second theme is that of framing smallholder farmers as a moral and cultural underclass that is either unwilling, uneducated or unable to meet their obligations and defined role in the PNPB – for example, by dishonouring multi-year production contracts or ignoring agricultural extension advice (Santos and Rathmann, 2009; Stattman and Mol, 2014; Xavier and Vianna, 2009).

State Coercion and Participation

While authors such as Rathmann and Padula (2011) argued that smallholder farmers and cooperative managers were participating in the PNPB due to their ignorance about the limited economic viability of the programme, more recent research noted that there is a level of state coercion to participation – both through informal and formal mechanisms. Informally, research conducted in agrarian reform settlements (Portuguese: assentamentos) (Ribeiro and Dias,

2016) emphasises the informal state control of physical and economic productive space[6] in these settings that results in an unspoken but strong social and political obligation on behalf of smallholder farmers to participate in the PNPB. The PNPB acts as more than just an economic activity, and this is considered a key factor of the success of the state's agrarian reform settlements and the fulfilment of the state policy goals. These coercive mechanisms operate throughout multiple facets. In Ribeiro and Dias' work the state had mandated the growing of transgenic soybean for biodiesel feedstock and state coercion extended to epistemic choices at macro and micro levels on the farms '(...) In the case that a family has favorable conditions for soybean cultivation and they do not [cultivate it], they are looked upon negatively, for not having adhered to the program. It disregards, therefore, the freedom of choice to participate or not in that particular program (...)' (2016: 18).

This lack of autonomy had flow-on effects – the use of transgenic soybean required the purchasing of external (off-farm) fertilisers, pesticides and herbicides and pushed farmers towards whole farm agronomic packages.

Formally, the Social Fuel Seal acted as an official coercive mechanism such that biodiesel refineries and biodiesel cooperatives had to accept the government pressures in order to gain access to benefits (Barros Ribeiro et al., 2018). Prior to 2020, biodiesel refineries that were not SFS-certified were effectively prevented from operating due to (a) the unviable restrictions on the volume of biodiesel they would be allowed to sell and (b) limited access to the public biodiesel auctions (Barros Ribeiro et al., 2018). This coercive mechanism meant that the relationship between the biodiesel plants and family farmers was primarily to fulfil commercial and business needs of the biodiesel refineries themselves, within the structure of the PNPB and government priorities, and effectively excluded family farmer autonomy, knowledge and agency.

Several authors have questioned the notion that smallholder farmers can be socially included through a government-led, export-oriented market mechanism. Indeed, their counter arguments include that a focus on export markets has led to economic exclusion for rural

---

[6]The state has strict protocols about productive land use and land conservation areas on agrarian reform settlements in Brazil.

communities and family farmers that the PNPB has contributed towards social exclusion by failing to acknowledge the heterogeneity of small-holder farmers and that inclusion can occur on adverse terms (Hospes and Clancy, 2011).

Sociological Approaches and False Consciousness

By applying a sociological lens to social inclusion (Allman, 2013), we can consider that the power of the state and the agro-industrial elite are reinforced through the PNPB as it relegates smallholder farmers to a weak, powerless position within the biodiesel production chain. The assumption that integration into the biodiesel value chains will support social inclusion of smallholder farmers equates with stepping away from challenging the social norms associated with power, class and landownership in Brazil[7] and fails to consider how demographics, particularly gender, and different access to capital affects individual farmers in the PNPB. According to Stattman and Mol '… marginal subsistence farmers have been sidelined in this rural development model because they are neither members of cooperatives nor profit from the social inclusion policies of the PNPB. In that sense, social inclusion works for only a portion of small family farmers' (2014: 292).

The PNPB by default defines social exclusion and its remedy in terms that are compatible with maintaining the status quo for those in power. By labelling smallholder farmers as socially excluded, the PNPB de-values the existing networks, local markets, production chains, structures and communities that form part of smallholder farmers' existing livelihoods and capitals. The PNPB fails to recognise that smallholder farmers may be happily socially included in communities and structures that fall outside the state policy and control. Indeed, it has been proposed that real commitment to social inclusion for Brazilian smallholder farmers would be better achieved via substantial agrarian and policy reform (Holanda et al., 2011). As a rural

---

[7]The northeastern state of Brazil has a higher percentage of subsistence smallholder farmers and higher rates of poverty (Rathmann and Padula, 2011) due to complex intertwined social, economic and political dimensions of the northeast which has a significant history of slavery, fazendeiros (large-landed estates), social discord, class divisions and violent conflict between smallholder farmers and landowners (Lehtonen, 2012; Wittman, 2009; Wolford, 2005).

development model, the combination of practical implementation issues, conceptual limitations and the shift towards support for agri-business in order to meet obligatory blending quotas has meant that the PNPB has been largely unsuccessful in meeting social inclusion outcomes and is widely considered unviable (Marcossi and Moreno-Pérez, 2017; Rico and Sauer, 2015; Selfa et al., 2015). Yet, as pointed out by Manzi (2013) – the PNPB has successfully functioned as a tool of state coercion and a way to incorporate agrarian and civil social movements into a state-controlled apparatus and to depoliticise family farmers. Structurally, the PNPB reinforces gendered and racialised approaches to rural development because it effectively reproduces structural power relations that locate family farmers as socially excluded through limited access to power (Manzi, 2013).

The structural power issues inherent in state coercion in the PNPB have been further reinforced by representation of the PNPB imple-mentation challenges as a moral failing of the family farmers – particularly so when farmers exercise choice that falls outside or in contradiction to the policy objectives. This includes actions such as choosing to not to opt-in, breaking multi-year contracts and ignoring agronomic advice in preference of local knowledge and farming practices.

By presenting family farmers, particularly those from the north-east of Brazil, as passive, uneducated and unable to make good farm management choices – it frames family farmers through the lens of false consciousness and buys into the falsehood of a restricted context of choice. That is, that under other circumstances other choices would be made (Cornwall, 2003). By citing farmers' low level of education, it suggests that more educated farmers would make other, necessarily better choices and delegitimises the agency of family farmers as valid in their own right. The false consciousness is further illustrated when family farmers' risk aversion is framed as a negative obstacle to improved livelihoods and full participation in the PNPB (Finco and Doppler, 2009). This overlooks the benefits to family farmers of being risk adverse, especially in nations such as Brazil that have limited social security, and a long history of failed agricultural development programs that were poorly adapted to the region and its people. Risk-averse farmers are protecting their liveli-hoods and risk-reducing innovation has long been considered a necessary characteristic by sustainable agriculture scholars (Altieri, 2002). Non-participation, non-fulfilment of contractual arrangements and non-adherence of prescribed technical advice can be framed as resistance to dominant structures and state coercion rather than antipathy, passivity, low education or poor farming practices. This transforms the conceptual lens from seeing these actions as failures by family farmers in the PNPB, to ways that family farmers resist, rebel, break the rules and pursue their own interests without being in direct, open conflict with the state (Cornwall, 2003; Scott, 1986).

Autonomy, Epistemic Injustice and Agrifood Transitions

As noted in the introduction, one path to support novel ways of theorising about farmers in agrifood transitions is to draw upon the philosophical concepts of autonomy and epistemic injustice to interpret how family farmers constructed their livelihoods in resistance to exogenous forces of the PNPB. This next section provides some theoretical background before moving to discussing how autonomy and epistemic justice are reflected in farmers' narratives about the PNPB.

Autonomy

Autonomy in the broad philosophical sense is defined as individuals having the entitlement to self-determining authority over their lives and the capacity for self-governance informed by their own values, morals and social context (Mackenzie, 2019). Autonomy is more than individual freedom or a liberal idealised version of rationally bound individualism. Instead, feminist relational autonomy scholars have argued that autonomy is socially, bodily and interpersonally bound. In using a theory of autonomy to interpret agrifood transitions, we need to ensure that the definition of autonomy aligns with how we conceptually imagine agrifood systems. For scholars engaging with agrifood systems as complex systems shaped by historical, cultural, social, economic and political forces, overlaid with intersecting sociological concepts, relational autonomy provides a way of being actor-centred, without disregarding the sociological dimensions of an individual's life. Philosopher Catriona Mackenzie best articulates this understanding of autonomy as:

An adequate conception of autonomy must therefore be premised on a thick socio-historical conception of individual identity. It must also recognise that our motives and commitments are often not transparent to us. The self-knowledge required for self-governing agency thus requires social interaction and dialogue with others as much as it requires introspective reflective skills. Moreover, relational theories recognise that since we are emotional, embodied, feeling, as well as rational creatures, self-governing agency involves the exercise of imaginative and emotional competences, not just practical rationality. In line with the commitment to a socio-relational ontology of persons, relational theories understand self-governing agency as a complex competence, the development and exercise of which requires ongoing interpersonal, social, and institutional scaffolding. (2019: 12)

Autonomy has been applied by a number of agrarian scholars to better understand how certain rural actors make decisions and act vis-à-vis exogenous and endogenous influences. Notably, Jan Douwe van der Ploeg's (2008) peasant principle drew heavily on theories of autonomy, though his application only partly aligns with the philosophical debates about autonomy. Van der Ploeg (2008) considers autonomy to be at the centre of what constitutes peasant agricultural practices and argues that this struggle for autonomy finds expression in the creation and development of a self-governed, resource base oriented towards improving peasant livelihoods.

Since his 2008 work, several other agrarian scholars have drawn on, expanded and adapted van der Ploeg's struggle for autonomy and peasant principle concepts (Nelson and Stock, 2016; Stock and Forney, 2014). Significantly, there has been a body of work that has expanded the struggle for autonomy to not just being in resistance to hegemonic, neo-liberal forms of agricultural development, but for autonomy to be recognised as an ongoing process of flux, that can include opting in, co-opting, adapting, incorporating and resistance to exogenous forces. Mackenzie's definition of autonomy (see above) is particularly important for the application of autonomy in agrarian contexts because it recognises individuals as more than rational decision-makers, more than single-dimensional decision-makers, and it reminds us that even in our pursuit of autonomy, we are messy human-beings, '...we are emotional, embodied, feeling...' (2019: 12). In this sense, the strength of autonomy as our starting point for imagining agrifood transitions comes to the fore, because we are able to let go of the fallacy of family farmers as financially driven, rational decision-makers that are socially excluded from their wider societies and emotionally disconnected from the land and waterways that support their livelihoods. Instead, we can philosophically embrace the messiness that the pursuit of autonomy entails and to widen our analytical lens to the question of 'what's going on here' in the pursuit of autonomy.

Epistemic Injustice

Epistemic injustice as articulated by Fricker (2007) has been widely embraced, though scholarly discussions about knowledge and whose knowledge counts preceded her authoritative text. As with the influence of feminist scholarship on the philosophy of autonomy, feminist scholars have shifted epistemology discussions towards the recognition that the creation and dissemination of knowledge is socially bound (McKinnon, 2016). Epistemic injustice refers to the ways in which the credibility of both knowers and their knowledges are either ignored or not acknowledged in any given space. Epistemic injustice occurs when either the knower or their knowledges are discredited and unable to be considered part of a wider collective knowledge – for instance, a scientific Western epistemology that excludes indigenous notions of nature as kin and treats indigenous knowledges, and the knowers of these knowledges, as less important or invalid (Weißermel and Azevedo Chaves, 2020). Epistemic injustice is particularly relevant for agrarian studies because Western scientific agricultural knowledge often underlies much agricultural policy that excludes other types of agrarian knowledges and its knowers.

Lessons From the PNPB

In terms of the PNPB and family farmers in Brazil, the two concepts of epistemic injustice and autonomy provide rich analytical lenses to the family farmers' narratives and experiences. It starts from the recognition that family farmers are morally autonomous beings that have ongoing processes of negotiating for autonomy – a process that is informed by internal factors, such as identity, shifting notions of the self and experiential knowledges and worldviews (Friedman, 2003). We understand that these internal processes are informed and changed by interactions with external structural and social context, and epistemological factors such as what family farmers consider being the choices available to them. Autonomy as self-governing agency inherently relies on epistemic justice because a sense of autonomy relies on the self as a knower and with faith in our own knowledges. Farming is a public display of farmer's knowledges and is closely linked to the farmer's identity – as noted by Wahlhütter and colleagues:

> Agricultural land can be seen as a 'display of the farmer's knowledge' and value system (Rogge et al., 2007). As soil and farmland activities are very visible to other members of the community, all visible activities and features that are not indicative of 'good farming' may restrict the generation of cultural capital, damage the reputation or status of the farmer and consequently, lower their access to social capital... (2016: 41)

In this way, it is not only natural and financial capital that inform farming decisions in the context of the PNPB, but social, human and cultural capital as well.

The family farmers in Brazil were not beholden to the PNPB and used acts of resistance to manoeuvre within the scheme – specifically drawing on their own knowledges to inform how the scheme could best contribute towards their livelihood. The high value placed on experiential knowledge by the farmers themselves led to actions such as breaking contracts and disregarding technical agronomic advice – actions that have been elsewhere misinterpreted in the literature as farmers ignorance or lack of understanding the benefits of such arrangements (Santos and Rathmann, 2009; Stattman and Mol, 2014; Xavier and Vianna, 2009).

Breaking multi-year contracts occurred because of a myriad of factors including better prices from the pharmaceutical industry, social obligations to community-based brokers and the decision to diversify resources towards other agricultural opportunities. Equally, ignoring technical agronomic advice occurred for a range of reasons: farmers were often more experienced than the technical staff and therefore trusted their own agricultural knowledge more than technical staff advice; farmers didn't want to plant mono crops and used their knowledge of co-planting and local weather patterns to plant beneficial companion plants; or farmers had followed technical advice in early years of the PNPB and found it lacking.

Farmers made decisions based on their knowledge that was in conflict with the PNPB guidelines because they prioritise their experiences and knowledge above that of an externally formulated programme. These decisions are not just functional – for instance, one farmer's account about long-term, dried bean storage as a livelihood strategy was explained as both 'being prepared' and 'being a good farmer'. It gave the farmer freedom from risk, represented choice and high moral standing in the community through potential food sharing and future food security. Even when the farmer's decisions did not result in the outcomes she anticipated – for instance when a farmer's sunflower crop production failed due to an experimental planting regime – the decision was still hers. This decision-making power reinforced other aspects of the farmer's identity as flexible, innovative and learning. 'We give special weight to our own present and past decisions... because (all other things being equal) we made them' (Christman, 2015: Section 2.1 para. 5).

Farmers' own sense of identity, social inclusion and autonomy was often in conflict with state-based interpretations within the PNPB. Farmers on agrarian reform settlements reported systemic social judgement, exclusion from government-led agricultural committees and multiple instances of discrimination when trying to purchase agricultural goods and services – in part because as landless peasants they were judged to not be fulfilling the ideals of the good farmer or to be doing good farming (Burton, 2021). Farmers on agrarian reform settlements were expected to be grateful, helpless and simultaneously dangerous and untrustworthy. Their life experiences of adaptability, strong social networks, resilience and intergenerational agricultural knowledge[8] was invisible to the structures and mechanisms of the PNPB. Epistemic injustice towards the farmers as knowers and towards their knowledges rendered their autonomy equally invisible.

In contrast to the PNPB's emphasis on economic maximization as an assumed driving force of family farmers' participation and as a key determinant of social exclusion, the farmers' narratives challenge this view with a much more nuanced and complex balancing of their livelihoods. Farmers weighed the participation costs (social, personal, financial) against their sense of autonomy and internal notions of epistemic injustice. Retired farmers eligible for government pensions

---

[8]Many came from farming families that were either itinerant workers or that had been displaced from their farms.

(and therefore with a source of stable income) were not enticed by the PNPB's profit-oriented cash crops that offered little in terms of community connections or development. Instead, these farmers were involved in their local agricultural cooperatives' diversification and value-adding activities because these activities benefited themselves and others in more than financial ways. These farmers' narratives challenge the logic of privileging financial maximization and income production as livelihood drivers and align with Nelson and Stock's assertion that '(. . .) Farmer practices are influenced by their room to manoeuvre, that is, what choices they have available to them physically, materially and financially, but also epistemologically (. . .)' (2016: 8)

Given the lack of official mechanisms for bottom-up knowledge and information sharing within the PNPB, the farmers incorporated their own knowledge through alternative information channels to access, observe and share information about the PNPB contracts, feedstock and harvest prices. These alternative pathways included the use of both localized social networks, such as neighbours, personal or family contacts in government; cooperative or farming organisations; and formalized knowledge channels, such as the internet, radio or television. This use of alternative channels debunks notions of family farmers as ignorant to the workings of the PNPB when choosing to disobey the formal PNPB rules and mechanisms – rather the farmers' knowledge and sense of autonomy indicated that these were preferable legitimate decisions based on a wider source of knowledge and information sharing. The farmers' narratives about valuing their own knowledge, experience and exercising their agency in ways that contradicted the PNPB advice can be reinterpreted through the lens of autonomy and epistemic injustice as choices that make sense in the context. Farmer's decisions and livelihood strategies are based on an understanding of their livelihoods from their own perspective, rather than top-down idealistic criteria.

Conclusion

In Brazil, the 2016 dissolution and absorption of the Ministry of Agrarian Development into the industrial focused Ministry of Agriculture has purposefully excluded smallholder farmer autonomy and knowledges, and reinforced agricultural modernization as the dominant paradigm. Globally, this paradigm has brought about many of the conditions that we now observe in the Anthropocene, with agriculture and food production contributing significantly to climate change, environmental stressors and unsustainable use of the earth's resources (Fanzo et al., 2020). The agricultural modernization paradigm conceptualizes agrifood production as being driven by Western-based technoscience, technological adaptation/innovation and linear dichotomous notions of undeveloped/developed, family farmer/modern farmer and a sustenance/profitable farming model.

The PNPB examined in this chapter largely conceived of family farmers as a homogenous group that was uneducated, unknowing of their own needs and in need of state intervention in order to modernize and link to global commodity chains with a primary objective of economic maximization (César and Batalha, 2010, 2013; César et al., 2013, 2015; Rathmann and Padula, 2011; Rico and Sauer, 2015; Silva et al., 2014a;). The PNPB structure emphasized economic incentives at farm, cooperative and refinery level through the provision of state subsidies and tax concessions. The normative assumption in the PNPB is that the desirable condition of social inclusion is an urban capitalist ideal and that family farmers must inevitably be transformed capitalist farmers (Lehtonen, 2012). This is evident in the PNPB through the use of the language of social exclusion and social inclusion whereby family farmers are eo ipso defined as socially excluded from the desirable capitalist mainstream (Hospes and Clancy, 2011; Gonçalves et al., 2013)

This discourse creates epistemic injustice because it disregards family farmers as morally autonomous beings capable of acting within and simultaneously changing the socio-political-economic context in which farmers are located. As noted by Burton and Wilson – agency-related factors accompany agrarian change but are (mistakenly) rarely considered as a driving force. '. . . the farming community has often been viewed as responding almost entirely to outside forces, with little acknowledgement of possible changes from within. . .' (Burton and Wilson, 2006: 96).

Farmers in this study offered a counter discourse as a way to acknowledge the messiness, and at times internal contradictions, that occur when farmers attempt to reflect and talk about their livelihoods. Autonomy is not a static concept; livelihoods are not set in a linear fashion; decisions can be messy, complex; identities are layered and shift. The concepts of autonomy and epistemic injustice offer a nuanced response both to better understanding of family farmers' livelihoods and to how we might better design policies for agrifood transitions in the Anthropocene. Valuing farmer autonomy and building in inherent epistemic justice in biofuel and agricultural development policies involves working with multiple epistemologies and ontologies and reaffirming farmers as knowers, with knowledges that must inform agrifood transitions if we are to ensure that the Anthropocene is not the last epoch of human existence on earth.

Disclaimer

This chapter is based on earlier work published in the open-access thesis Kilham (2017). Farmers, Autonomy and Sustainable Rural Livelihoods: Biodiesel Production in Brazil and Timor-Leste. Institute for Sustainable Futures. Sydney, Australia, University of Technology Sydney. PhD in Sustainable Futures. https://opus.lib.uts.edu.au/handle/10453/116897.

Data

The data from this research is open-access on the public data archive Figshare and can be found at: https://figshare.com/projects/Biodiesel_in_Brazil/115761.

References

Allman, D. (2013) 'The sociology of social inclusion'. *SAGE Open*, 3(1). (https://doi.org/10.1177/2158244012471957)

Altieri, M.A. (2002). 'Agroecology: The science of natural resource management for poor farmers in marginal environments'. *Agriculture, Ecosystems & Environment*, 93(1–3): 1–24.

Azevedo, A.M.M.D. and Müller Pereira, N. (2013) 'Conception and execution of an energy innovation program: Top-down and bottom-up analyses of the Brazilian National Program for production and use of biodiesel'. *Journal of Technology Management and Innovation*, 8: 13–25.

Barros Ribeiro, E.C., Moreira, A.C., Ferreira, L.M.D.F. and Da Silva César, A. (2018) 'Biodiesel and social inclusion: An analysis of institutional pressures between biodiesel plants and family farmers in southern Brazil'. *Journal of Cleaner Production*, 204: 726–34.

Blesh, J. and Wittman, H. (2015) '"Brasilience": Assessing resilience in land reform settlements in the Brazilian cerrado'. *Human Ecology*, 43(4): 531–46.

Borba, M.R.M.D. and Dias Paes Ferreira, M. (2019) 'Gross income variation of castor bean and land competition in the context of the PNPB in two Brazilian states'. *Revista Economica do Nordeste*, 50: 163–81.

Brands, H. (2011) 'Evaluating Brazilian brand strategy under Lula'. *Comparative Strategy*, 30: 28–49.

Burton, R.J.F. (2021) *The Good Farmer: Culture and Identity in Food and Agriculture.* London: Routledge, Taylor & Francis Group.

Burton, R.J.F. and Wilson, G.A. (2006) 'Injecting social psychology theory into conceptualisations of agricultural agency: Towards a post-productivist farmer self-identity?' *Journal of Rural Studies*, 22(1): 95–115.

Buvinic, M. (2004) 'Introduction: Social inclusion in Latin America'. In M. Buvinic, J. Mazza and R. Deutch (eds), *Social Inclusion and Economic Development in Latin America.* Washington, DC: Inter-American Development Bank, pp. 3–32.

Calmon, D. (2022) 'Shifting frontiers: The making of Matopiba in Brazil and global redirected land use and control change'. *Journal of Peasant Studies*, 49(2): 263–87.

César, A.D.S., Almeida, F.D.A., De Souza, R.P., Silva, G.C. and Atabani, A.E. (2015) 'The prospects of using Acrocomia aculeata (macaúba) a non-edible bio-diesel feedstock in Brazil'. *Renewable and Sustainable Energy Reviews*, 49: 1213–20.

César, A.D.S. and Batalha, M.O. (2010) 'Biodiesel production from castor oil in Brazil: A difficult reality'. *Energy Policy*, 38: 4031–9.

César, A.D.S. and Batalha, M.O. (2013) 'Brazilian biodiesel: The case of the palm's social projects'. *Energy Policy*, 56: 165–74.

César, A.D.S., Batalha, M.O. and Zopelari, A.L.M.S. (2013) 'Oil palm biodiesel: Brazil's main challenges'. *Energy*, 60: 485–91.

Christman, J. (2015). *Autonomy in Moral and Political Philosophy.* The Stanford Encyclopedia of Philosophy. (http://plato.stanford.edu/entries/autonomy-moral/)

Colares, J.F. (2008) 'A brief history of Brazilian biofuels legislation'. *Syracuse Journal of International Law and Commerce*, 35: 293.

Conejero, M.A., César, A.D.S. and Batista, A.P. (2017) 'The organizational arrangement of castor bean family farmers promoted by the Brazilian biodiesel program: A competitiveness analysis'. *Energy Policy*, 110: 461–70.

Cornwall, A. (2003) 'Whose voices? Whose choices? Reflections on gender and participatory development'. *World Development*, 31: 1325–42.

Costa, J.A.M. (2019) 'From sugarcane to ethanol: The historical process that transformed Brazil into a biofuel superpower'. *Mapping Politics*, 10.

Da Silva César, A., Conejero, M.A., Barros Ribeiro, E.C. and Batalha, M.O. (2019) 'Competitiveness analysis of "social soybeans" in biodiesel production in Brazil'. *Renewable Energy*, 133: 1147–57.

Da Silva Júnior, A.G., Leite, M.a. V., Clemente, F. and Perez, R. (2014) 'Contract farming: Inclusion of small scale farmers in the Brazilian biodiesel production chain'. In *Proceedings of 6th International European Forum (Igls-Forum) on*

System Dynamics and Innovation in Food Networks. 13–17 February 2012, Igls, Austria.

Dauvergne, P. and Neville, K.J. (2009) 'The changing North–South and South–South political economy of biofuels'. *Third World Quarterly*, 30: 1087–102.

De Oliveira, F.C., Lopes, T.S.A., Parente, V., Bermann, C. and Coelho, S. (2019) 'The Brazilian social fuel stamp program: Few strikes, many bloopers and stumbles'. *Renewable and Sustainable Energy Reviews*, 102: 121–8.

Exterckoter, R., Azevedo Da Silva, C. and Pujol, A.F.T. (2015) 'Family farmers as agents of resilience in the western region of Santa Catarina (Brazil)'. *Ager Revista de Estudios sobre Despoblacion y Desarrollo Rural*, 18: 115–38.

Fanzo, J., Hood, A. and Davis, C. (2020) 'Eating our way through the Anthropocene'. *Physiology & Behavior*, 222: 112929.

Finco, M.V.A. and Doppler, W. (2009) 'Jatropha curcas and ricinus communis in Brazilian cerrado: A farming and rural systems economics approach'. *Informe GEPEC*, 13: 54–69.

Fricker, M. (2007). *Epistemic Injustice Power and the Ethics of Knowing.* Oxford: Oxford University Press.

Friedman, M. (2003) *Autonomy, Gender, Politics.* Oxford and New York, NY: Oxford University Press.

Geraldes Castanheira, É., Grisoli, R., Freire, F., Pecora, V. and Coelho, S.T. (2014) 'Environmental sustainability of biodiesel in Brazil'. *Energy Policy,* 65: 680–91.

Gonçalves, Y.K., Favareto, A. and Abramovay, R. (2013) 'Estruturas sociais no semiárido e o mercado de biodiesel'. *Caderno CRH*, 26: 347–62.

Granco, G., Caldas, M.M., Bergtold, J.S. and Sant'anna, A.C. (2015) 'Exploring the policy and social factors fueling the expansion and shift of sugarcane production in the Brazilian Cerrado'. *Geojournal*, 82(1): 63–80.

Hira, A. and De Oliveira, L.G. (2009) 'No substitute for oil? How Brazil developed its ethanol industry'. *Energy Policy*, 37: 2450–6.

Holanda, M.C., Wichmann, B.M. and Pontes, P.A. (2011) 'The viability of the biodiesel program as an instrument of social inclusion'. In E. Amann, W. Baer and D.V. Coes (eds), *Energy, Bio Fuels and Development: Comparing Brazil and the United States.* New York, NY: Routledge, pp. 285–91.

Hospes, O. and Clancy, J.S. (2011) 'Unpacking the discourse on social inclusion in value chains'. in H. AHJBHJ and S. Vellema (eds), *Value Chains, Scial Inclusion and Economic Development: Contrasting Theories and Realities.* London: Routledge, pp. 23–41.

Johnson, F.X. and Silveira, S. (2014) 'Pioneer countries in the transition to alternative transport fuels: Comparison of ethanol programmes and policies in Brazil, Malawi and Sweden'. *Environmental Innovation and Societal Transitions*, 11: 1–24.

Kilham, S. (2014) *Social Sustainability in Biodiesel Production: Brazil and Timor-Leste.* SAGE Research Methods Cases. London: SAGE.

Kilham, S. (2017). *Farmers, Autonomy and Sustainable Rural Livelihoods: Biodiesel Production in Brazil and Timor-Leste.* PhD Dissertation. University of Technology Sydney, Sydney. https://opus.lib.uts.edu.au/handle/10453/116897

Lehtonen, M. (2009) 'Social sustainability of the Brazilian bioethanol: Power relations in a centre-periphery perspective'. *Biomass and Bioenergy*, 35(6): 2425–34.

Lehtonen, M. (2012) 'Power, social impacts, and certification of ethanol fuel: View from the Northeast of Brazil'. In A. Gasparatos and P. Stromberg (eds), *Socioeconomic and Environmental Impacts of Biofuels: Evidence from Developing Nations.* New York, NY: Cambridge University Press, p. 144.

Leite, J.G.D.B., Bijman, J., Van Ittersum, M.K. and Slingerland, M. (2014a). 'Producer organizations, family farms and market connection: Lessons for emerging biodiesel supply chains in Brazil'. *Outlook on Agriculture*, 43: 101–8.

Leite, J.G.D.B., Silva, J.V. and Van Ittersum, M.K. (2014b). 'Integrated assessment of biodiesel policies aimed at family farms in Brazil'. *Agricultural Systems*, 131: 64–76.

Leite, J.G.D.B., Justino, F.B., Silva, J.V., Florin, M.J. and Van Ittersum, M.K. (2015). Socioeconomic and environmental assessment of biodiesel crops on family farming systems in Brazil. *Agricultural Systems*, 133: 22–34.

Levitas, R. (1998) *Social Exclusion in the New Breadline Britain Survey. Perceptions of Poverty and Social Exclusion.* Bristol: Townsend Centre for International Poverty Research, University of Bristol.

Luiz, A. (2015) *Producao e uso do biodiesel e tema de evento regional, na Bahia.* Sobradinho Noticias Website. (http://www.sobradinhonoticias.com/2015/11/producao-e-uso-do-biodiesel-e-tema-de.html)

Mackenzie, C. (2019) 'Relational autonomy: State of the art debate'. In A. Armstrong, K. Green and A. Sangicomo (eds), *Spinoza and Relational Autonomy: Being with Others.* Edinburgh: Edinburgh University Press, pp. 10–32.

Manzi, M. (2013) *Agrarian Social Movements and the Making of Agrodiesel Moral Territories in Northeast Brazil.* PhD. Dissertation, Clark University.

Marcossi, G.P.C. and Moreno-Pérez, O.M. (2017) 'A closer look at the Brazilian Social Fuel Seal: Uptake, operation and dysfunctions'. *Biofuels*, 9: 1–11.

McKinnon, R. (2016) 'Epistemic injustice'. *Philosophy Compass*, 11(8): 437–46.

Ministério do Desenvolvimento Indústria e Comércio Exterior (2006) *O Futuro da Indústria: Biodiesel: Coletânea de Artigos. Série Política Industrial, Tecnológica e de Comércio Exterior – 14.* Brasília, DF: MDIC-STI/IEL.

Moreno-Pérez, O.M., Marcossi, G.P.C. and Ortiz-Miranda, D. (2017) 'Taking stock of the evolution of the biodiesel industry in Brazil: Business concentration and structural traits'. *Energy Policy*, 110: 525–33.

Mourad, C.B. and Zylbersztajn, D. (2012) 'Regulação Sobre Sistemas Agro-industriais De Produção de Biodiesel: Uma Análise Comparada'. *Organizacões Rurais & Agroindustriais*, 14(3).

Nelson, J. and Stock, P. (2016) 'Repeasantisation in the United States'. *Sociologia Ruralis*,58: 83–103.

Niederle, P.A. and Junior, V.J.W. (eds) (2021) *Agrifood System Transitions in Brazil: New Food Orders.* Abingdon: Routledge.

Pousa, G.P.A.G., Santos, A.L.F. and Suarez, P.A.Z. (2007) 'History and policy of biodiesel in Brazil'. *Energy Policy*, 35(11): 5393–8.

Rathmann, R. and Padula, A. (2011) 'The decision-making process of the agents belonging to the biodiesel production chain in southern Brazil'. *Journal of Agricultural Science and Technology A*, 865–73.

Ribeiro, D.D. and Dias, M.S. (2016) 'Efeitos do Programa Nacional de Producão e Uso de Biodiesel no território campones em assentamento rural'. *Interações*, 17: 15–21.

Rico, J.A.P. and Sauer, I.L. (2015) 'A review of Brazilian biodiesel experiences'. *Renewable and Sustainable Energy Reviews*, 45: 513–29.

Rocha, C. (2009) 'Developments in national policies for food and nutrition security in Brazil'. *Development Policy Review*, 27(1): 51–66.

Santos, O.I.B. and Rathmann, R. (2009) 'Identification and analysis of local and regional impacts from the introduction of biodiesel production in the state of Piauí'. *Energy Policy*, 37: 4011–20.

Schaffel, S., Herrera, S., Obermaier, M. and Lèbre La Rovere, E. (2012) 'Can family farmers benefit from biofuel sustainability standards? Evidence from the Brazilian social fuel certificate'. *Biofuels*, 3: 725–36.

Scott, J. (1986) 'Everyday forms of peasant resistance'. *Journal of Peasant Studies*, 13(2): 5–35.

Secretaria da Agricultura Familiar/Ministério do Desenvolvimento Agrário (2010) *Programa Nacional de Produção e Uso de Biodiesel inclusão social e desenvolvimento territorial*. Brazil: MDA.

Selbmann, K. and Ide, T. (2015) 'Between redeemer and work of the devil: The transnational Brazilian biofuel discourse'. *Energy for Sustainable Development*, 29: 118–26.

Selfa, T., Bain, C., Moreno, R., Eastmond, A., Sweitz, S., Bailey, C., Pereira, G.S., Souza, T. and Medeiros, R. (2015) 'Interrogating social sustainability in the biofuels sector in Latin America: Tensions between global standards and local experiences in Mexico, Brazil, and Colombia'. *Environmental Management*, 56(6): 1315–29.

Shortall, S. (2008). 'Are rural development programmes socially inclusive? Social inclusion, civic engagement, participation, and social capital: Exploring the differences'. *Journal of Rural Studies*, 24, 450–7.

Silva, M.S., Fernandes, F.M., Teixeira, F.L.C., Torres, E.A. and Rocha, A.M. (2014a) 'Biodiesel and the "Social Fuel Seal" in Brazil: Fuel of social inclusion?' *Journal of Agricultural Science*, 6(11): 212.

Silva, M.S., Teixeira, F.L.C., Torres, E.A. and Rocha, A.M. (2014b) 'Biodiesel e políticas públicas: Uma análise crítica do PNPB e das políticas do setor agroenergético no estado da Bahia'. *Revista de Desenvolvimento Economico*, 16(30): 20–34.

Stattman, S.L. and Mol, A.P.J. (2014) 'Social sustainability of Brazilian biodiesel: The role of agricultural cooperatives'. *Geoforum*, 54: 282–94.

Stattman, S.L., Hospes, O. and Mol, A.P.J. (2013) 'Governing biofuels in Brazil: A comparison of ethanol and biodiesel policies'. *Energy Policy*, 61: 22–30.

Stock, P.V. and Forney, J. (2014) 'Farmer autonomy and the farming self'. *Journal of Rural Studies*, 36: 160–71.

Van Der Ploeg, J.D. (2008) *The New Peasantries: Struggles for Autonomy and Sustainability in an Era of Empire and Globalization.* London and Sterling, VA: Routledge.

Van Der Ploeg, J.D., Jingzhong, Y. and Schneider, S. (2012) 'Rural development through the construction of new, nested, markets: Comparative perspectives from China, Brazil and the European Union'. *Journal of Peasant Studies*, 39: 133–73.

Veit-Wilson, J. (1998) *Setting Adequacy Standards: How Governments Define Minimum Incomes.* Bristol: Policy Press.

Vieira, L.P. (2015) 'Os (des)caminhos da agroenergia na Bahia: A participação da MRG de Irecê no circuito espacial produtivo do agrodiesel'. *Sociedade & Natureza*, 27: 67–79.

Wahlhütter, S., Vogl, C.R. and Eberhart, H. (2016) 'Soil as a key criteria in the construction of farmers' identities: The example of farming in the Austrian province of Burgenland'. *Geoderma*, 269: 39–53.

Weißermel, S.R. and Azevedo Chaves, K. (2020) 'Refusing "bare life" – Belo Monte,the riverine population and their struggle for epistemic justice'. *DIE ERDE – Journal of the Geographical Society of Berlin*, 151(2–3): 154–66.

Wilson, L. (2006). 'Developing a model for the measurement of social inclusion and social capital in regional Australia'. *Social Indicators Research*, 75, 335–60.

Wittman, H. (2009) 'Reworking the metabolic rift: La Vía Campesina, agrarian citizenship, and food sovereignty'. *Journal of Peasant Studies*, 36(4): 805–26. https://doi.org/10.1080/03066150903353991

Wolford, W. (2005) 'Agrarian moral economies and neoliberalism in Brazil: competing worldviews and the state in the struggle for land'. *Environment and Planning*, 37(2): 241–61.

Woods, M. (2014) 'Family farming in the global countryside'. *Anthropological Notebooks*, 20: 31–48.

Xavier, F.L.S. and Vianna, J.N.D.S. (2009) 'A atuação de grupos de pressão no cenário político e a viabilidade de participação da agricultura familiar no Programa Nacional de Produção e uso de Biodiesel'. *Revista Bahia Análise & Dados*, 18(4): 699–720.

10

Disasters and Catastrophes in Agrifood Studies

Elizabeth Ransom and Hope Raymond

Introduction

The study of disasters within social studies of agriculture and food (agrifood) literature has not featured prominently. The study of catastrophes in food systems has received even less attention. Yet, with climate change considered by some as a slow-moving catastrophe and growing concerns about other anthropogenic hazards (e.g., nuclear war, engineered pandemics), the field of agrifood studies may benefit from engaging more systematically with disaster studies (Ord, 2020; Pierrehumbert, 2006). This chapter sets out to provide a review of the existing literature that focuses on agriculture, food and disasters. We are particularly interested in what, if any, findings or recommendations speak to changing the way food is produced, distributed and consumed given that this is an imperative in the context of the Anthropocene (Loconto and Constance, this volume). In concluding, we focus on the types solutions proposed for addressing agriculture and food security post-disaster, and whether any of the solutions speak to a larger transformation of our food system (i.e., sustainable intensification, agroecology, food sovereignty).

Background

While the total number of deaths from natural disasters has declined (Ritchies and Roser, 2019), the occurrence of natural disasters, particularly weather-related events (i.e., droughts, floods and storms), has increased over the past three decades (FAO, 2015). Disasters are social events, not simply physical phenomena. In other words, the severity of a disaster is often measured by the magnitude of its societal impact (Tierney, 2019). While disasters used to be studied as discrete events, there is now recognition that disasters are better understood as arising from 'longer-term global and societal processes' (Tierney, 2019: 5).

Similarly, it is important to recognise the difference between disasters, emergencies and catastrophes (see Table 10.1). Understanding these differences can assist in thinking about organisational or institutional approaches to response and recovery or for considering potential mitigation strategies. For example, if the public is the only source of initial response post catastrophe, one might consider how to better empower and/or equip community members to effectively respond. Our interests in this chapter are focused on disasters and catastrophes as it relates to agrifood systems. Yet, most agrifood social science literature to date has focused on emergencies and disasters, rather than catastrophes. Undoubtedly, the lack of scholarly attention to catastrophes reflects the fortunate infrequency of such events. This also reflects that the social science literature often analyzes social conditions as 'outcomes emerging from the past, rather than as oriented to the future' (Welch et al., 2020: 439). As Jens

Table 10.1 How emergencies, disasters and catastrophes differ

Emergencies	Disasters	Catastrophes
Impacts localised	Impacts widespread, severe	Devasting physical and societal impacts
Response mainly local	Response is multi-jurisdictional, intergovernmental, but typical bottom-up	Response is initiated by central government because localities and regions are devastated
Standard operating procedures sufficient to handle event	Response requires activation of disaster plans; significant challenges emerge	Response challenges far exceed those envisioned in disaster plans
Vast majority of response resources are unaffected	Extensive damage to and disruption of key emergency services	Response system paralysed at local and regional levels
Public generally not involved in response	Public extensively involved in response	Public only source of initial response
No significant recovery challenges	Major recovery challenges	Massive recovery challenges and very slow recovery process

Source: Tierney (2019).

Beckert (2016: 49) puts it, 'The future, in the eyes of most sociologists, is a prolongation of the past'. Yet, the types of hazards that are threatening our global food system are increasingly novel or at least highly unusual events, for which prior experience may not exist.

There is growing recognition of anthropogenic hazards that threaten the destruction of humanity's long-term potential (Ord, 2020). In his estimation, Ord (2020: 67) argues that the likelihood of a natural catastrophe (i.e., supervolcano) occurring within the next 100 years is 1 in 10,000. By contrast, a human-created catastrophe – nuclear war, engineered pandemics, unaligned artificial intelligence – occurring within the next 100 years is estimated as a 1 in 6 chance. Ord (2020: 167) argues that the protection of humanity from these anthropogenic hazards should be considered a public good. He (2020: 58) asserts that, 'we can state with confidence that humanity spends more on ice cream every year than on ensuring that the technologies we develop do not destroy us'. In general, societies neglect supporting the protection of humanity and the environment as a public good, while simultaneously investing in technologies that threaten humanity and the planet. In the context of our focus, it could be argued that the food supply is considered a public good, in the sense that international and national governments have invested in seed saving through seed vaults (Fowler, 2008) and stockpiling of food (Wesseler, 2020). However, we also contend that far too little research has focused on response and recovery below the national level, at the individual, household, community and regional levels within agrifood studies. As indicated in Table 10.1, these are the levels at which most initial responses will occur post-disaster or catastrophe.

Disasters Versus Risks

Within the social sciences, especially sociology, whenever one speaks of disasters there is often reference made to risks, and yet it is important to acknowledge the ways in which these two concepts differ, both practically and theoretically. Practically, there is a time dimension, which also shapes our ability to study the two concepts. Disasters are often in the past and can be studied through direct or indirect measures. Risks are generally treated as possible future events; thus, detailed knowledge of such events are inferred but generally not known (Stallings, 1997).

Theoretically, risk has been a source of extensive theorising, most famously in the social sciences, via Ulrich Beck's (1992) theory of risk society. Beck viewed many of the most important risks facing society as global side-effects that are generated in the context of 'organised irresponsibility', where the originators of the risks are often able to avoid being held responsible for their damage (Curran, 2016: 4 citing Beck, 1995). For Beck, the unknown and unintended consequences come 'to be the dominant force in history and society of risk. Specifically, he argues that 'risk society is catastrophic society…the exceptional condition threatens to become the norm' (Beck, 1992: 24). In Beck's original formulation, the risk society was democratic in outcome, in that everyone was impacted. By contrast, Curran (2016: 11) adapted Beck to argue that 'risk society [is] intensifying key relational inequalities, in which the advantages of some are the cause of the disadvantages of others'. Curran's adaption of Beck's risk society as fundamentally undemocratic in its impact on diverse populations fits well with much social science literature that has focused on vulnerability and inequality, such as environmental justice and food insecurity. Below we summarise the disaster focused literature discussion of vulnerability amidst disasters and then in the discussion section we highlight similarities and differences between the disaster and agrifood studies literature.

Disaster-Focused Literature

In a review of three disaster-themed journals, Kuipers and Welsh (2017) found that over a third of all articles published in a 30-year period centred around natural disasters, with an emphasis on earthquakes, floods and hurricanes. While a wide range of topics were covered in their analysis, they found anthropogenic disasters received much less attention, particularly cybercrime, terrorism and public health concerns (i.e., virus outbreaks). In terms of themes identified, the three journals published extensively on community resilience and 'the operation and practical organisation of crisis and disaster mitigation, preparation, preparedness, and response' (Kuipers and Welsh, 2017: 278). They conclude that an analysis of the role of governance networks and the rise in importance of communication technologies is missing from the literature. In the case of the internet, there are potential opportunities in the midst of disasters, such as citizen-led responses, but there are also challenges, notably 'cascading effects of interdependencies', whereby an initial disaster can lead to other problems that significantly impact a larger population of people (Kuipers and Welsh, 2017: 280; Pescaroli and Alexander, 2015).

Existing research focused on the impact and recovery of disasters indicates that pre-existing inequalities are likely to be exacerbated by disasters (Bolin and Kurtz, 2018; Enarson et al., 2018; Tierney, 2019). Marginalised populations, including the poor, women and racial/ ethnic minorities, are more likely to be harmed by a disaster and are slower to recover (Nagel, 2012; Rahman, 2013; Tierney, 2019). For example, in the United States, extreme heat and heat-related deaths are associated with urban, low-income, predominantly minority communities (Harlan et al., 2006, 2013; Klinenberg, 2015). In the case of the 2004 Indian Ocean tsunami, children, older adults and females were the least likely to survive, which in part was attributed to the weaker physical strength, location of persons at the time the tsunami hit (e.g., at home versus work), and possibly the culturally accepted attire for women having restricted their mobility (Frankenberg et al., 2011).

Moreover, it is recognised that the pre-existing governance policies focused on mitigating or preparing for disasters at the state, national and international levels tend to be made by a fairly homogenous population of people (in terms of class, sex and socioeconomic standing). The composition of these governance bodies rarely represents the interests of those most vulnerable to disasters (Kaijser and Kronsell, 2014; Nagel, 2012). Disasters can also create challenges to the legitimacy and competency of governments and institutions (Tierney, 2019), which in turn can hamper organised recovery responses.

A final dimension to the disaster literature is the dramatic growth in so-called disaster resilience (Tiernan et al., 2019; Tierney, 2019). Although the concept of resilience has been applied in numerous disciplines throughout history, its application within disaster studies is a relatively recent phenomenon (Aldunce et al., 2015). The basis of this concept is often traced to its theoretical development and utilisation within the discipline of ecology, particularly due to the influential work of Holling in the 1970s (Holling 1973; see also Béné et al., 2016; Folke, 2006; Manyena, 2006; Walker et al., 2004). Since the early 2000s, the application of resilience within disaster research and policy has become increasingly common (Aldunce et al., 2015; Manyena, 2006; Tiernan et al., 2019).

There is no one agreed upon definition of the term, but Tierney (2019: 171) suggests there are two central ideas to most researcher's and practitioner's use of the concept. The first is that resilience as a concept involves resistance or absorptive capacity, whether at the individual, household or community scale. The second dimension is that resilience involves the ability to cope or adapt and to move on to recover. Similarly, Béné et al. (2012) discuss a resilience framework that is comprised of: (1) adsorptive coping capacity; (2) adaptive capacity; and (3) transformative capacity (see Figure 10.1). This expanded conceptualisation of resilience, which includes trans-formative capacity or the ability of a system to fundamentally trans-form in response to a shock or stressor, is pertinent particularly in the context of catastrophic events whereby a return to prior conditions is neither possible nor desirable (Béné et al., 2012).

The theoretical ambiguity in defining disaster resilience has resulted in a wide variety of interpretations and uses of the concept in practice (Aldunce et al., 2015). Among researchers and practitioners of disaster risk management, Aldunce et al. (2015: 252) found that the idea of 'bouncing back' is a common conceptualisation of resilience and is framed through three distinct themes. These dominant themes in the disaster resilience discourse include 'mechanistic/technocratic', 'sustainability' and 'community-based' (Aldunce et al., 2015: 259–61). The mechanistic/technocratic frame emphasises the role of govern-ment and institutions, whereas the community-based frame focuses on the role of social relationships and the community. Last, the sus-tainability resilience frame emphasises the role of interactions between

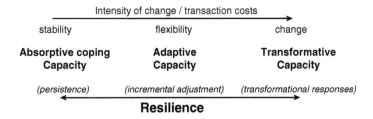

Figure 10.1 Conceptual framework of resilience capacities
Source: Béné et al. (2012).

society and the environment in disaster risk management. Although disaster resilience is framed differently among researchers and practitioners, there is a common recognition for the need to shift attention from 'response and recovery' to 'prevention and mitigation' (Aldunce et al., 2015: 6). Béné et al. (2016: 129) suggest that resilience emphasises prevention and mitigation due to scholars using 'ex ante attributes and abilities (including preventative measures and preparedness)'. Further, scholars have begun to adapt the construct of resilience as a 'bounce back' to a 'bounce forward' to broaden the focus on processes of transformation that accompany disasters (Aldunce et al., 2015; Manyena et al., 2011).

Somewhat surprisingly, little attention is paid to food and agriculture within disaster studies and urban policy and planning. For example, in Sylves (2019) *Disaster Policy & Politics: Emergency Management and Homeland Security*, there is no mention of food or agriculture, except in reference to the Food and Agriculture Organization (FAO) as an international organisation that issues early warnings of potential food crises. A similar lack of any significant treatment of the subject can be found in a recently published Handbook of Disaster Research, where mention of food (20 times) and agriculture (5 times) is limited in the sizeable 635-page volume (Rodríguez et al., 2017). In the context of the United States, Biehl et al. (2018: 39) observe that 'few U.S. cities have considered food systems in disaster preparedness or resilience planning'. Their study, while focused on the city of Baltimore, emphasises that cities must recognise ongoing food insecurity, as disasters will only make existing food insecurities worse (Biehl et al., 2018). The topic of disaster resilience is the one area where more attention is given to food and agriculture, particularly focused on livelihoods and food security (Tierney, 2019).

Resilience in Agrifood Context

The concept of resilience is also increasingly applied in the context of agriculture and food systems, especially as it relates to discussions surrounding climate change, natural disasters, sustainability and food and nutrition security (Béné et al., 2016; Berardi et al., 2011; Darnhofer, 2014; Darnhofer et al., 2010; Meuwissen et al., 2019; Rathi, 2020; Tendall et al., 2015). Traditionally, the application of resilience in the agrifood literature has primarily centred around coping strategies at the level of the farm or agricultural sector, rather than focusing on the entire agrifood system (Rathi, 2020; Tendall et al., 2015). Though, this has started to shift in recent years with the emergence of the concept of food system resilience within the literature (Béné, 2020; Hendrickson, 2015; Pingali et al., 2005; Rotz and Fraser, 2015; Tendall et al., 2015). Food system resilience, as defined by Tendall et al. (2015: 19), is the 'capacity over time of a food system and its units at multiple levels, to provide sufficient, appropriate and accessible food to all, in the face of various and even unforeseen disturbances'. Even more recently within the context of the COVID-19 pandemic, there has been a proliferation of journals that explore the resilience of local, national and regional food systems (Fan et al., 2021; Farrell et al., 2020; Moran et al., 2020; Worstell 2020).

In an assessment of its utilisation within the agrifood context, Béné et al. (2016: 124–6) argue that resilience is a valuable concept due to its 'integrative nature' or 'capacity to help link together and integrate sectors such as livelihoods, social protection, health, and nutrition that have traditionally been operating in a disconnected manner'. Thus, resilience may be an important mechanism to enhance communication and collaboration between disaster and agrifood scholars as well. Moreover, Berardi et al. (2011) contend that resilience is a useful framework to promote greater integration of adaptive capacity within agricultural policy and planning. There are also numerous critiques of the proliferated use of resilience, including the difficulty in studying resilience due to the dynamic nature of social systems (Béné et al., 2016). In addition, definitional disparities can lead to confusion and inconsistencies in what is meant or being studied, and practical differences in the implementation of resilience via practitioners and policymakers emerge as a result (Aldunce et al., 2015; Béné et al., 2016).

Another major challenge in the application of resilience as a concept to food systems is the difficulty of its measurement (Béné, 2020; Béné et al., 2016). The measurement of resilience is important in determining the most and least resilient individuals or groups to make decisions surrounding resource allocation and interventions, as well as in evaluating the effectiveness of interventions (Béné et al., 2016). Béné et al. (2016) identify several conceptual and operational challenges associated with the measurement of resilience. The first is the unforeseeable nature of shocks and the insufficient scale and frequency of measurement tools (i.e., surveys). The second is the issues of replicability of measurement indicators, as they tend to be specific to the context of the research and discipline of the researchers. Finally, although resilience is both multiscalar and multi-dimensional, measurement analyses tend to focus on one level or dimension of resilience.

We now turn to an examination of agrifood articles that have focused on disasters and catastrophes. We analyse the patterns that emerge in what has been published and consider how bringing agrifood studies into conversation with disaster studies might better inform future research, policies and practices. We also consider what, if any, types of alternative agricultural knowledge systems are proposed as solutions or responses to disasters and catastrophes.

Methods

Wave I: The search terms food security and disaster, food systems disaster, post-disaster food security, disaster responses, food security programming, food and catastrophe, food insecurity disaster and food security in disasters were used within the advanced search box 'with all of the words' in Google Scholar to identify relevant articles. We limited articles to those authored by social scientists, including but not limited to: anthropologists, cultural studies, development studies, economists, environmental studies and sociologists. A total of 71 article citations (see Appendix A for a list of articles) were downloaded within these criteria, and all of these were articles published in English. The year of publication ranged from 1981 to 2021. Then, Google Scholar was used to identify the number of times each article was cited by other scholars. After sorting the articles in descending order based on the number of times each article has been cited, the articles were read and coded. The range of citations was 1,828 to 0 citations, with the median number being 17 citations per article. Initial coding categories were created based on the knowledge of existing disaster literature. Subsequent coding categories were created as they emerged through an initial coding of ten articles.

The coding categories included the year of publication, the type of disaster (primary and secondary), the scale (e.g., individual, household, community), the type of data utilised in the article, the dimensions of food security (e.g., availability, access, etc.), the vulnerable population of focus, the geographic focus (e.g., Africa, North America), and if relevant, the type of food or commodity of focus.

There are a few limitations to our research, notably an English language bias and the search terms and databases utilised. There is obviously non-English scholarship that would fit within our search criteria but did not appear in our search using English words. In terms of search criteria, we began with a general search of disasters and agrifood studies. Future analysis will incorporate disaster-specific food and agriculture literature including: famine, climate change, nuclear accidents, flooding, earthquakes and COVID-19. Additionally, Scopus, an abstract and citation database was not used in the search for articles.

Results

General Trends

The results in this section are based on an analysis of these 71 articles. Overwhelmingly, the primary type of disaster that was focused on was climate change, with 25 percent of the articles having this as their primary focus. Of the climate change focused articles, 50 percent concentrated on extreme weather and 17 percent concentrated on natural disasters more generally as the secondary type of disaster. Other primary disaster types included general natural disaster (11 percent), flood (10 percent) and the COVID-19 pandemic (10 percent). The less common primary disaster types included drought (7 percent), hurricane (6 percent), earthquake (6 percent) and famine (6 percent). Of the articles categorised as focused on the generic category of natural disasters, 45 percent focused on climate change as the secondary disaster type.

Across all articles, the most common type of data utilised was commentary (34 percent), followed by qualitative data (e.g., interviews, focus groups, observations) (28 percent) and literature review (14 percent). Within specific types of primary disasters, specifically climate change, famines, drought and the COVID-19 pandemic, 50 percent or more of the articles were commentaries. What this means is that at least half of these articles did not contain data. Data was defined broadly as including: systematic literature reviews, surveys, qualitative methods, secondary data or multi-method approaches, including modelling. In other words, in articles without data, scholars made assertions using existing theory or with antidotal evidence, but in both instances without supporting evidence.

Of the articles with a geographic focus, the majority focused on countries considered to be part of low- and middle-income countries. In particular, the majority of articles focused on the regions of sub-Saharan Africa (18 percent), East Asia and Pacific (18 percent), and South and Central Asia (17 percent), as defined by the World Bank.[1] More generally, 11 percent of articles referenced low- and middle-income countries without geographic specificity. Of the three regions, South Asia has the highest number of articles that utilise data (92 percent), followed by East Asia and Pacific and sub-Saharan Africa (70 percent). Of the articles that referenced low- and middle-income countries more generally, the majority were commentary, without data (63 percent). There were a handful of articles focused on the United States, representing 9 percent of articles with a geographic focus. There were two articles (4 percent) that focused on countries in Latin America and the Caribbean, and both focused on Haiti. Additionally, there was only one article (2 percent) that focused on the Middle East and North Africa region, and the country of focus was Iran.

Given the large focus on vulnerable populations within disaster research, we coded for which groups receive attention within agriculture and food literature. The most common focus were poor people in low- and middle-income countries (38 percent). Within this subset of articles, 22 percent focused on rural communities as the secondary vulnerable population. Other primary vulnerable populations focused on among the 71 articles included: women (9 percent), children (4 percent), smallholders (4 percent) and urban communities (7 percent). Among the secondary vulnerable populations, rural communities (14 percent) and children (10 percent) were most frequently mentioned. Of the articles focused on the United States, 50 percent concentrated on poor people and 33 percent concentrated on urban communities as the primary vulnerable populations.

---

[1] 'World Bank Country and Lending Groups', *World Bank Group* (https://datahelpde sk.worldbank.org/knowledgebase/articles/906519-world-bank-country-and-lending-groups).

For articles with a specified scale, the largest portion of articles focused on a global or international scale (25 percent) followed by national (18 percent), multiscalar (17 percent) and community (16 percent). Fewer articles focused on a city (10 percent) or household scale (9 percent), while no articles focused on an individual scale. In general, most articles (89 percent) did not have a commodity or foodstuff focus. Of the few that did, the foodstuff of interest included: rice, cereal grain, maize and cardamom.

Thematic Overview[2]

The articles cover a wide-range of topics, including the role of markets and economic trade in ensuring food security, the positive and negative impacts of food aid post-disasters, the role of national governments, and, to a lesser degree, international governance in disaster recovery and community responses to disasters. We were particularly interested in how many of the articles advocated for changing 'the way food is produced, distributed, and consumed' in response to disasters, given that the problem of the Anthropocene demands solutions (Loconto and Constance, this volume).

Overall, no articles spoke of agroecology or sustainable intensification. Indirectly, there were a few articles that spoke to agroecology ideals. Specifically, one article (Jackson, 2019) focused on the negative impact that emergency food aid had on indigenous communities long term. The author finds that food aid decreased self-efficacy and traditional indigenous knowledge, while also increasing inequality in communities. Similarly, a study in Haiti (Forrester et al., 2017) focused on how community gardens could be used to expand access to food and enhance utilisation by community members post-disaster.

Several articles spoke to food sovereignty ideals. First, a few articles focused on the human right to food, noting that governments must provide more resources to adequately be prepared to provide food to people in the midst of an emergency (Belyakov, 2015; Rukundo et al., 2014). Second, several articles addressed community practices and ideals surrounding food sovereignty. For example, an article focused on Haiti (Shamsie, 2012) emphasised that Haitians view agriculture as

---

[2]All citations in this section are listed in Appendix A: Literature Review Articles Analysed.

multifunctional and serving more than just economic development, which the authors claim is in contrast to domination development initiatives in Haiti. Two articles centred in the United States, one situated in New York City post Hurricane Sandy (Chan et al., 2015) and the other New Orleans after Hurricane Katrina (Kato et al., 2014), focused on the role of community gardens. In the case of New York City, gardens provided food security for vulnerable members of the community, but the gardens also became spaces of healing and fostering a sense of collective efficacy (Chan et al., 2015). In the case of New Orleans, urban gardening served political ends as a way of countering 'neoliberal abandonment and disaster capitalism' and as a mechanism to 'reclaim space and identity' (Kato et al., 2014: 1845).

Urban agriculture and gardening were also mentioned by others as important responses to disasters, but not necessarily utilising a food sovereignty lens. For example, Dubbeling et al. (2019) and Barthel and Isendahl (2013) both discuss urban agriculture as having a place in combating climate change and creating more resilient cities. In the case of Dubbeling et al. (2019), they see urban planners and city management needing to facilitate and support urban agriculture, which is a different approach than other studies that speak of community members utilising gardening as an act of resistance and community efficacy.

There were several themes in this literature review that do not map easily on to transformative agrifood systems models or frames. Social capital was one topic that received a reasonable amount of attention, with a focus on how individuals and communities can better respond to disasters or how they failed to respond. One article focused on women gardening in the Philippines and the ways in which their peri-urban gardens can help build solidarity and improve food security (Ofreno and Hega, 2016). Other articles focused on changing social capital in protracted crises (Vervisch et al., 2013), resilience capacity among households in Bangladesh after flooding (Smith and Frankenberger, 2018), and the role of community social capital for food security after flooding in Vermont (Chriest and Niles, 2018). While social capital approaches may not be new, it could be argued that social capital has the potential to engage with a food sovereignty approach in terms of conceptualising rights in 'collective terms rather than the liberal conception of individual rights' (Constance and Loconto this volume citing McMichael, 2014).

Other notable recommendations that can be relevant for solutions in the agrifood and disaster literature are recommendations at the producer/farm level, including emergency sustainable agriculture kits (eSAKs) that focus on offering temporary supplies to assist farmers in beginning production again (Chapagain and Ralzada, 2017). Proposed items to include in eSAKs: agriculture grade plastics rolls, seed storage bins, inexpensive tools, food supplements and waterproof gloves (Chapagain and Ralzada, 2017). There are also studies that focus on farmer adaption post-disaster (DiCarlo et al., 2018) and the ways in which policies can incentivise farmer adaption, especially to climate change (Douglas, 2009; Bandara and Cai, 2014; Kotir, 2011). Finally, institutional capacity building at the regional, national and local levels to better respond to disasters is a major them identified in the literature (Babu and Mthindi, 1995; Cutter, 2017; Fitzpatrick et al., 2020; Islam and Ahmed, 2017; Tirivangasi, 2018; Ma et al., 2020).

With respect to vulnerable populations, the agrifood disaster literature clearly calls for targeted cash transfers for ensuring food security and the ability to recover from disasters (Ajaero, 2017; Béné, 2020; del Ninno et al., 2002, 2003; Kinsey et al., 2020; Shipton, 1990). This recommendation cuts across production and consumption, as smallholder farmers and poorer non-farming households are vulnerable, albeit in different ways, to food insecurity post-disaster. Moreover, poorer households are more likely to become in-debt while trying to recover from a disaster, which perpetuates their vulnerability moving forward.

Rural areas are highlighted as geographically vulnerable. Rural areas are thought to receive less assistance post-disaster than urban areas and yet assistance is usually very much needed to maintain livelihoods and food security (Chapagain and Raizada, 2017; Oluoko-Odingo, 2011). Moreover, while smallholders may be more resilient in the context of a disaster due to, for example, crop diversity, they have been found to be less effective at mitigating food insecurity due to low productivity (Adhikari et al., 2020).

The vulnerability of women and children is also a point of emphasis. Articles that focus on children often mention children in conjunction with women, although a few articles highlight the unique dimensions of disasters impact on children, notably long-term stunting and wasting due to poor nutrition, and increased rates of illness and death due to poor sanitation and contaminated drinking water (del Ninno et al., 2003; Kodish et al., 2019). One article focused on Zimbabwe is worth highlighting because it moves away from focusing solely on children's vulnerability and instead argues that children should be enroled in disaster planning and response (Manyena et al., 2008). Children are often uniquely impacted by disasters, and yet they are rarely enroled in consultation, either to gain their perspective or to appreciate what children can contribute to household food security. For example, boys in the Manyena et al. (2008) study said they would have gladly caught fish to sale to contribute income to their households. Similarly children reported that they were often chased away by aid workers, when they would prefer to try and assist.

Discussion

There are numerous reasons one would expect that research articles focused on agrifood systems and disasters to be disproportionately focused on the regions and countries in sub-Saharan Africa and South Asia. First, the majority of the population is engaged in agriculture in developing countries (Roser, 2018). Therefore, when extreme weather events occur, there are many more direct effects on the population. Second, the highest rates of food insecurity are located in sub-Saharan Africa and Southeast Asia (Smith and Meade, 2019). Third, disasters are much more devastating for developing nations, where deaths and injuries are more common by 'several orders of magnitude' (Tierney, 2019: 1). Developing nations also take longer to recover from disasters, at the individual, household, community and national level. Disasters can contribute to households becoming poor and it is much more difficult for those households to escape poverty (Hallegatte et al., 2016).

Conversely, there are reasons that a more geographically diverse literature would be beneficial when considering disasters and agrifood systems. Food insecurity exists throughout the world and disasters will continue contributing to increased food insecurity. Latin America and the Caribbean are a good example of a region that has made significant inroads into reducing food insecurity over the last few decades, but even prior to COVID-19, the region has recently seen a dramatic increase in food insecurity (FAO et al., 2019). In addition, industrialised countries, while employing a small percentage of the population in agriculture, produce a large quantity of the world's food supply. Depending upon the disaster, these centres of industrial production may be more severely impacted than smallholder agriculture. For example, modelling of extreme weather events predict production levels of cereals in industrialised agricultural systems of North America, Europe and Australasia will suffer more from drought than other regions of the world (Lesk et al., 2016). Moreover, industrialised agricultural systems are known for having longer supply chains. COVID-19 contributed to significant disruptions of these supply chains (Garnett et al., 2020; Thilmany et al., 2020). Such results raise questions about the role of shorter supply chains in contributing to resilience and adaptability in the context of disasters. Geographical diversity also extends to considering more urban and peri-urban spaces. While the vast majority of food is grown in rural areas, the vast majority of the population lives in urban locations.

There is also a more complicated dimension to studying disasters and agrifood systems, and that is the inequalities within nations, not simply between nations. The famous work of Amartya Sen (1981) called attention to the idea that people differ in their ability to command food through legal means in the midst of a famine. Recent data suggests inequality within nations is increasing, which implies urgency for studying how differences in social and material relations between individuals' and communities' impact the capacity to survive and recover from disasters (Derviş and Qureshi, 2016). Moreover, if you subscribe to Curran's (2016: 11) understanding of risk society as 'intensifying key relational inequalities, in which the advantages of some are the cause of the disadvantages of others', then there is a need within agrifood studies to attend to growing inequalities within nations. Our review of agrifood studies that have focused on disaster suggests a large majority of scholarship is not empirically informed, with limited to no analysis of household and individual data.

Another area for consideration in agrifood research is increasing analysis on anthropogenic risks to our food supply, such as supply chain disruptions or disruptions of other critical infrastructure. In addition, agrifood scholars should consider more deeply theorising similarities and differences across diverse disasters. While natural disasters are heavily studied, there may be a benefit to further segregating the different types of disasters and how they differentially shape agrifood systems. For example, comparing floods to wildfires to a pandemic will likely reveal unique challenges for agrifood systems, depending upon not only the scale of the disaster but also the type of disaster.

An area of convergence for agrifood scholarship and disaster studies is the focus on vulnerable populations. Much of the agrifood literature focuses on the poor, especially in developing countries, women, rural populations and children. There should be a continued focus on vulnerable populations. However, more empirical studies are needed to better understand vulnerable populations in the midst of disasters. A study focused on the important role of integrating children in disaster/food security plans as a mechanism to improve resilience of households and communities in a district in Zimbabwe is a good example of an empirical analysis of a vulnerable group (Manyena et al., 2008). Without data, agrifood studies risk homogenising what are clearly diverse populations. These studies also miss opportunities to not only think more strategically about the types of resources needed to assist vulnerable populations in recovery, but also the type of assets some populations may have (e.g. local knowledge of edible plants) that can facilitate recovery and transformation of our food system.

Conclusion

Agrifood scholars have called attention in recent years to the growing vulnerability of a neoliberal, industrialised food systems (Busch, 2010; Wolf and Bonanno, 2013). However, these accounts are not usually focused on considering agrifood systems in the context of disasters and catastrophes. By contrast, since the 1970s, there is a growing community of scholars that study disasters and catastrophes, although with a limited focus on food and agriculture.

The similarity between disaster studies and the 71 articles reviewed in this chapter is the recognition of the disproportionate impact of disasters on vulnerable populations. The literature has clearly established who is impacted and at present the most common recommendation is the targeting of cash transfers to vulnerable populations. The recommendation, while important, really speaks more to absorptive coping capacity, as opposed to adaptive or transformative capacity (see Figure 10.1).

In general, most of the articles focused on absorptive coping capacity and adaptive capacity. In other words, much of the focus is on incremental adjustments, such as policy coordination or more collaboration between researchers and policymakers, which aligns with a more mechanistic/technocratic framing of resilience. Overall, we found a limited focus on broader transformations to our food system long term. There were no explicit discussions of sustainable intensification, agroecology or food sovereignty. There were a few studies that focused on ideals embedded within agroecology or food sovereignty. For example, the role of indigenous knowledge and the ways in which food aid can diminish the use of indigenous knowledge (Jackson et al., 2020). Similarly, there were some articles that focused on the multifunctional role of agriculture and how food production post-disaster can contribute to healing and collective efficacy (Chan et al., 2015) or the recommendation that research shift towards being action-oriented (Campbell et al., 2016). All these concepts fit largely within a food sovereignty approach. And articles focused on the recent COVID-19 pandemic call for transformational approaches to enhancing food system resilience, but these articles remain limited in actual solutions offered.

There were also some possible solutions that do not map on to alternative knowledge systems. Instead these might be considered as mechanisms or tools that can assist individuals and communities in the midst of disaster or catastrophe recovery. These include a focus on social capital, mechanisms to support producers' recovery and adaption, and building more institutional capacity as all levels (local, regional, national and international). We would argue these mechanisms or tools do not determine the intensity of change, i.e. whether something is adaptive versus transformative, but rather speak to how food system actors might approach implementing changes.

Agrifood studies focused on sustainable food systems and alternative – often marginalised – knowledge systems can provide valuable insights for thinking about transforming our food system. Given the historic lack of focus on food systems in urban planning and disaster policy, agrifood scholarship can provide insights and inform policy and practices. Bringing these two areas of scholarship into conversation can provide new insights to scholars and policymakers in the context of living in the Anthropocene. Nonetheless, the limited number of articles focused on disasters and catastrophes in agrifood studies that offer insights into more transformational solutions to the growing problems in our food system suggests a critical overlooked area for research.

References

Aldunce, P., Beilin,R., Handmer, J. and Howden, M. (2015) 'Framing disaster resilience: The implications of the diverse conceptualisations of "bouncing back"'. *Disaster Prevention and Management.* (https://doi.org/10.1108/DPM-07-2013-0130)

Beck, U. (1992) *Risk Society: Towards a New Modernity.* London: SAGE.

Beck, U. (1995) *Ecological Enlightenment: Essays on the Politics of the Risk Society.* Atlantic Highland, NY: Humanities Press.

Beckert, J. (2016) *Imagined Futures: Fictional Expectations and Capitalist Dynamics.* Cambridge, MA: Harvard University Press.

Béné, C. (2020) 'Resilience of local food systems and links to food security: A review of some important concepts in the context of COVID-19 and other shocks'. *Food Security*, 12(4): 805–22.

Béné, C., Headey, D., Haddad, L. and von Grebmer, K. (2016) 'Is resilience a useful concept in the context of food security and nutrition programmes? Some conceptual and practical considerations'. *Food Security*, 8(1): 123–38.

Béné, C., Wood, R.G., Newsham, A. and Davies, M. (2012) 'Resilience: New utopia or new tyranny? Reflection about the potentials and limits of the concept of resilience in relation to vulnerability reduction programmes'. *IDS Working Papers*, 2012(405): 1–61.

Berardi, G., Green, R. and Hammond, B. (2011) 'Stability, sustainability, and catastrophe: Applying resilience thinking to US agriculture'. *Human Ecology Review*, 115–25.

Biehl, E., Buzogany, S., Baja, B. and Neff, R.A. (2018) 'Planning for a resilient urban food system: A case study from Baltimore City, Maryland'. *Journal of Agriculture, Food Systems, and Community Development*, 8(B): 39–53.

Bolin, B. and Kurtz, L.C. (2018) 'Race, class, ethnicity, and disaster vulnerability'. In H. Rodriquez, W. Donner and J.E. Trainor (eds), *Handbook of Disaster Research*, New York, NY: Springer, pp. 181–203.

Busch, L. (2010) 'Can fairy tales come true? The surprising story of neoliberalism and world agriculture'. *Sociologia Ruralis*, 50(4): 331–51.

Campbell, B.M., Vermeulen, S.J., Aggarwal, P.K., Corner-Dolloff, C., Girvetz, E., Loboguerrero, A.M., ... Wollenberg, E. (2016). 'Reducing risks to food security from climate change'. *Global Food Security*, 11: 34–43.

Chan, J., DuBois, B. and Tidball, K.G. (2015). 'Refuges of local resilience: Community gardens in post-Sandy New York City'. *Urban Forestry and Urban Greening*, 14(3): 625–35.

Curran, D. (2016) *Risk, Power, and Inequality in the 21st Century.* New York, NY: Springer.

Darnhofer, I. (2014) 'Resilience and why it matters for farm management'. *European Review of Agricultural Economics*, 41(3): 461–84.

Darnhofer, I., Fairweather, J. and Moller, M. (2010) 'Assessing a farm's sustainability: Insights from resilience thinking'. *International Journal of Agricultural Sustainability*, 8(3): 186–98.

Derviş, K. and Qureshi, Z. (2016) *Income Distribution within Countries: Rising Inequality.* Washington, DC: The Brookings Institution.

Enarson, E., Fothergill, A. and Peek, L. (2018) 'Gender and disaster: Foundations and new directions for research and practice'. In H. Rodriquez, W. Donner and J.E. Trainor (eds), *Handbook of Disaster Research,* New York, NY: Springer, pp. 205–23.

Fan, S., Teng, P., Chew, P., Smith, G. and Copeland, L. (2021) 'Food system resilience and COVID-19: Lessons from the Asian experience'. *Global Food Security*, 28: 100501.

FAO (2015) *The Impact of Natural Hazards and Disasters on Agriculture, Food Security and Nutrition.* Rome: Food and Agriculture Organization.

FAO, PAHO, WFP and UNICEF (2019) *Regional Overview of Food Security and Nutrition in Latin America and the Caribbean 2019.* Santiago: Food and Agriculture Organization.

Farrell, P., Thow, A.M., Wate, J.T., Nonga, N., Vatucawaqa, P., Brewer, T., Sharp, M.K., Farmery, A., Trevena, H. and Reeve, E. (2020) 'COVID-19 and Pacific food system resilience: Opportunities to build a robust response'. *Food Security*, 12(4): 783–91.

Folke, C. (2006) 'Resilience: The emergence of a perspective for social–ecological systems analyses'. *Global Environmental Change*, 16(3): 253–67.

Fowler, C. (2008) 'The Svalbard seed vault and crop security'. *BioScience*, 58(3): 190–91.

Frankenberg, E., Gillespie, T., Preston, S., Sikoki, S. and Thomas, D. (2011) 'Mortality, the family and the Indian Ocean tsunami'. *The Economic Journal*, 121(554): F162–F82.

Garnett, P., Doherty, B. and Heron, T. (2020) 'Vulnerability of the United Kingdom's food supply chains exposed by COVID-19'. *Nature Food*, 1(6): 315–18.

Hallegatte, S., Vogt-Schilb, A., Bangalore, M. and Rozenberg. R. (2016) *Unbreakable: Building the Resilience of the Poor in the Face of Natural Disasters.* Washington, DC: World Bank Publications.

Harlan, S.L., Brazel, A.J., Prashad, L., Stefanov, W.L. and Larsen, L. (2006) 'Neighborhood microclimates and vulnerability to heat stress'. *Social Science & Medicine*, 63(11): 2847–63.

Harlan, S.L., Declet-Barreto, J.H., Stefanov, W.L. and Petitti, D.B. (2013) 'Neighborhood effects on heat deaths: Social and environmental predictors of vulnerability in Maricopa County, Arizona'. *Environmental Health Perspectives*, 121(2): 197–204.

Hendrickson, M.K. (2015) 'Resilience in a concentrated and consolidated food system'. *Journal of Environmental Studies and Sciences*, 5(3): 418–31.

Holling, C.S. (1973) 'Resilience and stability of ecological systems'. *Annual Review of Ecology and Systematics*, 4(1): 1–23.

Jackson, G., McNamara, K.E. and Witt, B. (2020) 'System of hunger: Understanding causal disaster vulnerability of indigenous food systems'. *Journal of Rural Studies*, 73: 163–75.

Kaijser, A. and Kronsell, A. (2014) 'Climate change through the lens of intersectionality'. *Environmental Politics*, 23(3): 417–33.

Klinenberg, E. (2015) *Heat Wave: A Social Autopsy of Disaster in Chicago*. Chicago, IL: University of Chicago Press.

Kuipers, S. and Welsh, N.H. (2017) 'Taxonomy of the crisis and disaster literature: Themes and types in 34 years of research'. *Risk, Hazards & Crisis in Public Policy*, 8(4): 272–83.

Lesk, C., Rowhani, P. and Ramankutty, N. (2016) 'Influence of extreme weather disasters on global crop production'. *Nature*, 529(7584): 84–8.

Manyena, S.B. (2006). 'The concept of resilience revisited'. *Disasters*, 30(4): 434–50.

Manyena, S.B., Fordham, M. and Collins, A. (2008) 'Disaster resilience and children: Managing food security in Zimbabwe's Binga District'. *Children, Youth, and Environments*, 18(1): 303–31.

Manyena, B., O'Brien, G., O'Keefe, P. and Rose, J. (2011). 'Disaster resilience: A bounce back or bounce forward ability?' *Local Environment: The International Journal of Justice and Sustainability*, 16(5): 417–24.

Meuwissen, M.P.M., Feindt, P.H., Spiegel, A., Termeer, C.J., Mathijs, E., de Mey, Y., Finger, R., Balmann, A., Wauters, E. and Urquhart, J. (2019) 'A framework to assess the resilience of farming systems'. *Agricultural Systems*, 176: 102656.

Moran, D., Cossar, F., Merkle, M. and Alexander, P. (2020) 'UK food system resilience tested by COVID-19'. *Nature Food*, 1(5): 242.

Nagel, J. (2012) 'Intersecting identities and global climate change'. *Identities: Global Studies in Power and Culture*, 19(4): 467–76.

Ord, T. (2020) *The Precipice: Existential Risk and the Future of Humanity*. New York, NY: Hachette Books.

Pescaroli, G. and Alexander, D. (2015) 'A definition of cascading disasters and cascading effects: Going beyond the "toppling dominos" metaphor'. *Planet@ risk*, 3(1): 58–67.

Pierrehumbert, R.T. (2006) 'Climate change: A catastrophe in slow motion'. *Chicago Journal of International Law*, 6: 573.

Pingali, P., Alinovi, L. and Sutton, J. (2005) 'Food security in complex emergencies: Enhancing food system resilience'. *Disasters*, 29: S5–S24.

Rahman, S. (2013) 'Climate change, disaster and gender vulnerability: A study on two divisions of Bangladesh'. *American Journal of Human Ecology*, 2(2): 72–82.

Rathi, A. (2020) 'Is agrarian resilience limited to agriculture? Investigating the "farm" and "non-farm" processes of agriculture resilience in the rural'. *Journal of Rural Studies*, 155–64.

Ritchies, H. and Roser, M. (2019) *Natural Disasters*. OurWorldInData.org. (https://ourworldindata.org/natural-disasters#link-between-poverty-and-deaths-from-natural-disasters)

Rodríguez, H., Donner, W. and Trainor, J.E. (eds) (2017) *Handbook of Disaster Research*. Cham: Springer International Publishing AG.

Roser, M. (2018) *Employment in Agriculture.* OurWorldIn Data.org. (https://ourworldindata.org/employment-in-agriculture)

Rotz, S. and Fraser, E.D.D. (2015) 'Resilience and the industrial food system: Analyzing the impacts of agricultural industrialization on food system vulnerability'. *Journal of Environmental Studies and Sciences*, 5(3): 459–73.

Sen, A. (1981) 'Ingredients of famine analysis: Availability and entitlements'. *Quarterly Journal of Economics*, 96(3): 433–64.

Smith, M.D. and Meade, B. (2019) 'Who are the world's food insecure? Identifying the risk factors of food insecurity around the world'. *Amber Waves: The Economics of Food, Farming, Natural Resources, and Rural America.* (https://doi.org/10.22004/ag.econ.302721)

Stallings, R.A. (1997). *Sociological Theories and Disaster Studies.* Preliminary Paper #249, Newark, DE: University of Delaware Disaster Research Center.

Sylves, R.T. (2019) *Disaster Policy and Politics: Emergency Management and Homeland Security*: Washington, DC: CQ Press.

Tendall, D.M., Joerin, J., Kopainsky, B., Edwards, P., Shreck, A., Le, Q.B., Kruetli, P., Grant, M. and Six, J. (2015) 'Food system resilience: Defining the concept'. *Global Food Security*, 6: 17–23.

Thilmany, D., Canales, E., Low, S.A. and Boys, K. (2020) 'Local food supply chain dynamics and resilience during COVID-19'. *Applied Economic Perspectives and Policy*, 43(1): 86–104.

Tiernan, A., Drennan, L., Nalau, J., Onyango, E., Morrissey, L. and Mackey, B. (2019). 'A review of themes in disaster resilience literature and international practice since 2012'. *Policy Design and Practice*, 2(1): 53–74.

Tierney, K. (2019) *Disasters: A Sociological Approach.* Hoboken, NJ: John Wiley & Sons.

Walker, B., Holling, C.S., Carpenter, S.R. and Kinzig, A. (2004) 'Resilience, adaptability and transformability in social–ecological systems', *Ecology and Society*, 9(2): 1708–3087.

Welch, D., Mandich, G. and Keller, M. (2020) 'Futures in practice: Regimes of engagement and teleoaffectivity'. *Cultural Sociology*, 14(4): 438–57.

Wesseler, J. (2020) 'Storage policies: Stockpiling versus immediate release'. *Journal of Agricultural & Food Industrial Organization*, 18(1).

Wolf, S.A. and Bonanno, A. (2013) *The Neoliberal Tegime in the Agri-food Sector: Crisis, Resilience, and Restructuring.* Oxfordshire: Routledge.

Worstell, J. (2020) 'Ecological resilience of food systems in response to the COVID-19 crisis'. *Journal of Agriculture, Food Systems, and Community Development*, 9(3): 23–30.

Appendix A: Literature Review Articles Analysed

Adhikari, J., Timsina, J., Khadka, S.R., Ghale, Y. and Ojha, H. (2020) 'COVID-19 impacts on agriculture and food systems in Nepal: Implications for SDGs'. *Agricultural Systems*, 186: 102990.

Ainehvand, S., Raeissi, P., Ravaghi, H. and Maleki, M. (2019) 'Natural disasters and challenges toward achieving food security response in Iran'. *Journal of Education and Health Promotion*, 8. (https://doi.org/10.4103/jehp.jehp_256_18)

Ajaero, C.K. (2017) 'A gender perspective on the impact of flood on the food security of households in rural communities of Anambra state, Nigeria'. *Food Security*, 9(4): 685–95.

Alam, G.M., Alam, K., Mushtaq, S., Sarker, M.N.I. and Hossain, M. (2020) 'Hazards, food insecurity and human displacement in rural riverine Bangladesh: Implications for policy'. *International Journal of Disaster Risk Reduction*, 43: 101364.

Babu, S.C. and Mthindi, G.B. (1995) 'Developing decentralized capacity for disaster prevention: Lessons from food security and nutrition monitoring in Malawi'. *Disasters*, 19(2): 127–39.

Bandara, J.S. and Cai, Y. (2014) 'The impact of climate change on food crop productivity, food prices and food security in South Asia'. *Economic Analysis and Policy*, 44(4): 451–65.

Bang, H., Miles, L. and Gordon, R. (2018) 'Enhancing local livelihoods resilience and food security in the face of frequent flooding in Africa: A disaster management perspective'. *Journal of African Studies and Development*, 10(7): 85–100.

Barnett, J. (2011) 'Dangerous climate change in the Pacific Islands: Food production and food security'. *Regional Environmental Change*, 11(1): 229–37.

Baro, M. and Deubel, T.F. (2006) 'Persistent hunger: Perspectives on vulnerability, famine, and food security in sub-Saharan Africa'. *Annual Review of Anthropology*, 35: 521–38.

Barthel, S. and Isendahl, C. (2013) 'Urban gardens, agriculture, and water management: Sources of resilience for long-term food security in cities'. *Ecological Economics*, 86: 224–34.

Belyakov, A. (2015) 'From Chernobyl to Fukushima: An interdisciplinary framework for managing and communicating food security risks after nuclear plant accidents'. *Journal of Environmental Studies and Sciences*, 5(3): 404–17.

Béné, C. (2020) 'Resilience of local food systems and links to food security – A review of some important concepts in the context of COVID-19 and other shocks'. *Food Security*, 1–18.

Campbell, B.M., Vermeulen, S.J., Aggarwal, P.K., Corner-Dolloff, C., Girvetz, E., Loboguerrero, A.M., … Wollenberg, E. (2016) 'Reducing risks to food security from climate change'. *Global Food Security*, 11: 34–43.

Chan, J., DuBois, B. and Tidball, K.G. (2015) 'Refuges of local resilience: Community gardens in post-Sandy New York City'. *Urban Forestry and Urban Greening*, 14(3): 625–35.

Chapagain, T. and Raizada, M.N. (2017) 'Impacts of natural disasters on smallholder farmers: Gaps and recommendations'. *Agriculture & Food Security*, 6(1): 39.

Chriest, A. and Niles, M. (2018) 'The role of community social capital for food security following an extreme weather event'. *Journal of Rural Studies*, 64: 80–90.

Clay, E.J. (2003) 'Responding to change: WFP and the global food aid system'. *Development Policy Review*, 21(5–6): 697–709.

Cutter, S.L. (2017) 'The forgotten casualties redux: Women, children, and disaster risk'. *Global Environmental Change*, 42: 117–21.

Cutter, S.L. (2017) 'The perilous nature of food supplies: Natural hazards, social vulnerability, and disaster resilience'. *Environment: Science and Policy for Sustainable Development*, 59(1): 4–15.

De Haen, H. (2008) 'Food security strategies: Building resilience against natural disasters Stratégies de sécurité alimentaire: améliorer la résistance aux catastrophes naturelles Strategien für die Sicherung der Ernährung: Stärkung der Widerstandsfähigkeit gegen Naturkatastrophen'. *EuroChoices*, 7(3): 26–33.

De Haen, H. and Hemrich, G. (2007) 'The economics of natural disasters: Implications and challenges for food security'. *Agricultural economics*, 37: 31–45.

del Ninno, C., Dorosh, P.A. and Islam, N. (2002) 'Reducing vulnerability to natural disasters: Lessons from the 1998 floods in Bangladesh'. *IDS Bulletin*, 33(4): 98–107.

Del Ninno, C., Dorosh, P.A. and Smith, L.C. (2003) 'Public policy, markets and household coping strategies in Bangladesh: Avoiding a food security crisis following the 1998 floods'. *World Development*, 31(7): 1221–38.

DiCarlo, J., Epstein, K., Marsh, R. and Måren, I. (2018) 'Post-disaster agricultural transitions in Nepal'. *Ambio*, 47(7): 794–805.

Dilley, M. and Boudreau, T.E. (2001) 'Coming to terms with vulnerability: A critique of the food security definition'. *Food policy*, 26(3): 229–47.

Dirks, R., Armelagos, G.J., Bishop, C.A., Brady, I.A., Brun, T., Copans, J., ... Turton, D. (1980) 'Social responses during severe food shortages and famine [and comments and reply]'. *Current Anthropology*, 21(1): 21–44.

Dorosh, P., Malik, S.J. and Krausova, M. (2010). 'Rehabilitating agriculture and promoting food security after the 2010 Pakistan floods: Insights from the south Asian experience'. *Pakistan Development Review*, 167–92.

Douglas, I. (2009). 'Climate change, flooding and food security in south Asia'. *Food Security*, 1(2): 127–36.

Dubbeling, M. (2019). 'Urban agriculture as a climate change and disaster risk reduction strategy'. *Urban Agriculture Magazine*, (27): 3–7.

Farrell, P., Thow, A.M., Wate, J.T., Nonga, N., Vatucawaqa, P., Brewer, T., ... Andrew, N.L. (2020) 'COVID-19 and Pacific food system resilience: Opportunities to build a robust response'. *Food Security*, 12(4): 783–91.

Fitzpatrick, K.M., Harris, C., Drawve, G. and Willis, D.E. (2020). 'Assessing food insecurity among US adults during the COVID-19 pandemic'. *Journal of Hunger & Environmental Nutrition*, 1–18.

Forbes, S.L. (2017) 'Post-disaster consumption: Analysis from the 2011 Christchurch earthquake'. *International Review of Retail Distribution & Consumer Research*, 27(1): 28–42.

Forrester, I.T., Mayaka, P., Brown-Fraser, S., Dawkins, N., Rowel, R. and Sitther, V. (2017) 'Earthquake disaster resilience: A framework for sustainable gardening in Haiti's vulnerable population'. *Journal of Hunger & Environmental Nutrition*, 12(1): 136–49.

Gonzalez, C.G. (2011) 'Climate change, food security, and agrobiodiversity: Toward a just, resilient, and sustainable food system'. *Fordham Environmental Law Review*, 493–522.

Islam, M.M. (2017) 'Food security, livelihood, health and coping mechanism scenario in disaster Prone Villages of Bangladesh'. *OIDA International Journal of Sustainable Development*, 10(02): 45–56.

Islam, M.M. and Ahmed, S. (2017) 'Effects of natural disaster on food availability, accessibility and consumption in household level of Coastal Villages'. *Journal of Geography & Natural Disasters*, 7(3).

Jackson, G. (2019) 'The influence of emergency food aid on the causal disaster vulnerability of Indigenous food systems'. *Agriculture and Human Values*, 1–17.

Jackson, G., McNamara, K.E. and Witt, B. (2020). '"System of hunger": Understanding causal disaster vulnerability of indigenous food systems'. *Journal of Rural Studies*, 73: 163–75.

Kato, Y., Passidomo, C. and Harvey, D. (2014) 'Political gardening in a post-disaster city: Lessons from New Orleans'. *Urban Studies*, 51(9): 1833–49.

Kinsey, E.W., Kinsey, D. and Rundle, A.G. (2020) 'COVID-19 and food insecurity: An uneven patchwork of responses'. *Journal of Urban Health: Bulletin of the New York Academy of Medicine*, 1.

Klomp, J. and Hoogezand, B. (2018) 'Natural disasters and agricultural protection: A panel data analysis'. *World Development*, 104: 404–17.

Kodish, S.R., Bio, F., Oemcke, R., Conteh, J., Beauliere, J.M., Pyne-Bailey, S., ... Wirth, J.P. (2019) 'A qualitative study to understand how Ebola Virus Disease affected nutrition in Sierra Leone—A food value-chain framework for improving future response strategies'. *PLoS Neglected Tropical Diseases*, 13(9): e0007645.

Kotir, J.H. (2011) 'Climate change and variability in sub-Saharan Africa: A review of current and future trends and impacts on agriculture and food security'. *Environment, Development and Sustainability*, 13(3): 587–605.

Lassa, J.A., Teng, P., Caballero-Anthony, M. and Shrestha, M. (2019) 'Revisiting emergency food reserve policy and practice under disaster and extreme climate events'. *International Journal of Disaster Risk Science*, 10(1): 1–13.

Lesk, C., Rowhani, P. and Ramankutty, N. (2016) 'Influence of extreme weather disasters on global crop production'. *Nature*, 529(7584): 84–7.

Lioutas, E.D. and Charatsari, C. (2020) 'Enhancing the ability of agriculture to cope with major crises or disasters: What the experience of COVID-19 teaches us'. *Agricultural Systems*, 103023.

Ma, C.C., Chen, H.S. and Chang, H.P. (2020) 'Crisis response and supervision system for food security: A comparative analysis between Mainland China and Taiwan'. *Sustainability*, 12(7): 3045.

Manyena, S.B., Fordham, M. and Collins, A. (2008) 'Disaster resilience and children: Managing food security in Zimbabwe's Binga District'. *Children, Youth, and Environments*, 18(1): 303–31.

Masten, A.S. and Obradovic, J. (2008) 'Disaster preparation and recovery: Lessons from research on resilience in human development'. *Ecology and Society*, 13(1).

Mishra, A., Bruno, E. and Zilberman, D. (2020) 'Compound natural and human disasters: Managing drought and COVID-19 to sustain global agriculture and food sectors'. *Science of the Total Environment*, 754: 142210.

Mushtaq, S., Kath, J., Stone, R., Henry, R., Läderach, P., Reardon-Smith, K., ... Pischke, F. (2020) 'Creating positive synergies between risk management and transfer to accelerate food system climate resilience'. *Climatic Change*, 1–14.

Ofreneo, R.P. and Hega, M.D. (2016) 'Women's solidarity economy initiatives to strengthen food security in response to disasters'. *Disaster Prevention and Management*, 25(2): 168–82. (https://doi.org.ezaccess.libraries.psu.edu/10.1108/DPM-11-2015-0258)

Oluoko-Odingo, A.A. (2011) 'Vulnerability and adaptation to food insecurity and poverty in Kenya'. *Annals of the Association of American Geographers*, 101(1): 1–20.

Pingali, P., Alinovi, L. and Sutton, J. (2005) 'Food security in complex emergencies: Enhancing food system resilience'. *Disasters*, 29: S5–S24.

Rehman, A., Jingdong, L., Du, Y., Khatoon, R., Wagan, S.A. and Nisar, S.K. (2016) 'Flood disaster in Pakistan and its impact on agriculture growth (a review)'. *Environment and Development Economics*, 6(23): 39–42.

Rukundo, P.M., Iversen, P.O., Oshaug, A., Omuajuanfo, L.R., Rukooko, B., Kikafunda, J. and Andreassen, B.A. (2014) 'Food as a human right during disasters in Uganda. *Food Policy*', 49: 312–22.

Savage, A., Bambrick, H. and Gallegos, D. (2020) 'From garden to store: Local perspectives of changing food and nutrition security in a Pacific Island country'. *Food Security*, 12(6): 1331–48.

Savary, S., Akter, S., Almekinders, C., Harris, J., Korsten, L., Rötter, R., ... Watson, D. (2020) 'Mapping disruption and resilience mechanisms in food systems'. *Food Security*, 12(4): 695–717.

Shamsie, Y. (2012) 'Haiti's post-earthquake transformation: What of agriculture and rural development?' *Latin American Politics and Society*, 54(2): 133–52.

Sherman, M. and Ford, J.D. (2013) 'Market engagement and food insecurity after a climatic hazard'. *Global Food Security*, 2(3): 144–55.

Shipton, P. (1990) 'African famines and food security: Anthropological perspectives'. *Annual Review of anthropology*, 19(1): 353–94.

Skees, J.R. (2000) 'A role for capital markets in natural disasters: A piece of the food security puzzle'. *Food policy*, 25(3): 365–78.

Smith, K. and Lawrence, G. (2018) 'From disaster management to adaptive governance? Governance challenges to achieving resilient food systems in Australia'. *Journal of Environmental Policy and Planning*, 20(3): 387–401.

Smith, L.C. and Frankenberger, T.R. (2018) 'Does resilience capacity reduce the negative impact of shocks on household food security? Evidence from the 2014 floods in Northern Bangladesh'. *World Development*, 102: 358–76.

Takebayashi, Y., Murakami, M., Nomura, S., Oikawa, T. and Tsubokura, M. (2020). 'The trajectories of local food avoidance after the Fukushima Daiichi nuclear plant disaster: A five-year prospective cohort study'. *International Journal of Disaster Risk Reduction*, 46: 101513.

Tirivangasi, H.M. (2018) 'Regional disaster risk management strategies for food security: Probing Southern African Development Community channels for influencing national policy'. *Jàmbá: Journal of Disaster Risk Studies*, 10(1): 1–7.

Umar, M., Wilson, M. and Heyl, J. (2017) 'Food network resilience against natural disasters: A conceptual framework'. *SAGE open*, 7(3). (https://doi.org/10.1177/2158244017717570)

Vermeulen, S.J., Aggarwal, P.K., Ainslie, A., Angelone, C., Campbell, B.M., Challinor, A.J., … Wollenberg, E. (2012) 'Options for support to agriculture and food security under climate change'. *Environmental Science & Policy*, 15(1): 136–44.

Vervisch, T.G., Vlassenroot, K. and Braeckman, J. (2013) Livelihoods, power, and food insecurity: Adaptation of social capital portfolios in protracted crises – Case study Burundi'. *Disasters*, 37(2): 267–292.

Wentworth, C. (2020, April) 'Unhealthy aid: Food security programming and disaster responses to Cyclone Pam in Vanuatu'. In *Anthropological Forum* (Vol. 30, No. 1–2, pp. 73–90). Routledge.

Wheeler, T. and Von Braun, J. (2013) 'Climate change impacts on global food security'. *Science*, 341(6145): 508–13.

11

Food Systems in Europe and Sub-Saharan Africa: Critical Reflections on the Interface Between Food Systems and Ecosystem Services Using Social Practice Theory

Bernhard Freyer, Zerihun Yohannes Amare, Claudia Bieling, Jim Bingen, Marta Lopez Cifuentes, Pierre Ellssel, Valentin Fiala, Violet Kisakye, Lucia Diez Sanjuan and Christine Wieck

Introduction

Strong evidence points to food production as one of the largest driving forces of climate change (CC), biodiversity loss (BDL), land-system change, freshwater use and alterations in global nitrogen and phosphorus cycles (Brondizio et al., 2019; Rockström et al., 2009; Steffen et al., 2015). This development has tremendous negative impacts on socio-economic dimensions, e.g., limited food access, malnutrition or social injustice, and is fundamentally questioning the current dominant food system (FS) paradigm. Thus, food production and related FS are major drivers in shaping the so-called Anthropocene (Willett et al., 2019), culminating in multiple crises which are demanding fundamental change, i.e. transformation of FS.

To understand the relationships between environmental impacts, the socio-economic settings and FS (Borie et al.), we must capture the interdependencies across scales and contexts (Gatti et al., 2020). From this perspective, FS (Borie et al., 2020) are understood as socio-ecological systems (Marshall, 2015) in which Ericksen (2008) includes production, processing, retail sales and distribution, food quality and diets, actors, critical processes and other factors that influence social and environmental outcomes. FS are not only a driver of environmental changes but are also affected by their consequences. FS are weakened by BDL, which in turn can negatively impact human health (Chappell and LaValle, 2011; Crenna et al., 2019; Dalin and Outhwaite, 2019; Ingram, 2011; Johns and Eyzaguirre, 2006). In most cases, CC negatively impacts agricultural production, social systems and thus FS (Fraser, 2007; Fanzo et al., 2018; Myers et al., 2017; Niles et al., 2017), eventually leading to socio-ecological crises. The link of FS with socio-ecological crises can be described in relation to their impact on ecosystem services (ES),[1] as FS influence ES resilience and vulnerability (Biggs et al., 2015; Sarkki et al., 2017). ES assessment schemes can be used as an instrument for assessing the role of FS as drivers of socio-ecological crises (Mafongoya and Sileshi, 2020). Agriculture, forestry and fisheries are influenced and influence all types of ES including ecological and social dimensions (Lajoie-O'Malley et al., 2020).

The aforementioned characteristics that shape the Anthropocene put in question the current dominant FS and demand a more thorough understanding and shared learning processes on how the social and material dimensions of socio-ecological systems can be adapted, i.e. transformed (Berkes, 2017). With Reisman and Fairbairn (2020: 688), we argue that agri-FS serve as 'competing Anthropocene origin stories, a source of theoretical insight for the complexity of human–environment relations, and a site of agency for engaging alternative futures', where specifically the role of the social as a potential driver of the overall global crisis needs more in-depth studies. The global industrial shareholder-driven agri-food complex on one side, and the social movements-driven FS on the other, are framing the diverse FS and the related ES.

The relation between the social (including cultural and institutional dimensions) and the material (including nature/environmental and technical dimensions) is discussed from different theoretical standpoints. Moore et al. (2014) argue that technical transformation is closely linked with social transformation processes, and hence the material and the social are mutually dependent. In other words, there is inseparability of non-human nature and human society (Pellow and Nyseth Brehm,

---

[1]The Millennium Ecosystem Assessment (2005) defined Ecosystem Services as 'the benefits people derive from ecosystems'. The services comprise provisioning services (e.g., food, wood and other raw materials, plants, animals), regulating services (e.g., pollination of crops, disease regulation), supporting services (e.g., nutrient cycling) and cultural services (e.g., recreation and a sense of place).

2013). Palomo et al. (2016) underline the co-production of ES, rather than being only naturally produced, and thus ES have been and continue to be largely influenced by humans using different types of capital assets (human, social, manufactured and financial). Berbés-Blázquez et al. (2016) argue that most ES are co-produced by a mixture of natural capital and various forms of social, human, financial and technological capital. Raymond et al. (2018) introduce the concept of embodied ecosystem approaches, arguing that the human–nature relation is more complex than described by the co-production of ES research. They define embodied ecosystems as: '(1) relational – at any point in time embodied ecosystems are constituted by a web of relations between environment, culture, body and mind; (2) situational – at any point in time direct perception-action processes actualize relations between environment, culture, body and mind; and (3) dynamical – at any point in time embodied ecosystems and the value they provide change through pathways of actualized perception-action processes' (Raymond et al., 2018: 794).

Fischer and Eastwood (2016) suggest that identities and capabilities of people must be considered much more strongly than is currently the case in standard ES assessments, as these influence which ecosystem structures are eventually turned into benefits and give important insights into the environmental justice related to the distribution of ecosystem benefits. In the same direction, Díaz et al. (2015: 7) discuss the conceptual framework for the Intergovernmental Science-Policy Platform on Biodiversity and Ecosystem Services (IPBES). They classify anthropogenic drivers as those 'that are the result of human decisions and actions, namely, of institutions and governance systems', influencing all aspects of relationships between people and nature that are generated outside the ecosystem in question. Finally, social practice theory focuses on the interplay between the social and the material, arguing that any material – and at least behaviour change, i.e., transformation – depends on the social environment (Hargreaves, 2011; Standal and Westskog, 2022). We found this theoretical approach as the most adequate as social/cultural indicators as well as the material are both integrated in FS and ES assessment schemes. This interpretation of the social–material interface as introduced by social practice theory (Brand, 2011; Hargreaves, 2011) offers the starting point of this chapter. By providing evidence on the interrelations between FS and ES, representing both material and social dimensions, in this chapter, we study the role of the social dimension as a driver of material practices in FS. Therefore, we use social practice theory as a framework, analysing how far the social dimension of FS is framing the material, their impacts on ES cultural and material indicators and the role of the social indicators of ES.

Conceptual Framework and Approach

Referring to key literature and a discourse between the authors of this chapter, who offer different, but complementary scientific backgrounds,[2] we develop an indicative assessment framework to present and argue the interfaces between FS and ES. We use social practice theory to reflect on how the material/nature and the social practices are mutually dependent, which highlights the relationship between human and non-human natures, and we suggest how this concept can be used for a deeper understanding of undesirable social and ecological impacts for humans and nature. To study these linkages, the diverse FS and ES are organised via three matrices (Tables 11.1–11.3).

Social Practice Theory: Making the Material and Social Interdependencies Explicit

A sociological explanatory approach is applied to interpret the 'material' (agro-)ecological practices in their manifestations that contribute to specific ES. The role of social practices within FS and ES is specifically reflected in their role of structuring, initiating and enabling the material world and to better understand the systemic characteristics of the diverse FS (see Brand, 2011). Bourdieu's and Giddens's central theoretical strategic choice was to ground the 'locus of the social' in 'social practices' (Brand, 2011) and to make clear that material (technical and natural/(agro-)ecological) practices are embedded in not only one, but several social practices. The extent to which this approach is applicable to explaining the sustainability of FS is expressed through both FS and ES descriptions, presupposing a methodological framework, which is introduced below.

---

[2]The authors of this chapter are from different continents (Europe, Africa, North America) and countries (Austria, Ethiopia, Germany, Spain, Uganda, the United States) and have diverse scientific backgrounds.

Food Systems

Following Ericksen (2008), we argue that FS are more than a set of activities ranging from production to consumption, but also include multiple environmental, social, political and economic determinants and drivers that encompass the components of food availability and access, as well as natural resource use that influences the functioning and outcomes of FS (in terms of food sovereignty, food security, environmental impact, social welfare, and cultural adequacy, among others). FS should be understood as integrating all sub-systems and processes from farm to fork. Furthermore, the analysis of FS should integrate the role of these systems for the environment and society as a whole.

Based on these reflections, we formulated a typology of FS that allows for a differentiated assessment of the diverse impacts of FS on ES. In contrast to the three FS introduced by the *High-Level Panel of Experts on Food Security and Nutrition* (HLPE, 2017), or the typology proposed by Gómez and Ricketts (2013) with four FS types, but with a low differentiation of FS characteristics, we increased the number of characteristics for a more detailed differentiation into six FS types in the South and five FS types in the North (Table 11.2). This comparably high resolution into eleven FS types has its advantages as it is sensitive to multiple realities. The broad geographical scope responds to the global and interdependent character of many current FS, as well as to the global scope of current socio-ecological crises (Cadillo-Benalcazar et al., 2020). Sixteen characteristics of FS have been identified, adapted and expanded following the classification developed by the High-Level Panel of Experts on Food Security and Nutrition (HLPE, 2017). The differentiation of the FS follows a gradient from low input up to high input intensive farming systems as a guiding characteristic. This compilation of characteristics of the production and social/socioeconomic dimensions towards an FS type is a generalization, but necessary for the operationalization of any assessment procedure. Based on our experiences and key literature, we hypothesise that farming intensity is specifically contextualized with the four socially oriented indicators, which are (1) farmer-consumer relation, (2) relevance of FS's stakeholder values, (3) economic access for consumers and (4) social/community integration. In the language of social practice theory, the social enables the material and vice versa. What we further hypothesize are the characteristics of the stakeholder relationship in the respective FS: the more distant and hierarchised (decreasing governance/voice) the FS are, the more we can observe FS material practices with negative impacts on ES.

Ecosystem Services

Various ES assessment frameworks with different typologies exist[3] (Martínez-Harms and Balvanera, 2012). For our purposes, we use the ES framework as defined by FAO,[4] and the ES typology of TEEB (Sukhdev and Wittmer, 2008) on which the former is based. The ES concept with four types of services (Table 11.1) was also selected for its differentiation between supporting and regulating services as it allows for a more precise demonstration of the relationships between FS attributes and ES indicators.

Ecosystem Services – FS Interfaces

According to McElwee (2017), ES assessment frameworks face several methodological challenges. Taking the weaknesses and critical discourses on ES assessment frameworks into account, we do not refer to measured data that inform, e.g. about the impact of a herbicide on invertebrates expressed with the Shannon-Weaver index (Hennink and Zeven, 1990), or a certain crop rotation on humus content, expressed in tons of dry matter per hectare. Instead, rather we refer more broadly to the potential impacts on ES, characterised by the diverse attributes of FS regarding farming, processing, transportation, retail, consumption and cultural practices. Consequently, assessments of the impact of FS on ES can merely be an approximation based on preliminary research findings (Sperling et al., 2020). To gain insights into the ES–FS interfaces and the interplay between the material and social practices, we applied three different procedures. Using a descriptive approach, we first define the relationship between ES and relevant FS' attributes that can deteriorate, preserve or enhance ES, without specifically referring to a defined FS (see Table 11.1). This classification

---

[3]The Economics of Ecosystem and Biodiversity (TEEB) (Sukhdev and Wittmer, 2008), the US Environmental Protection Agency's (EPA) Final Ecosystem Services and Goods Classification System (FEGS-CS), the Millennium Ecosystem Assessment (Reid et al., 2005), the Intergovernmental Science-Policy Platform on Biodiversity and Ecosystem Services (IPBES) (IPBES, 2019) and the CICES classification (Czúcz et al., 2018; Haines-Young and Potschin, 2017; Haines-Young and Potschin-Young, 2018).
[4]http://www.fao.org/ecosystem-services-biodiversity/en

Table 11.1 Food system attributes' potential impact on ecosystem services indicators

		Food System Attributes that Affect the Different Ecosystem Services		
		Attributes that Deteriorate ES		Attributes that Enhance ES
No	Ecosystem Service[1]	+	++	+++
	Supporting services are necessary for the production of all other ecosystem services, e.g., by providing plants and animals with living spaces, allowing for diversity of species and maintaining genetic diversity			
S1	**Soil formation** (Organic matter accumulation, decomposition and humification)	Humus productivity is low due to low crop productivity and lack of biomass-rich diverse crops and lack of recirculation of animal manure; high soil tillage intensity	Humus production is maintaining site-specific levels with an increased crop diversity, cover crops and some circulation of animal manure; moderate soil tillage intensity	High humus productivity due to, e.g., forage legumes, alley cropping and recirculation of animal manure, moderate to low soil tillage intensity
S2	**Nutrient cycling** (Nutrients essential for life, including nitrogen and phosphorus, cycle through ecosystems and are maintained at different concentrations in different parts of ecosystems)	Often low level due to wind and water erosion; high leaching rates, soil erosion due to low soil cover; no animal manure circulation; low soil microbiological activity	Partly closed cycles of nutrients induced by erosion control measures and animal manure management; medium soil microbiological activity	Optimised animal manure management; low leaching rates and low soil erosion due to highly diversified cropping systems and biomass input; high soil microbiological activity

(Continued)

Table 11.1 Food system attributes' potential impact on ecosystem services indicators *(Continued)*

No	Ecosystem Service[1]	Food System Attributes that Affect the Different Ecosystem Services		
		Attributes that Deteriorate ES		Attributes that Enhance ES
		+	++	+++
S3	**Habitat for species** (Living spaces for plants or animals and maintaining a diversity of plants and animals)	Habitat diversity and share of land without crop use is low, low diversity of crop species, low diversity of animal species; high pesticide input	Maintenance of some habitats with a low diversity of plants; increased share of crops and animal species; partly pesticide input	High share of diverse habitats with high diversity of plants; high crop and animal diversity; pesticides excluded
S4	**Primary production** (Assimilation or accumulation of energy and nutrients by organisms)	High share of (temporary) bare land; biodiversity reduction and simplification of agricultural landscapes; low NPP**	Management practices that allow for some conservation of non-harvested biodiversity; medium NPP	Multi-functional agricultural biodiversity and landscape management practices, support of wild biodiversity; high NPP

Provisioning services are the material benefits people obtain from ecosystems for, e.g., supply of food, water, fibre, wood and fuels

No	Ecosystem Service[1]	+	++	+++
P1	**Water** (Availability)	Crops not adapted to water availability; bare soils; lack of irrigation/water storage;	Crops and farming practices partly adapted to water availability;	Crops adapted to water availability; optimised water management, high humus accumulation,

	dependence on external water resources	limited irrigation and water storage capacity	efficient irrigation approaches; high resistance against drought and flood due to highly diversified cropping systems and biomass input
P2 Food (Amount, quality and diversity of produced and 'wild' food)	(a) Low crop and animal productivity; no wild plant management or collection; low food quality; low diversity of cultivated and wild food (b) Temporary limited high food production accompanied by land degradation; low food quality; low diversity of cultivated and wild food; high livestock production and density	(a) Medium to high crop and animal productivity; some wild plant management or collection; medium food quality; medium crop and animal diversity (b) Increased sustainable production, better land management, medium diversity of cultivated and wild food; moderate livestock production and density	(a) Sustainable long-term medium to high production; wild plant collection including conservation management; high food quality (b) Sustainable production, high quality of land management, high diversity of cultivated and wild food; low livestock production and density
P3 Raw materials (Wood, biofuels, and fibre from wild or cultivated plant and animal species)	Low share of raw materials produced and used	Some wood, biofuels produced and used	High share of diverse raw materials produced, collected and used

(Continued)

Table 11.1 Food system attributes' potential impact on ecosystem services indicators (Continued)

No	Ecosystem Service[1]	Food System Attributes that Affect the Different Ecosystem Services		
		Attributes that Deteriorate ES	Attributes that Affect	Attributes that Enhance ES
		+	++	+++
P4	**Medicinal resources** (Pharmaceuticals, test and assay organisms)	No support/protection of medicinal wild plants; overuse; no cultivation of medicinal plants	Partly support/protection of medicinal wild plants and unsystematically used; cultivation of medicinal plants as an exception	Systematically support/ protection of medicinal wild plants and systematically used; cultivation of medicinal plants

Regulating services are the benefits obtained from the regulation of ecosystem processes, e.g., the regulation of air quality and soil fertility, control of floods or crop pollination

No	Ecosystem Service[1]	+	++	+++
R1	**Local climate** (Air quality, temperature, rainfall, pollutants)	Low positive impact on local climate due to low crop and habitat diversity and density, and the use of pesticides	Some positive impact on LC via tree planting	Highly positive impact on LC via highly diverse cropping systems, alley cropping, hedges and trees
R2	**Greenhouse gas (GHG) emission and carbon sequestration capacity (CSC)** (Emission of CO_2, CH_4 and N_2O; C	High GHG emissions with low CSC; due to low biomass production; negative carbon balances, high erosion risk; low crop/habitat	Balanced carbon sequestration capacity via cover crops and some alley cropping; medium livestock density, synthetic fertiliser use,	Low GHG emissions and high CSC via high crop diversity, biomass rich crops and trees; low livestock density; carbon surplus via forage

sequestration capacity in agricultural soils)	diversity; high tillage intensity; high livestock density; high synthetic fertiliser input; long distance between production, packaging and consumption	tillage intensity; reduced transportation distances/ increased transport efficiency	legumes, organic matter circulation and alley cropping; reduced tillage systems; low transportation distances, low material consumption
R3 Adaptation to and mitigation (AM) of extreme events (EE) (Crop and habitat diversity, soil cover, trees)	No specific activity to protect against EE: low crop and habitat diversity; high livestock density	Diversified cropping systems and some trees; medium livestock density	Highly diverse land use with biomass rich crops and trees; adapted livestock density according to the carrying capacity of the land
R4 Erosion prevention and maintenance of soil fertility (Technical and crop-based interventions)	Low soil cover and investment into soil fertility, high erosion rates and contamination of water bodies	Some erosion prevention-oriented activities supported by technical measures and tree planting, limited water contamination	High level of management activities to produce biomass via forage legumes, hybrid grasses, alley cropping and hedges and high quality of technical measures; no water contamination
R5 Biological control (Cropping system, habitat	No activities to support biological control, application of pesticides	Decreased level of pesticide use and establishment of habitats	Systematically established biological control through highly

(Continued)

Table 11.1 Food system attributes' potential impact on ecosystem services indicators *(Continued)*

No	Ecosystem Service[1]	Food System Attributes that Affect the Different Ecosystem Services		
		Attributes that Deteriorate ES		Attributes that Enhance ES
		+	++	+++
	diversity, pesticide use, alternative products)			diverse cropping systems and habitats; biological control by alternative industrial products
R6	**Water quality and regulation** (Impurities/purification capacity; runoff, flooding, storage potential)	Water contaminated by animal manure, fertilizers and pesticides, compacted soils, humus poor soils and low water holding capacity, water loss via erosion and inefficient irrigation technology; Drought and flood sensitive due to low biomass production and circulation; high stocking rate	Water partly contaminated, increased humus content, medium stocking rate; increased water holding capacity	No water contamination; cover crops, intercropping, permanent crops; terraces; fallow; stocking rate adapted to the farm internal food production

R7 **Pollination** (Distribution, abundance, and effectiveness of pollinators)	No or low share of pollinator plants; application of pesticides; low habitat and species diversification, and low share of habitats	Some pollinator plants; low rate of pesticide use	Diverse pollinators through habitats with species richness, and diversified crop rotations; high diversification of cropping system, species and habitats

Cultural services are non-material benefits people gain from ecosystems, e.g., aesthetic and engineering inspiration, cultural identity and spiritual well-being

C1 **Cultural aesthetic appreciation and inspiration** (Culture, parks, scenic drives, inspiration for art and design, folklore, national symbols, architecture, and advertising. . .)	No specific appreciation and inspiration; No social/community integration	Some elements sensitive to aesthetical issues are protected	Systematic use of nature's aesthetic potential; FS' adapted to local values; high level of social/community integration
C2 **Cultural heritage** (Maintenance of either historically important cultural landscapes/ culturally significant species; cultural driven diets)	No specific consideration of cultural heritage; No social/community integration	Selected CH values are protected	Systematic protection of cultural heritage; FS' adapted to local values; High social/community integration

(Continued)

Table 11.1 Food system attributes' potential impact on ecosystem services indicators *(Continued)*

No	Ecosystem Service[1]	Food System Attributes that Affect the Different Ecosystem Services		
		Attributes that Deteriorate ES		Attributes that Enhance ES
		+	++	+++
C3	**Educational and scientific values** (Formal and informal education, scientifically relevant value)	No specific consideration; low potential for educational and scientific use	Medium potential for educational and scientific use	High potential for educational and scientific use
C4	**Knowledge** (Traditional and formal and informal types of knowledge systems developed by different cultures)	No specific consideration of knowledge	Some activities to restore and foster knowledge	Systematic consideration and strengthening of knowledge
C5	**Recreation, mental and physical health** (Ecotourism, therapeutic activities, leisure time based in part on the characteristics of the natural or cultural landscapes)	No offer of recreational activities; no specific activities	Some specific offers of recreational activities	Systematic use of nature for offering recreational activities

C6 Social relations (Social relations induced by the FS' values)	Anonymous; the consumer doesn't know the farmer 'behind' the product; global prices often low in retail markets while higher in shops with a certain label like organic	Some organised events and relationships directed towards enhancement of social relations	Continuous relationship of farmers and consumer groups; local products adapted to the local income level; FS' adapted to local values; high level social/community integration; certification/control systems established by stakeholders for the whole food chain
C7 Spiritual and religious experience and sense of place (Symbolic value of sites or ecosystems elements (soil, plant, tree, animal, …) with historically spiritual significance)	No relevance of spiritual and religious experiences	Some species (e.g., trees or medicinal plants) or sites of spiritual/religious relevance	Understanding nature in its role for spirituality; (promotion of sense of place, of community); FS' adapted to local values; High level of social/community integration

Sources: IPBES (2019), Ingram (2011), FAO (2017), Johnson et al. (2007) and Hutchinson et al. (2007); adapted; *according to the farming method; **NPP-Netto primary production.

[1] http://www.fao.org/ecosystem-services-biodiversity/en/

we use in a second step to allocate FS' attributes to the 16 FS' characteristics of 11 FS types and execute the FS' characteristics linkage to the single ES (see Table 11.2). Finally, we reorganise these preparatory classifications and make explicit the linkage between ES, FS and their attributes using a qualitative approach (see Table 11.3).

Results and Discussion

In this section, FS characteristics, FS types and ES indicators are introduced and their interplay interpreted with reference to social practice theory. We argue that the embeddedness of the material in the social practices follows an inner logic of the respective FS. We primarily follow the idea that the social of FS enables the material, which has its correspondence in the ES, where there is a link between immaterial values (traditions, place-attachment) and favourable material outcomes (e.g., prevention of erosion or resource degradation). While the social enables and frames material practices, the latter creates options for the social practices. To make the diverse relationships visible, FS characteristics and ES indicators are organised in matrices (see Tables 11.1–11.3).

General Insights on How the Material and the Social Practices Are Interrelated

FS

FS are differentiated by ecological characteristics and related farming practices including the use of industrial inputs and the structure of the production (No. 1–3) (Tables 11.1 and 11.2); activities after harvest – logistics, market, administrative issues, technical standards, quantities of production, transportation and the site of sale (No. 4–11); and more socio-economic and social characteristics – the distribution of power, and communication characteristics – mainly integrating the consumer perspective (No. 12–16) (Table 11.2). Three characteristics are especially relevant for differentiating the material practices, i.e., the production (No. 1–3), in which farm input was used as a guiding characteristic, which also serves for labelling the FS.

FS characteristics, i.e., practices are driven by the social, i.e., the social settings of stakeholders specifically via community integration, farmer–consumer relations and stakeholder values (No. 14–16). An example from the South: low technical standards, no/low input practices, specific local value systems, close relationships between farmers and consumers, limited economic potential of the consumers and lack of certification are characteristics that represent a predominant FS; while the high-input conventional systems defined via high technical standards and a high degree of formalisation, globally oriented practices are related to distanced farmer–consumer relations. But we will not observe that high-input farming is embedded into/ driven by close farmer–consumer relations and farmer markets as social practices.

Ecosystem Services

ES are described via material practices, including nature (natural resources/biodiversity) itself and technologies applied by humans, which are in a close interplay with the cultural dimensions. Comparing material dimensions of ES (provisioning, supporting, and regulating services) with those of cultural services as the immaterial types of ES, the former seems much more elaborated in the scientific discourse, as well as within the ES framework itself than the latter (Plieninger et al., 2014). Similarly, this can be stated for FS reference to social/ socioeconomic characteristics like power, inequality, or food sovereignty. Cultural services directly or indirectly weaken or strengthen the supporting, provisioning, and regulating services, and can act to a certain degree as drivers, as far as they are influenced by human practices. Most cultural services (C1, C2, C4, C7) are directly related to biodiversity and production intensity, e.g. S3, S4, P2, P3, P4, R3, R5 and R7, enabling different contributions to the biophysical dimensions of ES. This influence on the material dimension is of systemic nature. For example, culturally embedded, diverse dietary practices and veganism/vegetarianism that are related to a certain degree with the diversity of cropping systems (Gaba et al., 2015) or limited shares of meat, might strengthen several biophysical and particularly regulating ES, while meat-based diets foster intensive livestock production and high livestock densities per land unit, which can have detrimental effects for these types of ES. Vegetarians tend to buy organic food as they share the ecological values as part of a social value set, often with fair trade certification, which is a further value set, integrating several aspects (e.g., labour, payment, health, gender). From a social perspective, C6 is specifically of importance as it conveys the option of farmer empowerment, which is often the social basis for any cultural practice, and with that certain material ES too. C1, C3 and C7 might be also driven by economic interest from outside of FS, thus informing about the dependency of FS stakeholders, i.e., of its hierarchical structures and its influence on governance characteristics that support or suppress ecologically favourable behaviour, i.e., practices.

The link between FS' characteristics and ES indicators

At a first glance, supporting, provisioning and regulating services are mainly driven by FS characteristics No. 1–3, which are material practices at the farm level (Table 11.2). Farm input (No. 1), crop and habitat diversity (No. 2) unite most direct relationships with the biophysical indicators of ES. The social/socio-economic characteristics of FS from harvest up to the consumer practices (No. 4–16) are those which create opportunities for improving production. The majority of indicators describing the cultural services of ES thematically overlap with the characteristics of FS or are closely related. Both the cultural services of ES and the social/socio-economic characteristics of FS create or frame the material practices of FS. Of course, at this level of aggregation, this classification into FS types via the combination of attributes of in total 16 characteristics into those that deteriorate/enhance ES cannot do justice to the diversity of, e.g. cultural systems, instead it can only make visible that socio-ecological crises or solutions are driven by FS as a whole where the social/socio-economic practices are the main driver.

Specifications of FS

FS in the Global South

Smallholder farming still dominates the southern FS production unit, but different production intensities are applied and relate to diverse characteristics from harvest to the consumer. Farming systems are increasingly characterised by maize-based cropping systems, low fertiliser input (low efficiency if combined with high rainfall, long dry periods and low soil humus content), overgrazing and loss of forests, thereby contributing to soil erosion, landslides, low soil fertility levels and management with high risk for the environment (Schader et al., 2021), and consequently low supporting, regulating, and provisioning services (Martínez-Harms and Balvanera, 2012). A high share of the food is sold in local and regional markets, while cooperatives, middlemen and companies collect products for the national and international market. These behavioural routines are physically anchored, so to speak, supported by a collective tacit knowledge and hence dominate current FS (Liedtke et al., 2013). Furthermore, a shift in diets can be observed away from traditional and diverse diets, which is among other factors, a result of the change towards maize-based production and the adoption of food consumption practices (e.g. increased intake of edible oils, caloric sweeteners, animal source-protein) based on the globalised FS of the multinational corporations (Mendenhall and Singer, 2019; Popkin et al., 2012).

Organic farming systems claiming for higher ecological standards can compete with the non-organic low/medium input system (No. 1, 2) yield level, if the main agroecological practices – crop rotation (crop and species diversity; low/no hybrid seeds), forage legumes and organic manure recirculation are consequently and systematically implemented. But it seems that the organic approach is culturally not well embedded, and therefore, the share of certified organic farms is still limited.

Organic medium input represents those FS that focus on a single product for the international market where the product must fulfil technical quality and certification standards defined by the North. In practice, these systems tend to use industrially produced organic fertilizers (input-driven) or biomass from outside the farm (Adamtey et al., 2016) to fulfil such standards. The fact that the different versions of organic FS are still underrepresented in the South has many reasons (Heryadi, 2018; Janjhua et al., 2019; Jouzi et al., 2017) (e.g., additional labour and costs, certification).

As farming practices are embedded in traditions and shared values in a community, innovations are confronted with cultural barriers. What hinders organic to become more mainstream is less the knowledge about successful practices than the lack of the social embeddedness (Gichure, 2020). The IFOAM (International Federation of Organic Farming Movements) value sets of organic agriculture are driven by the North, hence they might not be connected to any social practice in the South or are lacking a 'translation' into the cultural environment (Goldberger, 2008). New insights into these dynamics are offered by the latest discourse on bifurcation of organic FS in the South (Nikol and Jansen, 2021). As long as partners from production up to consumers are not able to link their traditions with the organic approach, and an organic movement is not established, the southern organic FS will be limited in its overall societal acceptance and impact. Smallholder farming still dominates the southern FS production unit, but different production intensities are applied and relate to diverse characteristics from harvest to the consumer.

FS in the Global North

Today, the conventional medium input FS is likely the most common FS in Europe, while it is in the conventional high input in the United States, with far reaching negative impacts on the environment (Guerrero Lara et al., 2019). Farmers of the conventional medium input system integrate single agroecological practices or so-called integrated methods (e.g. damage threshold principle) but decide not to convert to organic for various reasons (Constance and choi, 2010; Delbridge et al., 2017; Larsson et al., 2013; Xu et al., 2018). Social factors are one of the main barriers (Kociszewski et al., 2020; Xu et al., 2018) as conventional farmers are part of a different peer group than the organic farmers with their own value sets and differing material practices. Farmers fear the loss of their social environment. They are members of primarily farmer associations, where productivity and economic goals constitute the highest priority and value. The majority of conventional farmers are not connected with consumers nor is there any value discourse between farmers, consumers and the sub-systems of FS in between (processing, etc.). Large parts of conventional agriculture are driven by industrial complexes, where farmers are highly dependent via contracts and/or high investments, which does not allow ad hoc nor medium-term transformation towards organic farming and hence, more ecologically sound practices.

The organic low-input system represents the most supportive FS for a broad spectrum of particularly supporting and regulating ES. Of significance is their contribution to soil fertility. In contrast to other systems, the organic system integrates functions that are usually provided by industrial inputs (e.g., instead of herbicides and pesticides, using crop rotations to reduce the risk of weeds, pests, and diseases). The price of this approach is often a lower physical yield (Dufeu et al., 2020) but higher other ES. The organic medium FS replaces industrial mineral fertilizers with organic fertilizers from outside the farm on high application rates and produces mostly cash crops, and to a lesser extent those crops that aid in increasing soil fertility like forage legumes. These practices are still within the organic farming guidelines. They tend to better fulfil provisioning services in terms of higher yields, but the performance of supporting and regulating services is reduced.

It can be hypothesised that the more input-oriented organic farmers still sympathise with the agricultural logic of conventional farming, therefore share more values with the conventional farmers than with the organic community (see also the conventionalisation discourse) (Kociszewski et al., 2020). Again, the social embeddedness frames the material practices. Shared cultural services along the food chain obviously play a more important role in the low-input FS, while they are to a lesser extent part of a stakeholder-shared process, as far as they are defined by the industrialised FS types (Slámová and Belčáková, 2019; Špulerová et al., 2018). Organic farms tend to invest in the social within the context of their diversified marketing concept and increasing options for direct communications with consumers. By doing so, these social practices allow a high diversification of their production or/and a collaboration between other farms for product exchange, thereby increasing their social networks. Nevertheless, we can also argue that the diversification of production allows direct marketing and hence, closer consumer–farmer communications and relationships, while focusing on large production of one or a few products does not.

Robustness of the Social – Material Interface

At a first glance, it seems that FS follow a systemic logic, which means that a certain social/socio-economic environment opens spaces and opportunities for a specific production intensity, postharvest practice, administration, and market characteristics. But this is not always the case. The same social setting can lead to different material practices.

Around those FS types defined by the terms agroecological, traditional and organic farming methods, which are all discussed as low input, similar material practices are driven by different social settings. The traditional no/low input FS represents those farmers that might have been more ecologically oriented in former times (Gómez-Baggethun and Reyes-García, 2013). But due to changing socioeconomic conditions such as land pressure via urbanisation, traffic and infrastructure expansion, changing demands from the food market, and constantly shrinking farm sizes due to real division of the farmland, farmers moved away from farming methods that are, e.g., rich in biodiversity (Vignola et al., 2010). Therefore, we cannot generalise that traditional low-input FS protect their natural environments per se or build their relations with nature by spiritual values that contribute positively to the well-functioning of ES. In contrast, some communities, such as the Ethiopian Christian-Orthodox monasteries, in which food habits are structured by more than 180 fasting days per year, are known for protecting the last natural forests, since the monks respect the spiritual value of the forests (Bitewmekonen et al., 2019; Moges et al., 2017). However, due to largely economic reasons, this relation is also under pressure (Orlowska and Klepeis, 2018).

Agroecology became a fuzzy term with rather multiple significances. Agroecology is described as a science, a set of practices, and a social movement (Gliessman, 2018; Wezel et al., 2009), however without explicitly formulated general ethical principles or production rules as they are defined for organic farming (Luttikholt, 2007) or as the social standards for fair trade (Jaffee, 2010). Furthermore, any regulatory framework about the material practices is excluded, where one may argue that they should be defined by the people and not by top-down prescriptions of what is allowed and what is not. However, this opens the door for any kind of material practice, whether it is ecologically oriented or not. Agroecology overlaps in many ways in its material practices with organic farming, but also emphasises biological control methods that are part of integrated farming methods (e.g., integrated pest management). The latter represents the moderate version of conventional farming. The differentiation of integrated, conventional low/medium input and conventional high input (see Tables 11.2 and 11.3) expresses that not only organic farming FS are diverse (organic low input/organic medium input), but so too are conventional FS in which, for example, selected biological pest control methods are applied, or pesticides or simply nothing (Shields et al., 2019).

Looking at the social background, farmers might be organised in the same peer groups, but further socialized in different subgroups, e.g. where biological pest control methods are practiced while in others not. The intensity of soil tillage is not specifically related to a certain FS (not specifically listed as a differentiating characteristic, but highly influential on GHG emissions and carbon sequestration); farm size is not specifically a feature of organic or conventional farms, while livestock density (No. 3) is limited by the organic regulations, although there is no limitation with respect to other farms – we can find high stocking rates in small farms (animals also as a symbol of social status or as an important part of food security in dry periods), as well as in industrial farms, but with different impact on ES. Economic pressure, social and demographic drivers are responsible for the ongoing reduction of farm numbers, which is frequently associated with intensification processes of the surviving farms (Debolini et al., 2018), which confirms our assumptions that the material follows the social.

For storage, transport, processing, packaging, retail, and promotion, many FS use not only one but a set of practices, i.e., different attributes of the characteristics might be appropriate. In those cases, we decided to select attributes that are most often discussed and applied for defining a certain FS. Except in organic and traditional/low input systems in the South, seasonal-oriented consumption (No. 12) is not linked per se with other FS. There is consensus that conventional high-input FS include industrialised meat production, high livestock densities and meat-based diets, including national and international processing and trade processes, which are weakening ES (Jacob et al., 2020), while they are considered highly productive, at least in the short term, to the exclusion of external environmental/social ancillary costs. But also, postharvest practices do not necessarily exclude products from smaller farms in their processing and market system. On the consumer side, it is often the case that those with a certain preference for organic food also consume conventionally-produced food. As such they are part of more than one FS with rather different social contexts. As discussed in other studies, even if consumers favour their traditional food patterns, Western style fast food (Sherwood et al., 2001) is entering the traditional home-kitchen through pester power (Wertheim-Heck and Ranerids, 2020).

These examples demonstrate that it is not always possible to precisely delineate one FS type from the other with reference to some FS characteristic, and that specific social settings do not automatically lead to one and the same material practices. Furthermore, obviously several other FS types exist in between the defined ones, with a specific mix of mutually dependent social and material practices. This reality informs us that only the combination of all attributes of FS characteristics allows for a precise picture of how social and material practices interact and FS interrelate with ES.

Table 11.2 Typology of food systems, their characteristics and attributes and linkages to ecosystem services

No.	Food System Characteristics	South						North				
		Traditional No Input	Traditional/ AE[1] Practices Low/Medium Input	Organic Low Input	Organic Medium Input	Conv. Low/Medium Input	Conv. High Input	Organic Low Input	Organic Medium Input	Integrated Medium /High Input	Conventional Medium Input	Conventional High Input
	Attributes											
1	**Input I** (Use of industrial inputs per hectare) * ES: S1, S2, S3; P1[a]; R4, R5, R7; C2 [2]	No	Low	Low-medium	Low-medium	Medium-high	High	Low	Medium	Medium	Medium	High
2	**Crop and habitat diversity** (Planned and associated species diversity; species and varieties; share of hybrid varieties (reverse assessment) ES: S2, S3; P2, P3, P4; R2, R4, R5, R7[b]; C2	Low	Medium	High	Medium	Low	Low	High	Medium	Medium	Low	Low
3	**Farm size and livestock density** (Farmland ha, livestock density per ha) ES: P1, P2; R2; C6[c]	Low, low-high	Low, low-medium	Low, low-medium	Low, low-medium	Low-large, low-medium	large, low-high	Small-large, low-medium	Small-large, low-medium	Medium, medium	Low-medium, Low-medium	Large, low-high

		Low ST at farm, without DU	Low ST at farm, small DU	Medium ST at farm, medium DU	High ST outside farm; large DU	Medium ST at farm, medium DU	High ST outside farm; large DU	Medium ST at farm, small DU	High ST outside farm; medium/Large DU	High ST outside farm; medium/Large DU	Medium ST outside farm; medium DU	High ST outside farm; large DU
4	**Storage technology standards (ST) and distribution units (DU)** (Warehouses distribution) ES: P2; R1, R2; C6[a]											
5	**Transportation TT** (Means of transport used) ES: P2; R1, R2; C1, C6	Mainly animal traction and local	Mainly animal traction and local	Mainly small/medium size motor traction, regional/national	Mainly trucks, railway; national/international	Mainly small/medium size motor traction, regional/national	Mainly aircraft, trucks, global	Mainly small/regional and national	Mainly trucks, railway; national/international	Mainly trucks, railway; national/international	Mainly trucks, railway; national and international	Aircraft, trucks, global
6	**Processing** (Degree of modernisation; geographical distribution) ES: R2, R3	Local; manual	Local; mechanised	Mainly regional; mechanised	Mainly national; modernised	Mainly regional; mechanised	Mainly international; modernised	Local; modernised	Mainly national; modernised	Mainly regional/international; modernised	Mainly national/international; modernised	Mainly national/international; modernised
7	**Packaging** (Amount, (non)-renewable sources) ES: R2, R6	No/low	Low	Low	Low/Medium, higher share of renewable material	Medium higher share of non-renewable material	High material intensity PA	Low/Medium, higher share of non-ren. material	Medium, higher share of non-ren. material	Medium, higher share of non-ren. material	High material intensity	High material intensity
8	**Standards, certification and control system** (Formalisation degree) ES: C3, C6	No	No	Informal	(partly) Formal	Formal	Formal	Formal	Formal	Formal	Formal	Formal

(Continued)

Table 11.2 Typology of food systems, their characteristics and attributes and linkages to ecosystem services *(Continued)*

No. / Food System Characteristics	South						North				
	Traditional/AE¹ Practices										
	Traditional No Input	Low/Medium Input	Organic Low Input	Organic Medium Input	Conv. Low/Medium Input	Conv. High Input	Organic Low Input	Organic Medium Input	Integrated Medium /High Input	Conventional Medium Input	Conventional High Input
9 **Retail and market** (Diversity (DI) and density (DE) of markets, regionality, availability, proximity) ES: R3; C2, C4, C6 **	Mainly local informal low DI/ high DE	Mainly local informal low DI/high DE	Low DI/DE national	Low DI/DE national/ international	High DI/DE Local/national/ international	High DI/DE Local/ national/ international	High DI/ Medium DE local/national	Medium DI/ DE Local/ national/ international	Medium DI/ DE Local/ national/ international	Medium DI/ low DE Local/ national/ international	Low DI/High DE National/ international
10 **Promotion, advertising, and information** (Marking channel, consumer communication) ES: C1, C2, C3, C4, C6, C7	Mouth to mouth communication (MMC) in the market place	MMC	Classical media channels	Classical and new information channels³	Classical media channels	Classical and new information channels	MMC	Classical and new information channels	Classical media channels	Classical and new information channels	Classical and new information channels
11 **Food safety and (technical) quality standards** (Safety standards (SS), food quality standards (QS)) ES: P2; C3	Low SS, low/ high QS	Low/medium SS medium/ high QS	Low/High SS, medium/high QS	High SS/QS	Medium SS/QS	High SS/QS	High SS/QS	High SS/QS	High SS/QS	High SS/QS	High SS/QS

12	**Consumption patterns** (Adaptation to regional/seasonal product availability) ES: R2, R3; C4, C6, C7	High	High	High	Medium	Medium	Medium	High	Medium	Low	Low	Low
13	**Economic access** (Affordability for consumer) ES: P2; C6	High	High	Medium	Low	Medium	Medium	Medium	Low	Medium	High	High
14	**Social/ Community integration** (responsibility) ES: C1 – C7	High	High	Medium	Medium	Low	Low	Low/High	Low/medium	Low	Low	Low
15	**Farmer – consumer relation** (Trust, transparency, responsibility) [***] ES: C6, C7	Loose/very tight	tight/very tight	Very tight	Loose/tight	Loose/very tight	Loose	Very tight	tight	Loose/very tight	Loose	Loose
16	**Relevance of FS's stakeholder values** (Shared understanding of FS representatives) [****] ES: C1 – C7	Informal developed/ applied values	Informal developed/ applied values	High	Medium	Low	Low	High	Medium	Low/high	Low/high	Low/high

Source: Own; (Tscharntke et al., 2012); with reference to (Gómez and Ricketts, 2013; HLPE, 2017), adapted by the authors; [a] (Tilman et al., 2002); [b] (Kremen and Miles, 2012); [c] (Rosset, 2000); [d] (Forssell and Lankoski, 2015), also relevant for T; [e] (Pelletier, 2015), also relevant for PA; [*]mineral fertiliser; pesticides inclusive herbicides; [**]Diversity and density of markets, regionality, availability, proximity; [***]dependent on value chain structure; structures; [****]all stakeholder that are part of a food system.

[1]AE = Agroecology: practices like catch crops, farmyard manure application, biological pest control
[2]Short cut of ecosystem services see T; ecosystem services that are affected by FS characteristics specific attributes
[3]Classical media: newspaper, TV, broadcast, leaflets, etc.; new media: all kind of social media/

Table 11.3 Assessment of food systems impact/contribution to ecosystem services

No	Ecosystem Services	South						North				
		Trad. No/Low Input	Trad./AE Elements Low/Medium Input	Organic Low Input	Organic Medium Input	Conv. Low/Medium Input	Conv. High Input	Organic Low Input	Organic Medium Input	Integrated Medium/High Input	Conv. Medium Input	Conv. High Input
	Supporting services	-	++	+++	++	-	--	+++	++	++	-	--
S1	Soil formation	-	++	+++	++	-	--	+++	++	++	-	--
S2	Nutrient cycling	-	++	+++	++	-	---	+++	++	++	-	---
S3	Habitat for species	-	++	+++	++	-	---	+++	++	+	-	---
S4	Primary production	--	++	++	++	++	+++	++	++	++	+	+
	Provisioning services	-	++	+++	++	+	+	++	++	++	+	+++
P1	Water	-	++	+++	++	-	--	++	++	+		
P2	Food	-	+	+	++	++	+++	+	++	+++	++	+++
P3	Raw materials	-	++	++	++	+	++	++	++	++	++	+
P4	Medicinal resources	+	++	++	+	+	--	+++	+	.	+	--
	Regulating services	--	++	+++	++	-	---	+++	++	+	-	---
R1	Local climate	--	++	++	++	-	---	+++	++	+	-	---
R2	Carbon sequestration and storage	--	++	+++	++	-	---	+++	++	+	-	---
R3	Adaptation to/mitigation of extreme events	--	++	++	++	-	---	+++	++	+	-	---
R4	Erosion prevention/soil fertility maintenance	--	++	+++	++	-	---	+++	++	+	-	---
R5	Biological control	-	++	++	++	++	---	+++	++	++	-	---
R6	Water quality and regulation	-	++	+++	++	+	---	+++	++	+	-	---
R7	Pollination	+	++	+++	++	-	---	+++	++	+	-	---
	Cultural services	+	++	++	+	+	--	+++	++	+	-	-
C1	Aesthetic appreciation and inspiration	-	++	++	+	+	--	++	++	+	-	--

	C2/...										
C2 Cultural heritage	++	+++	++	+	+	--	+++	++	+	+	--
C3 Educational and scientific values	-	+++	++	++	++	-	+++	+++	++	+	+
C4 Knowledge	+	+++	++	++	++	+	+++	++	+++	+	+
C5 Recreation, mental and physical health	-	++	++	+	+	--	+++	++	++	-	-
C6 Social relations	++	++	++	+	+	--	+++	++	+	-	--
C7 Spiritual/religious experience/sense of place	++	++	++	+	+	---	++	+	-	-	--

Source: Own; legend: --- = negative / low; ...+++ = positive / high.

Conclusions

With this article, we aimed at creating an indicative framework on the linkage between FS and ES, to study the role and significance of social practices and their relation and impact on material practices that might support a transformative change of the current FS. Such transformations are urgent as current dominating FS is one of the main drivers of CC, soil degradation, BDL but also unhealthy diets. Our FS refer to the western world and the low-income countries in the South, to ensure that the framework is sensitive to the diverse ecological, environmental, economic and social conditions of developed and developing countries.

Guiding hypotheses include the notion that the intensity of farming correlates with social factors and the more distant and hierarchised (decreasing governance/voice) the FS are, the more we can observe FS material practices with negative impacts on ES. Findings should provide insights on FSs ES, and leverage points for a transformation of FS. As it is the human being who is the driver of environmental changes and its multiple crises in the Anthropocene, e.g., GHG emissions and CC, our specific interest was to put the social as a key dimension more in the centre. Hence, we elaborated a framework on the relation of different FS impacts on ES around social practice theory to highlight the interface between the social and the material (nature and technology), via a systematic and systemic integration of the linkages between FS, ES and socio-ecological crises.

We try to make explicit with several examples that material practices are socially embedded, take place in a lifeworld context, and fulfil a meaning driven by individual and collective values. We conclude that those FS that are based on valuing the social dimension are often also the driver of more ecological oriented FS, but as there are diverse factors a generalisation of this finding is not valid. One of the challenges was, that the differentiated description of FS requires substantial knowledge about them in order to understand the relation between the material and the social practice, which demands interdisciplinary knowledge along the whole FS as well as on ES, not at least to ensure an accurate assessment of the mutual implications and interdependencies of FS and ES. FS and ES are defined in terms of material (nature and technology) and social (including socioeconomic and cultural) factors, with the material and the social separated in their own categories for analytical reasons, but being aware that they are intertwined. This distinction is sensible as it makes the individual elements of FS and ES visible. However, in order to arrive at an overall understanding of FS and their linkages with ES, these representations are not sufficient.

There is much evidence that the close relationship and shared values of all stakeholders in FS enable positive impacts for ES, while hierarchical FS are more critical to assess in this context. The analysis of material and social characteristics (i.e., their attributes) points to the close relations between them and shows that the material dimensions impact can only be understood in its causes through the social context, except for those natural events that cannot be influenced by humans. Specifically, the cultural services frame, i.e. enable certain ecological based ES. Cultural ES represent the awareness of human–nature relationships and values that often defy monetisation, as well as sociocultural factors that frame the ecological (material) factors (Daniel et al., 2012; Dunne et al., 2002). Thus, the practices described via FS and ES denote a genuinely social, 'supra-individual' level that is expressed in material practices.

What is evident in this discourse on FS and ES is the still limited research with focus on the social dimension (Berbés-Blázquez et al., 2016; Bieling, 2014). Factors such as (in)equality, power and economics, which are underrepresented in the concept of cultural ES and FS descriptions, could inform ecological indicators of ES. For example, scholars have found that social inequality can be the cause of environmentally harmful practices (Bookchin, 2005; Boyce, 2007; Gaard, 1997), or that the food retail environment impacts traditional food consumption patterns (Wertheim-Heck and Raneri, 2019). The economic concerns and interests of all stakeholder groups along the entire food chain are also given limited attention in the current definition of FS. Similarly, the role of institutions, power distribution, and social justice, i.e. food security, food democracy and governance, are underrepresented and not integrated to seriously represent the role of the social for the material characteristics of FS/the respective ES. This also means that the social embeddedness of FS is inadequately analysed, consequently crucial social leverage points for an ecological transformation are not recognized, and thus the latter can hardly take place, as the material (nature and technology) practices are only made possible by social practices, and therefore also any transformative change of FS. Consequently, scientists should further investigate and apply systems-based research approaches that holistically integrate the social and material dimensions involved. Deeper knowledge of the relationship between FS and ES and its implications for socio-ecological crises could aid in further developing and justifying our conceptual framework. In other words, there is a need for a comprehensive revision, i.e., extension of the social (including cultural and socioeconomic) dimension of the ES approach if the aim is to inform on how transformative processes in society might happen. With that we conclude that the presented approach cannot be more than tentative; however, the systematic approach may serve for further development and investigations.

When it comes to the practical part at a policy level of how to initiate transformative changes of FS, we recognise that FS have been moved into the centre of global policy in these days, as – besides an energy crisis – not only developing but also developed countries are affected by a large food crisis. Latest global events together – global warming, the pandemic and military conflicts – can lead to a dramatic increase of poor people suffering hunger, which underlines the urgent need to act with an unprecedented sense of urgency. As documented in this chapter, the need for a transformative change of the majority of FS is comprehensive, as transformation means changes along the whole FS. Therefore, the social dimension provides an important starting point for further discussions beyond a purely ecological or material perspective while helping to understand the role of the social dimension in the Anthropocene's dominating FS, which is crucial for initiating transformation processes of FS. Policymakers must be aware of the different FS impacts on ES and the relevance of social practices and hence inform their decisions for policy development, legislation and subsidies accordingly. They can use these insights as a guide for the transformation towards those FS, that are both socially just, and in the meantime fulfil high ecological standards to prevent or reduce the potential for socio-ecological crises enhancing human and ecosystem health, and long-term food security.

References

Adamtey, N., Musyoka, M.W., Zundel, C., Cobo, J.G., Karanja, E., Fiaboe, K.K., ... Berset, E. (2016) 'Productivity, profitability and partial nutrient balance in maize-based conventional and organic farming systems in Kenya'. *Agriculture, Ecosystems & Environment, 235*: 61–79.

Berbés-Blázquez, M., González, J.A. and Pascual, U. (2016) 'Towards an ecosystem services approach that addresses social power relations'. *Current Opinion in Environmental Sustainability, 19*: 134–43.

Berkes, F. (2017) 'Environmental governance for the Anthropocene? Social-Ecological systems, resilience, and collaborative learning'. *Sustainability, 9*(7): 1232.

Bieling, C. (2014) 'Cultural ecosystem services as revealed through short stories from residents of the Swabian Alb (Germany)'. *Ecosystem Services, 8*: 207–15.

Biggs, R., Schlüter, M. and Schoon, M.L. (2015) 'An introduction to the resilience approach and principles to sustain ecosystem services in social-ecological systems'. In *Principles for Building Resilience: Sustaining Ecosystem Services in Social-Ecological Systems.* Cambridge: Cambridge University Press, pp. 1–31.

Bitewmekonen, A., Gebreslassie, B., Wassie, W.A., and Tsegay, B.A. (2019) 'Church forests – The green spots of Ethiopian highlands'. *Asian Journal of Forestry, 3*(2).

Bookchin, M. (2005) *The Ecology of Freedom: The Emergence and Dissolution of Hierarchy. 1982.* Oakland, CA: AKP.

Borie, M., Gustafsson, K.M., Obermeister, N., Turnhout, E. and Bridgewater, P. (2020). 'Institutionalising reflexivity? Transformative learning and the Intergovernmental science-policy Platform on Biodiversity and Ecosystem Services (IPBES)'. *Environmental Science & Policy, 110*, 71–6.

Boyce, J.K. (2007). 'Is inequality bad for the environment?' In *Equity and the Environment.* Amherst, MA: Emerald Group Publishing Limited.

Brand, K.-W. (2011). 'Sociological perspectives on sustainability communication'. In *Sustainability Communication.* Springer, pp. 55–68.

Brondizio, E.S., Settele, J., Díaz, S. and Ngo, H.T. (2019). *Global Assessment Report on Biodiversity and Ecosystem Services of the Intergovernmental Science-Policy Platform on Biodiversity and Ecosystem Services.* Bonn: IPBES secretariat.

Cadillo-Benalcazar, J.J., Renner, A. and Giampietro, M. (2020) 'A multiscale integrated analysis of the factors characterizing the sustainability of food systems in Europe'. *Journal of Environmental Management, 271*: 110944.

Chappell, M.J. and LaValle, L.A. (2011) 'Food security and biodiversity: Can we have both? An agroecological analysis'. *Agriculture and Human Values, 28*(1): 3–26.

Constance, D.H. and Choi, J.Y. (2010) Overcoming the barriers to organic adoption in the United States: A look at pragmatic conventional producers in Texas. *Sustainability, 2*(1): 163–88.

Crenna, E., Sinkko, T. and Sala, S. (2019) 'Biodiversity impacts due to food consumption in Europe'. *Journal of Cleaner Production, 227*: 378–91.

Czúcz, B., Arany, I., Potschin-Young, M., Bereczki, K., Kertész, M., Kiss, M., . . . Haines-Young, R. (2018) 'Where concepts meet the real world: A systematic review of ecosystem service indicators and their classification using CICES'. *Ecosystem Services, 29*: 145–57.

Dalin, C. and Outhwaite, C.L. (2019) 'Impacts of global food systems on biodiversity and water: The vision of two reports and future aims'. *One Earth, 1*(3): 298–302.

Daniel, T.C., Muhar, A., Arnberger, A., Aznar, O., Boyd, J.W., Chan, K.M., ... Gobster, P.H. (2012) 'Contributions of cultural services to the ecosystem services agenda'. *Proceedings of the National Academy of Sciences, 109*(23): 8812–9.

Debolini, M., Marraccini, E., Dubeuf, J.P., Geijzendorffer, I.R., Guerra, C., Simon, M., ... Napoléone, C. (2018) 'Land and farming system dynamics and their drivers in the Mediterranean Basin'. *Land use policy, 75*: 702–10.

Delbridge, T.A., King, R.P., Short, G. and James, K. (2017) Risk and red tape: Barriers to organic transition for US farmers. *Choices, 32*(4): 1–10.

Díaz, S., Demissew, S., Carabias, J., Joly, C., Lonsdale, M., Ash, N., ... Báldi, A. (2015) 'The IPBES Conceptual Framework—Connecting nature and people'. *Current Opinion in Environmental Sustainability, 14*: 1–16.

Dufeu, I., Le Velly, R., Bréchet, J.P. and Loconto, A. (2020) 'Can standards save organic farming from conventionalisation? Dynamics of collective projects and rules in a French organic producers' organisation'. *Sociologia ruralis, 60*(3), 621–38.

Dunne, J.A., Williams, R.J. and Martinez, N.D. (2002) 'Network structure and biodiversity loss in food webs: Robustness increases with connectance'. *Ecology Letters, 5*(4): 558–67.

Ericksen, P.J. (2008). 'Conceptualizing food systems for global environmental change research'. *Global Environmental Change, 18*(1): 234–45.

Fanzo, J., Davis, C., McLaren, R. and Choufani, J. (2018). 'The effect of climate change across food systems: Implications for nutrition outcomes'. *Global Food Security, 18*: 12–9.

FAO (2017). *The State of Food and Agriculture: Leveraging Food Systems for Inclusive Rural Transformation.* Food and Agriculture Organization of the United Nations.

Fischer, A. and Eastwood, A. (2016) 'Coproduction of ecosystem services as human–nature interactions—An analytical framework'. *Land use policy, 52*, 41–50.

Forssell, S. and Lankoski, L. (2015) 'The sustainability promise of alternative food networks: An examination through "alternative" characteristics'. *Agriculture and Human Values, 32*(1): 63–75.

Fraser, E.D. (2007). 'Travelling in antique lands: Using past famines to develop an adaptability/resilience framework to identify food systems vulnerable to climate change'. *Climatic Change, 83*(4): 495–514.

Gaard, G. (1997) 'Toward a queer ecofeminism'. *Hypatia, 12*(1): 114–37.

Gaba, S., Lescourret, F., Boudsocq, S., Enjalbert, J., Hinsinger, P., Journet, E.-P., ... Malézieux, E. (2015) 'Multiple cropping systems as drivers for providing multiple ecosystem services: From concepts to design'. *Agronomy for Sustainable Development, 35*(2), 607–23.

Gatti, R.C., Menéndez, L.P., Laciny, A., Rodríguez, H.B., Morante, G.B., Carmen, E., ... Schnorr, S.L. (2020). 'Diversity lost: COVID-19 as a phenomenon of the total environment'. *Science of The Total Environment, 144014.*

Gichure, J. (2020) 'ARTICLE Assessing the positions of actors in alternative food networks using connectedness and proximity: Kenyan organic vegetables'. *Discovery Agriculture, 6*(16): 127–34.

Gliessman, S. (2018) 'Defining agroecology'. *Agroecology and Sustainable Food Systems, 42*(6): 599–600.

Goldberger, J.R. (2008). 'Non-governmental organizations, strategic bridge building, and the "scientization" of organic agriculture in Kenya'. *Agriculture and Human Values*, *25*(2): 271–89.

Gómez, M.I. and Ricketts, K.D. (2013) 'Food value chain transformations in developing countries: Selected hypotheses on nutritional implications'. *Food Policy*, *42*: 139–50.

Gómez-Baggethun, E. and Reyes-García, V. (2013). 'Reinterpreting change in traditional ecological knowledge'. *Human Ecology*, *41*(4): 643–7.

Guerrero Lara, L., Pereira, L.M., Ravera, F. and Jiménez-Aceituno, A. (2019). 'Flipping the tortilla: Social-ecological innovations and traditional ecological knowledge for more sustainable agri-food systems in Spain'. *Sustainability*, *11*(5): 1222.

Haines-Young, R. and Potschin, M. (2017). '2.4. Categorisation systems: The classification challenge'. *Mapping Ecosystem Services*, *42*.

Haines-Young, R. and Potschin-Young, M. (2018). 'Revision of the common international classification for ecosystem services (CICES V5. 1): A policy brief'. *One Ecosystem*, *3*: e27108.

Hargreaves, T. (2011) 'Practice-ing behaviour change: Applying social practice theory to pro-environmental behaviour change'. *Journal of Consumer Culture*, *11*(1): 79–99.

Hennink, S. and Zeven, A. (1990) 'The interpretation of Nei and Shannon-Weaver within population variation indices'. *Euphytica*, *51*(3): 235–40.

Heryadi, D.Y. (2018) 'Why organic rice farmers switch back to conventional farming'. *Hasil Uji Kemiripan*, *9*(8).

HLPE (2017) *Nutrition and Food Systems. A Report by the High Level Panel of Experts on Food Security and Nutrition of the Committee on World Food Security.* Rome: Committee on World Food Security.

Hutchinson, J., Campbell, C. and Desjardins, R. (2007). Some perspectives on carbon sequestration in agriculture'. *Agricultural and Forest Meteorology*, *142*(2–4): 288–302.

Ingram, J. (2011). A food systems approach to researching food security and its interactions with global environmental change. *Food Security*, *3*(4): 417–31.

IPBES (2019) 'Summary for policymakers of the global assessment report on biodiversity and ecosystem services of the Intergovernmental Science-Policy Platform on Biodiversity and Ecosystem Services'. In S. Díaz, J. Settele, E. S. Brondízio, H. T. Ngo, M. Guèze, J. Agard, A. Arneth, P. Balvanera, K. A. Brauman, S. H. M. Butchart, K. M. A. Chan, L. A. Garibaldi, K. Ichii, J. Liu, S. M. Subramanian, G. F. Midgley, P. Miloslavich, Z. Molnár, D. Obura, A. Pfaff, S. Polasky, A. Purvis, J. Razzaque, B. Reyers, R. Roy Chowdhury, Y. J. Shin, I. J. Visseren-Hamakers, K. J. Willis, and C. N. Zayas (eds), *The Global Assessment Report on Biodiversity and Ecosystem Services: Summary for Policy Makers.* Bonn: IPBES Secretariat.

Jacob, M.C.M., Feitosa, I.S. and Albuquerque, U.P. (2020) 'Animal-based food systems are unsafe: Severe acute respiratory syndrome coronavirus 2 (SARS-CoV-2) fosters the debate on meat consumption'. *Public Health Nutrition*, *23*(17): 3250–5.

Jaffee, D. (2010) 'Fair trade standards, corporate participation, and social movement responses in the United States'. *Journal of Business Ethics*, *92*(2): 267–85.

Janjhua, Y., Chaudhary, R., Mehta, P. and Kumar, K. (2019) 'Determinants of farmer's attitude toward organic agriculture and barriers for converting to organic farming systems: Research insights'. *International Journal of Economic Plants*, *6*(2): 97–103.

Johns, T. and Eyzaguirre, P.B. (2006) 'Linking biodiversity, diet and health in policy and practice'. *Proceedings of the Nutrition Society*, 65(2): 182–9.

Johnson, J.M.-F., Franzluebbers, A.J., Weyers, S.L. and Reicosky, D.C. (2007). 'Agricultural opportunities to mitigate greenhouse gas emissions'. *Environmental pollution*, 150(1): 107–24.

Jouzi, Z., Azadi, H., Taheri, F., Zarafshani, K., Gebrehiwot, K., Van Passel, S. and Lebailly, P. (2017) 'Organic farming and small-scale farmers: Main opportunities and challenges'. *Ecological Economics*, 132: 144–54.

Kociszewski, K., Graczyk, A., Mazurek-Łopacinska, K. and Sobocińska, M. (2020). 'Social values in stimulating organic production involvement in farming – The case of Poland'. *Sustainability*, 12(15): 5945.

Kremen, C. and Miles, A. (2012). 'Ecosystem services in biologically diversified versus conventional farming systems: Benefits, externalities, and trade-offs'. *Ecology and Society*, 17(4).

Lajoie-O'Malley, A., Bronson, K., van der Burg, S. and Klerkx, L. (2020) 'The future (s) of digital agriculture and sustainable food systems: An analysis of high-level policy documents'. *Ecosystem Services*, 45: 101183.

Larsson, M., Morin, L., Hahn, T. and Sandahl, J. (2013). 'Institutional barriers to organic farming in Central and Eastern European countries of the Baltic Sea region'. *Agricultural and Food Economics*, 1(1): 1–20.

Liedtke, C., Hasselkuß, M., Welfens, M.J., Nordmann, J., and Baedeker, C. (2013) 'Transformation towards sustainable consumption: Changing consumption patterns through meaning in social practices'. In *Paper for Presentation at the 4th International Conference on Sustainability Transitions*, 19–21 June 2013, Zurich: Contribution No. 290, 702–29.

Luttikholt, L.W. (2007). 'Principles of organic agriculture as formulated by the International Federation of Organic Agriculture Movements'. *NJAS – Wageningen Journal of Life Sciences*, 54(4): 347–60.

Mafongoya, P.L. and Sileshi, G.W. (2020) 'Indices to identify and quantify ecosystem services in sustainable food systems'. In *The Role of Ecosystem Services in Sustainable Food Systems*. London: Elsevier Science, pp. 43–71.

Marshall, G. (2015). 'A social-ecological systems framework for food systems research: Accommodating transformation systems and their products'. *International Journal of the Commons*, 9(2).

Martínez-Harms, M.J. and Balvanera, P. (2012) 'Methods for mapping ecosystem service supply: A review'. *International Journal of Biodiversity Science, Ecosystem Services & Management*, 8(1–2), 17–25.

McElwee, P. (2017) 'The metrics of making ecosystem services'. *Environment and Society*, 8(1): 96–124.

Mendenhall, E. and Singer, M. (2019) 'The global syndemic of obesity, undernutrition, and climate change'. *The Lancet*, 393(10173): 741.

Moges, E., Masersha, G., Chanie, T., Addisu, A., bv Mesfin, E. and Beyen, C.W. (2017) 'Species diversity, habitat association and abundance of avifauna and large mammals in Gonde Teklehimanot and Aresema monasteries in North Gondar, Ethiopia'. *International Journal of Biodiversity and Conservation*, 10(4): 185–91. (https://doi.org/10.5897/IJBC2017.1136)

Moore, M.-L., Tjornbo, O., Enfors, E., Knapp, C., Hodbod, J., Baggio, J.A., ... Biggs, D. (2014) 'Studying the complexity of change: Toward an analytical framework for understanding deliberate social-ecological transformations'. *Ecology and Society, 19*(4).

Myers, S.S., Smith, M.R., Guth, S., Golden, C.D., Vaitla, B., Mueller, N.D., ... Huybers, P. (2017) 'Climate change and global food systems: Potential impacts on food security and undernutrition'. *Annual Review of Public Health, 38.*

Nikol, L.J. and Jansen, K. (2021) 'Rethinking conventionalisation: A view from organic agriculture in the Global South'. *Journal of Rural Studies, 86*: 420–9.

Niles, M.T., Ahuja, R., Esquivel, J.M., Mango, N., Duncan, M., Heller, M. and Tirado, C. (2017). *Climate Change and Food Systems: Assessing Impacts and Opportunities.* Washington, DC: Meridian Institute.

Orlowska, I. and Klepeis, P. (2018) Ethiopian church forests: A socio-religious conservation model under change'. *Journal of Eastern African Studies, 12*(4): 674–95.

Palomo, I., Felipe-Lucia, M.R., Bennett, E.M., Martín-López, B. and Pascual, U. (2016). 'Disentangling the pathways and effects of ecosystem service co-production'. *Advances in Ecological Research, 54*: 245–83.

Pelletier, N. (2015) 'Life cycle thinking, measurement and management for food system sustainability'. *Environmental Science & Technology, 49*(13): 7515–9.

Pellow, D.N. and Nyseth Brehm, H. (2013). 'An environmental sociology for the twenty-first century'. *Annual Review of Sociology, 39*: 229–50.

Plieninger, T., Van der Horst, D., Schleyer, C. and Bieling, C. (2014) 'Sustaining ecosystem services in cultural landscapes'. *Ecology and Society, 19*(2).

Popkin, B.M., Adair, L.S. and Ng, S.W. (2012) 'Global nutrition transition and the pandemic of obesity in developing countries'. *Nutrition Reviews, 70*(1): 3–21.

Raymond, C.M., Giusti, M. and Barthel, S. (2018) 'An embodied perspective on the co-production of cultural ecosystem services: Toward embodied ecosystems'. *Journal of Environmental Planning and Management, 61*(5–6): 778–99.

Reid, W.V., Mooney, H.A., Cropper, A., Capistrano, D., Carpenter, S.R., Chopra, K., ... Hassan, R. (2005). *Ecosystems and Human Well-Being-Synthesis: A Report of the Millennium Ecosystem Assessment.* Washington, DC: Island Press.

Reisman, E., and Fairbairn, M. (2020). 'Agri-food systems and the Anthropocene'. *Annals of the American Association of Geographers, 111*(3), 687–97.

Rockström, J., Steffen, W., Noone, K., Persson, Å., Chapin, III, F.S., Lambin, E., ... Schellnhuber, H.J. (2009). 'Planetary boundaries: Exploring the safe operating space for humanity'. *Ecology and Society, 14*(2).

Rosset, P. (2000). 'The multiple functions and benefits of small farm agriculture in the context of global trade negotiations'. *Development, 43*(2): 77–82.

Sarkki, S., Ficko, A., Wielgolaski, F.E., Abraham, E.M., Bratanova-Doncheva, S., Grunewald, K., ... Broll, G. (2017). 'Assessing the resilient provision of ecosystem services by social-ecological systems: Introduction and theory'. *Climate Research, 73*(1–2), 7–15.

Schader, C., Heidenreich, A., Kadzere, I., Egyir, I., Muriuki, A., Bandanaa, J., ... Lazzarini, G. (2021) 'How is organic farming performing agronomically and economically in sub-Saharan Africa?' *Global Environmental Change, 70*: 102325.

Sherwood, N., Story, M. and Neumark-Sztainer, D. (2001) 'Behavioral risk factors for obesity: Diet and physical activity'. *Nutrition in the Prevention and Treatment of Disease*, 517–37.

Shields, M.W., Johnson, A.C., Pandey, S., Cullen, R., González-Chang, M., Wratten, S.D. and Gurr, G.M. (2019) 'History, current situation and challenges for conservation biological control'. *Biological Control*, *131*: 25–35.

Slámová, M. and Belčáková, I. (2019) 'The role of small farm activities for the sustainable management of agricultural landscapes: Case studies from Europe'. *Sustainability*, *11*(21): 5966.

Sperling, F., Havlik, P., Denis, M., Valin, H., Palazzo, A., Gaupp, F. and Visconti, P. (2020) *Transformations within Reach: Pathways to a Sustainable and Resilient World: Resilient Food Systems.* Laxenburg: IIASA-ISC.

Špulerová, J., Petrovič, F., Mederly, P., Mojses, M., and Izakovičová, Z. (2018) 'Contribution of traditional farming to ecosystem services provision: Case studies from Slovakia'. *Land*, *7*(2): 74.

Standal, K., and Westskog, H. (2022) 'Understanding low-carbon food consumption transformation through social practice theory: The case of community supported agriculture in Norway'. *International Journal of Sociology of Agriculture and Food*, *28*(1): 25–41.

Steffen, W., Broadgate, W., Deutsch, L., Gaffney, O. and Ludwig, C. (2015) 'The trajectory of the Anthropocene: The great acceleration'. *The Anthropocene Review*, *2*(1): 81–98.

Sukhdev, P. and Wittmer, H. (2008) *The Economics of Ecosystems and Biodiversity.* Interim Report. European Union Commission for the Environment.

Tilman, D., Cassman, K.G., Matson, P.A., Naylor, R. and Polasky, S. (2002) 'Agricultural sustainability and intensive production practices'. *Nature*, *418*(6898): 671–77.

Tscharntke, T., Clough, Y., Wanger, T.C., Jackson, L., Motzke, I., Perfecto, I., … Whitbread, A. (2012) 'Global food security, biodiversity conservation and the future of agricultural intensification'. *Biological Conservation*, *151*(1): 53–9.

Vignola, R., Koellner, T., Scholz, R.W. and McDaniels, T.L. (2010) 'Decision-making by farmers regarding ecosystem services: Factors affecting soil conservation efforts in Costa Rica'. *Land use policy*, *27*(4): 1132–42.

Wertheim-Heck, S.C. and Raneri, J.E. (2019) 'A cross-disciplinary mixed-method approach to understand how food retail environment transformations influence food choice and intake among the urban poor: Experiences from Vietnam'. *Appetite*, *142*: 104370.

Wertheim-Heck, S.C. and Raneri, J.E. (2020) 'Food policy and the unruliness of consumption: An intergenerational social practice approach to uncover transforming food consumption in modernizing Hanoi, Vietnam'. *Global Food Security*, *26*: 100418.

Wezel, A., Bellon, S., Doré, T., Francis, C., Vallod, D. and David, C. (2009) 'Agroecology as a science, a movement and a practice. A review'. *Agronomy for Sustainable Development*, *29*(4): 503–15.

Willett, W., Rockström, J., Loken, B., Springmann, M., Lang, T., Vermeulen, S., … Wood, A. (2019) 'Food in the Anthropocene: The EAT–Lancet Commission on healthy diets from sustainable food systems'. *The Lancet*, *393*(10170): 447–92.

Xu, Q., Huet, S., Poix, C., Boisdon, I. and Deffuant, G. (2018). 'Why do farmers not convert to organic farming? Modeling conversion to organic farming as a major change'. *Natural Resource Modeling*, *31*(3): e12171.

12

'Planting Seeds' for 'Good Growth': Anthropocenic Performances of Responsibility

Allison M. Loconto

Introduction

All of the narratives described by Bonneuil (2015) argue that business as usual is insufficient for dealing with the societal challenges posed by the Anthropocene. Each narrative has a slightly different response to the question: who is responsible for ensuring the sustainability of agrifood systems so that humans will survive the current Epoch? Producers, who are tilling the earth with machines of variable complexity and are responsible for what toxins are entering the soil and water; or those companies who make the chemicals and machines responsible for the effects of their products on the environment? What about the processors who purchase the produce from the farms and turn these into products that can be consumed by people, animals and machines? What then is the responsibility of aggregators and distributors, who collect, pack and transport the produce and the products? Where is the responsibility of retailers and brands, which turn fresh and transformed products into consumables that are easily recognised by consumers? What role do consumers play when they decide to purchase something that has, through all of these steps, become a 'sustainable' product? Finally, where is the responsibility of researchers and actors in the agricultural knowledge and innovation systems (AKIS) who are creating and sharing knowledge about what is or could be sustainable? Or, for that matter, what is the responsibility of a State, and its various administrations working at different levels of engagement, who is supposed to govern what sustainability ought to be across geo-political boundaries?

In this chapter, I take up this challenge by comparing the two leading food manufacturers – Nestlé and Unilever – who control major portions of the global food system. Beyond their control of trade in food, in 2021, they were the largest investors in agricultural research and development (R&D), investing 1.6 billion and 800 million, respectively. Both companies have made 'responsibility' a fundamental aspect of their innovation agenda and they are at the forefront of the emerging 'sustainability' field. I focus on *how these MNCs are justifying the responsibility of their vision and technologies for the sustainability of agrifood systems.*

Responsibility for Sustainable Agrifood Systems

Sustainability and responsibility are 'essentially contested concepts' (Collier et al., 2006; Connelly, 2007; Gallie, 1955) because these terms are of great societal concern, yet they involve endless disputes by their users who can offer up a multiplicity of forms of proof to justify different interpretations (Boltanski and Thévenot, 2006 [1991]). As such, they pose fundamental ethical and political questions about how to live in the Anthropocene, what the future goal of that living ought to be (Jasanoff, 2004, 2015) and what cannot be accepted within the definition or application of the concept.

Scholars of political economy and ecology focus on the competing interests in control over the definition of sustainability (Constance et al., 2018; Levin et al., 2012), pointing out power struggles that can both reinforce existing systems of domination and provide opportunities for alternatives to emerge (Goodman et al., 2012; Levidow, 2015; McMichael, 2011, 2016). To date, the public controversies around sustainability have mostly been focused on the production-driven nature of the food system, where scientists and social movements have posed fundamental questions around the types of agriculture and knowledge (largely bio-technologies) needed to respond to the grand societal challenges (Bonneuil et al., 2008; Demortain, 2013; Dibden et al., 2013; Vanloqueren and Baret, 2009). Recent controversies in ecology and biology have brought to the fore the question of biodiversity and the best use of land (at individual, collective and territorial scales) to ensure the sustainability of production systems (Chappell et al., 2009; Desquilbet et al., 2017; Goulart et al., 2016; Phalan et al., 2011). These debates position different epistemic communities in opposition according to the types of knowledge they are producing and how they conceive human–nature relations (Chan et al., 2016; Dempsey, 2011; Díaz et al., 2015; Loconto et al., 2020).

Definitions of responsibility are likewise multiple but often remain embedded in an assumed rational actor. Weber considered the 'ethic of responsibility' as 'a political stance adequate to morally serious endeavour in a world characterised by inevitable and irresolvable value conflict' (Starr, 1999: 409). While debated in political theory, this interpretation pretends a consequentialist approach to ethics where outcomes may not always justify the means, but should always be considered within the political calculations (Nye, 1985). Thus, the notion of responsibility has been understood both in terms of acting responsibly and being held accountable for actions. But in the literature, the two terms are often used separately where account-ability is more closely tied to obeying rules and suffering conse-quences, and responsibility is more individual and open-ended (Selznick, 2008). These approaches are usually linked to legal con-cepts of liability and blame, and thus we see calls for transparency as a means to increase accountability (Biermann et al., 2012; Hale, 2008), but with uncertain results (Fox, 2007). Prospective responsi-bility attempts to account for something that may (or may not) happen in the future (Gorgoni, 2009; Stilgoe et al., 2013), while 'role-responsibility' is connected less to an individual virtue than it is to an obliged 'sense of responsibility', or stewardship (Hart and Gardner, 2008). Nesting and rotating these responsibilities have been shown to be effective means to manage common resources (Ostrom, 1990), while recent efforts to encourage 'responsiveness' in innovation seeks collective virtue (Grinbaum and Groves, 2013) and ethical choices in practice (Genus and Stirling, 2018; Stilgoe et al., 2013). The question here remains how individuals and collectives (particularly organisa-tions) become responsive to each other (Lindner et al., 2016), towards societal concerns (Von Schomberg, 2013), or inclusive and collaborative processes (EU Council, 2014) without rendering responsibility a 'thin' notion (Stirling, 2015) that reinforces incum-bent interests or becomes the 'green-washed' version of social responsibility (Enoch, 2007).

Sustainability is considered to be a fundamental aspect of respon-sible research and innovation (Von Schomberg, 2013) and the Euro-pean Commission has further framed sustainable agriculture and food security as the second societal grand challenge on the horizon.[1] Responding to this challenge requires research, innovation and action that contribute to more sustainable food and agriculture. Who then, is responsible for driving this research agenda and finding innovative solutions to the unsustainability of the current agrifood system?

According to a 2011 study by the United States Department of Agriculture (USDA), the private sector spent US$19.7 billion on food and agricultural research (56 percent in food manufacturing and 44 percent in agricultural input sectors) and accounted for about half of total public and private spending on food and agricultural research and development (R&D) in high-income countries in 2007 (Fuglie et al., 2011). According to the 2022 EU Industrial R&D Investment Scoreboard, food producers spent €8.17 billion while chemical companies (the largest of which – BASF and Syngenta – produce agro-chemicals) spent €25.14 billion.[2] Forty-six percent of the money spent on investment by food producers was spent by five companies and one third of the €8.17 billion was spent by only two companies – Nestlé and Unilever (Table 12.1). These large firms are multinational corporations (MNCs) who operate within global networks of both R&D and marketing and dominate global R&D landscape.

These numbers are significant not just because the private sector spends about as much on R&D as the public sector, but because there are publicly regulated responsibility and accountability mechanisms in place for the expenditure of public R&D funds, while there are no identical mechanisms for private R&D. Private R&D is regulated through controls internal to companies and in those spaces of hybrid control where public and private funds mix. Innovation processes are even less regulated as they are often occurring outside official R&D departments within organisations or through partnerships with start-ups, universities or other private organisations. Most mechanisms that are used to regulate private research and innovation are therefore voluntary instruments that are tied to international, sector-specific, professional or national agreements. This poses the empirical question of: *how is responsibility for sustainability governed within private research and innovation?*

---

[1]https://ec.europa.eu/programmes/horizon2020/en/h2020-section/societal-challenges, accessed 03/02/2022.
[2]2022 EU Industrial R&D Investment Scoreboard (https://iri.jrc.ec.europa.eu/scoreboard/2021-eu-industrial-rd-investment-scoreboard#dialog-node-5747), accessed 09/09/2023.

Table 12.1 R&D investments and net sales for the top five food producer companies investing in R&D in 2021

Company	Country	R&D	Net Sales	R&D Intensity (%)[1]	Significant Agricultural R&D	Countries with R&D Labs
		--- € Millions ---				
Nestlé	Switzerland	1,839.9	84,246.8	2.2	Cocoa, coffee, cereals, nutrition, packaging	Switzerland (~30 countries)
Unilever	UK	847	52,444	1.6	Tea, naturals, ice cream, jelly, reduced fat, packaging	The United Kingdom, India, China, the United States, the Netherlands
Vilmorin	France	406.2	1,476.6	27.5	Seeds	France, Brazil, China, Spain, Italy, Japan, Mexico, Turkey, the United States
Danone	France	338	24,281	1.4	Dairy, plant, water, nutrition, packaging	Benelux, Brazil, China, the Netherlands, Singapore, the United Kingdom
Kerry	Ireland	308.6	7,350.6	4.2	Taste and nutrition ingredients	Australia, Brazil, Canada, China, Costa Rica, Dubai, France, India, Indonesia, Ireland, Italy, Korea, Malaysia, Mexico, Philippines, South Africa, Singapore, Thailand, the United States, Vietnam

[1]R&D investments divided by net sales.
Source: 2022 EU Industrial R&D Investment Scoreboard. NB: The food producers are in the shaded rows.

Governing Responsible Research and Innovation

The concept of responsible innovation has been gaining much attention as the 'vanguard of both intellectual creativity and social responsibility' (Guston, 2006: 169). First defined as 'a transparent, interactive process in which societal actors and innovators become mutually responsible to each other with view on the (ethical) acceptability, sustainability and society desirability of the innovation process and its marketable products' (Von Schomberg, 2013: 9), the focus is moving towards incorporating democratic principles of governance into innovation processes and delivering the 'right impacts' (Owen et al., 2012), such as sustainability. Yet, what responsibility means in innovation processes is far from stabilised (Blok and Lemmens, 2015). Rather, it is highly contingent upon existing normative understandings and the discursive and material infrastructures that are already governing actors' interactions and practices.

This *de facto* governance (Rip, 2018) is what we can study empirically as we can find traces of these interactions in an organisational field (Dingwerth and Pattberg, 2009). Here, governance refers to 'self-governing' (Jessop, 2002), or more simply, the 'structuring of action and interaction that has some authority and/or legitimacy' (Rip, 2018: 76). It could be also seen as the way in which society defines and handles its problems (Voß et al., 2006), a type of 'self-steering' that has also be attributed to civil society and private actors (Cashore et al., 2007). These governance arrangements are heterarchical (hybrid vertical and horizontal networks) (Jessop, 2002), often formed by enrolling and entangling actors around specific matters of concern (Loconto and Fouilleux, 2014; Rip, 2010). But complex problem solving, particularly for food security and sustainable agriculture, is contentious, which, when managed, can also be productive (Duncan and Claeys, 2018).

Following from this line of thinking, we can trace the ideas, as inscribed in specific discourses, to their translations into the rules, material objects and collaborations that are used to govern how organisations take on responsibility for sustainability. This conceptualisation provides the basis for the analysis in this chapter, where I explore the *performation* (Callon, 2010) of the instruments used by each company to draw the boundaries around how they conceive of and control their responsibility for sustainability. That is, responsibility must be defined and put into action to be effective; what happens when it is enacted makes changes in turn to the activities and definitions. Therefore, analytically (see Table 12.2), we are attentive to how the governance arrangements are organised, including the specific actor landscapes, and the *de facto* governance practices. We also explore the legitimacy of these governance arrangements in terms of how 'well' the actors are doing in 'constructively' or 'productively' governing their responsibility for sustainability (Walhout et al., 2016).

Research for this chapter was conducted during two phases of qualitative research between 2007 and 2016. Formal interviews were conducted at different R&D sites of the two MNCs in Europe and Africa (five at Unilever and three at Nestlé) and interaction with key informants at both companies occurred throughout this period via participant observations during expert meetings on sustainable agriculture, including the Agri-food Task Force of the FAO/UNEP 10YP on Sustainable Consumption and Production, UN Global Compact's Food and Agriculture Business (FAB) Principles, sustainability standards conferences and invitation only events on sustainable value chains.

Table 12.2 Comparative case analysis

Company	Nestlé	Unilever
Governance Arrangements	**R&I:** Within a single Multinational organisation	**R&I:** Within a single Multinational organisation
	P: Making the business case	**P:** Mainstreaming sustainability
	PI: HR instruments, codes of conduct, CSR	**PI:** HR instruments, codes of conduct, CSR
	SE: Organisational chain of command	**SE:** Organisational chain of command
	WGL:	WGL:
	Vertical: National and International regulations	*Vertical:* National and International regulations
	Horizontal: NGO activism, Sector Associations, Multi-stakeholder fora	*Horizontal:* NGO activism, Sector Associations, Multi-stakeholder fora
Actor Landscape	External: National and International Regulators UN Global Compact	External: National and International Regulators UN Global Compact

(Continued)

Table 12.2   Comparative case analysis   *(Continued)*

Company	Nestlé	Unilever
	FAO/UNEP Sustainable Agri-food Task Force Scientific community Standard-setting organisations (4C) Donors (GIZ) SAI Platform Nestlé Foundation Suppliers Start-ups Internal: Innovation, Technology, R&D (including significant consumer research) Human Resources Corporate Relations	FAO Partnership Scientific community (Oxford and Cambridge Universities) Standard-setting organisations (Rainforest Alliance) SAI Platform Sustainable Food Labs The Unilever Foundation Suppliers Start-ups Internal: R&D (including consumer research) Human Resources Marketing and Communication Supply Chain
De facto Governance Practices	**DF:** Food security **S:** Integrating sustainability across the entire value chain **SI:** Expert meetings, multi-stakeholder initiatives, Scientific community **AM:** Nutrition and wellness of employees and consumers **RC:** LCA design tools **IU:** DJ Sustainability Index, Declaration of Abu Dhabi	**DF:** Food security **S:** People, Planet, Profit **SI:** Expert meetings, multi-stakeholder initiatives, Scientific community **AM:** Resource provision capacity building **RC:** Co-branding **IU:** DJ Sustainability Index, Declaration of Abu Dhabi
'Well-doing'	Constructive Responsibilisation Productive Contestation Management	Constructive Responsibilisation Productive Contestation Management

Governance Arrangements: Drawing the Boundaries of Responsibility

The wider governance landscape (WGL) extends both vertically and horizontally and is embedded in the notion of corporate social responsibility (CSR) (e.g., Carroll, 1979). CSR is well institutionalised within large companies and it has been the main pathway through which MNCs have expanded their consideration of and collaboration with a broad range of stakeholders. At the European level, CSR has been successively institutionalised since 2001 through multi-stakeholder meetings that resulted in a resolution by European Parliament[3] that identified existing guidelines and voluntary standards[4,5] as authoritative, internationally agreed sets of standards for corporate conduct for social and environmental responsibility. The EU focus on reporting requirements and existing policy instruments (PI) is the same approach used by MNCs.

A mix of PIs, including private soft regulation (private standards) and public voluntary laws and directives, are used and compliance with mandatory regulations is the foundation of their responsibility (see Table 12.3). For example, both companies had a version of a Code of Business Conduct or Code of Ethics for employees and codes of conduct for suppliers (both raw materials for products and for technologies). For example, at Nestlé, the values of 'integrity, honesty, fair dealing and full compliance with all applicable laws'[6] govern all aspects of their operations – including research and innovation. This code of conduct carries provisions for disciplinary action for non-compliance. The system of enforcement (SE) for responsibility follows the organisational chain of command internal to each company.

---

[3]European Parliament Resolution, (2006/2133/(INI)) (http://www.europarl.europa.eu/sides/getDoc.do?pubRef=-//EP//TEXT+TA+P6-TA-2007-0062+0+DOC+XML+V0//EN), accessed 03/09/2022.
[4]OECD Guidelines for Multinational Enterprises, (http://mneguidelines.oecd.org/), accessed 03/09/2022.
[5]ILO MNE Declaration (http://www.ilo.org/empent/Publications/WCMS_094386/lang–en/index.htm), accessed 03/09/2022.
[6]Nestlé's Code of Business Conduct (http://www.nestle.com/asset-library/documents/library/documents/corporate_governance/code_of_business_conduct_en.pdf), accessed 03/09/2022.

Table 12.3 Governance instruments

	Reactions to Regulatory Requirements		Reactions to 'Irresponsible' Industry Practices (Supplier Focused)	Global Sustainability Discourse (Not Directly Linked to Suppliers)
	Mandatory Measures	Early Compliance		
Nestlé	• The Agrivair Initiative	• Nestlé Policy on Environmental Sustainability • Baraka (bottled water), Egypt	• EcodEX Design Tool • Nespresso AAA • SuizAgua Colombia • The Nescafé Plan • Cocoa Plan • Grains and legumes in Central and West Africa	• UN Millennium Development Goal Participation • Preserving Balaton National Park • UN Global Compact's Food and Agriculture Business (FAB) Principles • Declaration of Abu Dhabi
Unilever		• Consumer Goods Forum (CGF) • Tropical Forest Alliance (TFA) • Sustainable Palm Oil Sourcing Policy • Unilever Sustainable Agriculture Code • Certification schemes for tea and cocoa and palm oil • Safety and Environmental Assurance Centre (SEAC) • Founding of MSC label	• Unilever Colworth Sustainability Research Centre • Sustainable Tea • Sustainable Soy and Oils • Sustainable Cocoa and Sugar • Sustainable Palm Oil • Sustainable Fruit and Vegetables • Sustainable Tomatoes • Sustainable Gherkins • Fairtrade Ben & Jerry's	• Forum for sustainable farming (FfSF) • UN Global Compact's Food and Agriculture Business (FAB) Principles • Declaration of Abu Dhabi

These instruments help govern responsibility in the following ways. First, as a reaction to existing regulatory requirements for agricultural research, new products and active ingredients, the MNCs have initiated specific collaborations, programs and tools. There are two types of reactions: *mandatory measures*, which is a situation in which legal obligations require that the company comply directly (own operations) or indirectly (through their customers) that translates into a market potential for the company. The second is a situation of *early compliance* where a future regulation seems possible due to an increased interest of the public and/or the public sector in the specific subject. The company thus reacts with voluntary standards or projects to pre-comply with upcoming regulation, shape possible regulation, increase investor confidence or get in contact with (local) authorities to facilitate future compliance.

Second, we see voluntary investments as corporate reactions to 'irresponsible' practices within the industry that are linked to their suppliers. This is a situation in which a company participates independent from legislation. The motivation emerges through reasons located in the production chain of a product and actions aim to reduce production costs, secure long-term availability/quality of production factors or enhance R&D.

Finally, we see the positioning of the organisation within global discourses of sustainability (i.e., social and environmental responsibility) through voluntary investments not linked to their direct supplies. This is a situation in which a company engages (usually external) partners through environmental and social initiative without having any direct connection between the investment and the daily business operations. They do this to generate financial return, as a CSR engagement to manage reputation and customer satisfaction, and to improve customer loyalty.

These instruments are used to frame the purpose (P) of the governance arrangement as ensuring responsibility for sustainability. The notion of responsibility is this justified in three approaches.[7] The first is *Regulatory Compliance*, which is in line with Carrol's pyramid of CSR priorities. This framing is largely linked to the definitional framing of *de facto* governance practices, which are explained in a subsequent section. The next two approaches require more

---

[7]These are found in both companies, the examples below are illustrative.

elaboration as they capture the particularities of how these companies justify their responsibility.

The Business Case

Making 'the business case' for responsibility was another dominant purpose for mobilising resources and personnel in an attempt to realise responsibility in research and innovation. Making the business case basically means that any research and innovation activity should contribute to the bottom line of the core business; the Unilever pledge to 'people, planet and profit' captures their focus on maintaining a triple bottom line. An interviewee at Nestlé noted that 'the last phrase of Von Schomberg's statement is key; research and innovation isn't there purely for their own sake, but for the marketable products'.

Nestlé uses an internal document called the 'Corporate Business Principles' to coordinate the company's responsibilities. This document incorporates the 10 principles of the UN Global Compact.[8] It lays out the responsibilities that the company has towards: Consumers (Nutrition, Health and Wellness, Quality assurance and product safety, Consumer communication, Human rights and labour practices, Human rights in our business activities), Employees (Leadership and personal responsibility, Safety and health at work), Suppliers and customers (Supplier and customer relations, Agriculture and rural development) and to the environment (Environmental sustainability and Water). Nestlé's main responsibility within its R&I processes is thus to ensure that its commercial products deliver nutrition, health and wellness: 'With the world's largest private nutrition and food research capability, we are continuously creating nutritional value and health benefits across our product range'.[9] This work includes investment in nutrition labelling and communication and primary research into nutrition and other types of research related to their core lines of business: cocoa, palm oil and sugar (for chocolate), coffee (Nescafé), water (infant formula) and other raw ingredients (Table 12.1).

---

[8]Nestlé's Corporate Business Principles (http://www.nestle.com/aboutus/businessprinciples), accessed 03/09/2022.
[9]Nutrition, health and wellness (http://www.nestle.com/nutrition-health-wellness), accessed 29/10/2018.

Nestlé takes a strategic approach in developing research lines and product development that can meet both the bottom-line calculations and contribute to broader health outcomes. Nestlé calls this its 'innovation sweet-spot'.[10] For sustainability, Nestlé has developed a design tool (EcodEX) that is based on a simplified life cycle analysis (LCA) and enables designers to make early-stage decisions in the design process about the environmental footprint of their products in order to make changes in their design and sourcing strategies.[11] Instruments like this, in combination with their value chain approach, facilitate the capacity of Nestlé to make its business case for sustainability.

Mainstreaming

The framing of the mainstreaming of responsibility and sustainability throughout the company is based on the belief that the success of a company and the health of the communities around it are interdependent; and that economic growth and progress come from capitalising on these interdependencies. It brings the notion of stakeholder participation to a different level of engagement. This notion also features prominently within Nestlé, who has made 38 commitments that support the company's long-term goal of creating shared value.[12] Unilever, however, is farther advanced in mainstreaming its responsibility for sustainability throughout its key supply chains (Table 12.3). The company claims that:

> We believe that as a business we have a responsibility to our consumers and to the communities in which we have a presence. Around the world we invest in local economies and develop people's skills inside and outside of Unilever.[13]

Unilever has joined the Blueprint for Better Business initiative,[14] which helped them to embed the company's purpose within its

---

[10]Nestlé Research: Vision, Action, Value Creation (https://www.nestle.com.eg/sitecollectio ndocuments/nestle-rd-brochure-2010.pdf), accessed 22/10/2018.
[11]Insight: how we're further building sustainability into our product design process (http:// www.nestle.com/media/newsandfeatures/ecodex-insight-blog), accessed 22/10/2018.
[12]Creating Shared value (http://www.nestle.com/csv), accessed 02/09/2022.
[13]About Unilever, Responsible Business (https://www.unilever.com/about/who-we-are/ about-Unilever/), accessed 22/10/2018.
[14]Blueprint for Better Business (http://www.blueprintforbusiness.org/), accessed 02/09/ 2022.

organisation. Unilever's approach for the past 15 years has been a successive restructuring of the company to ensure the incorporation of sustainability throughout their different product lines. While the global sustainability group consists of 12 people, Unilever has identified 'sustainability champions' in every R&D unit of the company: 'R&D find new sustainable technologies, marketers listen to consumers to help us make sustainable products consumers desire, supply chain implement our technologies and ideas in our factories, and ensure we source and manufacture in a sustainable way'.[15] They have driven this CSR approach from the company leadership by setting ambitious targets along 10-year timelines, including the ambitious goal of halving the environmental footprint of making and using their products by 2020. This is branded as the company's Sustainable Living Plan. The three goals of the plan are: (1) help more than a billion people to improve their health and well-being; (2) halve the environmental footprint of their products; and (3) source 100 percent of their agricultural raw materials sustainably and enhance the livelihoods of people across their value chain.[16] This mainstreaming approach has propelled them to be considered as one of the top green companies in the world.[17]

The main governance instrument used to organise this work is the voluntary standard, which is owned by an external NGO, but is used to 'co-brand' the products as being responsibly produced. Both companies use voluntary standards for sustainable sourcing, but Unilever has led this approach with its pioneering efforts to create the Marine Stewardship Council (MSC) certification together with the World Wildlife Fund (WWF) in 1995 (Constance and Bonanno, 2000). Unilever has subsequently established commitments for each of its product lines that include the adoption of voluntary standards by producers and innovations in packaging and transport, which enable the company to reduce its environmental footprint. This mainstreaming approach demonstrates a company-wide response to

---

[15]Interview – Global Director of Sustainability – Stefano Giolito (http://www.unileverg raduatesblog.com/2011/12/interview-global-director-of-sustainability-stefano-giolito/), accessed 22/10/2018.

[16]About Unilever, Responsible Business (https://www.unilever.com/about/who-we-are/ about-Unilever/), accessed 22/11/2015.

[17]Top 10 Green Companies in the World, 2015 (http://www.newsweek.com/green-2015/ top-10-green-companies-world-2015), accessed 02/09/2022.

responsibility, where the company has reflected on the stakeholder pressure that was received through both consumer research and NGO lobbying to restructure the priorities for the company's work. In an interview with a Unilever R&D employee, he highlighted the importance the MNC places on listening to stakeholder interests in designing the type of research that is done. For example, animal testing, while not illegal, is not accepted by many consumers, so this approach to product development is not used. Across its different product lines shown in Table 12.3, Unilever has selected the voluntary standards and lines of research that are the most responsive to consumer demand and stakeholder pressure – which represents significant flexibility and autonomy within its governance arrangement.

Actor Landscape

The two MNCs conduct research and innovation in as many as 14 different countries (Table 12.1) at the same time and sell products around the world. In this section, I briefly describe three unique sets of actors who are found across the three companies – R&D units, corporate affairs and foundations – as responsibility for research and innovation processes are distributed among these actors. Forging partnerships is the most often used approach for actor mobilisation (AM) and these partnerships take different forms, depending on the department that leads the effort. Partners include suppliers, start-ups, universities, donors, private research companies, NGOs, public actors (including extension) and intergovernmental organisations.

R&D Units

Nestlé employs 5,000 in their R&D operations that cover 14 different countries. They employ 'scientists, technologists, engineers and even anthropologists' (Nestlé, 2010: 4). Proprietary high-tech product development takes place in 34 Product Technology centres and R&D centres worldwide. Nestlé also has an Institute of Health Sciences that conducts fundamental research on health and disease related to nutrition, and a Nutrition Institute, whose mission is to share leading science-based information and education with health professionals, scientists and nutrition communities and stakeholders. This in-house network is complemented by corporate venture funds and research partnerships with business partners and universities.

Unilever has more than 6,000 scientists, engineers, chefs and technicians on staff in six strategic R&D laboratories, in 31 major development centres focused on development and implementation of product innovations and in 92 locations that implement innovations in countries and factories.[18] Unilever also runs a large consumer research unit that relies upon qualitative research.[19] Unilever also engages with start-ups, university and private research teams as well as maintaining a large 'open innovation' programme. In 2014, Unilever launched the Unilever Foundry, which is a web platform that offers a variety of programs and a range of partnership arrangements (crowd-sourcing, pilots, mentorships, venture funding, etc.) to stimulate and facilitate experimentation within their brands and functions.[20]

Corporate Affairs Units

Both companies maintain a corporate affairs unit that has the responsibility for developing and monitoring the CSR programs explained above. These corporate affairs units manage the relationships between the internal governance functions of the MNCs and the external partnerships. On the one hand they act as the public relations arms in communicating the responsibility of the company to the outside world, and on the other hand, collaborate internally to implement external programs that help the companies to act responsibly. For example, Nestlé interviewees explained that the MNC's core mission of health and wellness are also encouraged for Nestlé employees to create a more positive work environment. The interactions with the external voluntary standards are handled through these offices as are the official CSR programs like Nestlé's Corporate Business Principles for Creating Shared Value and Unilever's Sustainable Living Plan.

---

[18]Unilever's research webpage (http://www.unilever.com/about/innovation/working-in-unilever-r-and-d/), accessed 18/05/2015.

[19]Laybourne, Pete. 'Damned if you don't. Thoughts on the Unilever Accreditation Programme' (https://rwconnect.esomar.org/damned-if-you-dont-thoughts-on-the-unilever-accreditation-programme/), accessed 22/11/2015.

[20]Unilever Foundry (https://foundry.unilever.com/about-us#fpPanelItem2), accessed 22/11/2015.

Foundations

Each company also has a foundation, which engages in additional R&D activities. It was clear that there are strategic differences between the type of research conducted by each foundation and that of the core R&D departments of the MNCs. The foundations carry out research that is related to what Carrol would refer to as the 'philanthropic' layer of the CSR pyramid. Corporate foundations are funded and governed separately from the MNCs. The research agendas are broader than those of the MNCs that focus specifically on product development and related fundamental research, the foundations sponsor research and development projects that often have an 'international development' component. For example, Nestlé Foundation conducts research on human nutrition with public health relevance and provides access to funds and scientific publications for researchers in developing countries. The Unilever Foundation focuses on social investments that improve the quality of life through the provision of hygiene, sanitation, basic nutrition, access to clean drinking water and enhancing self-esteem. They do this primarily in communities where the company works and through partners in other countries.

de facto Governance of Responsibility

The *de facto* governance dynamics that we see in each of these MNCs are influenced by their internal framing of responsibility and external positioning with regards to the problem of food security, which is the common definitional frame (DF) in both companies (Table 12.2). While there are debates around the types of R&I needed to provide the solutions (S) to food insecurity (i.e., emerging biotechnologies, eco-friendly packaging and new ways to introduce micronutrients), the instruments used to verify the practices and the use of the technology are quite standardised. There is a general approach to integrating sustainability across entire value chains with the use of CSR programs, voluntary standards and involvement in multi-stakeholder initiatives at the global level.

There are two international communities that serve as spaces of interaction (SI). The first is the scientific community. In both MNCs, interviewees reported that their scientists are first and foremost scientists and therefore they follow the ethics of the scientific communities and professional organisations in which they were trained. Furthermore, they are constantly publishing in the peer-reviewed scientific journals and must follow the protocols and responsibility requirements of any other scientist in the academic community. At a scientific conference sponsored by Nestlé in 2015 – Planting Seeds for the Future of Food – there were participants from both MNCs and the debate about the role of scientists in society was raised. There was consensus that scientists themselves need to take responsibility for communication about new technologies and particularly about nutrition as consumers lack 'science education', which is exacerbated by a significant amount of 'bad information'.

The second is found in international multi-stakeholder initiatives. Voluntary standards are used for sustainable sourcing strategies by each of the companies; however, the MNCs are also involved in what might be called industry 'technical standards' committees whereby they set the analytical methods for safety in food and beverages (Nestlé – AOAC INTERNATIONAL) and standards for palm oil (Unilever – Roundtable on Sustainable Palm Oil). Additionally, these companies have both been involved in the UN Global Compact's Food and Agriculture Business (FAB) Principles. The FABs Principles draw a clear link between the MNCs' definitional frame (food security) and the concept of partnership: 'they [FAB Principles] were developed over two years, through over 20 consultations globally with over 1,000 businesses and other key stakeholders and offer a framework for principle-based partnerships to advance sustainable agriculture'.[21]

Finally, there are two *de facto* governance instruments that remain important. The first is the Dow Jones Sustainability Index.[22] Launched in 1999, this index tracks sustainability performance (using corporate responsibility reports) and selects the sustainability leaders. The second is The Declaration of Abu Dhabi,[23] which was launched and signed by the MNCs in 2014. This declaration is a global collaboration to develop a set of common good agricultural practices

---

[21]UN Global Compact FAB (https://www.unglobalcompact.org/what-is-gc/our-work/environment/food-agriculture), accessed 22/11/2015.
[22]DJ Sustainability Index (http://www.sustainability-indices.com/), accessed 22/11/2015.
[23]Declaration of Abu Dhabi (http://www.declaration-of-abu-dhabi.org/), accessed 22/11/2015.

(GAP) criteria that defines safe, environmentally sustainable and socially responsible agriculture and aquaculture. Along with this set of GAP standards, the partners will set up a system for uniquely identifying every certified farm, and a public reporting mechanism for supply chains. This system will be the foundation for delivering training, assessment and verification programs and measuring the impacts of more sustainable practices at farm level.

Responsibilisation, 'Doing Well'?

The richness of the above-described governance arrangements offers both pre-competition and competition incentives for companies, but are they effective and legitimate? To answer this question, we categorise the conditions where 'shared understanding' of responsibility are consistently found across the cases who are functioning at a global scale.

In both companies there has been a shift in their CSR policies from being *ad hoc* 'window dressing' to becoming integral parts of how they do business. This has included integrating CSR objectives into employee performance indicators and introducing design tools that can change the relationships between product designers, researchers and suppliers. There is also movement towards shifting some research centres to developing countries. In some cases, this is an attempt to be closer to the crop production areas (e.g., coffee, cocoa, tea), in other cases this may be to be closer to collaborating partners who are working on specific technologies, yet still in others it may be a way to conduct research that is not condoned elsewhere (e.g., genetic engineering is carried out in Brazil and India and not in Europe).

The work these MNCs are doing to align their governance instruments is moving them in the direction of productive responsibilisation. However, it would be naïve to declare that the MNCs have transformed action. The notion of 'good business' is the fundamental organisational principle for all activities within MNCs and this means that their main purpose of doing research and innovating is to create 'marketable products'. If they receive public backlash, or significant signs that their products will not make it to market, they will make changes to their R&D processes. However, these actions are part of a user responsive design process and not necessarily the result of efforts of a concerted responsibilisation process. Nonetheless, Unilever is the most advanced in this direction as its mainstreaming approach has indeed made the whole organisation more responsive towards meeting its sustainability goals.

The MNCs have become very responsive to stakeholder pressure and thus productively manage contestation. For example, in 2015, Unilever and Nestlé were ranked numbers 1 and 2 on Oxfam's 'Behind the Brands Scorecard'.[24] Gender was one of the concerns that was raised for both companies and in 2015 Nestlé hosted an expert consultation with the leading gender and value chain scholars and practitioners in order to gain advice on how to best promote gender equality in their cocoa value chain. Moreover, as explained earlier, both Unilever and Nestlé are making efforts to participate in multi-stakeholder initiatives and voluntary standards. As shown in Table 12.3, these two companies have been very effective in 'co-branding' with a number of voluntary standards. Therefore, this approach of responding and pro-actively engaging in the definitions of the collective rules for responsible behaviour have made these two companies very capable of managing contestation.

Conclusions

MNCs are a unique type of organisation who can influence the way in which responsibility is defined, constituted and taken up by other actors. The positioning of research within a private company, who is responsible not only for conducting new research but also product development and commercialisation, offers insights into how existing tools are being used and how responsibility for sustainability is governed in private research and innovation.

Through the analysis of these two companies' approaches to responsibility, the legacy of CSR emerges strongly and is well embedded in the infrastructures of the organisational field of sustainability. While the companies do take slightly different approaches to the actual placement of CSR incentives within their internal governance arrangements, CSR and existing regulatory regimes *de facto* dominate. CSR tools are often more important for the innovation processes than for the research processes, as the scientists working

---

[24]Oxfam, Behind the Brand Scorecard (http://www.behindthebrands.org/scorecard), accessed 12/11/2018.

within these companies view themselves primarily as scientists, and thus are also bound to the ethics and peer-review systems used in scientific communities.

The global scale at which MNCs work poses uncertainties about what happens to the governance of research and innovation processes outside headquarters. All interviewees confirmed that the internal codes of conduct are valid for all employees around the world. However, these companies also utilise the regulatory uncertainties and inconsistencies to their advantage by strategically positioning their research programmes within more permissive regulatory environments. This marks a displacement of responsibility from one geographic and regulatory context to another. It is not clear whether this approach strengthens or weakens the responsibility of the company, as it can be interpreted in one of two ways. Either as a strong responsibility for pursuing scientific endeavours and thus promoting the ethic of 'freedom of basic science', or to avoid citizen and public controversy over socially unsustainable practices and thus shirk the responsibility of responding to the needs of society.

In either case, the point is that we must move our understanding of governance of responsible innovation beyond fixed regulatory environments and towards fluid systems where there are multi-directional initiatives carried out by distributed actors in myriad spaces globally. This chapter shows clearly how responsibility for sustainability is closely tied to economic interests of 'core business' – which is a growth model that is fundamentally inconsistent with the conditions of the Anthropocene (Meadows et al., 2004). Responsibility is also linked to the strategic interests of balancing controversy with brand reputation, and company sustainability with the global societal challenges of sustainable agriculture and food security. The principle of 'shared benefits' recommended by informants suggests an expansion of responsibility to encompass outcome legitimacy or, more likely, towards a responsibility for maintaining the philanthropic aspect of CSR. While it is true that MNCs have taken on more responsibility within the sustainability field, they remain unable to change their R&D and business models in order to be responsive to the knowledge, environmental and governance challenges of the Anthropocene. If these actors continue to lead and control the creation of knowledge for agrifood systems, only contestations will be managed and transitions to sustainable agrifood systems will remain a discursive performance.

Acknowledgements

This research received funding from the European Union's Seventh Framework Program for research, technological development and demonstration under the Res-AGorA project (Responsible Research and Innovation in a Distributed Antici-patory Governance Frame. A Constructive Socio-normative Approach), grant agreement no 321427. The author acknowledges the contribution of Lara Rafaela Vogt in the company program analysis.

References

Biermann, F., Abbott, K., Andresen, S., et al. (2012) 'Navigating the Anthropocene: Improving earth system governance'. *Science*, *335*(6074): 1306–07.

Blok, V. and Lemmens, P. (2015) 'The emerging concept of responsible innovation. Three reasons why it is questionable and calls for a radical transformation of the concept of innovation'. In Koops B.-J., Oosterlaken I., Romijn H., et al. (eds), *Responsible Innovation 2*. Springer International Publishing, pp. 19–35.

Boltanski, L. and Thévenot, L. (2006 [1991]) *On Justification: Economies of Worth*. Princeton, NJ: Princeton University Press.

Bonneuil, C. (2015) 'The geological turn: Narratives of the Anthropocene'. In Hamilton C., Gemenne F. and Bonneuil C. (eds), *The Anthropocene and the Global Environmental Crisis*. Milton Park: Routledge, pp. 17–31.

Bonneuil, C., Joly, P.-B. and Marris, C. (2008) 'Disentrenching experiment: The construction of GM—Crop field trials as a social problem'. *Science, Technology & Human Values*, *33*(2): 201–29.

Callon, M. (2010) 'Performativity, misfires and politics'. *Journal of Cultural Economy*, *3*(2): 163–69.

Carroll, A.B. (1979) 'A three-dimensional conceptual model of corporate perfor-mance'. *Academy of Management Review*, *4*(4): 497–505.

Cashore, B., Egan, E., Auld, G., et al. (2007) 'Revising theories of Nonstate Market-Driven (NSMD) governance: Lessons from the Finnish forest certification experience'. *Global Environmental Politics*, *7*(1): 1–44.

Chan, K.M.A., Balvanera, P., Benessaiah, K., et al. (2016) 'Opinion: Why protect nature? Rethinking values and the environment'. *Proceedings of the National Academy of Sciences*, *113*(6): 1462–5.

Chappell, M.J., Vandermeer, J., Badgley, C., et al. (2009) 'Wildlife-friendly farming vs land sparing'. *Frontiers in Ecology and the Environment*, *7*(4): 183–4.

Collier, D., Daniel, Hidalgo, F. and Olivia, Maciuceanu, A. (2006) 'Essentially contested concepts: Debates and applications'. *Journal of Political Ideologies*, *11*(3): 211–46.

Connelly, S. (2007) 'Mapping sustainable development as a contested concept'. *Local Environment*, *12*(3): 259–78.

Constance, D.H. and Bonanno, A. (2000) 'Regulating the global fisheries: The World Wildlife Fund, Unilever, and the Marine Stewardship Council'. *Agriculture and Human Values*, *17*(2): 125–39.

Constance, D.H., Konefal, J.T. and Hatanaka, M. (2018) *Contested Sustainability Discourses in the Agrifood System*. Milton Park: Taylor & Francis.

Demortain, D. (2013) 'Regulatory toxicology in controversy'. *Science, Technology & Human Values*. (https://doi.org/10.1177/0162243913490201)

Dempsey, J. (2011) 'The politics of nature in British Columbia's Great Bear Rainforest'. *Geoforum, 42*(2): 211–21.

Desquilbet, M., Dorin, B. and Couvet, D. (2017) 'Land sharing vs land sparing to conserve biodiversity: How agricultural markets make the difference'. *Environmental Modeling & Assessment, 22*(3): 185–200.

Díaz, S., Demissew, S., Carabias, J., et al. (2015) 'The IPBES Conceptual Framework—Connecting nature and people'. *Current Opinion in Environmental Sustainability, 14*: 1–16.

Dibden, J., Gibbs, D. and Cocklin, C. (2013) 'Framing GM crops as a food security solution'. *Journal of Rural Studies, 29*(0): 59–70.

Dingwerth, K. and Pattberg, P. (2009) 'World politics and organizational fields: The case of transnational sustainability governance'. *European Journal of International Relations, 15*(4): 707–43.

Duncan, J. and Claeys, P. (2018) 'Politicizing food security governance through participation: Opportunities and opposition'. *Food Security, 10*(6): 1411–24.

Enoch, S. (2007) 'A greener Potemkin Village? Corporate social responsibility and the limits of growth'. *Capitalism Nature Socialism, 18*(2): 79–90.

EU Council (2014) *Rome Declaration on Responsible Research and Innovation in Europe*. Rome: Italian Presidency of the Council of the European Union.

Fox, J. (2007) 'The uncertain relationship between transparency and accountability AU - Fox, Jonathan'. *Development in Practice, 17*(4–5): 663–71.

Fuglie, K., Heisey, P., King, J., et al. (2011) *Research Investments and Market Structure in the Food Processing, Agricultural Input, and Biofuel Industries Worldwide*. Washington, DC: United States Department of Agriculture.

Gallie, W.B. (1955) 'Essentially contested concepts'. *Proceedings of the Aristotelian Society, 56*: 167–98.

Genus, A. and Stirling, A. (2018) 'Collingridge and the dilemma of control: Towards responsible and accountable innovation'. *Research Policy, 47*(1): 61–9.

Goodman, D., DuPuis, E.M. and Goodman, M.K. (2012) *Alternative Food Networks: Knowledge, Practice, and Politics*. New York, NY: Routledge.

Gorgoni, G. (2009) 'La responsabilità come progetto. Primi elementi per un'analisi dell'idea giuridica di responsabilità prospettica'. *Diritto e Societa, 2*: 243–92.

Goulart, F.F., Carvalho-Ribeiro, S. and Soares-Filho, B. (2016) 'Farming-biodiversity segregation or integration? Revisiting land sparing versus land sharing debate'. *Journal of Environmental Protection, 7*(7): 1016–32.

Grinbaum, A. and Groves, C. (2013) 'What is "responsible" about responsible innovation? Understanding the ethical issues'. In *Responsible Innovation: Managing the Responsible Emergence of Science and Innovation in Society*. Chichester: John Wiley & Sons Ltd. pp. 119–42.

Guston, D. (2006) 'Responsible knowledge-based innovation'. *Society, 43*(4): 19–21.

Hale, T.N. (2008) 'Transparency, accountability, and global governance'. *Global Governance: A Review of Multilateralism and International Organizations, 14*(1): 73–94.

Hart, H.L.A. and Gardner, J. (2008) *Punishment and Responsibility: Essays in the Philosophy of Law*. Oxford: OUP .

Jasanoff, S. (2004) *States of Knowledge: The Co-production of Science and Social Order*. International library of sociology. London and New York, NY: Routledge, pp. xii, 317.

Jasanoff, S. (2015) *Dreamscapes of Modernity: Sociotechnical Imaginaries and the Fabrication of Power*. Chicago, IL: University. of Chicago Press.

Jessop, B. (2002) *Governance and Meta-Governance: On Reflexivity, Requisite Variety, and Requisite Irony*. Lancaster: Department of Sociology, Lancaster University.

Levidow, L. (2015) 'European transitions towards a corporate-environmental food regime: Agroecological incorporation or contestation?' *Journal of Rural Studies, 40*: 76–89.

Levin, K., Cashore, B., Bernstein, S., et al. (2012) 'Overcoming the tragedy of super wicked problems: Constraining our future selves to ameliorate global climate change'. *Policy Sciences, 45*(2): 123–52.

Lindner, R., Kuhlmann, S., Randles, S., et al. (2016) *Navigating towards Shared Responsibility in Research and Innovation. Approach, Process and Results of the Res-AGorA Project Karlsruhe*, DE: Fraunhofer Institute for Systems and Innovation Research (ISI).

Loconto, A., Desquilbet, M., Moreau, T., et al. (2020) 'The Land sparing – Land sharing controversy: Tracing the politics of knowledge'. *Land Use Policy. 96*: 103610.

Loconto, A. and Fouilleux, E. (2014) 'Politics of Private Regulation: ISEAL and the shaping of transnational sustainability governance'. *Regulation & Governance, 8*(2): 166–85.

McMichael, P. (2011) 'Food system sustainability: Questions of environmental governance in the new world (dis)order'. *Global Environmental Change, 21*(3): 804–12.

McMichael, P. (2016) 'Commentary: Food regime for thought'. *Journal of Peasant Studies, 43*(3): 648–70.

Meadows, D.H., Randers, J. and Meadows, D.L. (2004) *The Limits to Growth: The 30-year Update*. White River Junction, VT: Chelsea Green Publishing Company.

Nestlé (2010) *Nestlé Research: Vision, Action, Value Creation*. Vevey, CH: Nestlé S.A.

Nye, J.S. (1985) 'Motives, means and consequences'. *Society, 22*(3): 17–20.

Ostrom, E. (1990) *Governing the Commons: The Evolution of Institutions for Collective Action*. Cambridge and New York, NY: Cambridge University Press.

Owen, R., Macnaghten, P. and Stilgoe, J. (2012) 'Responsible research and innovation: From science in society to science for society, with society'. *Science and Public Policy, 39*(6): 751–60.

Phalan, B., Om'al, M., Balmford, A., et al. (2011) 'Reconciling food production and biodiversity conservation: Land sharing and land sparing compared'. *Science (Washington) 333*(6047): 1289–91.

Rip, A. (2010) 'Processes of entanglement'. In Akrich M., Barthe Y., Muniesa F., et al. (eds), *Débordements: Mélanges offerts à Michel Callon*. Paris: Transvalor - Presses des MINES, pp. 381–92.

Rip, A. (2018) 'De facto governance of nanotechnologies'. In *Futures of Science and Technology in Society*. Wiesbaden: Springer Fachmedien Wiesbaden, pp. 75–96.

Selznick, P. (2008) *A Humanist Science: Values and Ideals in Social Inquiry*. Stanford, CA: Stanford University Press.

Starr, B.E. (1999) 'The structure of max weber's ethic of responsibility'. *Journal of Religious Ethics*, *27*(3): 407–34.

Stilgoe, J., Owen, R. and Macnaghten, P. (2013) 'Developing a framework for responsible innovation'. *Research Policy*, *42*(9): 1568–80.

Stirling, A. (2015) *Emancipating Transformations: From Controlling 'the Transition'to Culturing Plural Radical Progress. The Politics of Green Transformations*. Milton Park: Routledge, pp. 72–85.

Vanloqueren, G. and Baret, P.V. (2009) 'How agricultural research systems shape a technological regime that develops genetic engineering but locks out agroecological innovations'. *Research Policy*, *38*(6): 971–83.

Von Schomberg, R. (2013) 'A vision of responsible innovation'. In Owen R., Heintz M. and Bessant J. (eds), *Responsible Innovation*. London: John Wiley.

Voß, J.-P., Bauknecht, D. and Kemp, R. (2006) *Reflexive Governance for Sustainable Development*. Cheltenham: Edward Elgar.

Walhout, B., Kuhlmann, S., Ordonez-Matamoros, G., et al. (2016) 'Res-AGorA concepts and approach'. In Lindner R., Kuhlmann S., Randles S., et al. (eds), *Navigating towards Shared Responsibility in Research and Innovation. Approach, Process and Results of the Res-AGorA Project*. Karlsruhe, DE: Fraunhofer Institute for Systems and Innovation Research (ISI), pp. 47–54.

13

Interactive Innovation: New Ways of Knowing for the Anthropocene

Renée van Dis

Introduction

As introduced by Loconto and Constance (this volume), scholars are increasing questioning the types of knowledge that are needed to deal with the societal challenges posed by the Anthropocene. Modern economic optimists argue that there are a few key elements that provide the institutional arrangements necessary for humans to solve any problem that they may encounter specifically free markets, science and liberal democracy (Bowden, 2017). However, the breaking down of the human-nature binary that is implied by the Anthropocene, and the emergence of complexity theory in particular, challenges the idea that humans can solve planetary-level problems with their current institutions (Homer-Dixon, 2000). Moreover, Edwards (2017) claims that everything we know about the Anthropocene itself is based on the scientific knowledge infrastructures of the 20th century.

There have long been critiques in sociology's sub-disciplines that deal with rurality, the environment, science and technology that have highlighted how the exclusion of a diversity of knowledges has limited our ability to fully comprehend situations, and thus also develop appropriate responses (Gibson-Graham, 2006; Haraway, 1988). Political ontologies, participatory and action research perspectives, citizen science, the recognition of third spaces of research and inclusive innovations are approaches that have emerged over the last 30 years as researchers in the social sciences try to include alternative, lay, local and indigenous knowledge within science-policy dialogues, particularly around agriculture and food (Demeulenaere and Piersante, 2020; Lhoste, 2020; Peddi et al., 2022; van der Ploeg, 2014; Wynne, 1996). In the European Union (EU), there has been some success in introducing new knowledge infrastructures for agricultural research and innovation

(R&I); this is referred to as interactive innovation (II). This chapter is dedicated to exploring the emergence of this particular approach in order to respond to the calls from scientists to better engage with sociological perspectives in their studies of the Earth System (Ellis and Trachtenberg, 2014).

This chapter is structured as follows. The next section introduces the II concept and why it is an important object of research. The following section presents the conceptual framework, while the scientometric methodology used in this study will be detailed in Section 3. Sections 4, 5 and 6 describe the European vision of II, a multidimensional understanding and an explanation of II as policy approach in the EU. I conclude by linking this experience of a specific sectoral innovation policy to broader questions of the systems change needed to deal with the challenges posed to society by the Anthropocene.

Why Study II?

With the 'Horizon 2020' (H2020) framework programme, the European Commission made a conscious effort to fund research aimed at responding to crucial societal challenges of the Anthropocene, and strengthening the link between R&I in key sectors of the EU. For agriculture, this resulted in the launch of the European Innovation Partnership for Agricultural Productivity and Sustainability (EIP-AGRI) in 2012. EIP-AGRI finances innovation in EU agriculture and reflects a new interactive approach for sustainable agriculture to thinking about how innovation takes place, who innovates and what knowledge is needed for innovation (EU SCAR, 2012). This implementation has been advised by the Standing Committee on Agricultural Research (SCAR) working group on Agriculture Knowledge and Innovation Systems (AKIS).

II is the core concept of the EIP-AGRI and the approach creates conditions for successful innovation by supporting a multi-actor approach (MAA) that promotes cross-fertilisation of scientific and practical knowledge from different actors involved in agriculture, so as to integrate, co-produce and valorise their different skills, demands and knowledge (EU SCAR, 2013). As the concept of II in the EU is relatively new, a better understanding is needed of how the II EU policy approach emerged as a solution to a societal problem in agriculture: *Where did the ideas for this innovation concept come from and why did they get embedded in this particular policy approach? Considering the societal challenges of the Anthropocene, what are the changing needs for innovation?*

In the Science, Technology and Innovation (STI) literature a rediscovered policy paradigm referred to as 'transformative innovation policy' emerged over the past decade (e.g., Diercks et al., 2019; Kuhlmann and Rip, 2018; Weber and Rohracher, 2012). STI scholars not only argue for the need of new innovation policies that address solutions in response to current societal challenges but also stress the need for configurations in policy goals, policy instruments and involved actors in innovation processes. As such, innovation is seen as playing a key role in societal transformations (Weber and Rohracher, 2012). But in order to address societal challenges a change in setting innovation priorities is insufficient, it requires a change in the knowledge and innovation systems and the institutions that govern them (Kuhlmann and Rip, 2018).

With the introduction of II as a new policy paradigm for both STI and agricultural policy, the EU proposes a vision that interactive forms of innovation have the capacity to respond to societal challenges in agriculture. Understanding the emergence of this EU vision will teach us something about the agrifood transitions in the Anthropocene and the importance of policies that value different forms of knowledge. I draw from Borrás (2011) on policy learning whereby she argues that changes in innovation policy are a result of a co-evolution of theoretical ideas and policy. She states: 'the policy-learning school acknowledges the ability of the state and its bureaucracy to produce/make use of/accumulate knowledge and experience in processes of policy change. Therefore, the building block of this approach is that learning is an important source of policy change, and that learning is based on knowledge and experience produced and used through time' (p. 726).

Therefore, in this chapter, I explore the scientific emergence and conceptualisation of this new innovation concept, the II approach, in agriculture. This helps us to understand a shift in the political recognition in the EU of a different way of doing innovation in agriculture, in which farmers' knowledge and capacity to innovate are recognised, which is one of the proposals from scientists about how to know in the Anthropocene. The aim of this study is thus twofold. First, this research will shed light on the scientific knowledge on innovation processes that translated into this II policy approach to tackle societal challenges. And second, this study provides understanding how the EU expects to tackle societal challenges in agriculture through the II policy approach in the EIP-AGRI.

Analytical Perspectives: Tracing the Genealogy of an Innovation Policy

To explore the scientific emergence and conceptualisation of this new innovation concept in EU policy, our point of departure is based on three theory-inspired assumptions: (1) science, society and policy are interwoven in a dynamic, interactive relationship; (2) one way to establish this relationship and thereby to transfer scientific knowledge into policymaking processes is through knowledge brokerage; (3) the scientific emergence and conceptualisation of the II approach can be found by tracing its 'genealogy'. The combination of these three framings should enable us to understand the EU efforts in contributing to tackling the agricultural challenges of the Anthropocene.

Considering that the EIP-AGRI was created to respond specifically to societal challenges, it is important to understand the emergence of this science-policy-society interface. The idiom of 'co-production' represents how knowledge is co-produced between science, society and policy (Jasanoff, 2004). In other words, scientific knowledge is not independent from society nor from political thought and action: science is socially constructed. Jasanoff (2004) argues: 'what we know about the world is intimately linked to our sense of what can we can do about it [...] Science and technology operate, in short, as political agents [...] Legal and political institutions lead, as much as they are led by, society's investments in science and technology' (pp. 14, 16). If we follow Jasanoff's reasoning, we can find answers to interpreting a societal challenges policy approach in scientific literature that co-produced it.

I use 'knowledge brokerage' to understand the process of transferring science into the policymaking process through the bridges that are made between different types of knowledge and the knowledge producers and their users (Cummings et al., 2019; van Kammen et al., 2006). Knowledge brokerage is a complex process (Ward et al., 2011) that cannot be deepened here. Instead, I use it to describe the process of transferring and bridging scientific knowledge (knowledge producers) into policymaking processes (knowledge users) (van Kammen et al., 2006). As it was the SCAR-AKIS who advised the commission on the development of the II approach in the EIP-AGRI, I treat it as the knowledge broker in this process. SCAR-AKIS is an interdisciplinary working group consisting of researchers and decision-makers. They have a specific mandate to improve the implementation of the EIP, to integrate interactive approaches and better address knowledge flows.[1] In this regard, I study the scientific literature that has influenced the SCAR-AKIS and fed into developing the II approach.

To get his understanding of where the II approach emerged in science, I traced its 'genealogy', as describe by Foucault (1977). Concerning the production of knowledge, every theoretical concept has a genealogy. A genealogy is a historical approach to understanding how a currently used concept emerged – a 'history of the present' (Foucault, 1977). In this regard, a genealogy provides the analytical tools to study the relationship between knowledge and power (Olivier, 2000). To trace the genealogy of the II approach, I will analyse the discourse (i.e., the way knowledge is constituted (Foucault, 1972)) as produced by the SCAR-AKIS. Conducting a (complex) networked discourse analysis helps to identify where and by whom knowledge about II was produced, exchanged and discussed and to what other concepts it is linked. By tracing its genealogy, I explore the scientific emergence and circulation of knowledge around this new interactive innovation concept that has fed into the SCAR-AKIS. It will give us insight into the embedded type of science (knowledge, theories), and it helps thus to understand the emergence and conceptualisation of II as it emerged in the scientific literature, was used in policy advice by the SCAR-AKIS and finally was implemented in the EIP-AGRI as a different way of doing innovation in agriculture.

Methodology

The discourse analysis began with the examination of the studies that contributed to the conceptualisation of II as a policy instrument in the EU and thereby mapping its conceptual (knowledge) networks (Raimbault et al., 2016). I studied the discourse of the II approach by

---

[1]https://scar-europe.org/index.php/akis-mission-and-aims

doing a scientometric analysis, which is a qualitative analysis based on relationships, semantic and social networks (Biljecki, 2016; Ramin et al., 2016). Scientific fields and knowledge evolve over time; they emerge from different fields, merge, diffuse as well as disappear. Chavalarias and Cointet (2013) refer to these complex dynamic relations within scientific fields and knowledge production as *phylomemetic networks*. Consequently, I wanted to discover the phylomemetic patterns within the scientific fields that contributed to the development of the II approach by the EU. This is done in three steps.

Development of Corpus

The first step of the scientometric analysis is to develop the corpus of the network. The basis of the corpus lies in the written core documents (e.g., articles, reports, brochures) by the SCAR-AKIS (as the knowledge broker) and some of the European Commission (Annex I), in which they discuss and describe the concept of II as a policy approach in the EU. From these core documents I developed two corpora: (1) corpus 1 – the references used in the core documents when describing Interactive Innovations; (2) corpus 2 – I extracted all key-words and key notions in the core documents that describe the concept of II. This formed a search equation which I used in Scopus to develop the corpus of the literature related to II (search results until the end of 2017) – it led to 4,585 results.[2]

Co-citation Analysis

In the second step, I analysed co-occurrence within the corpus, to analyse the relations within scientific literature. For the purpose of this study, I did a co-citation analysis to prepare 'references-co-citation networks' (i.e., 'co-citation networks'). This analysis allowed us to

---

[2]Agriculture AND (Innovation AND [Interactive OR co-creation OR participatory OR Farmer-led OR cross-fertilisation OR holistic approach OR co-produc* OR multi-actor OR Participatory network OR 'Side by side network' OR responsible agri-rural OR Social OR multidisciplinary OR transdisciplinary OR Open OR demand-driven OR bottom-up OR Grassroots OR co-generation OR co-ownership] OR ['Innovation by "interaction in networks"' OR interactive innovation model OR Innovation networks OR System*Innovation OR Learning and innovation network* OR Social mechanism of innovation OR Innovation as interactive process OR Innovation partnership* OR Co-innovation OR Thematic Network* OR Multi Actor Approach* OR Operational Group*]).

analyse which references are co-occurring (co-cited) in the corpora as well as the strength of this relation. I thus analysed the co-citation frequency of references and their connections within the corpora. I assumed that the references that are most (centrally) co-cited represent and contain the major concepts and theories that contributed to the emergence and conceptualisation of the II approach. The patterns of co-cited references will be presented in the form of a co-citation network, which shows the relationship between the different co-cited references and thereby the relationship and connections between knowledge in the field of II (Chavalarias and Cointet, 2013; Small, 1973).

The co-citation analysis of corpus 1 was done by manually collecting all references, as the corpus is not homogenous enough to use a digital method like the CorTexT platform to analyse them. This resulted in a database of 2,373 citations. For corpus 2, I did the scientometric analysis digitally, whereby the social and linguistic (co-occurrence) clusters of the scientific articles found in the corpus were traced and mapped based on the textual traces of II, including the patterns of the development of concepts and knowledge over time. To facilitate the scientometric analysis I used the digital platform CorTexT.[3] By uploading the corpus, the CorTexT platform runs a linguistic network analysis based on the co-cited references. The developed network shows the references which are mostly co-cited in the scientific literature on II. Considering this large number of citations (1,000,000), only those citations that were cited three times or more were considered, which left a database of 29,406 citations.

Phylomemetic Networks

In the third step, for corpus 2, I prepared the co-citations networks, including a historical axis to study the phylomemetic patterns.[4] This resulted in a network map displayed on a historical scale, which shows the relations between the top-100 co-cited references. Each reference is presented as a node in the network and the lines represent the

---

[3]Breucker P., Cointet J., Hannud Abdo A., Orsal G., de Quatrebarbes C., Duong T., Martinez C., Ospina Delgado J.P., Medina Zuluaga L.D., Gómez Peña D.F., Sánchez Castaño T.A., Marques da Costa J., Laglil H., Villard L. and Barbier M. (2016). CorTexT Manager (version v2). URL: https://docs.cortext.net
[4]In CorTexT I ran the script 'network mapping'.

relationship between the different nodes. The larger the node, the more frequent the reference has been co-cited. The thicker the line between two nodes the higher the frequency of co-citation between the two references.

Each node is part of a cluster that can be studied as sub-networks. Each reference can be seen as a source of knowledge, which together with all co-cited references, form a network of the knowledge that contributed to the emergences of the concept of II for sustainable agriculture. As I created a historical network map that shows the structure of relationships of co-cited references, it allowed to analyse how these relationships and structures changed over time (Chavalarias and Cointet, 2013; Small, 1973).

To identify, for both corpora, the most central scientific literature and their position within the network, I examined for both corpora which references have the highest:

1. *Degree of relations*: node with a high degree is a node that is related to many (diverse) other nodes in the network;
2. *Weighted contribution to the literature*: Node which has many connections within the network but less divers;
3. *Betweenness*: central nodes in the network, as they are the link between different nodes and thereby connect knowledge and theories.

The content of those references were thoroughly analysed. Finally, qualitative interviews were conducted to discuss and verify the outcomes of the traced genealogy regarding the emergence and conceptualisation of II in the EU. Six scholars and policy experts in the field of interactive innovations for sustainable agriculture in the EU participated. Through semi-structured interviews, the co-citation network of scientific literature on II was discussed with the interviewees. Their quotes are used throughout the discussion of the scientific base for II to confirm or discuss various findings in relation to the actual concept of II.

A European Concept of II

The outcome of analysis of corpus 1 provided us with an understanding on the meaning of II, which has fed into the EU R&I policy approach (Table 13.1). The work and discussions of the SCAR-AKIS have been influenced by the evolving EU policy

Table 13.1   Top weight, degree and frequency of the main references from the co-citation analysis of Corpus 1

Nr.	Reference
1	Rogers, E.M. (1962) Diffusion of innovations
2	Rip, A. and Kemp, R. (1998) Technological change
3	Rotmans, J., Kemp, R. and van Asselt, M. (2001) More evolution than revolution. Transition management in public policy
4	Latour, B. (1987) Science in action
5	Kline, S.J. and Rosenberg, N. (1986) An overview of innovation. In: R. Landau & N. Rosenberg (Eds), The positive sum strategy
6	Giddens, A. (1984) The constitution of society: Outline of the theory of structuration
7	Kemp, R., Schot, J. and Hoogma, R. (1998) Regime shifts to sustainability through processes of niche formation: The approach of strategic niche management
8	Smits, R. and Kuhlmann, S. (2004) The rise of systemic instruments in innovation policy
9	Nonaka, I. and Takeuchi, H. (1995) The knowledge-creating company
10	River, W.M. and Zijp, W. (2002) Contracting for agricultural extension: International case studies and emerging practices

context, such as 'the financial and food crises, the EU 2020 strategy for a smart, sustainable and inclusive growth, the European Innovation Partnership initiative and the discussions on the CAP post-2013' (EU SCAR, 2012). Hence, I argue that the SCAR-AKIS can be seen as a knowledge broker and has influenced the emergence of the concept of II as developed in the EIP-AGRI. One of the interviewees (SCAR-AKIS member 2018) mentioned: 'The SCAR has been super important in the development of II. Before the EIPs started they already gave that message to DG-AGRI. If you are asking who in the beginning really kicked this off? It's the SCAR'.

What has been the message that the SCAR-AKIS gave towards II? The EU SCAR reports (EU SCAR, 2012, 2013) present the vision that technology and innovation diffusion cannot be seen outside their social, economic and political environment. They do not only pose the question on the impact of technology on society, but they also examine how technology is influenced by society. Innovations are therefore described as complex processes that cannot be seen as simple, linear models of diffusion. This idea is conceptualised as 'innovation journeys' by Van de Ven et al. (1999). They discuss innovation journeys as social processes; it's about the social organisation of knowledge as basis for the co-production of innovation. In this context, to understand the emergence in the EU, an interviewee (policy officer DG Agri 2018) stated the following:

> In agriculture, in the 1980s we still had a lot of public extension services which also served public goals, so they had a task to try to reduce environmental pollution etc. when they were providing individual advice to farmers. This whole public system is deteriorating and what is left are the private companies who profiled themselves as private advisors. So, they replaced in fact the old public extension services. Which makes the whole public knowledge system not turning around anymore. So, there is research published now in essence for the scientific publications, which the practitioners like the farmers themselves or their advisors hardly read. The concept of II emerged to change this situation: there is massive budget going to research and there is little coming to or implementable by practice.

This quote demonstrates the perception of policymakers who are out of touch with the diversity of pluralistic advisory services active across the EU (Cerf et al., 2011). It shows that through the II approach, policymakers are actually legitimatising societal change processes. Although science is seen as an important input to innovation, different types of knowledge are needed for innovation efficiency. Those different types of knowledge are difficult to manage as knowledge is embedded in complex social systems. This is in line with the recent publication by Van de Ven (2017) who found in his research that innovation journeys cannot be controlled. He states that only the odds of successful innovation journeys can be increased by developing skills to deal with and manage obstacles along the journey. The various types of knowledge, such as farmers' and scientists' knowledge, can only be integrated and co-produced if there are strong social relations among actors. Hence, there is a need for strong social capital: networks need to be set up for the knowledge to circulate.

Policy can play an important role in facilitating network building, by facilitating alignment, to develop innovations. In this regard, one of the interviewees (agronomist at a research institute 2018) confirmed:

> Why policy needs to take a more pro-active role is because there is a lack of coordination of the activities of the various actors within the agricultural system. The problem is that you have all kind of actors with all kind of different stakes and there is a lack of coordination of the efforts between them. So, you see a clash of the stakes. And policy is the only actor that in principle can have a more independent stake.

A Multidimensional Understanding of II

Where the previous section gave an idea of the meaning of II for the SCAR-AKIS, this section deepens the analysis of the scientific literature that has influenced this conceptualisation. Figure 13.1 shows the co-citation network of the scientific literature on II of the EIP-AGRI

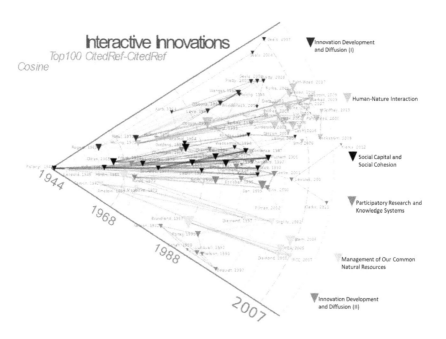

Figure 13.1   Co-citation network of scientific literature on II, presented on a historical axis. The larger the node, the higher the frequency of co-citation. The thicker the line between two nodes, the higher the frequency of co-citation

(corpus 2) as a result of tracing the genealogy. The network provides an interpretation of a multidimensional understanding of the II approach. I assume that the knowledge and theories from the references that are co-cited in this network have influenced the SCAR-AKIS and thereby fed into the emergence and conceptualisation of II as policy approach in the EU. Considering the theoretical framing about the relationship between science, policy and society (Jasanoff, 2004), the results provide insight into the societal problems and possible solutions to which the II could contribute, as well as where the need came from for such a policy approach. Table 13.2 gives an overview of the references which are co-cited with the highest degree, weight or betweenness within the network.

I defined five themes in the scientific literature, based on the clusters of Figure 13.1, that are feeding into a multidimensional understanding of II:

1. Management of our common natural resources
2. Human-nature interaction
3. Participatory research and knowledge systems
4. Social Capital and social cohesion
5. Innovation development and diffusion

Management of Our Common Natural Resources Cluster

The first central theme reveals scholarly preoccupation with the tensions between individualism and collective action in the management of our common pool of natural resources. The literature posits that by making self-centred and individual choices over collective choices with regards to the use of natural resources, human overuse and overexploit common natural resources that I need to live and make a living (of which the agricultural domain is a large contributor) which causes environmental degradation. Hence, this theme provides the problematisation – environmental degradation by agricultural practices – that contributed to the emergence of II in the EU – and thus there is a clear need for innovations that aim for sustainable agriculture. This was confirmed by an interviewee said about this body of literature: 'I would absolutely say that this literature is at the base of why we need II. This not only frames what happened in the scientific world, but also what happened in practice. I think that these articles are at the root of the dynamic in practice as well as at the root of the dynamic in science'.

Table 13.2 Overview of the references which are co-cited with the highest degree of relationships among co-citations, highest betweenness (connecting theories) or highest weighted contribution to the scientific literature

Nr. Co-citation	Highest Weight	Highest Degree	Highest Betweenness
1	Brundtland, G., (1987) Our common future	Dietz, T., Ostrom, E., Stern, P.C., (2003) The struggle to govern the commons	Stiglitz, J.E., (2002) Globalization and its discontents
2	Ostrom, E., (1990) Governing the commons: The evolution of institutions for collective action	Berkes, F., Colding, J., Folke, C., (2003) Navigating social-ecological systems: Building resilience for complexity and change	Hardin, G., (1968) The tragedy of the commons
3	Hardin, G., (1968) The tragedy of the commons	Holling, C.S., (1978) Adaptive environmental assessment and management	Rawls, J., (1971) A theory of justice
4	Stern, N., (2006) Stern review on the economics of climate change	Putnam, R.D., (2000) Bowling alone. The collapse of revival of American community	Costanza, R., d'Arge, R., deGroot, R., Farber, S., Grasso, M., Hannon, B., Limburg, K., vanden Belt, M., (1997) The value of the world's ecosystem services and natural capital

5	Ostrom, E., (2005) Understanding institutional diversity	Castells, M., (1996) The rise of network society	Diamond, J., (1997) Guns, germs, and steel: The fates of human societies
6	Folke, C., Hahn, T., Olsson, P., Norberg, J., (2005) Adaptive governance of social-ecological systems	Holling, C.S., (2001) Understanding the complexity of economic, ecological, and social systems	Granovetter, M., (1985) Economic action and social structure: The problem of embeddedness
7	Sen, A., (1999) Development as freedom	Ostrom, E., (2009) A general framework for analyzing sustainability of social-ecological systems	Putnam, R.D., (2000) Bowling alone. The collapse and revival of American community
8	Millennial Ecosystem Assessment, (2005) Ecosystems and human wellbeing: Synthesis	Rittel, H.W.J., Webber, M.M., (1973) Dilemmas in a general theory of planning	Dietz, T., Ostrom, E., Stern, P.C., (2003) The struggle to govern the commons
9		Olsen, M., (1965) The logic of collective action: Public goods and the theory of groups	Polanyi, K., (1944) The great transformation: The political and economic origins of our time
10		Berkes, F., & Folke, C. (1998). Linking social and ecological systems for resilience and sustainability	Carson, R., (1962) Silent spring

However, beyond just technological innovations, there is a need for institutional innovations through which I manage our resources in a multi-actor environment. The EIP-AGRI reshapes systems of global governance for common goods and addresses global environmental challenges: they bring together local actors, while funding is coming from a higher institution (EU). As shown in Figure 13.1, the environmental problems that are identified in the early 1960s (e.g. Carson, 1962; Hardin, 1968) have been influential the co-cited references published in the later part of the cluster which discuss solutions and actions required to mitigate the worse effects of environmental degradation. It's notable that many of these later co-cited references are reports developed by governmental organisations (e.g., Brundtland, 1987; IPCC, 2007; MEA, 2005). Apparently, there was a growing demand and mandate for governments to respond to the growing (human caused) environmental problems, but this process took a long time. One of the interviewees (agriculture innovation expert at a research institute 2018) responded:

> The mismanagement of our natural resources captures one of the big challenges that has become recognized in the early 1960s. In the mid-1970s some of these environmental problems became really drastic and could no longer be denied. The scientific thinking changed that innovation is not just to stimulate economic growth, but also to tackle problems that we face. And one of the problems were the natural resources. You see there is a very long lead time between when problems were first identified and when some actors and scientists are taking it up this new thinking and start to develop new ideas. Then it takes a long time before that is accepted in the scientific world and only then you see that also policy start to adopt those notions.

Human-Nature Interaction Cluster

As there is a need for recognition that natural resources are a common good and need to be managed collectively, the literature discusses the embeddedness of social and ecological contexts (e.g., the theory of 'social-ecological systems'). This literature stresses *how* human and nature interact in very complex systems, where human put high pressure on nature and cause environmental degradation. Also, costs of environmental degradation are a 'common' expense, while the provision of human welfare by ecosystems services is 'common' goods. This acknowledges that we should see natural resources as common, collective goods that impacts not just individuals, but society as a whole. Analysing the data from a temporal perspective shows how the early articles in this theme are about resilience, adaptive management and solutions related to ecological systems and environmental issues. Only the later co-cited references (after 2000) add a stronger human component in which the (complex) interactions between human and nature and socio-ecological systems are discussed. It reveals the relative recent addition of the human component in scientific literature on ecological systems.

The literature suggests that there is no 'one size fits all' solution to tackle the problem of high human pressure on nature or to deal with the complex social-ecological systems in general. Hence, this calls for proper governance of the commons: institutions through which we manage our natural resources such as property rights and access to natural resources. In this regard, one of the interviewees (agricultural innovation expert at a research institute, 2018) stated:

> What we need is institutional innovation, we need to change the rule of the game – the institutions through which we manage our resources, like pricing systems, legal rules, land tenure arrangements, certification systems. It's about moving away from the individual to collective action, it's about multi stakeholder approaches: not only collective action horizontally among farmers, but also coordinated action in a network of interdependent stakeholders.

Governance of natural resources includes many challenges that must not be overlooked, such as the complexity of social-ecological systems and the encouragement of dialogue between actors. As supported in the II approach, it needs a broad, multi-actor and multidimensional approach that includes interaction between different actors with disciplines, knowledge and skills. This is where the EU can fulfil an important role and is at the base of the need for a policy approach towards interactive sustainable rural development.

Participatory Research and Knowledge Systems Cluster

Yet, as discussed above, technologies alone are not the solution to solve the problem around the misuse and management of common natural resources, nor to manage the complexity of interaction between nature and human (well-)being. Instead, the scientific literature on II draws attention to the importance of mutual cohesion among human and of centring knowledge dissemination and production. An interesting point about this cluster is that two early publications (Freire, 1970; Rawls, 1971) are at its base. The general theories on social relations, human interaction and collective action discussed in those two publications are adapted specifically to the field of agricultural development and are found in the majority of the literature published from the mid 1990s to early 2000s. This resulted in the central theme of 'participatory rural development', as Leeuwis and van den Ban (2004) stated: '"Sustainability" cannot just be looked at in biophysical or ecological terms, because the state of "hard systems" depends crucially on interactions between multiple human beings'.

The co-cited references in this theme share knowledge in relation to agricultural knowledge and innovation systems, agricultural extension and agricultural research based on a participative approach. These areas are discussed in contrast to top-down research and innovation approaches. So, rather than just technological changes, the solutions lie in increasing dissemination and co-production of knowledge for innovation in agriculture, which should be farmer centred. Scientific and (local) farm knowledges are considered complementary. Interaction between farmers and researchers is required and such interaction can work if there is a culture of collective action and (strong) social relations. In this way farmers' actions and knowledge (i.e., farming and doing research) are not seen as separate and individual actions but are brought together to reach the same goal: sustainable agriculture. The validation of this outcome is at the root of the II approach and the EU approach could provide the policy instruments and the institutions that support participatory agricultural research and innovation. The interviews (agriculture innovation expert at a research institute 2018) confirmed this:

> The EU more and more came to recognize that there is an enormous gap between the research and farming side. Already in the 90s there were researchers who were working very closely with farmers to find new ways to address the sustainability challenges and they published about it. You might say this is at the root of the II approach. At a certain point the EU decided this is so important, we have to make this into a policy program.

Social Capital and Social Cohesion Cluster

From the previous themes it becomes clear that managing common natural resources in complex socio-ecological systems entail a high level of interactions. The literature feeding into this theme demonstrates that the complexity of social relations should not be underestimated. It requires flows of information, multi-actor approaches, collective action, strong connections and networks. There is a need for social capital intended for human interaction, engagement and collaboration, so that no individuals or actor groups are excluded from networks. To foster interactivity and support innovation, institutions are needed that can support the management and governance of the use of common natural resources. An interviewee (agriculture innovation expert at a research institute 2018) confirmed:

> Institutions can support interactions, such as: To bring together relevant stakeholders; Discover the complexities and make them reflexive; Build social cohesion. It's about the process to support innovation and fostering interactivity.

The references that are co-cited in this theme are spread over time, and almost none is specifically related to agriculture. The publications are rather about the social embeddedness of economy and science. For instance, they present evidence that the market economy has separated science from society and the conclusions push for a re-embedding of these relations. The interviewees confirmed that the II approach is legitimatising this science evidence, as one (policy officer DG Agri 2018) stated:

> II emerged as opposite to the still classical scientific publication-oriented research, so that we focus back to farmers' needs. Before, the things agricultural scientists researched were much more applied than the following generations when scientific publications became so important.

Yet, this literature around social capital and interactions discusses the social embeddedness of science and fed into the concept of II by discussing the need to re-embed science in society. The EIP-AGRI came up with the multi-actor II approach as opposed to the 'linear model of innovation'. The interactive character of II, the related EU policy instruments and support systems thus concentrate on the increase of social capital, that are needed to manage the 'commons' and complex social-ecological systems.

Innovation Development and Diffusion Cluster

Remarkable is the relative limited amount of literature related to development and dissemination of innovations. At the historical source of the co-citation network lies the reference of Rogers (1962) *Diffusion of Innovations*. Most of the earlier published co-cited references in this theme provide (general) theories about diffusion of innovations and technologies, about processes of learning and production of knowledge. While most of these publications don't relate specifically to agricultural or rural development, they are co-cited with more recent publications that are about agriculture and thus make the link with innovation and agriculture.

The literature in this theme on innovation brings together the knowledge and theories on innovation, agriculture and the need for collaboration and collective action. Two central terms are 'innovation systems' (which is about the organisation of the innovation process) and 'system innovation' (which is about transition). These approaches are seen as the basis of II, which one of the interviewees (agriculture innovation expert at a research institute 2018) confirmed:

> The concept of II is very present. Its interactivity is emphasized through the lens of innovation systems, but also through the lenses of system innovation (which emphasizes transition) which also emphasize multi stakeholder process.

To define the concept of innovation systems, in the EU SCAR (2012) gives the following description: 'AKIS is a useful concept to describe a system of innovation, with emphasis on the organisations involved, the links and interactions between them, the institutional infrastructure with its incentives and the budget mechanisms'. It's a concept that is used in various documents on public policies for innovations by the EU, and the term is often mentioned in the documents from the EIP-AGRI and SCAR-AKIS. The theories published in the bottom cluster provide the theoretical background of these ideas for public policies since the AKIS framework builds on the national innovation systems framework.

II as a Policy Approach for Innovation in the EU

The previous two sections have revealed the scientific genealogy of II as a policy concept in the EU. I illustrated how scientific knowledge fed into this innovation concept so to tackle societal challenges. In this section, I will bring all of this together to discuss how the II policy approach is characterised to respond to societal challenges in agriculture.

The EIP-AGRI is positioned within a larger set of EU instruments for innovation policy. Within the framework of the 'Innovation Union', launched in 2010, five European Innovation Partnerships (EIPs) (European Union, 2011).[5] The EIPs were developed to improve the EU's competitiveness and productivity, to respond to crucial societal challenges and to avoid fragmentation of innovation efforts by connecting various actors along the value chain (European Union, 2011, 2015). Each of the five EIPs defined their own objectives, priority areas and implementation mechanisms. There are various differences between the EIP-AGRI and the other EIPs. The EIP-AGRI has the II model as a central concept. Where the other EIPs are only implemented through the H2020 programme, the II model is implemented through two mechanisms: (1) the EU component: Multi-Actor Approach (MAA) projects of the H2020 Programme; and (2) the national and regional component: Operational Groups (OG) through the Rural Development Programs (RDP) of the Common Agriculture Policy (CAP) ('second pillar') (EU SCAR, 2013; European Union, 2014).

There are two important results that emerge from our analysis of the textual data that help understand the contextualisation of the II approach. First, from the perspective of science-society-policy co-production (Jasanoff, 2004), a surprising outcome of the traced genealogy is the importance of sociological theories, alongside natural resource management and development economics, in the core positions written into both scientific and policy documents. This heritage of II as innovation concept means that there is an understanding by the technocrats in the EU Commission that innovation goes beyond technical work to take into consideration the relations and interactions among actors. In addition, it captures the understanding that technology will not work if actors are not ready to integrate them into their practices. Second, the SCAR-AKIS, as a knowledge broker, has been

---

[5] (1) EIP on Active and Healthy Ageing – EIP on AHA; (2) EIP on Agriculture Sustainability and Productivity – EIP-AGRI; (3) EIP on Smart Cities and Communities – EIP-SCC; (4) EIP on Water; (5) EIP on Raw Materials.

quite influential in the EU innovation policy process. Indeed, their work in reaching across the boundaries created between sectors in the EU policy environment is unique in terms of opening up a pathway towards policies that might actually encourage innovative solutions to the problems that societies are dealing with in the Anthropocene, as I explore below.

Rethinking the Position of Researchers and Farmers in Research and Innovation Processes

The II approach is characterised by multi-actor collaboration. It recognises that innovation should go beyond the inclusion of science only in innovation and research and stresses a more central position of farmers, away from individualism to collective action. In the II approach innovation is perceived as interactive, multi-actor processes, which implies a change in the organisation of innovation processes and the reorganisation of knowledge networks by including all actors. Also, the need to incentivise agricultural research to respond better to the needs of practitioners/end users is recognised (EU SCAR, 2013). The II approach is implemented through initiatives such as multi-actor approaches (MAAs) (including thematic networks [TNs]) and OGs. This should lead to innovations that aim for sustainable agriculture using ideas, knowledge and tools coming from research and practical experiences.

However, this MAA requires strong interactions among the diverse food system actors. Each actor holds different (types of) knowledge, that is based on the actor type, beliefs, skills, experiences, material resources, etc. Interactions in learning processes could blend these different types of knowledge together into a process of co-creation.

Re-embedding Agricultural Sciences Into Society

The genealogy of the II concept highlighted the need of re-embedding or 'socialising' agricultural R&I in society. The II approach supports applied research that provides applicable solutions responding to challenges in farming systems, moving away from the scientific publication approach (Policy officer DG Agri 2018). This relationship between science and society requires interaction: for research and innovation to respond to societal challenges, and thereby in the contribution towards impacting society.

The II policy approach centralises 'interaction' in innovation processes between the various actors involved. As the new paradigm for R&I of the EIP-AGRI is implemented through its two pillars (H2020 and the RDPs), it is used at different levels of society: bigger institutes working at H2020 levels and for field-oriented actors working at regional level. In this regard, one of the interviewees (policy officer DG Agri 2018) stated:

When the EIPs were set up with the idea of speeding up innovation by bringing together the actors, there was an awareness that we should not only work with science, but get the other actors involved. The reason that it developed so well in the EIP-AGRI is that it has a second means of management through the Rural Develop Programmes (RDPs). The EIP-AGRI promotes the working together of researchers, farmers and advisors through the cooperation programs to work on issues that researchers had in mind or to work out innovative ideas that came from farmers.

In addition, another interviewee (a national focal point of the EIP-AGRI 2018) discussed:

On the EIP level, the EIP-AGRI is slightly different, because there are 2 pillars: on the one hand there is the H2020 which has a quite important impact, through the MAA. This is a new paradigm for research and innovation that is going beyond just having a committee with multiple stakeholders in the committee, but also in the projects. And the second aspect is the CAP and the capacity to influence the RDPs at regional level all over Europe. So EIP-AGRI really affects all territories and beyond national level, to spread it in the societies at all levels of Europe.

Embedding Innovation in EU Rural Development Programs (RDPs)

The implementation of the EIP-AGRI through the RDPs makes it directly impactful in the region: actors at all levels are involved in and impacted by the EIP-AGRI. Also, various measures of the RDPs can be used to stimulate innovation activities of the OGs (EU SCAR, 2013, 2015). This implementation approach of the EIP-AGRI explains the large stream of scientific literature inspiring II that comes from 'development studies' and indicates the direction of the EU towards a sustainable agriculture that meets societal challenges in rural areas. The increasing societal concerns in rural areas have changed the EU policy agenda. More emphasis is being put on the integration between agricultural policies and rural development. This results for instance in a shift in the CAP from direct support to farm production towards supporting common/public goods (EU SCAR, 2012). Also, policies (like the EIP-AGRI) support a better alignment between research and the practical context of farming (EU SCAR, 2012).

The EIP-AGRI aims to create synergies between various policies. In this case, the implementation of the II approach through the RDPs enables linking rural development plans with European research instruments, and innovation and research policy (H2020). In this way, the EIP-AGRI creates linkages between rural development and R&I. Since one of the aims of the RDPs 2014–2020 is to innovate at many places, the EIP-AGRI has also managed to be impactful through R&I at different layers of society through the projects carried out by the OGs during this period (EU SCAR, 2013; EIP-AGRI, n.d.). According to the EU SCAR (2013): 'Development projects – such as those funded by Rural Development policies – will increasingly mix different activities (research plus training plus extension) and diverse actors'.

Conclusions

The traced genealogy of the II approach for sustainable agriculture in the EU that is studied in this chapter shows that the need for policies that encourage sustainable agriculture innovations emerged from the recognition of the negative impacts of industrial agriculture in the Anthropocene. This genealogy of II reveals the scientific preoccupation with the tensions between individualism and collective action in the management of our common pool of natural resources and the type of the innovations needed for actually practice sustainable agriculture. Thus, rather than just technical innovations, the material and natural resources need to be included in the vision for society and managed as commons that impact society as a whole.

This article shows the influence of the SCAR-AKIS in guiding the EU in its R&I policy approach to reorienting R&I in response to societal challenges. By tracing the genealogy in the scientific literature this article contributes to the knowledge base of understanding how the II policy approach came up as a solution to societal challenges in agriculture. As I have shown what scientific knowledge has fed into this EU policy, I also identified the types of societal challenge it could contribute to and how it can direct innovations for agrifood transitions. Due to the two pillars of implementation of the EIP-AGRI, one at EU level through EU-wide calls for R&I and one at national level through the CAP incentives, actors at different levels are directly involved and impacted by the implementation of the II approach.

I thus argue that findings of the emergence of the II approach tell us something about the interlinkages between innovation and society. My findings suggest that this is not only about setting innovation priorities as a solution to societal problems, but innovation policy requires a change in the knowledge and innovation system (see Kuhlmann and Rip, 2018). These results demonstrate the EU policy response to a changing need for innovation to deal with challenges of the Anthropocene. In this regard, genealogy as a method has proven to reveal not only the societal problems that are at the basis of an innovative concept, but how this particular concept has been shaped by knowledge produced by social scientists. In particular, social scientists who have relied upon diverse knowledges to develop their own approaches. I thus suggest that the II approach goes beyond simply directing innovation towards certain outcomes and impacts, but that II changes the knowledge infrastructures and functioning of the innovation process. This transformative action is seen when comparing the genealogy results with the actual implementation of the II policy approach. II rethinks the position of researchers and farmers in research and innovation processes; it re-embeds agricultural sciences into society; and it embeds innovation in EU rural development programs. These three actions are needed if we, as societies, plan to find solutions to the complex and interrelated problems of the Anthropocene.

These conclusions suggest that there is a conscious effort by the EU to change who the innovators are and particularly how farmers and researchers engage each other to solve societal challenges. Considering the large body of literature on sociological theories about collective knowledge production that was traced in the genealogy of the II concept, it raises the question about the opportunities offered by the II approach for valuing this knowledge and interaction in innovation processes. Is the II approach in the EIP-AGRI simply implemented as an interactive policy instrument or is it about the actual valorisation of collective knowledge production that supposedly influenced the development of the policy in the first place? If we want to survive the Anthropocene, the response needs to be the latter.

Acknowledgements

The author worked on this Chapter under the supervision of Allison Loconto (Research Professor, INRAE) and Pierre-Benoit Joly (President, INRAE Centre at Toulouse). Thanks go to Marc Barbier (Research Professor at INRAE), Lionel Villard (Professor at ESIEE Paris) and the CorTexT team for their assistance with the CorTexT platform.

References

Biljecki, F. (2016) 'A scientometric analysis of selected GI science journals'. *International Journal of Geographical Information Science, 30*(7): 1302–35.

Borrás, S. (2011) 'Policy learning and organizational capacities in innovation policies'. *Science and Public Policy, 38*(9): 725–34.

Bowden, G. (2017) 'An environmental sociology for the Anthropocene'. *Canadian Review of Sociology/Revue canadienne de sociologie, 54*(1): 48–68.

Cerf, M., Guillot, M.N. and Olry, P. (2011) 'Acting as a change agent in supporting sustainable agriculture: How to cope with new professional situations?'. *The Journal of Agricultural Education and Extension, 17*(1): 7–19.

Chavalarias, D. and Cointet, J.P. (2013) 'Phylomemetic patterns in science evolution-the rise and fall of scientific fields'. *PLoS ONE, 8*(2): 54847.

Cummings, S., Kiwanuka, S., Gillman, H. and Regeer, B. (2019) 'The future of knowledge brokering: Perspectives from a generational framework of knowledge management for international development'. *Information Development, 35*(5): 781–94.

Diercks, G., Larsen, H. and Steward, F. (2019) 'Transformative innovation policy: Addressing variety in an emerging policy paradigm'. *Research Policy, 48*(4): 880–94.

Demeulenaere, E. and Piersante, Y. (2020) 'In or out? Organisational dynamics within European 'peasant seed' movements facing opening-up institutions and policies'. *Journal of Peasant Studies, 47*(4): 767–91.

Edwards, P.N. (2017) 'Knowledge infrastructures for the Anthropocene'. *The Anthropocene Review, 4*(1): 34–43.

Ellis, M.A. and Trachtenberg, Z. (2014) 'Which Anthropocene is it to be? Beyond geology to a moral and public discourse'. *Earth's Future, 2*(2): 122–5.

EU SCAR (2012) *Agricultural Knowledge and Innovation Systems in Transition – A Reflection Paper.* Brussels.

EU SCAR (2013) *Agricultural Knowledge and Innovation Systems towards 2020.* Brussels.

European Union (2011) *Report from the Commission to the European Parliament, the Council, the European Economic and Social Committee and the Committee of the Regions State of the Innovation Union 2011.* Brussels.

European Union (2014) *Outriders for European Competitiveness – European Innovation Partnerships (EIPs) as a Tool for Systemic Change. Report of the Independent Expert Group.* Brussels.

European Union (2015) *State of the Innovation Union 2015.* Brussels.

Foucault, M. (1972) *The Archaeology of Knowledge.* New York, NY: Pantheon Books.

Foucault, M. (1977) *Discipline and Punish.* New York, NY: Pantheon Books.

Freire, P. (1970) *Pedagogy of the Oppressed.* New York, NY: Penguin Books.

Gibson-Graham, J.K. (2006) *The End of Capitalism (As We Knew It): A Feminist Critique of Political Economy.* Minneapolis: University of Minnesota Press.

Haraway, D. (1988) 'Situated knowledges: The science question in feminism and the privilege of partial perspective'. *Feminist Studies, 14*(3): 575–99.

Homer-Dixon, T. (2000) *The Ingenuity Gap.* Toronto: Knopf.

Jasanoff, S. (2004) *States of Knowledge: The Co-production of Science and the Social Order.* London and New York, NY: Routledge.

Kuhlmann, S. and Rip, A. (2018) 'Next-generation innovation policy and grand challenges'. *Science and Public Policy, 45*(4): 448–54.

Leeuwis, C. and van den Ban, A.W. (2004) *Communication for Rural Innovation: Rethinking Agricultural Extension.* Oxford: Blackwell Publishing Ltd.

Lhoste, É. (2020) '« Les tiers-lieux peuvent-ils ouvrir la recherche à la société civile ? »'. *Cahiers de l'action, 55*(1): 13–9.

Olivier, B. (2000) 'Discourse, genealogy, social theory and a society in transition: The challenge facing the human sciences'. *Society in Transition, 31*(1): 45–57.

Peddi, B., Ludwig, D. and Dessein, J. (2022) 'Relating inclusive innovations to indigenous and local knowledge: A conceptual framework'. *Agriculture and Human Values.* (http://doi.org/10.1007/s10460-022-10344-z)

Raimbault, B., Cointet, J.P. and Joly, P.B. (2016) 'Mapping the emergence of synthetic biology'. *PLOS ONE, 11*(9): e0161522.

Ramin, S., Pakravan, M., Habibi, G. and Ghazavi, R. (2016) 'Scientometric analysis and mapping of 20 Years of glaucoma research'. *International Journal of Ophthalmology, 9*(9): 1329–35.

Rawls, J. (1971) *A Theory of Justice.* Cambridge, MA: Harvard University Press.

Small, H. (1973) 'Co-citation in the scientific literature: A new measure of the relationship between two documents'. *Journal of the American Society for Information Science, 24*(4): 265–9.

van der Ploeg, J.D. (2014) 'Peasant-driven agricultural growth and food sovereignty'. *Journal of Peasant Studies, 41*(6): 999–1030.

Van de Ven, A.H. (2017) 'The innovation journey: You can't control it, but you can learn to maneuver it'. *Innovation: Management, Policy & Practice, 19*(1): 39–42.

Van de Ven, A., Polley, D. and Garud, R. (1999) *The Innovation Journey.* Oxford: Oxford University Press.

Van Kammen, J., de Savigny, D. and Sewankambo, N. (2006) 'Using knowledge brokering to promote evidence-based policy-making: The need for support structures'. *Bulletin of the World Health Organization, 84*(8).

Ward, V., House, A. and Hamar, S. (2011) 'Knowledge brokering: The missing link in the evidence to action chain?'. *Evid Policy*, 5(3): 267–79.

Weber, K. M. and Rohracher, H. (2012) 'Legitimizing research, technology and innovation policies for transformative change: Combining insights from innovation systems and multi-level perspective in a comprehensive 'failures' framework'. *Research Policy*, 41(6): 1037–47.

Wynne, B. (1996) 'May the sheep safely graze? A reflexive view of the expert-lay knowlege divide'. In S. Lash, B. Szerszynski and B. Wynne (eds), *Risk, Environment and Modernity: Towards a New Ecology*. London: Sage Publications.

Annex 1: Reference List Core Documents EU and SCAR on Interactive Innovation

Reference List Core Documents

EIP-AGRI. (2014). Innovation support services.

EIP-AGRI. (2015). EIP-AGRI Seminar 'Promoting creativity and learning through agricultural knowledge systems and interactive innovation' (seminar report 3–4 December 2015).

EIP-AGRI. (2015b). Participatory approaches for agricultural innovation.

EIP-AGRI. (2016). Operational groups turning your idea into innovation.

EIP-AGRI. (2017). Horizon 2020 multi-actor projects.

EIP-AGRI. (2018). Agricultural knowledge and innovation systems stimulating creativity and learning.

EU SCAR. (2009). Some of the key messages raised in the 2nd SCAR-Foresight into priorities for building the agricultural research agenda of the coming years.

EU SCAR. (2012). Agricultural knowledge and innovation systems in transition – a reflection paper. Brussel.

EU SCAR. (2013). Agricultural knowledge and innovation systems towards 2020 – an orientation paper on linking innovation and research. Brussel.

EU SCAR. (2015). Reflection paper on the role of the standing committee on agricultural research.

EU SCAR. (2017). SWG SCAR-AKIS Policy Brief on New approaches on Agricultural Education Systems.

European Commission. (2009). New challenges for agricultural research: Climate change, food security, rural development, agricultural knowledge systems 2nd Scar Foresight Exercise. Brussel.

European Commission. (2014). Guidelines on programming for innovation and the implementation of the EIP for agricultural productivity and sustainability.

European Commission. (2015). EIP-AGRI Common format for interactive innovation projects.

European Union. (2013). Knowledge Transfer and Innovation in Rural Development Policy (EU Rural Review).

Poppe. (2012). Akis 1 presentation final report. Education.

Moreddu, C., & Poppe, K. J. (2013). Agricultural research and innovation systems in transition. EuroChoices, 12(1), 15–20.

Poppe, K. (2014). Linking Innovation and Research in Agricultural Knowledge and Innovation Systems.

(Continued)

Annex 1: Reference List Core Documents EU and SCAR on Interactive Innovation   *(Continued)*

Reference List Core Documents

Poppe, K. (n.d.a). The European Agricultural Knowledge and Innovation System (AKIS) towards an interactive innovation model.

Poppe, K. (n.d.b). The European Agricultural Knowledge And Innovation System (Akis) Towards An Interactive Innovation Model Scar-swg Agricultural Knowledge and Innovation Systems.

Poppe, K. (2012). Agricultural Knowledge and Innovation Systems in transition: Findings of the SCAR Collaborative Working Group on AKIS. Improving Agricultural Knowledge and Innovation Systems.

Prager, K. (2015). How can advice and knowledge be better organised to support farmers? Presented at EIP-AGRI Seminar 'Promoting creativity and learning through agricultural knowledge systems and interactive innovation', Dublin, Ireland.

Szabelak, P. (2013). How can National Rural Networks fit into the existing AKIS and help organise knowledge Flows? Presented at EIP-AGRI Seminar 'Promoting creativity and learning through agricultural knowledge systems and interactive innovation', Dublin, Ireland.

van Oost, I. (2015). The European Innovation Partnership (EIP) 'Agricultural Productivity and Sustainability. Presented at EIP-AGRI Seminar 'Promoting creativity and learning through agricultural knowledge systems and interactive innovation', Dublin, Ireland.

van Oost, I. (2017). The European Innovation Partnership 'Agricultural Productivity and Sustainability' (EIPAGRI): Speeding up innovation. Presented at Annual PLATFORM event: session Co-creation and responsible research, Rome.

Vuylsteke, A. (n.d.). Experiences with interactive innovation approaches in European countries. SCAR.

Weber, M., and Georghiou, L. (2010). The future of the European innovation Policy. EU Commission.

14

Why and How to Observe Agroecological Transitions in the Anthropocene?

Marc Barbier, Claire Lamine and Nathalie Couix

Introduction

Agroecology as a syncretic notion and moreover agroecological as a qualifier to indicate a certain direction or type of transitions in agri-food systems clearly appeared as a strong signal concomitantly – if not before – to the growing and mundane reference to the Anthropocene. In front of us are the issues of autonomy, resilience and rapid change in agriculture. These must be considered at the level of practices and policy, from farm to fork as much as from local to global, and vice versa. Agroecological transitions represent such a strategy for farming in the Anthropocene (Altieri and Nicholls, 2020) as well as for international agricultural policy framing (Bicksler et al., 2023).

Many scholars in sociology of food and rural sociology or sociology of natural resources (see the Introduction) as well as in many other disciplines of social sciences have for decades been studying changes, contradictions, resistances and innovations in the agrifood sector with a sustainability transition lens (Barbier and Elzen, 2012; Sage et al., 2021). They have also framed many debates around the relevance of the ecological-modernisation perspective (Barbier, 2010), while many contesting sustainability discourses were blossoming (Constance, 2018). All that took place before the current agrifood transitions studies arose in association to the Anthropocene but has to be nevertheless re-harnessed in our attempt to reframe agrifood systems (Reisma and Fairbairn, 2020) with an inevitable motion of presentism articulating critiques of 'capitolocene' (and sometimes 'plantationocene') with the defence of alternative food networks. The research agenda for such a perspective is then muddled via many epistemic hopes (or dys-hopes). With these hopes come many tensions concerning the policy relevance of social studies accounts of transitions or of lock-in mechanisms.

The question of whether agroecological transitions should be open-ended or deterministically driven paying attention to the diversity of transitions pathways and to the complexity of mechanisms of change has been activated (Lamine et al., 2021). This question is also addressing a matter of reflexivity in relation to the governance of discontinuation of the existing agrifood regime. This is not a vague supplementary question when one considers that the call for 'public sociology' (Burawoy, 2005) should be coupled with engaging participatory research practices. This is clearly a way of doing research that echoes the idea of taking into account our own position towards the dominant knowledge-environment-governance nexus that is vivid enough to encompass agriculture in a post-industrial Anthropocene (Newman et al., 2023), as it is still difficult for agroecology to be considered substantially in terms of human and social values (Bezner et al., 2022) that go beyond niches or peasant agriculture.

In light of this programmatic and general element of discussion, one difficulty lies in the fact that some policy instruments, sociotechnical experiments and transformative projects are carrying the 'eye of the state' (Scott, 2020) towards agroecological transitions in the making. They use values, objectives, statements and also our own work to exist. Should we stay outside so not to be trapped in a new kind of agroecological-anthropocenic modernisation? Should we close our eyes, delivering simply scientific knowledge, then just see what happens?

Certainly, like many scholars, we try to find a pathway in between, also because this is how we might find matters of fact, areas for empirical investigation and levers to fuel a reasonable critique of policy instruments. This chapter precisely illustrates such a position while reporting a longitudinal and collective social research based on the sociological and participatory observation of the design, the implementation and the impacts of a public policy instrument dedicated to agroecology in France at the heart of the incumbent agricultural knowledge and innovation system.

The Landing of Agroecology in France

After the conceptualisation of agroecology by Wezel et al. (2009) as the triplet of scientific discipline, social movement and set of practices, it is worth reconsidering the progressive synchronicity of these three prongs in light of the promise and effects of public policies that have targeted the development of agroecology. In France, agroecology first appeared as social movements in the 2000s and then emerged within academic agronomy leading to the constitution of an epistemic community (Bellon and Ollivier, 2018). It then concomitantly became an agricultural policy (Arrignon and Bosc, 2017) and a structuring axis in agronomic research policy (Ollivier et al., 2019). Scientific expertise has contributed to the foundation of the new agricultural policy launched in 2012 with the Agro-Ecological Project for France and then the Law on the Future of Agriculture and Forestry (LAAF) in 2014. Agroecology was, thus, also to be defined and established by law leading to many definitional struggles at the cross-road of science, policy and agriculture (Barbier et al., 2022b). This political choice took place in a context where agriculture was subject to the growing imperative to 'green' agricultural practices and was also questioned by various international programs, networks and initiatives. The French Agriculture Ministry's 'Producing Differently' policy carried at that time the promise of agroecology as a paradigm for driving a strong greening of agriculture in order to articulate the transformation of agricultural practices and systems with the global issues of food security, limitation of greenhouse gases, loss of biodiversity and adaptation to climate change.

This choice of agroecology very quickly gave rise to debates, reappropriation and re-differentiation within the agricultural world and civil society (Arrignon, 2020; Lamine, 2015). It was supported by the deployment of a set of public measures aimed, for some, in continuity with previous programs, to promote or supervise approaches aiming at reducing the use of synthetic pesticides (Guichard et al., 2017), or at supporting forms of ecological agriculture, such as organic farming, agroforestry and conservation agriculture. This new policy also initiated a movement of quite radical reorientation of agricultural technical education and instituted new mechanisms to support collective approaches by farmers.

In 2013, shortly after the launch of the agroecological project, the Ministry of Agriculture launched a call for tenders entitled Collective Mobilisation for Agro-Ecology (MCAE). This was seen by the government as a form of socio-technical experimentation in order to prefigure the delivery of a label for farmers' groups that would target sustainable agriculture initiatives: Environmental and Economic Interest Groups (GIEE), which was to be launched with the 2014 Agricultural Law. If public funding by call for tenders has become ordinary in many sectors, this MCAE call for tenders carried a rather unprecedented mode of action for agricultural development since it directly financed collectives of actors involved in innovative approaches, and by widely opening the field of these eligible collectives beyond the agricultural organisations usually targeted through public programs. This call was addressed very directly to groups of farmers and possibly other actors involved in a development and innovation action in the name of agroecology that can be described as a form of grassroots innovation (Seyfang and Smith, 2007), following a modality of direct contracting between the ministry and these groups of farmers. Through this call for tenders, 469 projects were submitted and 102 projects were ultimately funded (average of 65 k Euros per project) representing 3,300 farms to be engaged, the Ministry of Agriculture being even 'forced' to increase the budget base to 6.6 million euros.

The Research Framework

Objectives and Design

The existence of this MCAE dispositive in a transformative momentum of French Agricultural Policy was a relevant opportunity for social scientists to study it both as a specific public action instrument and as a catalyst for emerging dynamics that needed to be characterised. It led to a collective research project, whose objective was to lay the foundations of a sociological observatory of agroecological transitions (ObS-TAE), see Barbier et al. (2022a). To achieve this objective of experimenting the foundation of an observatory, we decided to set up a collective survey that was qualitative and quantitative, multi-site and based on embedded studies.

From 2015 to 2019, we carried out a longitudinal real-time survey of a set of 16 projects supported by this Collective Mobilisation for Agroecology (MCAE) dispositive, over three years, which allowed to compare them as they were enforced and at play. We established a common methodological framework and a thematic analysis focused on three main dimensions: (1) meanings of agroecology, (2) knowledge production and (3) dynamics of collective action. These analytical dimensions obviously echo what had already – but partially – been established by scholars to depict the emergence of agroecology as a concept, as a goal and as a principle of action (Wezel et al., 2018). Notwithstanding our own professional commitment to produce knowledge in social sciences, the aim was also to make it possible for the collectives themselves to reflect on what these projects allowed them to do and to envisage, and also the difficulties that their actions entailed.

This work, thus, took into account a diversity of research questions concerning both the characteristics of the public action instrument and what it achieves when mobilised by a diversity of actors with their specific sources of knowledge and horizons of action. This boundary-work approach (Clark et al., 2011) was essential for dealing ambitiously, but in a way that is rooted in the realities of doing (by actors and researchers alike), with these agroecological transitions that climate change is now forcing upon us. Indeed, it was not only a matter of stating possibilities or promises but also a matter of confronting the agroecological purpose of a policy design with the conditions and effects of its implementation. Thus, this 'à la Dewey' pragmatic orientation was clearly not an evaluative, top-down institutional orientation, and our comprehensive approach of the instrument and the projects had to be negotiated as such with the Ministry, that renounced to the idea of using our research work for a mean of evaluating projects and ended up seeing it as a possible external outlook on its own practices.

In this chapter, we firstly present the three levels of analysis of our observatory, we then discuss the feedbacks from projects leaders and the lessons learnt for accompanying transitions. Finally, we suggest some generic proposals for the construction of a sociological observatory of agroecological transitions.

Three Analytical Entrees: Meanings, Knowledge and Collective Dynamics

The first level of analysis in the research project and the book based on our primary results (Barbier et al., 2022a) focused on the construction of meaning in the MCAE call for tender. The contested nature of the meanings of agroecology has been addressed by many authors (Levidow, 2015; Montenegro de Wit and Iles, 2016; Rivera-Ferre, 2018). In our project, we considered this construction of meaning to be internal to the group under study and, just as much, a process that was constantly in contact with the 'outside' and even explicitly directed towards the 'outside'. The analyses of the cases show that the production of meaning is part of a legitimisation process that takes several forms and links to articulate agroecology visions and practices with 'existing' models of agriculture, which are more or less legitimised and serve, at least initially and partially, as a framework for the construction of the meaning given to the action. This analysis also emphasised the way in which autonomy, an underlying but structuring principle of agroecology, is worked on in the groups studied, through a diversity of situations and interpretations. This notion of autonomy appears as polymorphic, referring both to the technical-economic sphere and to the social sphere of farms' activities.

The second level of analysis deals with the production, circulation and institutionalisation of agroecological knowledge. Diverse studies have addressed the specificity of knowledge production and circulation in agroecology and highlighted their situated and collective nature (Compagnone et al., 2018; Girard and Magda, 2018). We analysed the different trajectories of knowledge production and mobilisation in order to grasp, on the one hand, the type of knowledge at stake in collective action, and on the other hand, the commitments of groups caught up in institutional injunctions to resolve local problems and capitalise on their learning. The search for legitimacy based on the knowledge drawn from the experience of agroecology in practice is very present in the groups. This experience is not limited to on-farm experimentation but also concerns the conduct of projects and their management, with the assumed effects of questioning the re-composition of the professional space around the group. This search for legitimacy in the orientation of what to be experienced conveys the idea of an inversion of the prescription relationships usually at play in between farmers and technical advisors when technical packages have to be demonstrated in field trial.

Finally, the third level of analysis deals with the processes of collective action that emerged with these projects and that the members of the groups had to 'manage' in order to create a community. In our project, we took a cross-cutting look at all of the projects studied and analysed the way in which these collectives were formed, maintained and evolved, in line with other recent studies focused on the role of collective dynamics in agroecological transitions (Cardona et al., 2021; Derbez, 2018), as well as the way in which the motion of the project was expressed in the various collectives. There is no standard profile of collectives that emerged, neither according to the structures that support them nor to the themes they tackle, but on the contrary, a highly diverse variety of ways of 'making a collective' according to the objects and practices at the heart of the projects as well as to pre-existing routines. The collectives also show a form of gradient in participation, ranging from a strong commitment of farmers in the governance of the project, supported by significant contributions, to more moderate membership and contribution. Finally, this perspective reveals a trend towards the transformation of the modalities of agricultural consulting and, in particular, a shift from prescription to a micro-policy of various forms of support. This is an important point for understanding the professional sociabilities at work in agroecological transitions.

Feedbacks From Groups' Leaders and Their Partners

The seminars during which the research group met with the group leaders and their partners (farmers, advisors, facilitators) allowed us to discuss our analyses with these actors, who were both the object of observation and participants in the collective reflexive process. The collectives were often made up of nuclei of farmers who were committed to the project in close proximity to one or more facilitators. Around these nuclei, a more or less dense network was formed for the construction of the project.

Collective or Community?

This question was being discussed in the groups because the collective could open up or wither away over the course of the project, which is a fairly classic dynamic in the world of agricultural and rural development driven by numerous working groups (technical, economic, union, etc.). Notwithstanding this intrinsic difficulty, the groups also had to support themselves in relation to the public action mechanism itself, both in terms of its political component of 'producing differently' and of the more technocratic requirements that presupposed a justification of their action. It is, therefore, by taking into account this situation of enunciation for the groups that we had to apprehend the restitution of our work along the way and during a final conference held in November 2018 which allowed the collectives to expose their achievements and their points of view in the presence of the actors of the ministry at the origin of the public action instrument. From these seminars and the final conference, we retain and share the following potentially generalisable statements.

Analysis and Action Do Not Always Go Together

In all the projects, in various forms, the participants contribute to the implementation of the intentions of their respective projects, with a difficulty in inscribing innovative practices in the field of ordinary practices. It is through the meaning that individuals and groups give to the action coordinated within the framework of their project that this tension between the ambition of the objectives and the reality of their inclusion in ordinary action can become a source of learning and fruitful sharing of experiences. Here again, the facilitation of the group is a key dimension.

A Reflection on the Technique Is Required to Found the Shared Experiential Knowledge

Whatever the technical orientations at work in the collectives (cultivation technique, mechanisation technique, self-training technique, experimentation technique, breeding technique etc.), the members of the various collectives distance themselves from the search for immediate direct operational effectiveness of these techniques. In other words, the relationship with the technique is not conceived as a prescription resulting from the choice of a tool that is adequate for a given purpose, but rather from the implementation of an experimentation to be shared: '*the tool must not be the consequence of a single theoretical reflection*', said a facilitator. The commitment of the groups is made of a search for a more global mastery of the technique and of adaptation according to the contexts that are often specific to their production orientation '*It is necessary to master the technique first, and then to choose the tool which can be appropriate*', said a farmer. In other words, farmers tend to form groups of technologists when they are involved in an agroecological transition.

The Group's Journey Is Made Up of Milestones

Group dynamics are multi-speed and indecision or overly broad actions can sometimes undermine collective dynamics. The collectives are therefore in tension in the conduct of the actions implemented. However, the social dynamics of the collectives are carried by adjusted leaderships:

'If we had left it open, the decisions would have been difficult to make, the members would not have wanted it either, and I, as president, had a lot of power. You don't want to be too broadly framed, because it can be scary, and members can back out. Getting rid of tillage was scary. We had to make compromises', said a farmer as president of a professional association. Such an approach of compromise, supported by adjustments and intermediate milestones, is an important dimension for the success of the projects.

Lessons Learnt for Accompanying Agroecological Transitions

Recognising the Open-Endedness Nature of Agroecological Transitions

MCAE, in contrast to more conventional policy instruments such as agri-environmental schemes, input reduction plans, subsidies for organic conversion, is innovative for three main reasons: its target is not individual farmers but groups with a multi-actor approach trying to involve not only farmers also other food systems actors; its approach is territorial; and it allows the groups to build their own trajectory of change. This last characteristic is linked to the fact that it combines both a deterministic and an open-ended perspective to agroecological transitions (Lamine et al., 2021) in the way it is conceived and through the frame it provides to the groups' projects (normative effect) and, at the same time, allows an articulation of these two perspectives through the way the groups use the instrument and adapt its potentialities to their own situation (performative effect).

Taking Into Account the Reversal of the Direction of the Prescription in Agricultural Advisement

The work of the groups takes place in various forms of relationships with facilitators and prescribers of change, sometimes placed under emerging collective action, sometimes placed under more incumbent agricultural development settings. The dynamics of the groups were often based in the case of bottom-up projects on an inversion of the prescription relationships whereby farmers would define what they expect from advisors and extensionists rather than the contrary. It is from the progress of the groups in the treatment of the problem or the ambition chosen with the project that they wish to become themselves prescribers of knowledge and recommendations that they consider relevant to their development and progress. This is a striking fact that goes hand in hand with the need for autonomy discussed above.

Thus, our studies are also micro-observatories of the effects of the re-composition of local advisory networks and of such processes of 'inversion' of prescription. They bear witness to the development of intermediation activities that focus as much on the provision of resources for action as on methods of support and empowerment of the collectives (Cardona et al., 2021).

Considering Territorial Re-compositions

The working context of the groups is marked by a larger territorial re-composition of agricultural development actors and new intermediaries. Despite the fact that the projects that we studied were not located at the heart of the incumbent agricultural development system, their actors are affected by policy changes at European, national or territorial levels. In what farmers often experience as a whirlwind of norms, an important condition for the maintenance of projects is the sustainability of the resources allocated to the intermediation activities carried out by the supportive structures. This question of the sustainability of approaches initiated with or sometimes before the MCAE call was raised in many of our discussions. The discussion that took place during the last seminar also brought to light the work of reflection that is necessary – and in progress – in the agricultural and rural development organisations, in particular in the network of incumbent advisory structures, both on the modalities of advising (who, how, etc.) and on its financing supports.

Towards a Sociological Observatory of Agroecological Transitions

Our analyses of the content of definitional texts, administrative databases and practices put into text as well as of these agroecological projects in the making, converge to support the need for the type of research we have conducted in this project. Our collective experience and reflection also aimed at laying the methodological and practical foundations of an observatory, which would couple a genealogical approach to the institutionalisation of a concept, and an analytical approach to the writings of bureaucratic action to ascribe a transformative dispositive. Thanks to the design of the this observatory, agroecology is not reduced to a simplistic and determinist technological fix that would be defined by science and applied by policymakers.

Beyond this project, the perpetuation of a sociological observation of agroecological transitions is then posed. In light of the experience gained from this collective survey, such an observatory could take the form of a mechanism that links research and action, bringing together researchers, collective actors, institutional and territorial actors with the aim of making the changes that make up the agroecological transition visible and intelligible. The outcomes of a pluralistic re-thinking of agroecological projects or initiatives could, thus, feed the reflection for public action and territorial policies as well as for groups and collectives in action.

Why Continue?
The objective of long-term observation is all the more pertinent since the question of reducing inputs and, more broadly, of greening agriculture calls for many transformations. These must be approached in the context of the relocalisation of food production as well as in the context of stopping biodiversity loss, the ongoing quantification and economisation of soil carbon and water resources management. It therefore seems essential to us not to confine the report to the dynamics of transformation within the framework of the measurement of good agroecological technical practices and their diagnosis in the form of a score. The entire dimension and scope of the systemic approach, which the groups studied clearly emphasised, must be central. It is not a technical-economic issue, but a professional demand.

Though the idiom of agroecology has become mundane in many narratives, the future of the French Agroecological policy has become uncertain due to several retrograde developments on pesticide reduction and water management. First of all, the political changes of 2017 changed the way the programme was carried, then new issues were brought to the forefront with pesticides reduction and the Etats Généraux de l'Alimentation (General Assembly on Food), while the impact of climate change on agriculture became more and more present in the debates. Finally, the Covid19 pandemic has greatly impacted the entire population, notably putting into light advantages of short food supply chains.

Nonetheless, the studies carried with this research project still seem relevant, so it is worth restating it here. Many of the actors in the groups that were mobilised in this MCAE call for proposals very quickly questioned the continuity of the dynamics established by the action instruments of the Agroecology government plan. They were cautious about the changes in regional agricultural policies from the point of view of the greening of agricultural policies and their inclusion in the revision of the European support system. Current evolutions concerning the impossible reduction of pesticides and the pressing issues of income composition or difficulties in succession can still prove them right today. Farmers, but also many intermediary actors, apprehend the positive or negative impact of these re-compositions through the prism of rural territories' policies. Territorial Food Projects are supported by a new policy instrument in which the agroecological transition as an aim is not very present despite its inscription in the 2014 agricultural law based on agroecology; the same goes for Territorial Climate-Air-Energy Plans, which increasingly concern agriculture in its expected contribution to the management of greenhouse gases as well as to the valorisation of bio-energy. In addition, one has also to bear in mind the effects of numerous initiatives in rural areas carried out by the Social and Solidarity Economy movement, which are certainly still too invisible.

Which Lessons Are Worth Following?

In this context, we would like to highlight three lessons learnt from this action-research project at the interface of social science research and reflection on the design and evaluation of public action instruments. Our discussions and interviews with representatives of the Ministry, who initiated or piloted the MCAE instrument, show that it was similar to a socio-economic intelligence mechanism. This mechanism, and then the following GIEEs dispositive, form a capacity to explore, construct and evaluate a re-engagement of the State in agricultural development according to a less neo-corporatist and more delegative model, which therefore re-engages the state in deconcentrated services for intersectoral public action logics. This movement seems to be slowly ongoing, but it is muddled through debated evolutions of differentiation, decentralisation and de-concentration of territorialised public action. The challenge of simplifying local public action is, however, one of dealing with the complexity of the transitional situations that need to be governed and the skills required at the decentralised level to do so.

First, the MCAE projects have been – and continue to be through the GIEEs – the bearers of collective experiences of a bottom-up approach to a re-composition of the themes and the modes of organisation of their treatment. This preliminary work suggests that there is a differentiated and more or less intense bottom-up demand for agricultural development, depending on the region. A statistical treatment crossing the MCAE project submissions and then the GIEE projects with data on the structure and orientation of production and with data on the results of professional consular elections would be relevant to the continuation of our project. This statistical processing could be coupled with in-depth work on a comparative history of regional and even departmental agricultural development policies, which should take into account the changes and mutations of agricultural cooperation.

Second, without presuming an analysis that would concern all the funded MCAE projects, the 16 groups that we have chosen to follow for their particularly innovative approach are deploying activities to explore, experiment and report on their own experimentations, knowledge exchange and building processes, and achievements. These activities are marked by the search for a certain autonomy in the way of posing problems and making them treatable, with an effect noted on several occasions of inversion of the prescription relation. We can thus hypothesise that the projects generated by the MCAE call have effects beyond their own space of action by generating configurations of agricultural development organisation that, even if they are not always new in their object, solicit agricultural development actors in more symmetrical relationships. Thus, it can be argued that a programme such as MCAE has been a source of learning that goes beyond the level of projects, and has made it possible to construct a prospective view of the dynamics of agroecological transitions.

Finally, from the point of view of what the Ministry can expect to learn from the analysis of such a system, we would like to emphasise two possible directions for reflection. On the one hand, the MCAE call appears to be an innovative lever for public action if we consider the more standard methods of distributing public aid for agricultural development. It assumes both an allocative dimension by taking into account the multifunctionality of agriculture for sustainable development and a redistributive dimension by directing support to groups that are able to ensure a certain economic and social cohesion on projects with an assumed territorial impact. From this point of view, the MCAE mechanism is partly similar to that of the Territorial Farming Contracts (CTEs, in operation between 1999 and 2002 and discontinued in 2003), because it targets dynamics now described as agroecological which have great similarities with those that targeted multifunctionality at the time. It does indeed combine allocative and redistributive strategies, but by shifting the point of application of the aid from farms to collective projects that are nexuses of organisation driven by various structures.

What Would a Sociological Observatory of Agroecological Transitions Be Made Of?

Based on these preliminary observations drawn from our collective action-research experience, we think it is necessary to have a space for the production of knowledge on these dynamics over the long term, associated with a consortium of organisations that would be sensitive to the idea that research and actors could propose and share their views in a way that would stay at a distance from evaluation stances. The project that we carried out established such a framework for conducting case studies according to a model that allows for the stylisation of a reporting format without preventing the capture of the variety of objectives or contexts. This is how the accumulation was made possible in our own research project and, above all, how it has been debated for the cross-case analysis. Of course, many frames of reference can be thought of on a formal level, but the fairly advanced reflection that the research group conducted leads us to promote the need to specify the association of a clear frame of reference that articulates the objectives, the questions and the modalities of the collective work with minimal and unavoidable prescriptions for the description of cases.

Establishing and maintaining such a capacity would, thus, address three main objectives:

- to acquire a capacity for sociological analysis, comparison and collective reflection on the collective dynamics of agroecological transition;
- to animate a network of researchers and actors concerned by these issues, defining together shared research-action questions;
- to constitute, in connection with higher and technical education, a support for student work and the construction of pedagogical content.

As for the use of the knowledge produced by such an observation, it leads to the definition of a set of key issues that can then contribute to enlightening the decision, orient the debates on the modalities of the development of agroecology and finally allow an evaluative relationship to the instruments of public action based on qualitative evidence. We present below these key issues that the creation and implementation of such an observatory could help addressing.

Key Questions for a Sociological Observatory of Agroecological Transitions

What Difference Do Projects Make to Exchange and Learning Practices?

Depending on the project, we observe more or less re-compositions in the modes of exchange, support, and mobilisation of different forms of expertise (endogenous/exogenous): the trajectories of mobilisations reveal the work of articulating actionable knowledge and situated knowledge. It is also important to know how they are transformative in situations and contexts that are, in fact, very varied.

Do the Projects Stimulate Transitions From the Bottom-Up?

There is a variable combination of continuity (previous achievements, local context) and new approaches (various configurations linking type of mobilisation and partnership with type of objective and problem addressed). It is important to note what constitutes a form of generative tension between the launch and perpetuation of bottom-up approaches and the adjustment work based on top-down approaches proposed by national or regional public action.

What Are the Agroecologies at Work?

The study of the diversity of the cases studied (chosen with the objective of studying innovative approaches and not with the objective of sampling) shows that the implementation of ministerial agroecology corresponds to very varied visions and conceptions, more or less compatible with the modernising reference system. The challenge is to work on the definitions of agroecology and on the (self-)evaluation of the greening processes and changes in practices by the actors in these groups. From this point of view, the evaluation frameworks of the systems have counter-intuitive effects and lead to decoupling operations between the way of approaching the reality of the work carried out and that which is appropriate for justifying the use of resources and public funding schemes.

What Difference Do Projects Make to the Way Actors Interact?

The projects show more or less open partnerships, sometimes expressing conflicts of legitimacy with the structures present: the projects, in their set-up, selection and implementation, have changed the interplay of local actors while the innovative objectives were calling for intermediary activities facilitating structures. This is an important feature, particularly in order to consider the current GIEE dynamic and, above all, the relevance of a two-pronged public action: supporting collective mobilisation initiatives for innovation and labelling groups for their capacity to innovate.

What Are the Transformations Induced by the Mobilisations at the Level of Agricultural Development and Change Intermediation?
The projects were carried out through intense animation and intermediation work in configurations linked to different forms of agricultural development. The analysis of the modalities and forms of knowledge production linked to the innovations carried out by these projects leads us to note the importance that farmers give to knowledge drawn from experience and even to claims of capacity to prescribe the objects or actions of advice following an inversion of the prescription relations. This affirmation goes hand in hand with the emergence and institution of groups claiming a certain autonomy of peer-to-peer development. These transformations need to be studied in order to contribute to the renewal of professional training plans and curricula in the sector. Understanding them would also contribute to the establishment of proactive support strategies for agroecology.

What Are the Feedback Effects of the Experiments Carried Out on the Form of Public Action Instruments and on the Scope of Their Evaluation?
If the monitoring of collective mobilisations provides experiences and knowledge for farmers and not only for researchers, it is also a source of « food for thought » for the Ministry about the design of instruments and their decentralised implementation in internal networks operating around agroecology training. But it is also certainly a source of reflection for the evaluation of the relevance of these instruments and their administration, despite our own aim and perspective were not evaluative ones. Finally, the principle of linking the exploratory instrument of MCAE to other policy instruments (and for instance to the labelling of sustainable initiative like GIEE) seems to be entirely relevant as a principle of experimenting public action itself. The fact remains that the frame of reference of what could define innovations in agroecological transition must certainly be re-assed along processes of change because it is not just a matter of establishing a public policy frame of reference but also of

formulating the questions that could be addressed by an Observatory, whether they are ecological, technical-economic, organisational or professional.

Conclusion

This chapter intended to discuss the main outcomes of the ObS-TAE research project. As far as the status of agroecology is concerned at the international level and notably during its (although temporary) relative legitimation during the FAO global dialogue between 2013 and 2018 (Loconto and Fouilleux, 2019), our project is a contribution to a better understanding of the transformative effects of agroecological policies, bearing in mind the challenges enlightened for Europe by Wezel et al. (2018) and for Latin America. Numerous scholars are mobilising agroecology as an epistemic claim, as a sociotechnical promise, as a normative frame or as an evaluation referential, to study change or lock-in mechanisms in agrifood systems. But few studies report about socio-technical devices or policy supports focused on agroecological transitions. Few countries in the world have undertaken directional public policies or specific policy support in favour of full and explicit recognition of agroecology, especially in Europe (France and Hungary) and Latin America (Brasil, Bolivia, Mexico, Nicaragua and Costa-Rica). This is why this chapter offers a rather unique view of what the experience of purposeful agroecological transitions-in-the-making does and means for actors and how to observe this for analytical purposes.

At the end of this research, we are convinced that founding an Observatory of Agro-Ecological Transitions today cannot be done without reviewing the parameters of a sectoral approach centred on agronomic innovation, which would be understood on a technical level alone. This was not the spirit of the 2014 French law, but it seems to us that this line of slope has been too widely prioritised. Many of those who are studying agricultural development will not be surprised; this deviation calls for transformative and multi-level reorientations for agroecological transitions in the making (Elzen et al., 2017).

The space for exploration and debate carried by the actors seems to us to be much wider and de facto far more interesting and transformative with such a de-sectoralisation, including, and even especially, in order to understand the multiple pressures of change that the agricultural world must face. The issue of inclusion in a low-carbon economy is not the least of these and is even more complex than the acknowledged issues of water management, environmental health or cultivated biodiversity because it is clearly putting an entire profession in motion. This project as a singular experience, but also the possible Agroecological Transition Sociological Observatory that could emerge, both echo the objective claimed in this book about the necessity to empower transitions pathways in the Anthropocene by raising definitional, technological and political struggles at the heart of the knowledge-environment-governance nexus.

Acknowledgements

The work presented in this chapter has been realised thanks to the project « *Observatoire sociologique des transitions agro-écologiques et réseau d'échange autour de collectifs lauréat de l'appel à projets Mobilisation Collective pour l'Agro-écologie* », funded by the « *Compte d'affectation spéciale 'développement agricole et rural' relatifs à l'exécution du Programme 775 'Développement et Transfert en Agriculture' du Ministère de l'Agriculture* ». Special thanks to Hervé Bossuat, Hacina Benhamed and Pierre Schwartz. Thanks for the helpful and precise comments from the editors of the book.

References

Altieri, M.A. and Nicholls, C.I. (2020) 'Agroecology: Challenges and opportunities for farming in the Anthropocene'. *Ciencia e investigación agrari a: revista latinoamericana de ciencias de la agricultura, 47*(3): 204–15.

Arrignon, M. (2020) 'La transition agro-écologiqu e: une politique de développement durable comme les autres?'. *VertigO – la revue électronique en sciences de l'environnement, 20*(1). (https://doi.org/10.4000/vertigo.27869)

Arrignon, M. and Bosc, C. (2017). 'Le plan français de transition agroécologique et ses modes de justification politique. La biodiversité au secours de la performance agricol?'. In D. Compagnon (ed), *Les politiques de biodiversité*. Paris: Presses de Sciences Po, pp. 205–224. (https://doi-org.inshs.bib.cnrs.fr/10.3917/scpo.compa. 2017.01.0205)

Barbier, M. (2010) 'The ecologization of agricultural development and the treadmill of sustainable development. A critique in a state of transition'. *Przegląd Socjologiczny (Sociological Review), 59*(2): 9–28.

Barbier, M. and Elzen, B. (eds) (2012) *System Innovations, Knowledge Regimes, and Design Practices towards Transitions for Sustainable Agriculture*. Paris: INRA Edition.

Barbier, M., Lamine, C. and Couix, N. (eds) (2022a) *Pratiques et savoirs agricoles dans la transition agroécologique*. Editions des Archives contemporaines. (https://doi.org/10.17184/eac.9782813003560)

Barbier, M., Ollivier, G. and Lamine, C. (2022b) 'L'agroécologie en textes'. In M. Barbier, et al. (ed), *Pratiques et savoirs agricoles dans la transition agroécologique.* Editions des Archives Contemporaines, pp. 17–58. (https://doi.org/10.17184/eac. 5947)

Bellon, S. and Ollivier, G. (2018) 'Institutionalizing agroecology in France: Social circulation changes the meaning of an idea'. *Sustainability*, *10*(5): 1380. (https:// doi.org/10.3390/su10051380)

Bezner Kerr, R., Liebert, J., Kansanga, M. and Kpienbaareh, D. (2022) 'Human and social values in agroecology: A review'. *Elementa: Science of the Anthropocene*, *10*(1): 00090. (https://doi.org/10.1525/elementa.2021.00090)

Bicksler, A.J., Mottet, A., Lucantoni, D., Sy, M.R. and Barrios, E. (2023) 'The 10 Elements of Agroecology interconnected: Making them operational in FAO's work on agroecology'. *Elementa: Science of the Anthropocene*, *11*(1).

Burawoy, M. (2005). 'For public sociology'. *American Sociological Review*, *70*(1): 4–28.

Cardona, A., Cerf, M. and Barbier, M. (2021) 'Carrying out public action to reduce pesticides use: Recognizing intermediation activities'. *Cahiers Agricultures*, *30*(33). (https://doi.org/10.1051/cagri/2021020)

Cardona, A., Brives H., Lamine C., Godet J., Gouttenoire L. and Rénier L., (2021) 'Supports for collective action in agroecological transitions. Insights from the study of five groups of farmers in the Rhône-Alpes region'. *Cahiers Agricultures*, *30*: 21.

Clark, W.C., Tomich T.P., van Noordwijk M., Guston, D., Catacutan D., Dickson N.M. and McNie E. (2011) 'Boundary work for sustainable development: Natural resource management at the consultative group on international agricultural research (CGIAR)'. *Proceedings of the National Academy of Sciences of the USA*, *113*(17): 4615–22, (http://www.pnas.org/content/early/2011/08/11/0900231108)

Compagnone, C., Lamine, C. and Dupré, L. (2018) 'La production et la circulation des connaissances en agriculture interrogées par l'agro-écologie. De l'ancien et du nouveau'. *Revue d'anthropologie des connaissances*, *12*(12–2). (http://journals. openedition.org/rac/767)

Constance, D.H. (2018). 'Contested sustainability discourses in the agrifood system: An overview'. *Contested Sustainability Discourses in the Agrifood System*, 3–16.

Derbez, F. (2018) 'D'un maïs, l'autre – Enquête sur l'expérimentation collective d'agriculteurs rhône-alpins autour de variétés de maïs population'. *Revue d'anthropologie des connaissances*, *12*(2). (https://journals.openedition.org/rac/911)

Elzen, B., Augustyn A.-M., Barbier, M. and van Mierlo B. (eds) (2017) *AgroEcological Transitions. Changes and Breakthroughs in the Making.* WUR. (https://edepot.wur.nl/407609)

Girard, N. and Magda, D. (2018) 'Les jeux entre singularité et généricité des savoirs agro-écologiques dans un réseau d'éleveurs'. *Revue d'anthropologie des connaissances*, *12*(2). (https://doi.org/10.3917/rac.039.0199)

Guichard, L., et al. (2017) 'Le plan Ecophyto de réduction d'usage des pesticides en France: décryptage d'un échec et raisons d'espérer'. *Cahiers Agricultures*, *26*(1): 14002. (https://doi.org/10.1051/cagri/2017004)

Lamine, C. (2015) 'Sustainability and resilience in agrifood systems: Reconnecting agriculture, food and the environment'. *Sociologia Ruralis*, 55(1): 41–61. (https://doi.org/10.1111/soru.12061)

Lamine, C., Magda, D., Rivera-Ferre, M. and Marsden, T. (eds) (2021) *Agroecological Transitions, between Determinist and Open-Ended Visions*. Peter Lang International Academic Publishers. (https://library.oapen.org/handle/20.500.12657/51366)

Levidow, L. (2015) 'European transitions towards a corporate-environmental food regime: Agroecological incorporation or contestation?'. *Journal of Rural Studies*, 40: 76–89. (https://doi.org/10.1016/j.jrurstud.2015.06.001)

Loconto, A.M. and Fouilleux, E. (2019) 'Defining agroecology: Exploring the circulation of knowledge in FAO's global dialogue'. *International Journal of Sociology of Agriculture and Food*, 25(2): 116–37.

Montenegro de Wit, M. and Iles, A. (2016) 'Toward thick legitimacy: Creating a web of legitimacy for agroecology'. *Elementa: Science of the Anthropocene*, 4: 000115. (https://doi.org/10.12952/journal.elementa.000115)

Newman, L., Newell, R., Dring, C., Glaros, A., Fraser, E., Mendly-Zambo, Z., … KC, K.B. (2023) 'Agriculture for the Anthropocene: Novel applications of technology and the future of food'. *Food Security*, 1–15.

Ollivier, G., Bellon. S., et al. (2019) 'The boundaries of agroecology. Research policies of two public agricultural institutes in France and Brazil'. *Natures Sciences Sociétés*, 27(1): 20–38.

Reisman, E. and Fairbairn, M. (2020) 'Agri-food systems and the Anthropocene'. *Annals of the Association of American Geographers*, 111(3): 687–97. (https://doi.org/10.1080/24694452.2020.1828025)

Rivera-Ferre, M.G. (2018) 'The resignification process of Agroecology: Competing narratives from governments, civil society and intergovernmental organizations'. *Agroecology and Sustainable Food Systems*, 42(6): 666–85. (https://doi.org/10.1080/21683565.2018.1437498)

Sage, C., Kropp, C. and Antoni-Komar, I. (2021) 'Grassroots initiatives in food system transformation: The role of food movements in the second 'great transformation''. In *Food System Transformations*. Taylor & Francis. (https://library.oapen.org/handle/20.500.12657/46853)

Scott, J.C. (2020) *Seeing Like a State: How Certain Schemes to Improve the Human Condition Have Failed*. New Haven, CT: Yale University Press.

Seyfang, G. and Smith, A. (2007) 'Grassroots innovations for sustainable development: Towards a new research and policy agenda'. *Environmental Politics*, 16(4): 584–603.

Wezel, A., Bellon, S., Doré, T., Francis, C., Vallod, D. and David, C. (2009) 'Agroecology as a science, a movement and a practice. A review'. *Agronomy for Sustainable Development*, 29: 503–15. (https://doi-org.inshs.bib.cnrs.fr/10.1051/agro/2009004)

Wezel, A., Goris, M., Bruil, J., Félix, G.F., Peeters, A., Bàrberi, P., … Migliorini, P. (2018) 'Challenges and action points to amplify agroecology in Europe'. *Sustainability*, 10(5): 1598. (https://doi.org/10.3390/su10051598)

15

Contested Agrifood Knowledge Transitions Into the Anthropocene: The Case of CGIAR

Douglas H. Constance and Allison M. Loconto

Given that food systems are the major driver of poor health and environmental degradation' in the Anthropocene, 'the need for a global transformation of the food system is urgent. [It will] require a rapid adoption of numerous interventions and unprecedented global collaboration and commitment: nothing less than a Great Food Transformation. (Willett et al., 2019)

Introduction

The industrial agrifood system is in the midst of a legitimation crisis regarding its negative ecological, economic and social externalities (Constance et al., 2018; Gardner, 2009; Magdoff et al., 2000). This crisis has accelerated steadily over the past 20 years and has now reached a tipping point based on the realisation that the agrifood system is a major contributor to global climate change. The climate impacts of the Anthropocene make it imperative that we change the way food is produced, distributed and consumed (Campbell et al., 2017; IPES-Food, 2016; Rockstrom et al., 2017). The problem is well understood, yet the solutions are difficult and contested (Almas and Campbell, 2012; Holt Gimenez and Shattuck, 2011; Scoones, 2016). The challenge is how to feed 10 billion people by the year 2050 without expanding the agricultural land base and at the same time reduce the negative environmental impacts.

In response to this challenge, two competing agrifood models have emerged as the better path forward: (1) sustainable intensification and (2) agroecology (Levidow, 2015, 2018). These two transition paths are the outcome of a long history of competing visions regarding the preferred model of the agrifood system: the agrarian ethic and the industrial ethic (Thompson, 2010a). These visions are grounded in different agrifood ontological frames, which manifest as different knowledge systems: food security and food sovereignty (McMichael, 2014). This critical agrifood studies approach reveals the role of agrarian social change and development in the ecological crisis of the Anthropocene (Reisman and Fairbairn, 2020).

The chapter begins with an overview of the historical tension between the 'agrarian' and 'industrial' visions of US agriculture, followed by a presentation of the current manifestation of these visions, sustainable intensification and agroecology. This section ends with a presentation of the competing ontological frames that ground the proposed transition paths: the food security versus food sovereignty discourses. Next, we present the case of the Consultative Group on International Agricultural Research (CGIAR) to illustrate and contextualise these competing agrifood knowledge systems in the Anthropocene. Data were collected for this case by both authors through extensive document analysis and interviews by the second author during participant observations at FAO – in her role as a Visiting Scientist – between 2013 and 2021. Finally, we analyse the events of this case informed by a sociology of agriculture and food conceptual framework.

Agriculture in the Anthropocene

Industrial agriculture is a leading contributor to climate change in the Anthropocene, accounting for between one-fourth and one-third of GHG emissions (Campbell et al., 2017; Godfray and Garnett, 2014; Kuyper and Struik, 2014). About 12K years ago the Neolithic Revolution starts the process as early agriculturalists reshaped their environs for food production. The Industrial Revolution institutionalised this process in much of Europe, followed by the spread of national and global capitalism into the developing world and the 'Great Acceleration' after World War II (Hamilton et al., 2015).

Concerns about the sustainability of industrial agriculture and its role in sustainable development were raised by the Brundtland Report in 1987 (Velten et al., 2015). Since then, the term sustainability has come into play as competing interests manoeuvre to capture the definition (Buttel, 2006; Constance, 2010; Scoones, 2016). The ecological crisis of industrial agriculture was the first to manifest, followed by social and economic crises regarding food production and consumption (Constance et al., 2014; Magdoff et al., 2000). The productivist model based on intensive, specialised monoculture combined with intensive, concentrated livestock production created a metabolic rift – the geographic separation of the nutrient/waste cycle – which contributed to pollution and ecological degradation. This model was coordinated by the nation-state through the US Department of Agriculture (USDA) and the Land Grant Universities through public research on mechanisation, genetics and breeding, and chemical inputs, along with powerful com-modity groups linked to agribusiness corporations (Hightower, 1973; Buttel and Newby, 1980). The ensuing treadmill of production rendered US agriculture ecologically, economically and socially unsustainable (Buttel, 2006). This industrial model was diffused globally as part of development projects through the Green Revolution and organisations such as the CGIAR (McMichael, 1996). The food shocks of 2008–2009 accelerated sustainability concerns as calls grew louder for the transition to a new paradigm based on agroecology (IPES-Food, 2016). To complicate the scenario, by the year 2050 the agrifood system needs to feed a world population of 10 billion people without expanding the agricultural land base, and while reducing negative environmental impacts such as greenhouse gas (GHG) emissions, chemical contami-nation, and species extinction (Feed the Future, 2015; Campbell et al., 2017).

In response to this realisation, two competing visions and systems emerged as the better path forward to sustainably feed the world: sustainable intensification (SI) and agroecology (Levidow, 2015). These two transitions paths are the outcome of historically competing visions and contested discourses regarding the preferred model of the agrifood system. Modern agriculture in the United States has been characterised by two competing visions grounded in the 'agrarian ethic' and the 'industrial ethic' (Thompson, 2010a). The industrial perspective views agriculture as just another part of industrial society where commodities are produced using positivist science at the lowest cost possible. The trend towards consolidation in farms and firms is just economies of scale at work to increase efficiency and lower costs. Landscapes are viewed in terms of the commodities they can produce and any concerns regarding labour, community, environment, and animal welfare externalities can be addressed through incremental technological changes rather than major departures from the model. From this perspective, sustainable equals produce more with less inputs. This system must be exported to ensure sustainable food production for the world.

The agrarian ethic views agriculture as a virtuous social structure with unique cultural norms that enhance quality of life for rural peoples (Berry, 1978; Thompson, 2010a). Sometimes called alternative and/or multifunctional, agriculture has important social functions beyond its efficient production of commodities, such as providing positive ecological services, protecting the integrity and functioning of the ecosystem, and contributing to healthy rural communities. Agriculture should be embedded in the local community. Farm and agribusiness consolidation negatively impacts community quality of life (see Lobao and Stofferahn, 2008). This view advocates for agroecology and calls for a transformative departure from the conventional agriculture, which is extractive and unsustainable.

The evolution and prevalence of these two perspectives are linked to the development of the Land Grant University (LGU) system (Constance, 2014). During the Civil War the US government took several actions to modernise agriculture (Danbom, 1979): the USDA and the LGU system (LGUs) were created; the Homestead Act of 1862 was passed to populate the land with farmers; immigration policies provided industrial workers and prospective farmers; the transcontinental railroad was subsidised; and the Native Americans were subdued. The actions, policies, and programs accelerated the extensification and intensification of modern agriculture across the landscape.

The agrarian ethic tended to be supported by Rural Sociologists and Institutional Agricultural Economists in LGUs and the USDA. The industrial ethic was supported more by natural (soil, animal, plant) scientists, neo-classical Agricultural Economists, and urban elites. The agrarian view first aligned with preservationist sentiments that privileged the rural over the urban due to its moral superiority linked to attachment to the land and conservative values. The industrial view aligned with modernist perspectives that saw traditional rural beliefs and institutions as anachronisms of the past that must be modernised to improve rural quality of life. Though the preservationist position tended to dominate into the mid-1900s and occupied substantial academic and political space in the LGUs and the USDA, during and after WWII the preservationists were purged as part of the Cold War and the modernists came to power (Danbom, 1979; Gilbert, 2015; McMichael, 1996).

After World War II, and especially during the Cold War, the modernist – now productivist – approach dominated the LGUs. Productivism combined the mechanisation of the industrial revolution, selective breeding and hybrid seeds, and chemical pesticides and fertilisers to maximise yield per acre. The resulting food surplus was employed as a weapon to counter the spread of communism. This adoption-diffusion model of agricultural modernisation based on technological improvements embraced by modern, innovative farmers was spread to the world through the Green Revolution as 'packages' of agricultural intensification through international agricultural research organisations such as the CGIAR. The US diet based on that model of agriculture was spread through the world through food aid programs (Buttel and Newby, 1980; McMichael, 1996).

In the 1970s the productivist model was criticised as a system whereby the USDA and the LGUs were coopted by agribusiness (Buttel and Newby, 1980; Hightower, 1973). In the 1980s the pendulum swung back towards the preservationists, but this time in the form of critical Rural Sociology approaches that documented the negative environmental, economic, and social impacts of industrial agriculture on rural communities. At the international level the value-neutral modernisation/productivist framework was challenged by the value-laden dependista/World Systems framework focusing on neocolonialism, whereby the Global North continued to exploit the Global South through corporate domination (Buttel and Newby, 1980; McMichael, 1996). These two perspectives remain today, represented by the tension between positivist and critical positions within the Land Grant System and the USDA (Constance, 2014).

The current manifestation of these competing knowledge systems is the tension between sustainable intensification and agroecology as the better path to feed the world in the Anthropocene. The term 'sustainable intensification' (SI) originated in Africa in the 1990s as an agro-ecological programme designed to increase food production (intensification) in developing countries without bringing more marginal and/or pristine land into production (extensification), while at the same time reducing negative environmental externalities on the existing cultivated lands (see Levidow, 2015; Pretty, 1997). This first vision was synonymous with the French approach called 'ecological intensification' that was being promoted at the same time in West Africa (Tittonell, 2014). Utilising appropriate technologies informed by indigenous, knowledge-based, agro-ecological methods, SI would increase yields, conserve soil and water, and manage nutrients and pests through local processes of innovation whereby the byproducts of each cycle become the inputs to another. In this context SI is a culturally-sensitive, lower tech alternative to high-tech Green Revolution approaches that have proven unrealistic and/or problematic for much of the developing world (Patel, 2013; Shiva, 1992).

In 1996, the Food and Agriculture Organization of the United Nations (FAO) sponsored a World Food Summit that called on governments to support a new round of intensification to feed the world, but also to avoid the negative environmental consequences of industrial agriculture ala the Green Revolution (FAO, 1996). The World Bank (2006) defined SI as a combination of production practices such as Integrated Pest Management, Conservation Farming, Low External Input and Sustainable Agriculture, Organic Agriculture, and Precision Agriculture. After the world food crisis in 2007, the United Nations (2008) incorporated SI into the discourse on global food security as an approach to move small-holder peasants past subsistence production by linking them to improved marketing channels and national and international supply chains through a combination of biotech and Conservation Agriculture. Technologies developed in the global North would be part of the 'tool kit' transferred to producers in the global South to maximise production per acre while conserving soil and water resources. The Royal Society of the United Kingdom (2009) echoed the SI agenda to reduce reliance on non-renewable inputs through increased adoption of agroecology and GM techniques to increase yields without adverse environmental impacts and without the cultivation of more land. As evidence of industrial agriculture's contribution to global climate change increased, SI became the model for all of agriculture – the new paradigm to feed the world sustainably (FAO, 2009).

SI became the dominant discourse for national and international organisations, such as the 'Feed the Future' programme of the USDA, the CGIAR, the FAO, the Montpellier Panel and the Sustainable Development Solutions Network and international donor organisations such as the Gates Foundation (Constance and Moseley, 2018;

Tittonell, 2014). The molecular biology (GMO) transnational corporations (TNCs) embraced the food security discourse from a SI perspective. For example, in 2014 Monsanto's Chief Technology Officer stated that 'sustainable intensification is key to meeting food security needs for our growing planet while also reducing agriculture's impact on the environment' (Monsanto, 2014: 20). Other major GMO firms had similar pronouncements regarding food security and sustainable intensification (Constance and Moseley, 2018).

As the SI agenda gained prominence, it was criticised for being too focused on intensifying production rather than minimising ecological externalities and social justice disparities (Garnett et al., 2013). Critics maintained the term was not well defined and had 'become a buzzword' that allowed people to put 'a positive spin' on unsustainable solutions (Nink, 2015; Petersen and Sieglinde, 2015). For many agricultural researchers, while SI was necessary in the face of climate change, population growth, and ecological constraints, it was fraught with conceptual and programmatic inconsistencies, which tended to privilege agricultural intensification over ecological sustainability (Kuyper and Struik, 2014; Petersen and Sieglinde, 2015; Struik et al., 2014). The politics of the possible tended to push SI towards an incremental greening of the dominant system and away from any transformative agenda. Agricultural ethicist Thompson noted, 'The upshot is the debate over agricultural intensification has ideological overtones that one neglects at one's peril' (Thompson, 2010b: 7).

For civil society critics, SI should not be a modest greening of industrial agriculture, but rather should be a radical rethinking of the agrifood system to not only reduce environmental externalities, but also to enhance animal welfare, human nutrition, and sustainable rural development. But its current application is dominated by the Green Revolution focus on high-technology solutions applied to specialised monocultures designed for growing more food on less land with more efficient use of resources (Garnett et al., 2013; Levidow, 2015; Petersen and Sieglinde, 2015; Rockstrom et al., 2017; Struik et al., 2014). As the critique of SI progressed, the agrifood TNCs, agro-exporting states and the Gates Foundation 'sought to recapture control' of the discourse on and the governance of the global agrifood system through the framework of 'climate smart agriculture' (CSA) grounded in a 'market liberal frame' utilising technologies and private property rights to address climate change and food security (Newell and Taylor, 2018: 113).

For agroecology proponents, 'business as usual is not an option' (IAASTD, 2008). What is required is a fundamentally different model of agriculture based on diversifying farms and farming landscapes, replacing chemical inputs, optimising biodiversity and stimulating interactions between different species, as part of holistic strategies to build food security through long-term soil fertility, healthy agro-ecosystems and secure livelihoods, i.e., diversified agroecological systems (IPES-Food, 2016). The approach focuses on honouring indigenous cultures and appropriate technologies that support a decentralised agrifood system aligned with concepts of ecological resilience, food sovereignty, fair trade and social justice (Altieri, 2002; Fernandez et al., 2013; IAASTD, 2008; IPES-Food, 2016; Wittman et al., 2010). Agroecology is a science, practice and social movement, which stands in direct contrast to the standardised package of the Green Revolution (Gliessman, 2015; Wezel et al., 2009).

In 2015, delegates representing diverse organisations and international movements of small-scale food producers and consumers gathered in Mali for the 'Declaration of the International Forum for Agroecology' to promote agroecology as a key element in the construction of food sovereignty and defend it from co-optation. The cooptation that the declaration refers to was the Global Dialogue on Agroecology organised by FAO between 2014 and 2018. The meeting in Mali allowed civil society to prepare a strong definition of agroecology, which they introduced at each subsequent meeting of the dialogue: (Brasilia, Dakar, Bangkok in 2015; La Paz, Kunming, Budapest in 2016; Rome in 2018; Loconto and Fouillieux, 2019). The Declaration claims that 'agroecology is the answer to how to transform and repair our material reality in a food system and rural world that has been devastated by industrial food production and its so-called Green and Blue Revolutions'.[1] In 2017, as part of a separate process, the UN Committee on World Food Security (CFS) convened the High-Level Panel of Experts on Food Security and Nutrition (HLPE) to produce a report on agroecological approaches and other innovations for sustainable agriculture and food systems to enhance

---

[1]Nyeleni Declaration (https://www.foodsovereignty.org/wp-content/uploads/2015/02/Download-declaration-Agroecology-Nyeleni-2015.pdf), accessed 20/08/2022.

food security and nutrition. The first recommendation of the report states that all stakeholders involved in food systems 'should learn from agroecological and other innovative approaches concrete ways to foster transformation in food systems by improving resource efficiency, strengthening resilience and securing social equity/responsibility' (HLPE, 2019: 21). The final report was obstructed by proponents of industrial agriculture until the term 'other innovations' was added to the title and covered in the report, which allowed the inclusion of genetic engineering and 'greening' technologies as some of the other innovations (Anderson and Maughan, 2021).

In 2018, at the end of the Global Dialogue, the FAO defined agroecology as 'an integrated approach which simultaneously applies ecological and social concepts and principles to the design and management of food and agricultural systems' (2018: 1). To support political decision-making and accelerate progress towards sustainable agrifood systems, it approved the 10 Elements of Agroecology as an analytical framework to support the design of differentiated paths for food system transformation. The 10 Elements framework takes into consideration the differing contexts at a range of levels on a number of scales and is specifically designed to be a consensus frame that avoided strong terms like principles or criteria (Loconto and Fouillieux, 2019).

Food Security and Food Sovereignty: The Ontological Tension

The ontological tension between the food security and the food sovereignty visions aligns with these competing agrifood transition pathways in the Anthropocene (Constance and Moseley, 2018). The food security discourse begins in the 1940s when the FAO was created to establish global food security. Although the FAO embraced the scientific modernisation of world agriculture (extensification and intensification), it also included the UN's Universal Declaration of Human Rights, which held that food was an essential right of life rather than a commodity. The Cold War subverted FAO multilateralism as the United States employed bilateral food aid to counter the spread of communism. The FAO vision of food as a right was formally replaced in 1986 when the World Bank redefined food security as the ability to buy food. Part of this change included moving the locus of international agricultural research out of the FAO and into the CGIAR (ETC Group, 2009). In 1994, the World Trade

Organization (WTO) institutionalised the global free trade regime and this market vision of food security, whereby countries grow and trade agrifood products based on comparative advantage and people buy these foods instead of grow them. As part of this Corporate Food Regime (McMichael, 2005), the WTO's 2008 Agreement on Agriculture furthered this vision by defining the 'new agriculture' as system of global entrepreneurial farmers employing sustainable intensification practices linked to agrifood TNCs in flexible arrangements governed by sustainability standards (Ingram et al., 2010; McMichael, 2014).

In contrast, the food sovereignty movement posits a counter frame to food security approaches. Created by La Via Campesina, a global, broad-based, peasant-centred, social movement committed to social justice and human rights, this view from the global South challenges the Corporate Food Regime through protests where it denies the validity of the WTO-sanctioned food security framework based on free trade, corporate intellectual property rights, and land grabs (McMichael, 2014). Their protest inside the FAO building at the 1996 World Food Summit set a precedent for subsequent food protests by civil society and led, with the help of institutional entrepreneurs inside the FAO, to the reform of the World Committee for Food Security in 2009 (Loconto and Fouillieux, 2019; McKeon, 2014). Instead, Via Campesina builds coalitions to create agrifood self-sufficiency through land reform, indigenous knowledge and agro-ecological principles (Desmarias, 2007; Fairbairn, 2012; Rosset, 2008; Wittman et al., 2010). This perspective proposes to heal the global metabolic rift of industrial agriculture through repossession and regionalisation of agrifood systems.

The food security and food sovereignty discourses are grounded in opposing ontological assumptions (Desmarais, 2007; McMichael, 2014). Food security embraces a land commodification ontology that assumes that the problem of food supply can be solved through ecological modernisation and sustainable intensification, a high-tech repackaging and greening of the modernist adoption and diffusion approaches of the productivist paradigm. This bio-capitalist Second Green Revolution links entrepreneurial global farmers practicing sustainable intensification to agrifood TNC constructed global value chains governed by the WTO free-trade regime. Friedmann (2005) calls this system of green consumers linked to green companies the Corporate Environmental Food Regime.

In contrast, the land sovereignty ontology views land through a multifunctional lens rather than the commodity lens. Food sovereignty embraces a triple-bottom line, full-cost accounting approach that internalises the environmental externalities and embraces a rights-based rather than market-centred framework, where rights are defined in collective terms rather than the liberal conception of individual rights (McMichael, 2014). This ontology requires a repossession of the land in the face of the continuing enclosures based on accumulation through dispossession (Moore, 2017). The intellectual property rights/copy right framework advanced by the WTO is countered by the copy-left, creative commons and open-source framework of La Via Campesina. Domestic agrifood production is the better path to food security rather than global commodity chains (de Schutter, 2008). Moderate and smaller scale agro-ecological farming is more resilient to climate shocks. The battle between La Via Campesina and the GMO seed TNCs over seed sovereignty is a crucial example of the ontological fracture (Kloppenburg, 2010).

The food security and food sovereignty frames proceed from non-reconcilable ontological differences (McMichael, 2014). The food security discourse separates the social and physical sciences and casts traditional agriculturalists as primitive laggards, whereas the food sovereignty frame values interdisciplinary approaches, honours indigenous knowledge and pursues social justice (Rivera-Ferre, 2012). The food security approach lacks a social justice and human rights component, which is a central feature of the food sovereignty perspective (Guthman, 2008; Fairbairn, 2012).

The food security path is based on neo-productivist, high-tech solutions using all available tools and technologies, including intellectual property and GMOs (Almas and Campbell, 2012; Marsden, 2013; McMichael, 2014). The food sovereignty path is based on agroecology and a social justice framework. The food security path is patterned on consequentialist philosophy grounded in utilitarian assumptions about agrifood science and rurality. The greater good for the most people outweighs the negative impacts on the few. The agroecology path employs a rights-based rhetoric grounded in de-ontological assumptions to support its social justice agenda. The food security path includes incremental, 'green' reforms to the existing system, while the food sovereignty path pushes for transformative change to the system (Holt-Gimenez and Shattuck, 2011; Thompson,

2010b). Where the current system promises to sustainably intensify, the agroecologists prefer to intensify the sustainable. The agroecologists warn that sustainable intensification is an oxymoron at least (Eckard, 2015), and more probably a 'wolf in sheep's clothing' (FOE, 2012). The neo-productivists promise their green solution can feed the world, while the low-tech agroecology approach cannot. While food sovereignty advocates argue for a transition path informed by deep agroecology, conventional agriculture proponents have countered with food security discourses focusing on ecological modernisation, sustainable intensification, and CSA (Levidow, 2015).

The Case of CGIAR

The CGIAR celebrated its 50th anniversary in 2021. Created in 1971, the original CGIARs were the culmination of experiments with numerous organisational models of international agricultural research and development reaching back to the early twentieth century. The CGIARs became 'the model' for foreign assistance in agriculture as part of the Green Revolution (Byerlee and Lynam, 2020). Today, the CGIAR is the governance structure for a system of 15 international agricultural research centres (IARCs), focusing on research in support of development and food security in the tropics and subtropics. Six of these IARCs existed prior to the formalisation of the CGIAR in 1971 as previous efforts carried out by the Ford and Rockefeller Foundations (FF and RF), the FAO, the US National Academy of Sciences (NAS), the Pan-American Union (now the Organisation of American States) and remnants of colonial research institutes of the British and French (mostly) in Africa.

The IARC model was designed as centres of excellence to carry out fundamental multidisciplinary research to generate agricultural technologies (originally germplasm and seeds), which through economies of scale and scope would be diffused via research networks across different countries and ecological regions. IARCs were designed originally to substitute for underdeveloped agricultural research facilities in developing countries through capacity building, training local scientists, and supporting national university programs in agricultural modernisation. They targeted research on specific commodities (rice, wheat, corn, beans, livestock, etc.) designed to be public goods and reduce hunger. Additionally, the governance structure of the IARC model strove to reduce bureaucratic and political interference by operating as autonomous, non-governmental centres with independent and international boards. Finally, the funding structure was designed to be long-term and sourced from richer countries through the official foreign aid (agencies) and philanthropical organisations, which would align with those organisations' humanitarian and *political objectives* (*italics added*; Byerlee and Lynam, 2020: 2).

The Genesis of the IARC Model

The structure and mission of the IARC system can be traced to the LGU model developed in the United States in the late 1800s, in collaboration with the USDA, and then embraced by the foundations and the FAO after World War II. The three-pronged LGU research, teaching and cooperative extension model was designed to develop and diffuse agricultural innovations. The USDA maize (corn) improvement programme started in the 1920s at the University of Minnesota. The institutional innovation of cooperative research – organised teams at different locations studying the same topic – accelerated the rate of technological innovations of genetically-improved hybrid maize seed. In 1943, the UN held its first conference on food and agriculture; in 1945 the FAO was formed to modernise food and agriculture and feed the world (well, at the time they only meant to feed Europe) (Loconto, 2022). After World War II, the United States used its scientific forces to address the Malthusian challenge and to use food as a weapon in the Cold War (see Perkins, 1997). The USDA/FAO coordinated a hybrid maize programme to rebuild European agriculture (Byerlee and Lynam, 2020).

The USDA international wheat programme started in the 1950s in response to a stem rust epidemic, linking to the RF Mexico Agricultural Programme (MAP) led by Norman Borlaug (from the University of Minnesota), and then creating similar research sites in Australia, India, Kenya, South Africa, and Spain. Following the European maize model, it formalised as the FAO Near East Wheat and Barley Association, where it fostered breeding programs in North Africa and Pakistan and then cross-country diffusion of resistant strains. The early organisational and monetary support from foundations, USDA, and FAO set a strong base, which later morphed into the first IARC – CIMMYT (the International Maize and Wheat Improvement Centre) (Byerlee and Lyman, 2020).

The international rice improvement programme originated in India (International Rice Study Group) after World War II, then was formalised as an IARC in 1948 in the Philippines as the International Rice Commission (IRC). Coordinated by FAO, it followed the cooperative research model of maize in Europe and wheat and barley in the Near East to develop hybrids that transferred the increased fertiliser-induced growth rates of the temperate japonica varieties to the indica varieties of the tropical and sub-tropical regions. The IRC laid the groundwork for the second IARC – IRRI (the International Rice Research Institute) (Byerlee and Lynam, 2020).

Following a different trajectory, after World War I, another group of scientists, governments and industry from the United States organised to support regional agricultural research centres for the Latin American tropics. The group included Latin American countries dependent on tropical exports and US corporations looking to source tropical commodities in response to increased competition in US markets by Dutch and British Empire imports from Asia. The Tropical Plant Research Foundation (TPRF, 1924–1931) operated under the National Academy of Sciences, headquartered in Washington, D.C. It was governed by a mix of private and academic interests from the US, with most of the funding from US food companies. The founding director was a LGU-trained USDA plant pathologist. The global depression in 1930 eliminated the funding stream for the TPRF, but the interest in tropical commodities persisted (Byerlee and Lynam, 2020).

As World War II disrupted US supplies of tropical commodities, in particular rubber, the tropical research centre agenda resurfaced, supported by the Pan-American Union and Henry A. Wallace, US Secretary of Agriculture. Headquartered in Costa Rica near a USDA rubber research station, the Inter-American Institute of Agricultural Sciences (IICA) was founded in 1942 with an Iowa State University-trained USDA agronomist as its director. After the war ended, the funding stream changed from the US government back to private US corporations sourcing tropical commodities. In the 1960s, the IICA got a new Latin American director from Colombia, changed its name and switched its focus to Central American research and teaching (Byerlee and Lynam, 2020). Over the years, IICA has come to dominate the agricultural development project grants in the region, often in direct competition with FAO and other specialised, IARCs that are not based in the sub-region.[2]

In the early 1960s another IARC venture was proposed to counter communist insurgency in Latin America. The Kennedy Administration, with support from the RF and NAS, announced the Alliance for Progress, a USAID programme to create a series of regional institutes with special attention to Latin America. The NAS-funded feasibility study conducted by the University of Minnesota suggested the creation of the Tropical Research Foundation (TRF) to establish research stations in three ecological zones of the tropics, each staffed by twenty US scientists. The TRF was Washington conceived, staffed and funded, largely due to the LGU scientists' collective view that developing countries could not conduct agricultural research and feed themselves. Alliance for Progress partner countries such as Brazil pushed back against the TRF for not integrating with ongoing efforts in the regions. The TRF proposal was rejected by a NAS-appointed, high-level panel for these reasons. It was replaced in 1967 with Centro Internacional de Agricultura Tropical (CIAT) headquartered in Palmira, Colombia, and mostly funded by the RF. Although the original CIAT mandate was to develop sustainable cropping systems for tropical lowlands, over time it became led by the Brazilian research organisation Embrapa, founded in 1973, which had transformed Brazil's tropical savannahs into the soy breadbasket of the world (Byerlee and Lynam, 2020).

The IARCs in Africa followed a different path grounded in the colonial histories of Britain and France. The colonial model consisted of regional research centres supporting export crops for the core country. With independence, the model shifted to smallholder farming systems, especially the challenges associated with shifting cultivation and animal diseases, but insufficient infrastructure and lack of stable funding hampered these efforts. After preliminary initiatives by NAS, USAID and the foundations in anglophone West Africa, in the 1960s the International Institute for Tropical Agriculture (IITA) was created following the IICA model in Latin America. The RF and FF provided majority funding, and a University of Minnesota agricultural scientist was in charge. Headquartered in Ibadan, Nigeria, IITA cooperated with francophone African scientists on farming systems research,

---

[2]Interviews with FAO and IICA staff in Costa Rica in February 2019.

particularly on the issue of declining yields in the shifting cultivation system. IITA is the only one of the four African IARCs that gave serious attention to farming systems research. Longer-term formula funding from the FF allowed it to do this, as most other IARCs had to focus on crop-oriented research to show quicker results and pay-off (Byerlee and Lynam, 2020).

West Africa Rice Development Association (WARDA) was preceded by British and French post-colonial research institutes. In the late 1960s, the French network of six stations faced budget problems. West African countries wanted increased domestic rice production to reduce imports and provide an urban wage food. The USAID and newly formed United Nations Development Programme (UNDP) were interested in pursuing a regional rice project. UNDP coordinated the creation of WARDA in 1970, led by a French and a Vietnamese economist who specialised in rice and the Green Revolution in Vietnam. The decentralised French model based on strengthening existing institutions conflicted with the US centralised model. Politics over WARDA (centralised or decentralised) was heated, resulting in a hybrid model that struggled, and then was reorganised as the Africa Rice Centre, which retained a hybrid form of an IARC model aligned with existing research centres (Byerlee and Lynam, 2020).

After independence the importance of cattle in Africa as a protein source increased to combat malnutrition. Africa's colonial history created special barriers to the IARC model, as noted above in the WARDA story. Eventually, in 1973 International Laboratory for Research on Animal Diseases (ILRAD) was sited in East Africa and in 1974 the International Livestock Centre for Africa (ILCA) was based in West Africa. The RF was the prime organiser for both centres with USAID and UNDP support in anglophone East Africa and USAID and francophone support in West Africa. Both ventures had to navigate the 'centre versus regional' organisation form. At the organisation meetings, the French representatives argued that these IARCs should complement and strengthen the existing national and regional efforts. These discussions shifted to the CGIAR after its creation in 1971. After some difficulties with blending the two models, ILRAD was created as an autonomous centre based in Nairobi, Kenya, and ILCA, based in Ethiopia with a French director, was approved and designated to function in a complementary role to the existing national and regional centres in West Africa. In 1995,

CGIAR merged ILRAD and ILCA into International Livestock Research Institute (ILRI) (Byerlee and Lynam, 2020).

By the late 1960s, the logistics and costs of running the four existing IARCs pushed the foundations and USAID to consider a comprehensive plan for the IARCs. Several more IARC centres were coming online. The first two IARCs – CIMMYT and IRRI – were credited with much of the success of the Green Revolution in wheat and rice. The FF, RF, UNDP, aid agencies from the US, Great Britain, Canada, Sweden, Japan and other countries, plus the Asian Development Bank and the Inter-American Development Bank, and other interested parties held a series of conferences at the FF's villa in Bellagio, Italy in the late 1960s. The IARC model had significant traction as 'the model' of agricultural development. At the same time, the OECD Development Assistance Committee was supporting multi-donor cooperation. Then, the World Bank, through its president Robert McNamara, entered the negotiations. As a trustee of the FF McNamara supported the Green Revolution and brought that agenda to the World Bank as a Cold War tool to blunt the spread of communism. He wanted to scale up the IARCs with World Bank as majority funder. He proposed five new centres and offered the World Bank's unrestricted grant funding. USAID promised to cover 25 percent of total costs. The IARC model dominated the discussions, championed by the FF as 'a new form of truly international organisation' (Byerlee and Lynam, 2020: 14). But it was still opposed by the French representatives and other attendees who preferred supporting existing research institutes.

In summary, the IARC organisational model, culminating in CGIAR, originated in the US LGU system around hybrid maize. That model was based on LGU centralised control of multiple trials at once to speed up the genome testing and bring better producing cereal varieties to market. LGU agricultural scientists staffed the FF, RF and USDA. After World War II the growing global concerns about eliminating hunger and feeding the world prompted the foundations to expand their investments in the agricultural sciences. The FAO, USAID, and UNDP supported the model, which was replicated famously by the RF and Borlaug in Mexico for wheat and maize (CIMMYT) and then again for rice in Southeast Asia (IRRI). The model was diffused overseas by the foundations, USAID, UNDP, and then the World Bank as part of the development project – the Green

Revolution – where it encountered remnants of colonial models of agricultural development. The French model was based on decentralised national and regional centres, instead of the centralised US-based IARC model. The French often pushed back in negotiations over the structure and form of the IARCs and CGIAR. The IARCs – in the form of CGIAR – were seen as critical for progress in developing countries that had neither the resources nor the infrastructure to carry out agricultural development. The IARC model was also seen as a critical tool in the Cold War to counter the success of communism in the developing world.

The Creation of CGIAR

The CGIAR was formalised in December 1971 as a network of independently managed IARCs that worked together to create and disseminate improved plant varieties to alleviate hunger and poverty. Sponsorship of the four original centres (CIMMYT, IRRI, IITA and CIAT) was transferred to the CGIAR and its Technical Advisory Committee (TAC), with offices at the World Bank in Washington, D.C. (Correa, 2009; Ozgediz, 2012). CGIAR was based on four principles: informal, consensus decision-making; donor sovereignty; centre autonomy with autonomous governing boards; and science based.

The first two decades were the golden years of CGIAR. Stable core funding of unrestricted funds (from the World Bank), TAC control, autonomous boards, and political consensus about its mission and founding principles allowed the TACs to prioritise research agendas (Petit, 2022). By 1975 there were seven new centres, two more policy centres were added by 1980 (IFPRI and ISNAR), and from 1972 to 1980 donors had increased from 17 to 29 and funding from \$21M to \$141M. The research agenda also changed from strictly genome improvement to include farming systems, natural resource management (NRM), livestock, and institutional constraints on agricultural development (Ozgediz, 2012).

System reviews started in the mid-1970s. The 1981 review prompted the clarified corporate functions of the CGIAR system, enacted rolling five-year plans for each centre, and better specified the roles and duties of trustees on boards. Influenced by the Brandt Report (1980) and Brundtland Report (1987), the CGIAR mission shifted to increasing sustainable food production in developing countries to enhance nutrition and quality of life for low-income people. This new sustainability concern forced more attention to NRM aspects of the centres and added five more centres: water, irrigation, agroforestry, plantain/banana, and forestry research. In the late 1980s, the increased need for cross-centre coordination regarding NRM and cropping systems combined with new donor preferences to expand the IARC focus beyond agriculture into water and forestry issues began to change the funding structure from the unrestricted model to a restricted project-based model. Donors wanted greater control, accountability, and short-term pay-offs for their contributions, which started the trend towards bilateral projects with specific centres and shifted the decision-making power from the TAC to the donors. Bilateral funding imposed a contract approach to research staff instead of a long-term team approach (Ozgediz, 2012).

By 1991, CGIAR staff numbered 12,000, with 1,300 internationally recruited. Funding needs were $332M, but only $251M was secured. The expected increase in funding did not materialise, as donor monies increasingly went to bilateral contracts with new centres at the expense of older centres, which created turmoil in the system. The two livestock centres were combined to reduce costs (as noted above), other centres were downsized, and two standing donor committees for oversight and finance were created to support funding. The new CGIAR chair secured a one-time $20M donation from the WB, which allowed full funding for 1994. In the 1990s, CGIAR membership increased with more developing country members and from the old Eastern Bloc. There was also a new gender initiative (Gender and Diversity Programme) and a new policy arena (genetic resources, intellectual property and biotechnology). The mission statement was adjusted again to 'to contribute, through its research, to promoting sustainable agriculture for food security in developing countries' (Ozgediz, 2012: XIV).

The 1990s also brought new calls for accountability and performance evaluations and shifts to cross-cutting programmes to address global issues, but these programs were funded by unrestricted funds, which continued to decrease to about 20 percent of total funding. The changes brought increased transaction costs for each centre running multiple bilateral projects and gathering assessment data. As funding shifted away from long-term stability and plant genome research to NRM and bilateral contractual projects, the centres lost many of their career scientists who were the basis of the centres of excellence IARC model. The World Bank changed its funding system from 'balancing' to 'matching donors', which further eroded unrestricted funds. The locus of power continued to shift from the TAC to the CGIAR Chair, the CGIAR centre Directors Committee and the donors. As a result, the donors' pet programs got funded rather than what the TAC thought was most needed scientifically (Ozgediz, 2012).

Funding problems persisted prompting another system review in 1998, which suggested that the CGIAR establish as a legal corporation with a central board, executive committee, and full time CEO. The suggestions met with strong resistance from within CGIAR, as had previous recommendations for centralisation. The European donors again suggested a regional structure by reorganising the centres into four regional programs linked to national and regional actors on time-fixed projects. Climate change and nutritional health came under the purview of CIGIAR, further complicating missions and funding (Ozgediz, 2012).

In CGIAR's 4th decade, it continued to struggle with how to organise the CGIAR system to meet higher order needs and still retain the positive attributes of the IARC model. In the end, the 'one model fits all' approach did not work well for much of what needed to be done – climate change, poverty and nutrition. Finding stable funding to do the research to deliver the public goods continued to be the challenge (Ozgediz, 2012). CGIAR's research financing shifted from funding centres to funding Challenge Programs (CPs) to better coordinate CGIAR with other research actors and mobilise additional funding. Other changes included transforming the TAC into a Science Council, establishing a CGIAR system office, adopting the Charter of the CGIAR system and establishing regular performance assessments. The Donor group reached 62 members by 2002, and they liked the performance measurement system, but Centres disliked it for the increased transaction costs, especially as restricted funding continued to rise. With this new model, staff positions were no longer secured funding but were completely tied to resource mobilisation by the researcher to pay their salaries, very much in the image of the American-Dutch model of competitively funded research.[3]

---

[3]Interview with staff member of the Alliance Bioversity-CIAT in October 2020. This Alliance was forged during the most recent series of mergers within CGIAR in 2019 that is focused on reorienting the entire CGIAR system around 'food systems'.

The centres perceived the CP system, with no restriction on who could submit proposals, as a threat. To mollify the centres, the first pilot CPs funded were submitted by the centres: *Water and Food* – grow more food with less water; *Harvest Plus* – reduce micronutrient deficiency to breed staples with micronutrients (e.g., Golden Rice); and *Generation* – molecular biology (GMOs) to create a new generation of plants to meet farmer needs. The next CP, submitted by the Forum for Agricultural Research in Africa, was *Livelihoods and Natural Resource Management in Sub-Saharan Africa: Securing the Future of Africa's Children*. 'The final CP approved by the CGIAR, after a few years of freeze, was on a much-anticipated subject: climate change', *Climate Change, Agriculture, and Food Security*[4] (Ozgediz, 2012: xvii).

The CGIAR approved more changes at the 2008 meeting, again adjusting its mission to: reduce poverty and hunger, improve human health and nutrition and enhance ecosystem resilience through high-quality international agricultural research, partnership and leadership (Ozgediz, 2012: XVIII). The major outcome of these changes was the separation of 'doers' and 'funders'. The centres (doers) created a new organisation – the Consortium of IARCs – with a board and an executive office located in Montpellier, France, that established global programs called CGIAR Research Programs (CRPs) through the Strategy and Results Framework (SRF). The counterpart (funders) was the CGIAR Trust Fund with the Fund Council performing executive duties. The SRF provided the roadmap for achieving a new vision and strategic outcomes through the CRPs and requested funding for each CRP from the Fund. Final approval for these changes occurred in 2009 when the Bill and Melinda Gates Foundation joined the CGIAR; the foundation had been a major donor to Centres. At this meeting the donors requested and secured a third tier of funding: (1) pooled contributions (unrestricted); (2) restricted – donor to pet project CRP to Centre through CGIAR; (3) centre direct – donor money passes CGIAR, goes directly to the centre, which is 'essentially a by-pass mechanism to channel donor funds to individual centres' (Ozgediz, 2012: XX). These changes brought an end to the original CGIAR system as a network of

---

[4]CGIAR Research Program on Climate Change, Agriculture and Food Security – CGIAR (https://www.cgiar.org/research/program-platform/climate-change-agriculture-and-food-sec urity/), accessed 03/09/2022.

consulting IARCs; the Consultative Group would no longer exist, but the CGIAR name would still be used. The 2009 major restructuring transformed the loose coalition of centres with separate research agendas and donors to 'a coherent, business-like whole' (CGIAR, 2016a).

The new CGIAR became operational in January of 2010 with the CGIAR Trust Fund established at the World Bank, followed by the inaugural meetings of the Consortium and Fund Council. During the transition two CRPs were approved for funding: the Global Rice Science Partnership and the Climate Change, Agriculture, and Food Security ($100M and $65M annually, respectively). By the end of 2011 24 donors had contributed $332M to the CGIAR Fund. In 2012, the Fund Council approved 15 CRPs for funding, each led by a CGIAR Centre. The new CGIAR focused on three new principles: separation of doers and funders, harmonisation of research funding and implementation and managing for results (Ozgediz, 2012).

In 2016, the CGIAR adopted another governance structure, called the CGIAR System Framework, which provides a System Council and CGIAR System Organization (CGIAR, 2016b). In December, the CGIAR's 2011–2016 research portfolio of CRPs came to an end, and the System Council approved the 2017–2022 Portfolio of Research Programs and Platforms. 'CGIAR remains the world's leading partnership on sustainable crop and animal agriculture, forestry and fisheries, with annual System revenue of $919 million' (CGIAR, 2016b: 3). Windows 1 (no restrictions) and 2 (funders to specific CRPs) funding was $220M (down 15 percent from 2015). Window 3 (funders to specific centres) funding was $323M (up 10 percent from 2015), and bilateral project funding was $346M (down 11 percent from 2015). Centre funding was $30M, up from $28M in 2015. At the end of 2016, CGIAR's 15 centres and the CGIAR System Organisation employed 10,270 staff in 96 countries.

In summary, the success of the Green Revolution, especially the increase in Mexican wheat and Asian rice, is attributed to the IARC model and the CGIAR as the exemplar (Renkow and Byerlee, 2010). While the original centres focused on single-crop genome research to increase productivity and reduce poverty, later centres researched farming systems, NRM and agricultural policies. Because crop productivity is easier to quantify, some centres were more successful than others at generating positive measurable impacts. As a result, through a series of governance reforms, the donors and CGIAR central administration put increasing pressure on the CGIAR research managers and centres to demonstrate that the money was well spent, eventuating in a shift in power from the TAC to the donors. Reforms in 2015/2016 addressed the continuing disconnect between donor demands and scientific achievability, between 'delivery and uptake of new knowledge' and 'production of international public goods'. The CGIAR struggled to be both a research and development mechanism and failed because you cannot draw a cause–effect line straight from agricultural research today to development tomorrow (Leeuwis et al., 2018).

The long-term view of the SRF conceptual frame operationalised through CRPs and the short-term model of bilateral contracts attached to yearly budget cycles created unrealistic quantitative promises of development impacts by researchers – to secure funding – that could be accomplished (or measured in the short term), which then led to a poor review and more calls for reforms and accountability. Long-term strategic research did not fit with short-term development success and the yearly budget cycles. The result was that the new CGIAR model is geared towards quick wins instead of the kind of work needed for long-term transformations to combat poverty, enhance global food security and address climate change. Being responsive to donors, national partners, and place-based contexts distracts from the CGIAR original mandate to produce international public goods (Leeuwis et al., 2018).

The IARC model proved not as useful for NRM activities, such as farming systems, soil erosion, water conservation, nutrient depletion, land degradation and climate change, which are site/region-specific. The newer IARCs do have a broader focus on sustainable intensification of farming systems, but as mentioned above, NRM and farming systems are harder to quantify, find the pay-off and see the wide-spread impacts and benefits of the donor's investment for that research. After the 1992 Earth Summit and Brundtland and Brandt reports, the CGIAR refocused towards a sustainability agenda, which took it outside its normal agricultural research boundaries into NRM and farming systems. For example, IITA developed techniques to sustainably intensify shifting bush/fallow agriculture but needed a 'new type of farmer' to adopt these techniques and integrate them into its farming operations. CGIAR is searching for organisation models to do both, especially as such 'a model has become essential to a global agenda focused on mitigation and adaptation to climate change, zero deforestation, sustainable use of freshwater resources, and other aspect of the SDGs' (Byerlee and Lynam, 2020: 15).

The 2030 CGIAR goals highlight: health (malnutrition and food safety); reduced GHG; sustain NRM; poverty and hunger, which are all indivisible. 'We need to find ways of generating healthy diets that are affordable, desirable, environmentally sustainable, and poverty reducing in their generation' (Lawrence, 2020: 1). To do this, the CGIAR needs new alliances with upstream and downstream political economy of food choices researchers. CGIAR is good at doing the science but not as good on why science-based policies are not enacted. CGIAR 'needs to understand the terrain between food and fork much better than is does now' (Lawrence, 2020: 2).

CGIAR and Sustainable Intensification

As noted above, the 2010 changes to the CGIAR included a CRP on Climate Change, Agriculture and Food Security funded at $65M annually over several years (Ozgediz, 2012). Recommendation #3 of the Final Report of the CGIAR Commission on Sustainable Agriculture and Climate Change was to 'Sustainably intensify agricultural production while reducing greenhouse gas emissions and other negative environmental impacts of agriculture' (Beddington et al., 2012: 33). The report noted that 'sustainable intensification is potentially the most promising means of simultaneously increasing food production while achieving land-based mitigation...' (Beddington et al., 2012: 33).

The first project was SIMELSA – the Sustainable Intensification of Maize-Legume Cropping Systems for Food Security in Eastern and Southern Africa (2010–2018) (Siamachira, 2018). Coordinated by the International Maize and Wheat Improvement Centre (CIMMYT), its main goal was to aid smallholder farmers to reach their resources' full potential through the development of Conservation Agriculture-based sustainable intensification options and thereby increase their farm-level food security, productivity and incomes in the context of reduced climate risk and change.[5]

---

[5]SIMLESA (https://simlesa.cimmyt.org/what-we-do/), accessed 03/09/2022.

The second project was Africa RISING – Africa Research in Sustainable Intensification for the Next Generation – supported by USAID as part of its Feed the Future Initiative with a focus on cereal-based, crop-livestock and maize-legume-livestock farming systems.[6] Coordinated by IITA and ILRI, Africa RISING's aim was to reduce smallholder farmers' hunger and poverty through sustainable intensification farming systems that improve food, nutrition, and income security, particularly for women and children, and conserve or enhance the natural resource base. The goal was that by 2021 at least 300,000 smallholder farm households would have had access to Africa RISING technologies.

The third project was the USAID-funded Feed the Future Innovation Lab for collaborative research on sustainable intensification.[7] It was coordinated by CIAT from 2014 through 2019 with a focus on sustainable intensification, food safety, gender integration, and dietary diversity in Tanzania, United Republic of Burkina Faso, Ethiopia, Senegal, Bangladesh, Cambodia. The overall aims were to sustainably increase the production of nutritious food and encourage dietary diversity of smallholder and women farmers and to increase food production through improved crop production technologies while minimising environmental impact.

The final project was LivestockPlus – The Sustainable Intensification of Forage-based Agricultural Systems to Improve Livelihoods and Ecosystem Services in the Tropics (Arango et al., 2013). It was coordinated by CIAT from 2014 to 2020 with a regional emphasis on Colombia and Brazil with the aim to improve mixed-crop-forage-livestock-tree systems by achieving social, economic and environmental security through sustainable intensification on improved forages. The overall goal was to reduce the ecological footprint of livestock production and generate a diversity of ecosystem services, such as improved soil quality and reduced erosion, sedimentation and GHG emissions, through three interrelated intensification systems: genetic intensification – the development and use of superior grass and legume cultivars for increased livestock productivity; ecological intensification – the development and application of improved farm and NRM practices; and

---

[6]Africa Rising (https://africa-rising.net/), accessed 03/09/2022.
[7]Feed the Future Innovation Lab for Sustainable Intensification (https://blogs.k-state.edu/siil/), accessed 03/09/2022.

socio-economic intensification – the improvement of local and national institutions and policies, which enable refinements of technologies and support their enduring use.

The French Position: Agroecology

An important part of the recent changes in the CGIAR system is the geo and techno-politics revealed through tensions between national and international research (Hainzelin, 2022; Petit, 2022), as well as the most recent conflicts over the agroecological transition (see Barbier et al., this volume).

The move of the new global centre to Montpellier in 2009 was part of an effort to legitimate both the CGIAR system as an international organisation and the power of France as an international leader in agricultural research (Hainzelin, 2022). By moving to Montpellier, the headquarters of the CGIAR system is now physically located in the same campus as one of the four branches of International Centre for Advanced Mediterranean Agronomic Studies (CIHEAM), an inter-governmental organisation created in 1961 to focus on agriculture in the Mediterranean region. This campus is also the site for Agropolis Foundation, which was created in 2007 by the three specialised national agricultural research institutes in France: National Research Institute for Agriculture, Food and Environment (INRAE), the Centre for International Cooperation in Agricultural Research for Development (CIRAD), Research Institute for Development (IRD) and the Agricultural Engineering School of Montpellier (Montpellier SupAgro).

The foundation was created to consolidate and increase collabo-ration within the immense French scientific community working on agriculture, food, the environment and development within the country and so to create a single interlocutor for international nego-tiations with the Rome-Based Agencies (FAO-IFAD-WFP) as part of France's political ambitions in the agrifood sector (Loconto and Fouillieux, 2019). One of the key ambitions is to promote the agro-ecology paradigm not only within France but also in international agricultural research, which has meet with serious resistance, partic-ularly in Africa (Hainzelin, 2022; Petit, 2022). This ambition also cost France the directorship of FAO as the French candidate was perceived by the United States and China (and the numerous African countries who voted for the Chinese candidate) as being too weak in supporting the productivist agenda.[8] Nonetheless, the proposed research mandate is clear – interdisciplinary research that will support the agroecological transition is the future of international agricultural research (Caquet et al., 2019; Soussana, 2021).

In 2021, Agropolis International produced its 26th dossier entitled '*Agrological transformation for sustainable food systems: Insight on France-CGIAR research*' devoted to research and partnerships in agroecology in support of the CGIAR 2030 Research and Innovation Strategy and the nascent 'One CGIAR' (Atta-Krah et al., 2021). The dossier is the collective work of Agropolis International, CIRAD, INRAE, CGIAR and IRD. Following a year-long process of a series of scientific workshops organised among the four organisations, the dossier includes contributions from 500 French and CGIAR agroecology scientists and experts from 100 national and international universities and research organisations to demonstrate that agroecology is now a key focus of the scientific community in the critical work on transformative food systems approaches to address climate change and food security for all. The objective of the dossier is to link the different dimensions of the CGIAR 2030 elements 'in a holistic and transformative approach to food systems, *beyond the usual focus of CGIAR research teams on agricultural production*' (italics added; Atta-Krah et al., 2021: 8).

Agropolis dossier #26 builds upon the work of the FAO and the High Level Panel of Experts (HLPE) on Food Security and Nutrition of the UN Committee on World Food Security (CFS) to reflect 'the enormous opportunity ahead' for the 'transdisciplinary research needed to respond to the challenges facing our food, land, and water systems now, in the 21st century' (Atta-Krah et al., 2021: 5). The 'urgency of the agroecological transformation of agriculture and food systems' documented in the dossier is provided in support of the upcoming UN Food Systems Summit to illustrate the 'variety of agroecological transitions pathways' necessary to achieve 'genuinely sustainable food systems' and to avoid the simplification of 'one size fits all' conventional agricultural models that focus on sustainable intensification but too often

---

[8]Review of the official statements of the member states during the vote in 2019, interviews with observers of the vote at FAO and an interview with a member of the French candidate's campaign.

neglect 'socioeconomic power asymmetries' and thereby fail to develop 'inclusive cooperative systems' (Atta-Krah et al., 2021: 8).

The current approach that has been set out by France and CGIAR is to gradually strengthen linkages between national and international systems in strategies and funding. However, the current reform towards a One CGIAR was carried out without giving a particular place to the regional forums that make up Global Forum for Agricultural Research (GFAR) unlike the 2010 reform (Moreddu, 2022). GFAR was established by FAO, IFAD, the World Bank and CGIAR in 1996 as a project for resource sharing among national, international, private sector, farmer and civil society research organisations.[9] Housed by FAO, it has also undergone its own series of reforms that have made it more responsive to farmers' needs, more focused on participatory and interdisciplinary research and more inclusive of broader stakeholders in its forum. However, the main national research centres of the G20 countries do not participate.[10]

Within the OECD countries, which are the main donors of international agricultural research including the CGIAR system and the GFAR members, there is no general coordinating institution. Only the European Union has been successful in consolidating investment in research at a regional level, and increasingly internationally with its new Horizon Europe programme that finally allows third-party countries to receiving funding.[11] During this period, specifically in 2012, a new multi-donor fund called the AgroEcology Fund was developed and now includes 15 foundations and awards about USD 1.2 million biannually.[12] This is just a drop in the bucket compared to what is mobilised by Gates Foundation annually (USD 6.87 billion in total, USD 398 million for agricultural development in 2021).[13] But both of these private foundations are not typically financing research, but rather simply funding the application of their respective technical packets (Boillat et al., 2022).

---

[9]GFAR – About Us. (https://www.gfar.net/about-us), accessed 07/09/2022.

[10]Partners in GFAR. (https://www.gfar.net/about-us/partners?keys=&field_geographic_sc ope_value=All&field_countries_target_id=All&field_gfar_constituency_target_id=15205), accessed 07/09/2022.

[11]Horizon Europe. (https://research-and-innovation.ec.europa.eu/funding/funding-opportu nities/funding-programmes-and-open-calls/horizon-europe_en), accessed 07/09/2022.

[12]AgroEcology Fund. (https://www.agroecologyfund.org/history), accessed 07/09/2022.

[13]Bill & Melinda Gates Foundation. Annual Report 2021. (https://www.gatesfoundation. org/about/financials/annual-reports/annual-report-2021), accessed 07/09/2022.

A number of national countries have raised questions about the multiplication of international networks and initiatives, requesting a stronger emphasis on collaborative approaches in funding and evaluation of research (Moreddu, 2022). One proposal has been to return the CGIAR system to be housed within FAO, as this organisation tries to increase its role in knowledge management and reduce its role in development projects.[14] However, this type of a move would most likely put the recent shift towards agroecology at risk, considering that this topic is only one of the recent initiatives, and is programed to last only three years (in line with the dedicated budget line).[15] Indeed, the recent appointment of Dr. Ismahane Elouafi – formerly the Chief Scientist at FAO – to the position of Executive Managing Director suggests that this shift might become a real possibility.[16]

Conclusions

The global food and climate crisis we face today is 'not spontaneous but rather the consequence of a long struggle over the governance of global food systems' (Canfield et al., 2021: 2). In this chapter, we document the long struggle grounded in the original contrasting ethical positions of agrarianism and industrialism and ending with the current ontological tension between rights-based food sovereignty and market-centred food security proponents, aligned with agroecology and sustainable intensification, respectively. The chapter highlights the role of the LGU system – and the USDA – as a key venue where the competing interests of preservationist versus productivist, world systems versus modernisation and critical versus positivist knowledge systems played out; first in the United States and then in the world as the Green Revolution and the CGIAR.

The original IARC model and CGIAR vision and mission embraced the industrial ethic and modern, productivist system of agriculture. The CGIAR, supported by the foundations, government

---

[14]Interview with a staff member of FAO legal services in 2020.

[15]Initiative: transformational Agroecology Across Food, Land and Water Systems. (https://www.cgiar.org/initiative/31-transformational-agroecology-across-food-land-and-water-systems/), accessed 07/09/2022.

[16]CGIAR. 2023. Visionary leader, strategic thinker: CGIAR appoints Dr. Ismahane Elouafi as Executive Managing Director. (https://www.cgiar.org/news-events/news/emd-elouafi-2023/), accessed 09/09/2023.

agencies and business interests, became 'the model' to diffuse modern agricultural innovations in the developing world to enhance food security and support geopolitical agendas. The 'one size fits all' model was resisted by the French, who advocated for regional research centres focusing on NRM and farming systems. CGIAR system reviews starting in the 1970s led to a series of reorganisations and mission drift from a narrow focus on genome technologies for the public good decided by and administered by the TAC scientists to a corporate model and increasing bilateral contracts between donors and research centres. These changes accelerated after 1990 when the World Bank relinquished its role as the major funder and the foundations, in particular the Gates Foundation, filled the void. The foundation model expected short-term pay-offs for their research dollars, which compromised the kind of long-term research necessary for poverty reduction and system change. By 2010, the consultant group model of collaborating centres had been replaced by the centralised corporate model, but the name 'CGIAR' was kept. In the 2000s, climate change became the driving concern, and CGIAR developed various programs on sustainable intensification. In 2021, the French pushed back against sustainable intensification and the 'one size fits all' model through the Agropolis dossier, and thereby put agroecology – and farming systems – in the centre of the discourse.

The competing agrifood knowledges systems detailed in this chapter continue to play out in the current discourse and negotiations over the Anthropocene (see Chapter 1). The academic and political discourse on the Anthropocene can be divided into two 'knowledge' camps (plus, the climate deniers) (Hamilton et al., 2015). The 'good Anthropocene' camp is represented by Eco-Pragmatism and Eco-Modernisation proponents which promise that reflexive modernisation technology will solve the crisis and humans will gain control over the earth's systems. The food security model linked to sustainable intensification aligns here. The 'bad Anthropocene" camp is represented by Eco-Marxists and Eco-Catastrophists. The Eco-Marxists make global capitalism – the 'Captilocene' (Moore, 2017) – the culprit and the Eco-Catastrophists call for preparation for a frugal, 'post-growth society' (Semal, 2015). The food sovereignty and agroecology model align here. For philosophers, the Anthropocene – and its 'telluric' Anthropos – calls into question the modernist, Cartesian ontological assumptions of the dualist separation of humans and nature (Hamilton et al., 2015). The ontological crisis of the Anthropocene speaks again to the food sovereignty versus food security tension. While earth scientists scream that the evidence of the human-caused climate change crisis is overwhelming and undeniable, they lament that the politics of unsustainability prevents the needed transformative changes in favour of public policy incrementalism guided by eco-modernisation (Hamilton et al., 2015).

The United Nations Food Systems Summit (UNFSS) is the current venue for the contested control of the global food system where the battle between the corporate model of private interest versus the peoples' coalition model of public interest is being played out. Announced on World Food Day in 2019 as part of a UN 'Decade of Action' to deliver on the Sustainable Development Goals, the UNFSS was convened in late 2021 under the auspices of the World Economic Forum (WEF) instead of the UN CFS. Representing the interests of multinational corporations, export-oriented countries and philanthropies, the WEF promotes a 'Great Reset' to 'allay opposition to neoliberal globalisation' through a new vision of multistakeholder global governance (Canfield et al., 2021: 2; Schwab, 2021). The food sovereignty counter movement, led by La Via Campesina and the Civil Society and Indigenous Peoples' Mechanism (CSM), is pushing back against the UNFSS, criticising it as an organised attempt to subvert democracy and maintain colonial and corporate control of the agrifood system in the Anthropocene (Canfield et al., 2021).

References

Almås, R. and Campbell, H. (eds) (2012) *Rethinking Agricultural Policy Regimes: Food Security, Climate Change and the Future Resilience of Global Agriculture.* Bingley: Emerald Group Publishing Limited.

Altieri, M. (2002) 'Agroecology: The science of natural resource management for poor farmers in marginal environments'. *Agriculture, Ecosystems & Environment,* *93*: 1–24.

Anderson, C.R. and Maughan, C. (2021) '"The innovation imperative": The struggle over agroecology in the international food policy arena'. *Frontiers in Sustainable Food Systems,* *5*: 619185.

Arango, J., Cook, S., White, D., Guimaraes, E., Tohme, J., Blummel, M., Douxchamps, S., Rincón, A., Bungenstab, D.J., Villanueva, C., Subbarao, G.V., Rudel, T. and Searchinger, T. (2013) 'LivestockPlus: Sustainable intensification of tropical forage-based systems for improving livelihood and environmental benefits'. Paper presented at the *International Workshop on Pastures, Climate Change and Sustainable Intensification*, CIAT, Colombia. May 28−29.

Atta-Krah K., Chotte J.-L., Gascuel C., Gitz V., Hainzelin E., Hubert B., Quintero M. and Sinclair F. (eds) (2021) *Agroecological Transformation for Sustainable Food Systems. Insight on France-CGIAR Research, Vol. 26.* Les dossiers d'Agropolis International. Montpellier: Agropolis International, p. 148. (https://doi.org/10.23708/fdi:010082500)

Beddington, J., Asaduzzaman, M., Clark, M., Fernandez, A., Guillou, M., Jahn, M., Erda, L., Mamo, T., Van Bo, N., Nobre, C.A., Scholes, R., Sharma, R. and Wakhungu, J. (2012) 'Achieving food security in the face of climate change: Final report from the Commission on Sustainable Agriculture and Climate Change'. In *CGIAR Research Program on Climate Change*. Copenhagen: Agriculture and Food Security (CCAFS). (http://www.ccafs.cgiar.org/commission)

Berry, W. (1978) *The Unsettling of America: Culture and Agriculture.* San Francisco, CA: Sierra Club Books.

Boillat, S., Belmin, R. and Bottazzi, P. (2022) 'The agroecological transition in Senegal: Transnational links and uneven empowerment'. *Agriculture and Human Values*, 39(1): 281–300.

Buttel, F.H. (2006) 'Sustaining the Unsustainable: Agro-food systems and the environment in the modern world'. In P. Cloke, T. Marsden, and P.H. Mooney (eds), *Handbook of Rural Studies*. London: SAGE, pp. 212–29.

Buttel, F.H. and Newby, H. (1980) *The Rural Sociology of Advanced Societies: Critical Perspectives*. Montclair: Allenheld, Osmun.

Byerlee, D. and Lynam, K. (2020). 'The development of the international center model for agricultural research: A prehistory of the CGIAR'. *World Development*, 135: 105080. (https://doi.org/10.1016/j.worlddev.2020.105080)

Campbell, B.M., Beare, D.J., Bennett, E.M., Hall-Spencer, J.H., Ingram, J.S.I., Jaramillo, F., Ortiz, R., Ramankutty, N., Sayer, J.A. and Shindell, D. (2017) 'Agriculture production as a major driver of the Earth system exceeding planetary boundaries'. *Ecology and Society*, 22(44): 8.

Canfield, M., Anderson, M.D. and McMichael, P. (2021) 'UN Food Systems Summit 2021: Dismantling democracy and resetting corporate control of food systems'. *Frontiers in Sustainable Food Systems*, 5: 661552. (https//:doi.org/10.3389/fsufs.2021.661552)

Caquet, T., Gascuel, C., Tixier-Boichard, M., et al. (2019) *Réflexion prospective interdisciplinaire pour l'agroécologie*. Rapport de synthèse, p. 108.

Constance, D.H. (2010) 'Sustainable agriculture in the United States: A critical examination of a contested process'. *Sustainability*, 2(1): 48–72.

Constance, D.H. (2014) 'Rural sociology'. In N.K. Van Alfen (ed), *Encyclopedia of Agricultural and Food Systems, Vol. 5.* San Diego, CA: Elsevier, pp. 62–74.

Constance, D.H., Renard, M.C. and Rivera-Ferre, M. (eds) (2014) *Alternative Agrifood Movements: Patterns of Convergence and Divergence*. Bingley: Emerald Group Publishing Ltd.

Constance, D.H., Konefal, J. and Hatanaka, M. (eds) (2018) *Contested Sustainability Discourses in the Agrifood System*. New York, NY: Routledge/Earthscan.

Constance, D.H. and Moseley, A. (2018) 'Agrifood discourses and feeding the world: Unpacking sustainable intensification'. In D.H. Constance, J. Konefal and M. Hatanaka (eds), *Contested Sustainability Discourses in the Agrifood System*. New York, NY: Routledge/Earthscan, pp. 59–74.

CGIAR (2016a) *History of CGIAR*. (http://www.cgiar.org/who-we-are/history-of-cgiar/cgiar-reform/)

CGIAR (2016b) *CGIAR Financial Report, 2016*. Montpellier: CGIAR System Management Office. (https://www.cgiar/org/impact/finance-reports/)

Correa, C. (2009) *Fostering the Development and Diffusion of Technologies for Climate Change: Lessons from the CGIAR Model*. San Francisco, CA: International Center for Trade and Sustainable Development (https://citeseerx.ist.psu.edu/viewdoc/download?doi=10.1.1.394.2062&rep=rep1&type=pdf)

Danbom, D.B. (1979) *The Resisted Revolution: Urban America and the Industrialization of Agriculture: 1900–1930*. Ames: Iowa State University Press.

de Schutter, O. (2008) *Production and Protection of All Human Rights: Civil, Political, Economic, Social and Cultural Rights, Including the Rights to Development*. New York, NY: United Nations.

Desmarais, A.A. (2007) *La via Campesina: Globalization and the Power of Peasants*. London: Pluto Press.

Eckard, R. (2015) 'Sustainable intensification: Oxymoron or unavoidable imperative'. *The Age*, June 10. (http://www.theage.com/au/action/printArticle?id=6586069)

ETC Group (2009) *Who Will Govern Rome's Food Summit May Determine Who Decides Who Will Eat*. (http://www.etcgroup.org/content/who-will-govern)

FAO (1996) *World Food Summit: Rome Declaration on World Food Security*. November 13–17. (http://www.fao.org/docrep/003/w3613e/w3613e00.htm)

FAO (2009) 'Global agriculture towards 2050'. In Paper Presented to the *High-Level Expert Forum on "How to Feed the World in 2050*. Rome, October 12–13. (www.fao.org).

FAO (2018) *The 10 Elements of Agroecology: Guiding the Transition to Sustainable Food Systems and Agricultural Systems*. (https://www.fao.org/3/i9037en/i9037en.pdf)

Fairbairn, M. (2012) 'Framing transformation: The counter-hegemonic potential of food sovereignty in the US context'. *Agriculture and Human Values, 29*(2): 217–30.

Feed the Future (2105) *Feed the Future*: The U.S. Government's Global Hunger and Food Security Initiative. Washington, DC. (https://feedthefuture.gov/progress2015/)

Fernandez, M., Goodall, K., Olson, M. and Mendez, V.E. (2013) 'Agroecology and alternative agri-food movements in the United States: Toward a sustainable agri-food system'. *Agroecology and Sustainable Food Systems, 37*(1): 115–26.

FOE (Friends of the Earth) (2012) *Wolf in Sheep's Clothing: An Analysis of the Sustainable Intensification of Agriculture*. (http://www.foei.org/resources/publications/publications-by-subject/food-sovereignty-publications/a-wolf-in-sheeps-clothing)

Friedmann, H. (2005) From colonialism to green capitalism: Social movements and the emergence of food regimes'. In F.H. Buttel and P. McMichael (eds), *New Direction in the Sociology of Global Development: Research in Rural Sociology and Development. Vol. 11*. Oxford: Elsevier, pp. 227–64.

Gardner, B. (2009) *Global Food Futures: Feeding the World in 2050.* London and New York, NY: Bloomsbury.

Garnett, T., Appleby, M.C., Balmford, A., Bateman, I.J., Benton, T.G., Bloomer, P., Burlingame, B., Dawkins, M., Dolan, L., Fraser, D., Herrero, M. Hoffmann, I., Smith, P., Thornton, K., Toulmin, C., Vermeulen, S.J. and Godfray, H.C.J. (2013) 'Sustainable intensification in agriculture: Premises and policies'. *Science, 341*(6141): 33–4.

Gilbert, J. (2015). *Planning Democracy: Agrarian Intellectualism and the Intended New Deal.* New Haven and London: Yale University Press.

Gliessman, S. (2015) *Agroecology: The Ecology of Sustainable Food Systems.* Boca Raton, FL: CRC.

Godfray, H.C.J. and Garnett, T. (2014) 'Food security and sustainable intensification'. *Philosophical Transactions of the Royal Society B, 369*(1639): 20120273.

Guthman, J. (2008) 'Neoliberalism and the making of food politics in California'. *Geoforum, 39*(3): 1171–83.

Hainzelin E. (2022) 'L'orchestration de la recherche agricole internationale par les partenariats scientifiques'. In: Goulet F., Caron P., Hubert B., et al. (eds), *Sciences Techniques et Agricultures. L'impératif de la transition.* Paris: Presses des Mines, pp. 71–7.

Hamilton, C., Bonneuil, C. and Gemenne, F. (eds) (2015) *The Anthropocene and the Global Environmental Crisis: Rethinking Modernity in the New Epoch.* New York, NY: Routledge.

Hightower, J. (1973) *Hard Tomatoes, Hard Times.* Cambridge, MA: Schenkman Publishing Co.

HLPE (2019) *Agroecological and other innovative approaches for sustainable agriculture and food systems that enhance food security and nutrition.* A Report by the High-Level Panel of Experts on Food Security and Nutrition of the Committee on World Food Security, Rome. (https://www.fao.org/fileadmin/user_upload/hlpe/hlpe_documents/HLPE_Reports/HLPE-Report-14_EN.pdf)

Holt-Gimenez, E. and Shattuck, A. (2011) 'Food crises, food regimes, and food movements: Rumblings of reform or tides of transformation'. *The Journal of Peasant Studies, 38*(1): 109–44.

IAASTD (2008) *International Assessment of Agricultural Knowledge, Science and Technology for Development.* (http://www.fao.org/fileadmin/.../Agriculture_at_a_Crossroads_Global_Report_IAASTD.pdf)

Ingram, J., Erikson, I. and Liverman, D. (eds) (2010) *Food Security and Global Environmental Change.* London: Routledge/Earthscan.

IPES-Food (International Panel of Experts on Sustainable Food Systems) (2016) *From Uniformity to Diversity: A Paradigm Shift from Industrial Agriculture to Diversified Agroecological Systems.* (http://www.ipes-food.org)

Kloppenburg, J. (2010) 'Impeding dispossession, enabling repossession: Biological open sourcing and the recovery of seed sovereignty'. *Journal of Agrarian Change, 110*(3): 367–88.

Kuyper, T.W. and Struik, P.C. (2014) 'Epilogue: Global food security, rhetoric, and the sustainable intensification debate'. *Science Direct, 8*: 71–9.

Leeuwis, C., Klerkx, L. and Schut, M. (2018) 'Reforming the research policy and impact culture of the CGIAR: Integrating science and systemic capacity development'. *Global Food Security, 16*: 17–21.

Levidow, L. (2015) 'European transitions towards a corporate-environmental regime: Agroecological incorporation or contestation?' *Journal of Rural Studies, 40*: 76–89.

Levidow, L. (2018) 'Sustainable intensification: Agroecological appropriation or contestation?' In D.H. Constance, J. Konefal and M. Hatanaka, M. (eds), *Contested Sustainability Discourses in the Agrifood System.* New York, NY: Routledge/Earthscan, pp. 19–41.

Lobao, L. and Stofferahn, C. (2008) 'The community effects of industrialized farming: Social science research and challenges to corporate farming laws'. *Agriculture and Human Values, 25*(2): 219–40.

Loconto A. (2022) 'Gouverner par les métriques: Un exercice dans l'intermédiation des connaissances'. In Goulet F., Caron P., Hubert B., et al. (eds), *Sciences Techniques et Agricultures. L'impératif de la transition.* Paris: Presses des Mines, pp.139–50.

Loconto, A. and Fouillieux, E. (2019) Defining agroecology: Exploring the circulation of knowledge in FAO's Global Dialogue. *International Journal of Sociology of Agriculture and Food, 25*(2): 116–37.

Magdoff, F., Foster, J.B. and Buttel, F. (eds) (2000) *Hungry for Profit: The Agribusiness Threat to Farmers, Food, and the Environment.* New York, NY: Monthly Review Press.

Marsden, T. (2013) 'From post-productivism to reflexive governance: Contested transitions in securing more sustainable food futures'. *Journal of Rural Studies, 29*: 123–34.

McKeon, N. (2014) *Food Security Governance: Empowering Communities, Regulating Corporations.* New York: Taylor & Francis.

McMichael, P. (1996) *Development and Social Change.* Thousand Oaks, CA: Pine Forge Press.

McMichael, P. (2005) 'Global development and the corporate food regime'. In F.H. Buttel and P. McMichael (eds), *New Directions in the Sociology of Global Development, Research in Rural Sociology and Development, Vol. 11.* Oxford: Elsevier Press, pp. 265–300.

McMichael, P. (2014) 'Rethinking the land grab ontology'. *Rural Sociology, 79*(1): 34–55.

Monsanto (2014) *From the Inside Out: Monsanto 2014 Sustainability Report.* (www. monsanto.com/.../csr_reports/monsanto-2014-sustainability-report.pdf)

Moore, J.W. (2017) 'The Capitalocene, Part I: On the nature and origins of our ecological crisis'. *The Journal of peasant studies, 44*(3): 594–630.

Moreddu, C. (2022) 'La coopération internationale pour mobiliser la recherche agricole: enjeux de gouvernance'. In Goulet F., Caron P., Hubert B., et al. (eds), *Sciences Techniques et Agricultures. L'impératif de la transition.* Paris: Presses des Mines, pp. 97–105.

Newell, P. and Taylor, O. (2018) 'Contested landscapes: The global political economy of climate-smart agriculture'. *Journal of Peasant Studies, 45*: 108–29.

Nink, E. (2015) *Harvesting the Research: Ecological Intensification Can Feed the World*. Food Tank. (http://foodtank.com/news/2015/08/harvesting-the-research-ecological-intensification-can-feed-the-world)

Ozgediz, S. (2012) *The CGIAR at 40: Institutional Evolution of the World's Premier Agricultural Research Network*. Washington, DC: CGIAR Fund Office. (https://cgspace.cgiar.org/handle/10947/2761)

Patel, R. (2013) 'The long green revolution'. *Journal of Peasant Studies*, *40*(1): 1–63.

Perkins, J.H. (1997) *Geopolitics and the Green Revolution: Wheat, Genes, and the Cold War*. Oxford: Oxford University Press.

Petersen, B. and Sieglinde S. (2015) 'What is sustainable intensification? Views from experts'. *Land Use Policy*, *46*: 1–10.

Petit M. (2022) 'Gouvernance internationale de la recherche agronomique: nécessité d'un consensus minimum'. In: Goulet F., Caron P., Hubert B., et al. (eds), *Sciences Techniques et Agricultures. L'impératif de la transition*. Paris: Presses des Mines, pp. 79–87.

Pretty, J.N. (1997) 'The sustainable intensification of agriculture'. *Natural Resources Forum*, *21*(4): 247–56.

Reismann, E. and Fairbairn, M. (2020) 'Agri-food systems in the Anthropocene'. *Annals of American Association of Geographers*, *111*(3): 687–97.

Renkow, M. and Byerlee, D. (2010) 'The impacts of CGIAR: A review of recent evidence'. *Food Policy*, *35*(5): 391–402.

Rivera-Ferre, M.G. (2012) 'Framing of agri-food research affects of the analysis of food security: The critical role of the social sciences'. *International Journal of Sociology of Agriculture and Food*, *19*(2): 162–75.

Rockstrom, J., Williams, J., Daily, G., Noble, A., Matthews, L.G., Wetterstrand, H., DeClerck, F., Shah, M., Steduto, P., de Graiture, C., Hatibu, N., Unver, O., Bird, J., Sibanda, S. and Smith, J. (2017) 'Sustainable intensification of agriculture and human prosperity and global sustainability'. *Ambio*, *46*(1): 4–17.

Rosset, P. (2008) 'Food sovereignty and the contemporary food crisis'. *Development*, *51*(4): 460–3.

Royal Society (2009) *Reaping the Benefits: Science and the Sustainable Intensification of Global Agriculture*. London. (https://royalsociety.org/topics-policy/publications/2009/reaping-benefits/)

Scoones, I. (2016) 'The politics of sustainability and development'. *Annual Review of Environmental Resources*, *41*(1): 293–319.

Schwab, K. (2021) *Stakeholder Capitalism: A Global Economy that Works for Progress, People, and the Planet*. Geneva: John Wilkes and Sons.

Semal. L. (2015) 'Anthropocene, catastrophism, and green political theory'. In C. Hamilton, C. Bonneuil, and F. Gemenne, F. (eds), *The Anthropocene and the Global Environmental Crisis: Rethinking Modernity in the New Epoch*. New York, NY: Routledge, pp. 87–99.

Shiva, V. (1992) *The Violence of the Green Revolution: Third World Agriculture, Ecology, and Politics*. New York, NY: Zed Books.

Siamachira, J. (2018) *End of Eight-year Project Leaves Farmers Ready to Tackle Climate Change in Africa*. CIMMYT. (https://www.cimmyt.org/end-of-eight-year-project-leaves-farmers-ready-to-tackle-climate-change-in-africa-2/)

Soussana J.-F. (2021) *International Science Foresight Workshop: Global Challenges and Research Gaps*. The Royaumont process.

Struik, P.C., Kuyper, T.W., Brussaard, L. and Leeuwis, C. (2014) 'Deconstructing and unpacking the scientific controversies in intensification and sustainability: Why the tensions in concepts and values'. *Science*, 8: 80–8.

Thompson, P. (2010a) *The Agrarian Vision: Sustainability and Environmental Ethics*. Lexington: University of Kentucky Press.

Thompson, P. (2010b) *The Ethics of Intensification: Agricultural Development and Social Change*. New York, NY: Springer.

Tittonell, P. (2014) Ecological intensification of agriculture – sustainable by nature. *Current Opinion in Environmental Sustainability*, 8: 53–61.

United Nations (2008) *High-level Task Force on the Global Food Crisis. Comprehensive Framework for Action*. (http://www.un/org/ga/president/62/letters/cfa160708.pdf)

Velten, S., Leventon, J., Jager, N. and Newig, J. (2015) 'What is sustainable agriculture? A Systematic review'. *Sustainability*, 7: 7833–65.

Wezel, A., Bellon, S., Doré, T., Francis, C., Vallod, D. and David, C. (2009) 'Agroecology as a science, a movement and a practice. A review'. *Agronomy for Sustainable Development*, 29(4): 503–15.

Willett W., Rockström J., Loken B., et al. (2019) 'Food in the Anthropocene: The EAT–Lancet Commission on healthy diets from sustainable food systems'. *The Lancet*, 393(10170): 447–92.

Wittman, H.K., Desmarais, A. and Wiebe, N. (eds) (2010) *Food Sovereignty: Reconnecting Food, Nature and Community*. Oakland, CA: Food First Books.

World Bank (2006) *Module 4: Investments in Sustainable Agriculture Intensification*. (http://siteresources.worldbank.org/EXTAGISOU/Resources/Module4_Web.pdf)

Index

www.ingramcontent.com/pod-product-compliance
Ingram Content Group UK Ltd.
Pitfield, Milton Keynes, MK11 3LW, UK
UKHW030040181224
452424UK00003BA/43